The Jewish Legacy
and the
German Conscience

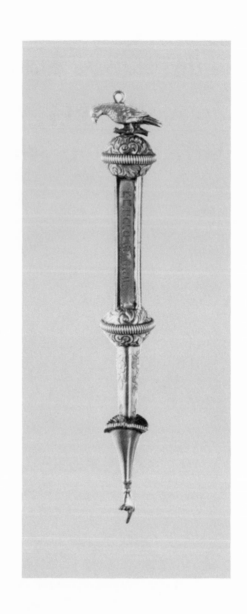

THE JEWISH LEGACY AND THE GERMAN CONSCIENCE

Essays in Memory of Rabbi Joseph Asher

*Edited by Moses Rischin
and Raphael Asher*

THE JUDAH L. MAGNES MUSEUM
BERKELEY, CALIFORNIA

Published by: The Judah L. Magnes Museum
2911 Russell Street, Berkeley, California 94705

Cover and book design: Sarah Levin
Cover illustration: Sara Glaser
Typesetting: Canterbury Press, Berkeley

Frontispiece: German Torah pointer with the German eagle
perched on top, early twentieth century (B. M. Ansbacher's
Zeugnisse jüdischer Geschichte und Kultur).

ISBN: 0-943376-48-3 (paperback)
ISBN: 0-943376-47-5 (hardcover)
Library of Congress Catalog Card Number: 91-062518

Printed in the United States of America
10 9 8 7 6 5 4 3 2 1

CONTENTS

Illustrations

PREFACE

The Jewish Legacy and the German Conscience is a book of essays honoring Joseph Asher. Joining religious learning with secular scholarship, a group of distinguished authors have collaborated to make this volume both a tribute to my father and what we trust will be an important contribution to the study of modern Jewish history.

We are most grateful to Congregation Emanu-El in San Francisco for its generous support and to Rabbi Robert Kirschner for his direction and good counsel. My gratitude extends also to the leadership of my Congregation B'nai Tikvah in Walnut Creek, California, for recognizing the importance of this extra-congregational activity, and to Lance Canter, Virginia Fried, and Sally Cohen of the Temple staff.

Seymour Fromer, Director of the Magnes Museum, has aided us at every turn. Alan Snyder, Susan Katz-Snyder, and Mordecai Ansbacher added an extra artistic dimension. Laura Steuer's skillful editing helped shape the variegated essays of this volume into their final form. Nelda Cassuto's and Ruth Rischin's keen editorial eyes were indispensable. And Yehudit Goldfarb prepared the index with discrimination and dispatch.

Of the many people who were consulted in the course of the book's preparation, I would like to single out Rabbi Robert Jacobs and Diane Spielmann of the Leo Baeck Institute in New York, Rabbi Lewis Barth of the Hebrew Union College in Los Angeles, and Consul General Walter Koenig and Michael Koch of the German Consulate in San Francisco. We are especially indebted to Charlotte Fonrobert who translated much of the German material. A doctoral candidate at the Graduate Theological Union, Charlotte first met my father as his student at the *Kirchliche*

ix

Hochschule in Berlin in 1985 and represented for him the promise of reestablishing a vital interest in Judaism on German soil among the younger generation of Germans.

Two contributors, Ludwig Altman and Simcha Kling, both among my father's closest friends, passed away before this volume went to press. Simcha's essay was given a few final touches by his daughter Reena and Ludwig's memoir was supplemented with excerpts from his oral history, for which we must thank Emmie Altman, Eleanor Glaser, and the Western Jewish History Center.

Professor Moses Rischin provided the benefit of his wisdom and experience and ensured that our work met high standards. Our family also owes him a tremendous debt for his determination to establish and clarify the historic role that Joseph Asher played in exploring the potential for a postwar German-Jewish dialogue.

With my father's death in May 1990 this volume lost its principal contributor. The living embodiment of the charm, humor, and vitality of German Jewry, in the waning months that were given him he found deep fulfillment in the making of this book. To the great sorrow of his family, he was not able to share in its realization. In his absence, my wife Jennifer's patience and concern, my brother Daniel's support, and my mother Fae Asher's words of encouragement all have been essential. May this cooperative effort do justice to my father's memory and to the rich legacy of German Jewry.

—*Raphael Asher*

THE GERMAN IMPERATIVE AND THE JEWISH RESPONSE

Moses Rischin

The Jewish Legacy and the German Conscience speaks to a portentous theme, one that weighs heavily upon all of us but that haunted Joseph Asher and his fellow Jews of German birth in the extreme. Were they, the survivors of the Holocaust, heirs of a glorious legacy that was both Jewish and German, or were they the dupes of a fatal delusion? For a thousand years Jews had inhabited Europe's heartland whose German-speaking regions had shaped their lives, their demeanor, their ways, and their very souls. Rooted in Middle High German, their Judeo-German idiom reached out to Eastern Europe where, deepened and Slavicized, it flourished as Yiddish and became the *lingua franca* of a vaster number of Jews than has any other language, including English, in all of Jewish history. And with the dawn of emancipation and for nearly a century and a half thereafter, Germany's Jews, indeed, virtually all modernizing Jews, would regard German accomplishment as uniquely and self-evidently coextensive both with their own subculture and with the best of modern European culture.

Until Adolf Hitler plunged their beloved homeland down the road to neo-barbarism, an apparent German-Jewish or Jewish-German symbiosis, as it came to be called, promised to be the paradigm for a high European civilization infused with Jewish ingredients that provided an added warranty for German excellence and for a European Germany envisioned by its best. Even the great historian Gershom Scholem, who

1

adamantly denied that a German-Jewish symbiosis had ever been remotely possible, was to avow in 1966 that "only if we seek to get to the bottom of their relationship...[can] the atmosphere between Jews and Germans...be cleansed."[1]

"Their relationship," of course, had formally ended, if not in 1933, 1938, or 1942, then with the Final Solution, that ultimate bureaucratic euphemism for the unspeakable and incomprehensible murder of six million Jews, among them virtually all of Joseph Asher's kin. "Auschwitz remains unique," proclaimed the president of the Federal Republic in 1988 in his opening address before an assemblage of mostly revisionist German historians who questioned German responsibility for Auschwitz and who seemed to have lost the moral capacity to distinguish even between Nazism and Zionism. "It was perpetrated by the Germans in the name of Germany," continued President Richard von Weiszäcker. "The truth is immutable and will not be forgotten."[2]

However tormented by the specters of the past, Joseph Asher had resolved to look beyond Auschwitz and to reaffirm the lost promise of the German-Jewish symbiosis. A "monumental and mutually beneficial common history" and "cultural and intellectual creativity...put their stamp on both Judaism and West-European civilization," declared Asher to a distinguished audience at San Francisco's German Consulate on April 5, 1989. Honored on that occasion by the Federal Republic for his historic efforts to promote "German-American and German-Jewish understanding," Asher insisted that only if the entire past is remembered would there be hope for reconciliation between Germans and Jews. And for Asher, as for his mentor, Leo Baeck, Jews of all traditions, including non-Jewish Jews, and those who regarded themselves solely as citizens of "the supranational republic of culture," were all integral to that past as they were to the German and European past.[3]

In this closing decade of the twentieth century, the striving for reconciliation and remembrance is momentous in its implications for both Germans and Jews, as it well ought to be for all mankind. "Of all the shameful divisions that tear men asunder from their fellow men," concluded Harvey Cox, the noted American Protestant theologian, in 1965, "perhaps the split between Jews and Germans is the most dramatic and spectacular,"[4] for theirs was an extraordinary relationship. "This ambivalently intense relationship," as Erich Kahler once described it, informed by "a dramatic dialectical exchange on both sides, touching the nerve of existence,"[5] agitated Joseph Asher to the core of his being. As the opening essays testify, Asher, driven to bridge the gap between Germans and Jews, was determined that this volume advance that enterprise by focusing particular attention on its religious dimension.[6]

Less than a decade after being forced to flee his homeland, Joseph Asher inadvertently entered upon a mission that was to be cut short only by his death forty-three years later. In 1947, at the bidding of Leo Baeck, the heroic-souled leader of Germany's Jews in the Hitlerian era and the president of the World Union for Progressive Judaism, the 27-year-old Asher spent six weeks helping to reconstruct Jewish life among the survivors in the British-occupied zone of Germany where he served as liaison for displaced persons. In an exhausting whirlwind marathon "to save the soul and conscience of Jewry here," as he put it at the time, the special representative of the World Union found nothing that was hopeful. Wiesbaden, Cologne, Frankfurt, Bremen, Bonn, Hamburg, Hanover, Düsseldorf, not to mention Bergen-Belsen, all appeared waystations on the Jewish journey to oblivion. Mangled in body and spirit, the Jewish remnant in that Nazi-infested hell left Asher aghast. "The human eye cannot fathom such horrible sights as I had to see," he reported to Lily Montagu of the World Union. Nowhere did he detect even the barest trace of the great traditions of the Central European Jewish communities that he had once known.[7] Did he then quite realize that "the monstrous experiences" of those weeks would impel him to pursue the great task of reconciliation between Germans and Jews that was to grace the last decades of his life?

During the next few years, Asher immersed himself in America and in American Jewish life and exulted in the privilege of becoming an American. But the German question continued to trouble him. Before departing England for America in 1947, he had proposed at a meeting of rabbis that Germany be placed "off limits" for Jews. Thereafter, Asher continued to wage a pitched rearguard battle against establishing any ties with the new German republic and he himself refused to visit Germany. But a change came in 1955 when a trip to Europe that included his former homeland, now in a state of breathless renewal, inspired Asher to reconsider and to reformulate his ideas in an unpublished article, "Let's Be Jewish About the Germans," in which the rabbi called for "a reorientation of the Jewish relationship with Germany," for the sake of all concerned, that would be informed by "pure and simple Judaism" and "an especially keen sense of history."[8]

For the next few years, as Joseph Asher continued to ponder further on how to "be Jewish about the Germans," he found himself thrust into the midst of the burgeoning civil rights movement. In February 1960, in Greensboro, North Carolina, where he had become rabbi of Temple Emanu-El, Asher and a Baptist minister alone among the local clergy came to the support of the nation's first sit-ins at a Woolworth lunch counter, actions which "remade history, inaugurating the civil rights revolution of the 1960s and setting in motion the most turbulent decade of our nation's history." It was just at this time that the Eichmann trial in Jerusalem focused world attention on the Holocaust. That tragedy, which long had remained submerged in the Jewish and the public mind, one which Asher had hesitated to address earlier, became in 1961 the theme of his Rosh Hashanah eve sermon. "The horror story of which I would speak today," began Asher, "should have been told years ago and told again and again. Yet it took the emergence of one man to splash it into the forefront of the world's attention. That man, of course, is Adolf Eichmann...."[9]

A trip to Europe with his family the following year, which included a visit to Wiesbaden, his hometown, opened the way to the second phase of a mission inadvertently begun seventeen years earlier. In 1964, aided by Dr. Heinrich Kappstein, German ambassador to the United States, Joseph Asher returned to Germany at the invitation of the German government. This time, he came to take a measure of the New Germany and to learn especially what the new generation of German youngsters at the Gutenberg, formerly the Staatliche, *Gymnasium* in Wiesbaden, his alma mater, knew of the Holocaust, of Jews, and of Judaism. In the course of his trip, he also visited the Schoolbook Institute at Braunschweig, which published history texts for the schools; was welcomed at the Max Planck Institute in Berlin, specializing in research in educational methods; and met with the Commissioners of Education of the Federal Republic and of the state of Hesse.

Never before had Joseph Asher experienced life so piercingly and been so stirred to find deepest meaning in his own life. Walking down the corridors of his old school, he was assailed by nightmarish memories of his childhood and youth at every turn. Yet to encounter perplexed teachers, speak with 250 youngsters who knew neither their past nor a single Jew, and be reunited with his old deskmate, rival for class honors and Nazi youth movement enthusiast, now a repentant physician, vested Asher with new-found authority to measure the fine linkages between memory and conscience.

On returning to the United States, Asher proceeded to write what proved to be an extraordinary article, one in which he sensitively and dramatically depicted his historic visit to Wiesbaden and masterfully drew out its implications for future German-Jewish relations. Splashed across the outsize pages of *Look,* the weekly pictorial magazine, and sensationally packaged, "A Rabbi Asks: Isn't It Time We Forgave the Germans?" was read by millions. Catapulting a virtually unknown American rabbi onto the world stage, the *Look* article touched an exposed nerve, eliciting hundreds of troubled letters from Jews and non-Jews, Germans and Americans, few of them complimentary.

In reply to a distraught Jesuit scholar in Indiana, the rabbi denied that "forgiveness" signified "condescension" and insisted that "remembrance," not forgetting, was essential to laying "the foundation for a better future." To a professor in Marburg, Asher pronounced "Homogeneity ...the passion only of the lower species," and reiterated his commitment to "religious, ethnic, and racial pluralism...for the benefit of all men." To an Orthodox Jewish compatriot of his Australian days who impugned the rabbi's religious legitimacy and personal authority, Asher resignedly responded "no further public debate." But an especially poignant letter from a genuine soulmate proved tonic and assured Asher that his faith in the younger generation was well-placed. Judith Dietz, a German major at Wellesley College of "mixed Conservative-Reform background," had been selected two years earlier to be an American Field Service exchange student and was returning to serve as a counselor at a new international music camp in Berlin. To this sensitive young woman perplexed about her capacity to speak as a Jew, Asher wrote that he was "confident that, when you return to Germany, you will represent the best of which our tradition makes us capable."[10]

Critical above all for Asher was the simple mandate calling for reconciliation with which he had closed his article in *Look* magazine and which he reinvoked a year later in an interview with a reporter for *Aufbau,* German America's leading Jewish weekly: "Forgiving and forgetting are not the same. A new generation is growing up that was not born when the horrible crime was committed and for which they cannot be held responsible. The only positive thing we can do is to acquaint them with the Jews, their teachings, customs, and history, which they have not had the opportunity to know."[11]

The response to Asher's proposal was immediate. Endorsed by Berlin's Mayor Willy Brandt, soon to become chancellor of the German

Federal Republic, it was implemented by the Commission on Interfaith Activities of Reform Judaism which dispatched four German-speaking American rabbis, including the noted biblical scholar and American-born Professor Samuel Sandmel of Hebrew Union College, to lecture in Germany on Jewish life and Judaism. On this visit, Asher alone met with some 8,000 teachers-in-training and students in Berlin and Hanover and helped prepare the first curriculum on the Holocaust for secondary schools. Contrary to a "completely false impression" that the pilot project was a bridgehead for a "crusade...to convert Nazis to a humanitarian attitude," the German ambassador to the United States made it clear that the rabbis' objective was to enter into "a humane confrontation with the young generation...which does not know who and what Jews and Judaism are, because it no longer knows Jews."[12]

For the next quarter century, Asher remained singularly dedicated to that "humane confrontation with the young generation," a task for which his remarkable capacity for empathy, commitment, temperament, and German background equipped him second to none. An inveterate visitor to Judaic studies departments at German universities, in the last years of his life Asher attained special distinction as a visiting professor at the *Kirchliche Hochschule* in Berlin where he lectured on modern Jewish life and Reform Judaism to hundreds of pastors and theological students and did so with his incomparable flair for his native language, a delight in his able and receptive German students, and a pride in his subject matter. In recognition for his unique services, Asher was appointed in 1980 to the United States Holocaust Memorial Council, entrusted with overseeing the projected Holocaust Memorial Museum in Washington. Ironically, on the eve of President Reagan's visit to the Bitburg cemetery in 1985 (an affair that propelled Elie Wiesel, on receiving the Congressional Gold Medal at the White House, to reprove the President, "That place...is not your place. Your place is with the victims of the SS"), Chancellor Helmut Kohl invited Asher to serve on the Joint United States-West Germany Committee to explore the lessons of the Holocaust in "the long and painful process of reconciliation between the Jewish people and the New Germany." Subsequently, Asher participated in an international meeting of scholars representing Austria, Germany, Israel, Poland, and the United States to plan a Holocaust memorial at Wannsee Villa near Berlin where in January 1942 the decision had been made to implement "the Final Solution of the Jewish Question." Along with a number of Americans, Asher also met with

German schoolbook publishers to discuss how the central historic issues between World War I and World War II might best be presented in German texts.[13] To his last days, Joseph Asher persisted in this mission.

The Jewish Legacy and the German Conscience consists of an introduction, eight parts, and an afterword that are intended to bring into focus those themes that illuminate the German-Jewish relationship from the late eighteenth to the late twentieth century. Each of the segments addresses an important movement or phenomenon, episode or era, development or trend in the history of Germany's Jews in what has justifiably come to be regarded as one of the most obsessive and perplexing colloquies in human history. Men and women, Christian and Jew, German and Israeli, Canadian, English, and American—the contributors' varied interests, disciplines, personae, and expertise extend across the entire gamut of relations between Germans and Jews.

Part I portrays Joseph Asher, American rabbi, primarily in his role as reconciler of German and Jew. His own essays, the second of which was drafted in the final weeks of his life, and the reminiscences by two of his closest associates—his son, Raphael Asher, and his successor at San Francisco's Temple Emanu-El, Robert Kirschner—endow this book and its theme with the inspirational force and breadth of spirit that was Joseph Asher.

Part II begins with Peter von der Osten-Sacken's pivotal survey of the Christian-Jewish encounter in Berlin from its inception in the age of Lessing and Mendelssohn to its extinction in the Hitlerian era and to its subsequent revival in the years after World War II. Throughout his discussion, von der Osten-Sacken makes clear that the spokesmen for Judaism, in their supreme effort to accommodate their history to German Christianity, remained outsiders, German Christianity remaining virtually deaf to Jewish tradition and to religious dialogue. When German Christianity did begin to approach Judaism in the 1920s, it proved far too weak and far, far too late. It is with supreme irony that von der Osten-Sacken pays tribute to Leo Baeck as the finest exemplar of dialogue between Jew and Christian and to Baeck's towering *The Gospel as a Document of the History of the Jewish Faith*—apparently the last Jewish book to be published in Germany before the mass pogroms in 1938—as without equal for its appreciation of the Christian Gospels as quintessentially Jewish books.[14] From another perspective, David Ellenson makes richly evident the profound effect on Orthodox Jewish thinkers of their encounter with the German philosopher Immanuel Kant, whose non-dogmatic Christianity and moralistic outlook proved so congenial to Judaism, if not quite receptive to it in its own terms.

In Part III, "Historical Judaism," David Dalin and Herbert Strauss give special attention respectively to the impact of German-Jewish *Wissenschaft* on Anglo-Jewish scholarship en route to America and on German-Jewish history as a test case in the modernization of Judaism. In Part IV, "The People," Gunther Plaut, Werner Weinberg, and Trude Maurer provide scholarly studies of ordinary Jewish folk in Mendelssohn's day, of the persistence of the Judeo-German idiom among Germans into the second half of the twentieth century, and of the anomalous position in which East European Jews found themselves in Weimar Germany. Part V consists of four essays by Immanuel Jakobovits, Jakob Petuchowski, Simcha Kling, and Karl Richter that illuminate diverse Jewish religious legacies, specifically: *Torah im Derekh Eretz* as propounded by the founder of Neo-Orthodoxy; the vicissitudes in the making of the *Einheitsgebetbuch*, a Reform prayerbook whose reforms were most responsible to the tradition; the impressive role of Zionism in Germany before World War I; and the place of the German refugee rabbinate on the American scene.

In Part VI, "The God-Seeking Intellectuals," Michael Weinrich and Paul Mendes-Flohr focus on the cosmopolitan religious humanists gathered around Judah L. Magnes at the Hebrew University in Jerusalem, on their stellar figure, Martin Buber, and on their collective religious expression as it was briefly incorporated in the society *Ha'ol*, or The Yoke. In Part VII, "The Arts," Ziva Amishai-Maisels' incisive study of the history of painting and the problem of Jewish identity is accompanied by a rare memoir by Ludwig Altman depicting the musical life of a Jewish organist in the Nazi era.

Finally, in Part VIII, "Finis and Beyond," Gerhard Weinberg, Barry Katz, Winston Pickett, and Fred Rosenbaum bring their scholarship to bear upon such issues as the supreme price in human liberties exacted of all Germans by the Nazis, the incapacity of American intelligence personnel to influence government policy—whether with respect to the Holocaust or other matters—and the grimly problematic condition since World War II of Germany's few Jews. Lastly, Elie Wiesel, literary laureate of the Holocaust and its premier statesman, lends his resonant voice as witness in "Memory and Reconciliation."

Taken together, these essays give special, if by no means exclusive, attention to the religious component in German-Jewish life. In a pronouncedly secular age, a great nation, Germany, failed, as had no nation of its exalted standing, to address the problem of religion and civilization and so brought disaster upon itself, upon Europe, and upon much of the world. Europe's Jews, and most notably the highly integrated Jews of Germany, were the most vulnerable of its peoples. Their tragic fate has raised gnawing doubts regarding the viability of civilization itself. In the last two generations, Germany assuredly has distanced itself from the darkest episode of its past and become a model democratic nation. *The Jewish Legacy and the German Conscience* is intended to contribute to that fulfillment, as well as to enunciate the vital role that German Jewry played in creating Jewish institutions and forms that have singularly helped to define the parameters of modern Jewish life.

NOTES

1. Gershom Scholem, *On Jews and Judaism in Crisis*, ed. Werner J. Dannhauser (New York, 1976), 73.

2. Ansprache des Bundespräsidenten, *Richard von Weiszäcker: zur Eröffnung des 37 Historikertages in Bamberg am 12 Oktober 1988 (Presse- und Informations-amt der Bundesregierung*, n. 451-488), 12. Also see Charles Maier, *The Unmasterable Past: History, Holocaust, and German National Identity* (Cambridge, Mass., 1988), 1-8, 29-9, and 82 on this point.

3. Response by Rabbi Joseph Asher to Consul General Walter Koenig April 5, 1989, *Ansprache anlässlich der Überreichung des Grossen Verdienstkreuzes des Vereinsordens der Bundesrepublik Deutschland an Rabbi Joseph Asher im General Konsulat April 5, 1989*. Leo Baeck, *This People Israel: The Meaning of Jewish Existence*, ed. Albert H. Friedlander (New York, 1964), xxii, 339.

4. Harvey Cox, "The Statute of Limitations on Nazi Crimes: A Theological and Ethical Analysis" (Background Reports National Conference of Christians and Jews, June 1965), 11.

5. Eric Kahler, "The Jews and the Germans," in *Studies of the Leo Baeck Institute*, ed. Max Kreutzberger (New York, 1967), 25.

6. See Peter Gay, *Freud, Jews, and Other Germans* (New York, 1978), vii, 165; George L. Mosse, *Germans and Jews* (New York, 1970), 77-78, 204-5; Mosse, *German Jews Beyond Judaism* (Bloomington, 1985); Abraham J. Peck, ed., *The German-Jewish Legacy in America, 1938-1988* (Detroit, 1989); Jehuda Reinharz and Walter Schatzberg, eds., *The Jewish Response to German Culture* (Hanover, 1985). Herbert A. Strauss and Werner Röder, eds., *International Biographical Dictionary of Central European Emigres, 1933-1945*, 4 vols. (New York, 1980-1983), is a magisterial statement about the manifold gifts of some 9,000 German exiles, over four-fifths of whom were Jews. Michael Meyer, *Response to Modernity: A History of the Reform Movement in Judaism* (New York, 1988) is the best single volume of its kind. Shulamit S. Magnus, "German-Jewish History," *Modern Judaism* 11 (February 1991), 125-46, is a fine historiographical appraisal.

7. Leo Baeck to Joseph Asher, May 1, 1947; Joseph Asher to Lily Montagu, May 28, June 18, July 2, 1947. (All letters to and from Joseph Asher and other cited unpublished materials are to be found in the Joseph Asher Collection at the Western Jewish History Center of the Magnes Museum.)

8. Joseph Asher, "Let's Be Jewish About the Germans," November 1956.

9. William H. Chafe, *Civilities and Civil Rights: Greensboro, North Carolina, and the Black Struggle for Freedom* (New York, 1980), vii; Joseph Asher, Sermon on the eve of Rosh Hashanah, 1961.

10. Joseph Asher to Rudolf Furchtenicht-Boening, May 13, 1965; Joseph Asher to Werner Kummel, May 7, 1965; Joseph Asher to Elias Munk, May 13, 1965; Judith A. Dietz (Lurie) to Joseph Asher, June 5, 1965; Joseph Asher to Judith A. Dietz (Lurie), June 9, 1965.

11. *Aufbau,* March 11, 1966.

12. Willy Brandt to Joseph Asher, June 8, 1965; Balfour Brickner, *Report on Commission on Interfaith Activities Sponsored Project in Germany* (Summer 1966); Heinrich Kappstein to Joseph Asher, February 24, 1966. See Wolfgang Scheffler and Werner Bergmann, eds., *Lerntag über den Holocaust als Thema im Geschichtsunterricht und in der Politischen Bildung: Zentrum für Antisemitismusforschung gemeinsam mit der Research Foundation for Jewish Immigration, New York, November 8, 1987* (Berlin, 1988); and Chaim Schatzker, "Education on the Holocaust: West Germany" in vol. 2, *The Encyclopedia of the Holocaust,* ed. Israel Gutman, 4 vols. (New York, 1990).

13. Elie Wiesel to Joseph Asher, May 17, 1985; Joseph Asher to Elie Wiesel, May 29, 1985.

14. Volker Dam, "Das Jüdische Buch im Dritten Reich, II: Salmon Schocken und sein Verlag," *Archiv für Geschichte des Buchwesens XXII* (1981), 850. For a brilliant selection and translation of Baeck's writings, see Walter Kaufmann, trans., *Judaism and Christianity: Essays by Leo Baeck* (Philadelphia, 1959); and for a valuable, more recent effort, see Fritz A. Rothschild, ed., *Jewish Perspectives on Christianity* (New York, 1990) which reprints a number of Baeck's most important writings. Also see Otto Kulka and Paul Mendes-Flohr, eds., *Judaism and Christianity under the Impact of National Socialism* (Jerusalem, 1987), especially Flohr, "Ambivalent Dialogue: Jewish-Christian Theological Encounter in the Weimar Republic," and Lenore Siegele-Wenschkewitz, "The Relationship between Protestant Theology and Jewish Studies during the Weimar Republic," for superb depictions of the problematics of the Jewish-Christian encounter.

PART I

German and Jew:
A Portrait of Joseph Asher

ISN'T IT TIME?[*]

Joseph Asher

I AM A RELIGIOUS JEW who grew up in Germany and felt the terror of Nazism. Yet I feel that the time has come for those who hate Germany and the Germans to take a new look at their feelings.

My own new look came recently when I journeyed to a German secondary school—one that I myself had attended in the early days of Hitler—to see what young students today are being taught about the Hitler era. I did so not to recapture the joys of my boyhood, because these were few, but to see if a nation had changed.

My old school, the Staatliche *Gymnasium,* is in Wiesbaden, Germany. Now called Gutenberg *Gymnasium,* it includes grades 5 through 13. My father was an Orthodox rabbi in Wiesbaden, a Rhine River city, and I, like my grandfather, great-grandfather and great-great-grandfather before him, was destined to become a rabbi. I attended religion classes twice a week after school, but most of each day was spent in the Staatliche *Gymnasium.* When Hitler took over as chancellor in January 1933, there were only seven Jews in our student body of around 600. Three years later, I was the last student to be expelled for the "crime" of being a Jew.

Today, I am a Reform rabbi in a pleasant Southern city in the United States. I got there via a seminary in London, a wartime internment camp for "enemy aliens" in Australia, a chaplaincy in the Australian Army and a seminary in Cincinnati. I have been a rabbi in Melbourne, Australia; Sarasota, Florida; Tuscaloosa, Alabama; and for the past six years, Greensboro, North Carolina. From my various pulpits, I have often discussed the German responsibility for crimes against Jews. I felt the need to keep alive the memory of these years among American Jews. But I also often wondered how the German youth of today react to those crimes. What do they know of the Hitler years? How do they feel about them? I thought that if I returned to my old classrooms and saw for myself, I could learn more of the truth about a controversial and oft-debated topic. I believed that if I listened to German boys who were as yet unborn when Hitler and his regime committed their crimes, I could determine if Germany has really changed.

The German Ambassador in Washington, Dr. Heinrich Kappstein, was intrigued to hear of my project. He arranged for the principal and students of Gutenberg *Gymnasium* and other educators to provide me full cooperation. Not long after my arrival, I found myself walking to my old school down Wiesbaden's Kaiser Friedrich Ring, just as I had so many times in the past. The memories, good and bad, came flooding back as I strode along the traffic-choked street.

In 1935, I was marching down this same street with a class of 48 boys on a field trip to the nearby State Museum. I was the only Jew in the class, and by now hardly any of my classmates spoke to me. Once, I used to do my homework in classmates' homes, but no more. The students looked quite military as they marched briskly along, singing one of the songs of the times: *"Köpfe rollen, Juden heulen, als das Blut vom Messer spritzt!"* This meant: "Heads roll, Jews weep, as blood spurts from the dagger!" I broke from the ranks and, weeping bitterly, ran home. "I'll never go back again," I vowed. My father, who was later to be sent to the infamous Buchenwald concentration camp, comforted me. "Do you think I was never teased or persecuted in the Kaiser's Germany?" he asked. "You must go back." The next day, I returned to school.

I was the only student who was allowed to keep a textbook atop my desk whenever the teacher ordered all desk tops cleared "immediately, without fail." The textbook was there to cover the word JUDD, carved there in the wood two inches deep and starkly outlined with black ink. I had found that word, which means "kike," when I came to school one morning in 1933.

Because I was a Jew, I was exempted from saying *"Heil Hitler!"*, required six times a day when we had to give the Nazi salute in class. I still had to raise my right arm, left hand rigidly at my belt buckle, while the others thundered a Nazi greeting to the various teachers.

My Latin teacher was kind enough to suggest that I pass him by, should we meet on the street, with no sign of recognition, even though school rules required us to greet all teachers in a prescribed fashion. The law prohibited us from saying "good morning"; instead, we had to give the Nazi salute. My teacher feared that this might infuriate any loyal Nazis who saw me walking with my bearded father. Other teachers were not so understanding. To avoid disaster when meeting them on the street, I would have to duck into a doorway or peer intently into a shop window, pretending I hadn't seen them.

Inside the old brick school building, the classrooms nowadays are not too different. It is easy to turn the clock back more than 32 years and reconstruct the scene as it was in 1932. "Ernst," as I shall call him, shares my double desk. He has done so for years. We boys are seated in order of the grades we receive. Ernst and I have been constant rivals for first place, so we always share the first desk; sometimes, he sits in the No. 1 position, and other times, I win it back from him. We despise each other. During exams, we build a high wall of books between us to prevent the other from copying answers. Hitler hasn't yet taken power, and there is no need for 12-year-old Ernst to be a Nazi. Nevertheless, he is an enthusiastic follower of the Hitler Youth movement. Our parents try to have us mend our differences, but nothing can make us friends now that Ernst is a Nazi.

One day, just before the biology teacher is scheduled to come into our classroom, Ernst draws a swastika that covers the entire blackboard. The teacher is known to have been a member of the National Socialist party since the 1920s. He still has to wear his Nazi membership pin concealed on the reverse side of his coat lapel. A thunderous chorus of *"Heil Hitler!"* greets him as he walks in. He is elated. "Are you all good Hitler Youths?" he asks. Eager Ernst, currently the class spokesman, jumps to his feet and replies, "Yes, sir, all except the Jew, Joseph." The room reverberates with raucous laughter. My mortification is complete. I realize that I am alone, with 47 enemies. But the old Nazi teacher (who was interned by U.S. occupation forces after the German surrender) comes to my rescue. "That's enough!" he orders. "If all of you were like Joseph, I would not have the grief with this class that is turning my hair gray." I still am grateful for the way he soothed my wounds on that terrible day.

Revisiting my old school, I found that the arrangements made by the German Ambassador were excellent. The students and faculty had been eagerly awaiting my coming for eight weeks. The principal organized 250 of the older students—those from ages 17 to 19—into groups of about 50

In *Gymnasium* class picture, the future Rabbi Asher (no. 32) sits in
front row, not far from Ernst (no. 22), who had scrawled "Judd!!"
in his yearbook opposite Rabbi Asher's old German name.
Wiesbaden, 1934. (*Look* magazine)

IV b.

(Studienrat Dr. Steingräber)

1. Adolph, Gerd
2. Ansbacher, Joseph
3. Aumann, Kurt
4. Beisheim, Fritz
5. Bind, Klaus —
6. Brukſch, Hans
7. Charles, Kurt

each. I was to meet with each section for two hours. I was also to meet with 20 teachers.

When I was introduced to the students, one by one, I heard the last name of my old classmate, Ernst. The name belonged to a 19-year-old boy who looked just as I remembered Ernst: tall, straight and blond—the ideal Aryan German. "Are you related?" I asked the youth. "Yes, sir," he answered. "He is my father. I'll tell him you're here. He will want to see you."

Within an hour, I was summoned to the telephone. The Germans love titles. I heard from someone who called himself *Herr Doktor* So-and-So. It was Ernst! He was a prosperous professional man. *"Sieg und Heil,"* he greeted me. "We must get together at once. How about coming to my apartment at four o'clock? I'm putting the champagne on ice right now."

I could hardly wait. When Ernst opened the door of his elegant apartment, we were both visibly shocked. It was not so much that we had both aged by 28 years; all class reunions have this built-in surprise. But where was the tall, lean, straight, blond-haired model of the Aryan superman? Instead, I saw a shortish, stocky, slightly debilitated and quite bald middle-aged man, showing every bit of his 44 years, and then some. He was no less stunned by me, and said so. "When did you grow like that?" he asked. (I happen to be 6 feet 4 inches tall and weigh around 160.) "I remember you as short and stocky." I realized what had happened. He recalled me as the caricature of the Jew that had been drummed into him by the obscene literature of his day. And I remembered him as the fearsome ideal of the superrace who could administer pain to me and yet remain inviolate. When I commented on this observation, we both had a hearty laugh. "That must be it!" he chuckled as he poured me some champagne.

Ernst produced a photo album, with some of the same class photos I had in my own album back home. But here Ernst was also in a variety of uniforms: Hitler Youth, the Labor Service and the *Wehrmacht,* the army. Here was Ernst before leaving for the Eastern Front, and here was Ernst just back from the Eastern Front. What a difference! The Eastern Front must have had quite an impact on Ernst; in those photos Ernst seemed to develop his run-down appearance.

I talked about the persecutions of my youth. Ernst was unbelieving. "I know things were bad for the Jews, but not in our old class. Sure, I was a Nazi, and loved it. I wouldn't kid you about that. But I couldn't have been that cruel to you. Nor could our old classmates."

I felt that Ernst was telling the truth as he saw it. It is a quirk of nature that a victimizer rarely remembers torturing, while his victim retains

17

every detail. Ernst agreed in principle with my recollections, but he remained skeptical about the particulars. But Ernst's mood was to change abruptly. I recalled that at home I had our school yearbook for 1933-34, which that year for the first time displayed a swastika atop the eagle on the cover. I asked Ernst to bring out his copy. At the back of the 78-page book was a list of our classmates. Eagerly, we pored over the names, mentally conjuring up the boyish faces. Suddenly, as though the book had become something repulsive, it dropped from Ernst's hand. There beside my old name (it was Ansbacher before I changed it after leaving Germany) was penciled the word *Judd!!* Two exclamation marks. "Whose handwriting can that be?" Ernst muttered unbelievingly. "That's not mine." He apparently had not looked at the book for years and had forgotten what was there.

I had no animosity in my heart, only compassion. The incident had brought back to Ernst's mind the whole forgotten nightmare of the past—more so than all the accounts of the war-crimes trials, which meant nothing to him and with whose horrors he had never identified himself. Ernst knew that I had not exaggerated the recollections of my torture. It was *his* memory that lacked exactitude. Could he help being as mortified today as I was in that biology class 32 years ago? Then, I had had a Nazi to soothe my aching soul. As a religious Jew, I would surely be magnanimous now in my compassion for him.

We changed the subject. He told me of attending our class's 25th annual reunion. Of the 48 students when I was expelled in 1936, only 16 graduated three years later, and of these, only nine survived the war. When we said our good-byes, Ernst pressed his copy of the yearbook into my hands. "Surely it means more to you than it does to me," he said. I promised to mail him my own unmarked yearbook.

Upon returning to my hotel, I found pencil-written notes on other pages of the yearbook. One note referred to a professor who had been transferred. "Penal transfer," it said. "Not a party member as late as March, 1933. Proud of my part in bringing it about." Alongside a listing of members of the parents' council was written: "Despite my efforts, not a single party member among them. I ascribe this to the 21-year-old assistant teacher who was charged to watch the situation. He has been a miserable failure."

True, none of these examples measured up to the chaos that engulfed millions of victims. Yet they represented the beginnings, which, if seen in their correct perspective, foreshadowed what was to come.

I had also told Ernst that my first impressions of the school program were most favorable, and that the students appeared well-informed about events of the Nazi period. "Nonsense," Ernst replied. "They didn't know a thing about the Nazis until eight weeks ago, when your visit was announced. Then they began boning up on it. I know. I happen to be on the parents' council and heard all this discussed."

Now it was my turn to express disbelief. No curriculum can be put together in only eight weeks, nor can textbooks be published in such a short time. I suspected that Ernst's feelings were characteristic of a German posture that can be described: "As a nation, we are no good; individually, we are beyond reproach. The more we whip our nation, the more believable is our individual innocence." This is not surprising. The German poets Goethe and Heine had utmost contempt for the nation's chauvinism, and expressed it repeatedly in their writings.

When I returned to school the next day, I saw additional evidence that facing facts can be unpleasant. The superintendent of schools for the state of Hesse, which oversees my alma mater, told me of a new school subject called *Gemeinschaftskunde,* which can best be translated as "community study." It incorporates the history of the rise and fall of the Third Reich and gives a measure of political education. The very name of the course, "community study," reveals a painful dilemma. Germans have always been reluctant to express true meanings. In the phrase "final solution," for example, the Germans found respectable words for annihilation. "Protective custody" meant illegal arrest and indefinite detention.

The superintendent was eager, however, to prove that "now we do not beat about the bush." He held up a curriculum outline, indicating the word *Judenmorde,* or Jew-murder. It is true that the only subject in Germany devoid of euphemism is the treatment of the Jews. A word-association test given the students would link the word Jew or Judaism with one of the following: anti-Semitism, destruction, tragedy, annihilation, murder, victim, etc. I questioned the wisdom of this approach, particularly since there was a complete absence of teaching about Jews or Judaism in any positive sense. I told him that I feared these intelligent young students might conclude that where there has been so much smoke, there must be a little bit of fire. They might ask, "Why have the Jews been so maligned and so persecuted if there really wasn't something wrong with them?"

It did not surprise me that none of the 250 students I met had any personal knowledge of Jews. According to the *American Jewish Year Book,* the Jewish population of both Germanys is estimated at 31,000 out of a total population of about 75 million. In all of West Germany, there

19

cannot be more than 30,000 Jews. In Wiesbaden, a city of 250,000, there are less than 100—with many of them the products of mixed marriages and only vaguely connected with Judaism. None of the students had ever seen a rabbi. Only a few had ever seen a Jew.

"The contribution of the Hebrew prophets in devising the concept of the universal God laid the foundation for the birth of Christianity and Islam," I told them. "It is not accidental that both these religions sprang from Judaism. The mission of Judaism is not to convert the world to its particular views, but rather to spread the Truth of One Eternal God. As God's attributes are infinitely varied, so can our understanding of an approach to Him reflect the infinite variety of Man's inventiveness.

"The so-called chosenness of the Jewish people imposes special responsibilities on Jews, rather than privileges. Israel is not the master race, but the people who chose to dedicate themselves to the Master."

One of the instructors asked that I please inform the class about the religious rituals of home and synagogue. "Tell the class that it is not true that Jews drink a Christian child's blood as part of the Passover ritual," he requested. Shocked into disbelieving silence, I asked him to repeat his question. I was astounded that after all that has happened to Jews as a result of this medieval libel, which was repeated again and again in the Nazi publications, a denial was still required. I am not questioning this teacher's goodwill; he genuinely regretted having to make such a request.

"Why do the Jews persist in remaining a separate people?" asked several of the students. Anti-Semitism, they believed, stems from what they call the *Andersartigkeit*, "differentness" of the Jews. It had not been made clear to them, I replied, that nowhere in Europe had the Jew been assimilated as thoroughly as in Germany. Jews were in politics, the theater, journalism and in the professions. Yet the scourge of modern anti-Semitism originated in this same Germany.

"But isn't there anti-Semitism in America today?" asked a student. "Yes, to a certain extent," I answered. "But rabid anti-Semitism is confined to the lunatic fringe. Americans have never found the need to build gas ovens. Prejudices are still rampant among all men. None of us is entirely free of them. The trick is to contain prejudices, not to allow them to run amok as they did in Germany of the 1930s."

Another recurring question was: "Do you consider yourself an American or a Jew?" Here again the students seemed unaware that America is strong *because* of its pluralism, that unlike most European countries, we blend diverse cultures, religions and philosophies. "You wouldn't ask a German if he considered himself a Lutheran or a

German," I answered. "In America, under the same sky, you can find Polish-Americans, Irish-Americans, Protestant-Americans and Catholic-Americans. But we are all of us Americans."

I had thought it impossible that I would ever feel an overwhelming compassion for Germany or the Germans, but this feeling surged forth as I talked with three teachers of contemporary history. They told me that before starting their courses, they felt compelled to explain their stand on Hitlerism to their students.

The first teacher reported that he usually begins by saying: "Now, gentlemen, I want you to know, even before you ask the question, 'Where were you in all this?' that I had no part in it." The teacher may be telling the truth, but some arrogant student invariably retorts, "That's what they all say!" His classmates, who don't have the courage to articulate the same sentiment, join in the snickering. The teacher's effectiveness is destroyed.

The second teacher told me that he usually starts his first lecture by berating himself, by beating his breast because of his guilt and thus proving himself repentant. This doesn't seem conducive to establishing a good teacher-student relationship, either. The students wonder where truthfulness begins and where falsehood and cynicism end. If the professor was so gullible in the 1940s for swallowing Nazism, what proof is there that his present devotion to democratic principles is not due to the same gullibility?

The third teacher, barely 35 years old, said he tells his classes: "I wasn't old enough to have participated in all this. Nor was I old enough to protest it." He then condemns the whole generation as maniacal and depraved. Invariably, one of the students rises to protest: "Sir! You insult my father and mother!"

When I first returned to the scene of my youth, suspicion and even loathing were my strongest sentiments. Having seen the Hitler tragedy in all of its enormity, I was neither willing to forgive nor forget. But has not the time come to forgive? Can we—especially those of us with religious motivations—hold all of the German people responsible for what happened? Can we blame a new generation that was not even alive in the Hitler era?

One of the students couldn't understand the difference between forgiving and forgetting. He asked, "Is not the ultimate gesture of forgiveness of a wrong the act of forgetting it ever had been perpetrated?" I was profoundly troubled by the question. I tried to distinguish between the wrong occurring between individuals and the evil arising from a misguided philosophy that entrapped a whole nation. I said that "while the wronged need muster a measure of magnanimity that encompasses both forgiveness and forgetfulness, the wrongdoer, by his own choice, shall not forget his evil deed, lest he repeat it."

An instructor who heard my answer cut in: "No rabbi can answer this question to your satisfaction. His religion subscribes to a God of punishment, while the Christian ethic speaks of a God of love. His religion is based on the *lex talionis*—an eye for an eye and a tooth for a tooth. Ours is based on the Golden Rule. In the Jewish sense, there is a distinction between forgetting and forgiving that is incomprehensible in the Christian sense."

I stood up to object: "Besides the *lex talionis,* the Jewish Bible also speaks, and with much greater frequency and emphasis, of loving one's neighbor (Leviticus 19:18). It also establishes the principle of the brotherhood of man (Malachi 2:10) and of God's equal love of all mankind (Amos 9:7). Does not the Bible speak of magnanimity toward one's enemy (Proverb 25:21), and doesn't the rabbinic literature define the highest form of heroism as turning an enemy into a friend (*Abot de R. Nathan,* Chapter 23)?"

One of the classes I visited had made a field trip to Frankfurt-am-Main only 10 days earlier to witness one day of the trial of Auschwitz concentration-camp officials. The students had deliberately delayed their discussion of what they saw until my arrival. "Why prosecute them?" asked one student. "They are no more guilty than all of the Germans." The principal lost his composure. "That is not true!" he shouted. "They *must* be prosecuted and punished. All Germans are not guilty of their crimes."

"Well, Rabbi," asked another student, still shaken by his experience in Frankfurt. "Do you consider *me* guilty?"

"Of course, I cannot burden you with the guilt of the past," I answered. "You were not even born when all this horror occurred. Your question weighs me with great sorrow. For I ask myself, what could I have said or done that could conceivably make you feel that I hold you responsible? I, too, must search my heart, lest I commit the historic error of unending retribution."

How much of a burden of guilt can you lay on the shoulders of an 18-year-old boy without damaging his soul almost beyond repair? Is he not entitled to the benefit of the doubt? Didn't he ask what must be on the minds of so many who are either unable or unwilling to ask themselves the same question? What kind of hostility must there be hidden under this involuntary assumption of guilt by the German people? How indeed would someone feel in whose mind, even if only subconsciously, there arose the question of that 18-year-old boy: "Am I guilty?" There must always remain a bill of particulars, but there must also come a time—and the time may very well be now—when we must stop presenting it for payment.

Looking at Germany, I can see that there can be no genuine and lasting rehabilitation without rehabilitation on a person-to-person level. The horror of it all is too great to grasp; it eludes us. The small inhumanities, however, are within our power to heal.

I was pleased when, after returning home to North Carolina, I received a warm letter from my old seatmate, Ernst. He wrote: "I was overjoyed after nearly 30 years to sit across from a contemporary, one whom I should have respected, but because of a false or at least one-sided education, I have stigmatized....Your visit has somehow made me feel my own inadequacy, which surely must have shocked you.

"Now that I look back upon your visit and question myself concerning the sentiments that were evoked in me, I know that it was a sense of shame that arose in me about the times that lie behind us. Therefore, your visit was a valuable experience that I shall long remember. I was especially pleased that you have overcome all those great difficulties and have become an open-minded person whom I was allowed to get to know again."

Because I had this chance to see Ernst again, I learned the truth that time heals many wounds. It is truer still that individual relations transcend relations between anonymous masses. As the mass murderers could not see their crimes, so the mass healers cannot see the effect of their handiwork.

The spiritual victory I feel that I have won lies in the reducing of bitterness and converting it into the stuff of which civilized human relations are made. Beyond retribution for evil lies compassion for the wrongdoer. "God desires not the death of the wicked, but that he return from his evil ways and live." That is the Jewish concept of God. Since man is created in His image, it behooves him to desire likewise. As wickedness springs from small and individual acts, thus does compassion begin in a single man's heart.

NOTES

*This article, originally entitled "A Rabbi Asks: Isn't It Time We Forgave the Germans?" appeared in *Look* magazine on April 20, 1965.

Rabbi Jonah Ansbacher (1880-1967).
c. 1930 (private collection)

AN INCOMPREHENSIBLE PUZZLEMENT

Joseph Asher

WE HAVE CHOSEN as the central theme of this Festschrift the legacy of German Jewry from the era of the Enlightenment in the mid-eighteenth century to the annihilation of virtually all of European Jewry by the Nazi Regime. We propose that the Jewish responses to modernity have continued to be models for the contemporary Jewish community, models for its religious pluralism, for its social institutions, for its cultural innovations and dilemmas and for its integration into American and Western civilization. We trust that this volume will make a contribution to historical scholarship as well as to a wider readership, for whom the rise and fall of German Jewry remains an incomprehensible puzzlement.

There are at least two vantage points from which to view this "incomprehensible puzzlement." The first asks how Germany with its high culture, as she was universally perceived, could literally engineer the genocidal instruments of the *Shoah*. More puzzling still is the second angle: how can we understand German Jewry's failure to anticipate the fate that was to overtake it and the rest of European Jewry? German Jews were certainly not unaware of anti-Semitism for a common and popular phrase among German Jews was: *"Frühling ist's und der Rischess blüht."* (It is spring and anti-Semitism blossoms.) *Rischess* was a Judeo-German word for anti-Semitism, literally "evil." This phrase was a kind of "inside" caution raising a mild warning signal against overconfidence.

To illumine that second puzzlement I submit a brief biography of my family, focussing on my father. Jonah Ansbacher represented the fifth direct generation of rabbis whose predecessors served communities in Southwest Germany, Bavaria and Franconia, from such small agrarian towns as Dinkelsbuhl to the city of Nuremberg where my grandfather built a magnificent synagogue, one of the many architectural treasures of this medieval city.

Grandfather Solomon Ansbacher and father Jonah were the first in the family to respond to the mandates of Enlightenment. In addition to their intense Jewish and rabbinic education, they were steeped in secular studies, as had become the standard practice in the 1800s for all prospective rabbis. A candidate for the rabbinate was expected first to gain a doctoral degree from a secular university in a subject most often quite unrelated to his future career. Thus my father wrote his doctoral dissertation at the University of Erlangen on a work by a thirteenth-century Arab cosmologist, translating and annotating it in German. (Copies are still available in the Harvard Library, as well as in that of the Hebrew Union College in Cincinnati.) His minor was mathematics, in which he excelled all his life, leading him to a hobby in astronomy.

My grandfather was not yet convinced of the efficacy of this emphasis on a secular education. He is reported to have said: "Since rabbis have become doctors, the Jewish people have become sick." As was the custom at the time, the young, aspiring rabbis, now armed with their doctoral sheepskins, would go abroad for their first year of training. My father went to a famous Hungarian yeshiva in Deutschkreuz and from there proceeded to the Hildesheimer Seminary in Berlin. In Frankfurt-am-Main, he received his ordination, hand-written by Rabbi Solomon Breuer, known as the *"Alte Rav,"* the son-in-law of Samson Raphael Hirsch, the founder and spiritual father of Neo-Orthodoxy.

A touching phrase in my father's *semicha* (ordination) certificate describes him as a link in *"shalshelet rabbanim"* (a chain of rabbis). At his behest, the *semicha* I received from an Orthodox Beth Din (Rabbinical Court) in London of which my father was a member, included that same phrase, thus binding me, at least symbolically, to my forebears.

The symbiosis between one's intense Jewishness and one's commitment to German culture and patriotism was quickly fashioned for the laity as well as the rabbis. The centuries of Jewish sojourn in the German territories provided ample precedent for peaceable existence as well as, unfortunately, for virulent hostility. Their eligibility for German citizenship, if not unlimited, provided the Jews with an awareness of their privilege. They viewed this privilege as a responsibility to be exercised with grace and correctness. The conventional wisdom of the German Jews' "super-patriotism" can only be understood in the context of the novelty of their status and the mutual benefits it bestowed both upon Jews and Germans. Moreover, when compared with their brethren in Eastern Europe, the German Jews were treated immeasurably better and naturally supported the society that allowed them their relative freedom.

German patriotism—any patriotism—could almost always be brought into harmony with an uncompromising adherence to Jewish tradition. For example, when two of grandfather Solomon's sons, David and Jonah, served their time as conscripts in the German Imperial Army, Solomon took upon himself a private fast-day, Monday and Thursday of each week for the duration of their service. It was meant to atone for a possible transgression of the dietary laws or observance of the Sabbath which they may have been compelled to commit in the pursuit of their military duties. The rabbinic allowance that in some cases the Law of the Land prevails over Jewish ritual needed to be balanced with every effort to safeguard the integrity of Jewish law.

A partially hand-written commendatory letter addressed to my father from the last of the German emperors, Kaiser Wilhelm II, who fled to Holland at the end of World War I, is in our family archives and illustrates yet another example of this patriotism. The letter refers to a sermon my father delivered at the conclusion of the Battle of Verdun, using a text from the Torah portion of that week, the story of Noah and the flood, a most propitious reference. The letter commends my father for his patriotism and his loyalty to the Crown. He mounted this treasured document in a frame displaying the Imperial colors: black, white and red. The colors were later outlawed by the Weimar Republic and replaced by black, red and gold.

A young teenager when the Nazis grabbed power, I argued with my father about keeping this framed document which now represented the worst kind of infamy. He could not comprehend the connection I attempted to draw. I cannot bring myself to speak ill of my father but this incident is a small example of the German Jews' myopia which a young teenager could simply ignore or disdain. Such deeply rooted patriotism is hard to dislodge. It took a much more dramatic experience to accomplish that.

In his professional life my father personified the strictest adherence to Neo-Orthodoxy. He served one of the few congregations, perhaps four or five in all of Germany, which followed the example set by Samson Raphael Hirsch—secession from the unified Jewish community which was the organizational standard throughout the country. This meant that all Jewish institutions in each city functioned under one organizational roof financed by a religious tax collected by the government. That was also the standard of Protestant and Catholic institutions. As part of that unified Jewish community, the *Gemeinde,* there were Liberal, Reform and Orthodox synagogues, social welfare agencies, cultural facilities, schools, cemeteries, and other organizations. The secessionists, while continuing to pay taxes to the government without remaining its beneficiaries, decided to safeguard their total independence by avoiding any and all concessions which membership in the *Gemeinde* might exact from them.

As the years of the Nazi regime proceeded and the Jewish communities became ever more impoverished, the secessionists suffered most severely. I heard my father state on many occasions in the mid-1930s that secession was a horrendous mistake—not only because of the financial burdens it imposed, but just when the German-Jewish communities needed to mobilize their maximum unity, the secessionists were sounding a discordant note.

If at the end of his career my father had any regrets, it was regarding the idea of secession. He had come to view it as a violation of the rabbinic injunction as stated in the *Mishnah* ("Sayings of the Fathers"): "Do not separate yourself from the community." Of course, Samson Raphael Hirsch was as familiar with this text as anyone but believed that it was the community that had separated itself from authentic Judaism, and was therefore the culprit.

My sister Sulamith and I were born in Heilbronn-am-Neckar in 1913 and 1921 respectively. Our mother, the former Rosa Menke, was the daughter of a religious functionary in the first congregation my father served after his ordination in the small town of Labischin in the province of Posen. My mother's father acted as *shochet* (ritual slaughterer), *mohel* (circumciser), cantor, and religious teacher. Mother therefore came to this marriage fully prepared in knowledge and experience to assume the role of a full-time rabbi's wife.

Posen, an area caught in the geopolitical contention between Prussia and Poland, was ceded to Poland after World War I and became known as the Polish Corridor separating West and East Prussia (now part of Poland). Grandfather was consequently somewhat apprehensive about this union. As a Bavarian he viewed all people living east of the River Elbe as somewhat tainted by their proximity to Poland. My mother and her family proved to be at least as patriotic and as German as those born west of the Elbe. Nevertheless, she could never shake the epithet of being an *Ostjude* (East European Jew).

It was not uncommon for sons of rabbis to follow their fathers into the pulpits they had served. Grandfather Solomon, however, saw his son Jonah as not strong or strict enough to meet the standards he had set and did not encourage a succession for his son.

While my father may have been perfectly content to stay in Heilbronn, Mother was much more ambitious for him. She was aware of his great talents as a scholar and teacher, a reputation he gained over the years. His own humility and Mother's driving ambition led to many a conflict because he found fulfillment surrounded by his books at home whereas Mother wanted a broader public to share his gifts. In 1925 we moved to Wiesbaden, a city world-renowned as a spa, where people from all over Europe and elsewhere came for physical restoration and mental stimulation.

Wiesbaden abounded in scores of fine hotels, among them two fine kosher establishments monitored by my father. Not unlike the Michelin Guide, these kosher hotels displayed an illuminated sign showing a black eagle with the word "kosher" in one of its claws. While the owners may not have been observant Jews, they were expected to engage the services of a supervisor, usually a woman who, in turn, was responsible to the rabbi. She saw to the purchase of food supplies, the separation of meat and dairy kitchens, the separate storing of china and silverware and many other requirements of a kosher establishment. At the Hotel Kron-Prinz, a premier kosher hotel in Wiesbaden, the Supervisor's title *shomeres* (guardian) was slightly changed to *shomreuse*. A Hebrew word was transformed into a French version, perhaps to match the fancy wine list and the menu.

One *shomreuse,* Miss Katz, a frequent visitor to our home, often complained about the pressures from the proprietors to relax her strictness. In his supervision Father took into consideration the economic factors, especially after the rise of Hitler, when keeping the strictest *kashrut* became ever more difficult and costly. Indeed, my father belonged to the school of rabbis whose religious decision-making would go beyond the cold letter of the law. He would take into account the impact of his decisions on the total picture of the life of those affected.

Unlike Mother who was quick to counsel, "Down with the Eagle," regardless of how that would affect the business, Father would provide opportunities to remedy the situation. (Grandfather would have perhaps been more receptive to have my mother succeed him than my father.) That is not to say that Father was lax or indifferent to the mandates of halakhah (Jewish Law). He simply sought ways to preserve both its integrity and the livelihood of the operators of the hotels.

One of the first prohibitions against Jews decreed by the Nazi regime was the outlawing of *shechita* (ritual slaughter), the new law demanding that all animals be anesthetized before slaughter, which was contrary to halakhah. The Conservative movement, however, agreed to abide by that stipulation, and the meat sold under those conditions was described as "new kosher." In one of his sermons excoriating the Conservatives for this compromise, my father asked "What is new kosher? It is old *treife.*" I cite this to demonstrate that my father might have been a little more tolerant than other rabbis, but that even tolerance had its limits.

What is often misunderstood or overlooked about the Jewish experience in Germany is the extent of Jewish integration into the general community. Although rabbinic discourse was always part of the daily fare at our home, we were equally familiar with discussions over the latest cultural events. Equally broad was our experience at school, where a classical education, with Latin, Greek and the literary masters of many cultures were as familiar to us as the three Rs. Among my friends, as well as those of my family, were as many non-Jews as Jews. Throughout my school career I was always the only Jew in my class. It was only natural for me to spend a good deal of my leisure time and to pursue extra-curricular activities with non-Jews.

Therefore it came as a traumatic shock when the Nazis assumed power on January 30, 1933. A curtain came down between us and our life-long friends. Virtually the next day, I was shunned at school by my classmates. The teachers, some of them sheepishly, confined their relationship with me only to the most essential contact demanded between student and teacher. I was devastated. When I complained to my parents and insisted that I would not return to school they explained first that it was never easy to be a Jew and, second, that I did not go to school to be sociable but to get an education.

When quotas for Jewish students were established in 1934, a large number of Jewish students in many schools were expelled and Jewish teachers dismissed. In response, Jewish communities established Day

Schools with teaching staffs recruited largely from unemployed Jewish professionals. I survived the first two quota regulations, the first I suspect because of the prominence of my family and the quiet help of some of my teachers, the second based on grade status because the top students were permitted to remain. It was not until 1936 when all Jewish students were expelled that I transferred to a Jewish Day School located in Frankfurt-am-Main, about an hour's train ride from Wiesbaden, to which I commuted every day. This school by coincidence was called the Samson Raphael Hirsch School, a name that wielded great influence upon my family.

During a few weeks in the darkest of winter, I boarded in Frankfurt at the home of Dayan Eliezer Posen. (The title Dayan is given to such rabbis as function in rabbinical courts deciding issues of ritual and personal status.) Posen was Chairman of the Frankfurt Rabbinical Court, perhaps Germany's foremost Jewish legal authority. This hiatus in my daily commute was not to spare me the exposure to the bitter cold. My regular departure time in winter was long before daybreak, before it was permitted to don the phylacteries for the morning prayers. Living in Frankfurt simply allowed for the punctilious observance of the morning prayer schedule.

After one year there I had to transfer to Hamburg's famous Talmud Torah School for my first year of secondary education. It is no exaggeration to say that the Hamburg Talmud Torah, an all-boys' school, could boast of a faculty unmatched by any similar school in Germany before or since. Next to Berlin, Hamburg was the most cosmopolitan city in Germany; these were also the last two cities in Germany to submit to Nazification. The Hamburg school attracted the most talented professionals in every field. The roster of teachers read like a Who's Who of German-Jewish literati, scientists, linguists and philosophers, among them such luminaries as Martin Buber who visited our school on a fairly regular basis to teach the Senior class.

The curriculum, consisting of fairly equal portions of secular and religious subjects, qualified its graduates for at least two years' credit toward a Baccalaureate degree, which in my case was intended to be at the University of London. In Hamburg I boarded with several other out-of-town boys at the home of an observant family, but spent virtually every Sabbath at the home of the Chief Rabbi of Hamburg, Dr. Joseph Carlebach, his wife and their six children. These Sabbath celebrations with their most cordial piety remain etched in my memory as among the most cherished experiences of my youth. The Carlebach family, except for three children, perished in the Holocaust.

The Carlebach family, not unlike my own, was one of several rabbinic dynasties in Europe. Our families were intimate friends. Several years earlier, my father had received a call to succeed the former Chief Rabbi of Hamburg, Dr. Joseph Spitzer. My mother's most cherished ambition was about to be realized; however, Spitzer, despite prodding from the community, refused to retire at his appointed time. When, as was customary, several candidates were invited to preach before the congregation, Dr. Spitzer refused to allow the candidates to occupy his pulpit for this purpose. Although the congregation rented a large auditorium in order to circumvent his objection, my father immediately withdrew his candidacy. His respect for his colleague and the prospect of starting a new career with this foreshadowed tension violated his sense of propriety.

Between 1933 and 1936, attending school was for me a daily torture. Most of my fellow students appeared in class in their Hitler youth uniforms. The greeting for our teachers as they entered class was now a lusty *"Heil Hitler,"* with left hand grasping the belt buckle and the right raised in the Nazi salute. Although I was exempt from participating in this ritual one can only imagine the humiliation a young Jewish boy suffered several times each day. Quite aside from this experience there was total ostracism from every social contact with fellow students. The handful of remaining Jewish students clustered together at recess seeking the lowest visibility.

During one of our field trips, to which we marched with military precision, singing the current military and Party songs, the class broke into a popular melody.

> *Köpfe rollen*
> *Juden heulen*
> *Wenn das Blut*
> *vom Messer spritzt*
>
> (Heads are rolling
> Jews are screaming
> As the blood
> Spurts from the knife.)

I broke ranks, not an inconsequential breach of German discipline in itself, and ran home with hot tears of fear and anger streaming down my face. It was surely the last straw. My father, hardly able to restrain his own distress, still insisted I return to school the next day. I believe he lodged a blistering complaint to the Principal. While no penalties were administered to the class or its ringleader, there were several days of embarrassed silence on this issue.

My own unqualified, vocal and activist commitment to the civil rights movement in the early 1960s, when we lived in North Carolina, is traceable to these experiences. I could not remain silent in the face of the vicious racism our black fellow-citizens were compelled to endure, having felt its painful sting in my own person thirty years earlier. Each manifestation of racism and other forms of discrimination, even now, conjures up the pain I suffered and drives me to seek a remedy for it.

Lest I give the impression that we were entirely passive as these events unfolded, we did make provisions for escape. My parents had in their possession immigration visas for England for themselves and their children from as early as 1933. Due to my father's prominent status in the European rabbinate, colleagues in England helped procure these papers on his behalf. When my sister, at age twenty, completed her secondary education in 1933, my parents sent her to London as an *au pair* for a Jewish family. When I graduated from the Talmud Torah in Hamburg in the spring of 1938, just before Hitler's annexation of Austria, I was sent to London to enter rabbinical college. My father insisted on staying on, citing the principle of the captain being last to leave a sinking ship.

It is crucial to remember here how indifferent the world was to the fate of the Jews in Europe. Immigration opportunities were sparse. In addition to the agony such indifference imposed upon the Jews, it also sent a message to the Nazi regime that the world cared little about what was inflicted upon the Jews. When each cautious restraint was imposed at first, and little protest was heard from abroad, Hitler became even bolder, culminating in the Conference at Wannsee, legitimizing the Final Solution.

What is often cited as a fatal mistake by the Jews of Germany—trying to preserve a semblance of Jewish life during the early years of the Third Reich from 1933 to '38—could also be used to demonstrate the Jews' resilience to bend to the most severe pressures. Panic or capitulation would not only have demoralized the Jewish community, but would have condemned the physical as well as the spiritual architecture of a great and innovative Jewish world to immediate self-destruction by self-immolation. Instead, the Jews held on to whatever remnants of their lifestyle that could be salvaged, at least for the foreseeable future.

No matter what storms assaulted the Jewish community in the

outside German world, within the confines of the synagogue and the community the Jews attempted to uphold a sense of calm and dignity, of decorum and even elegance. At each Sabbath service the men were expected to wear their silk top hats. The Sabbath was still a truly celebratory occasion. At our synagogue, as in most throughout the country, one could not be given an *aliyah* (a calling to the Torah) unless one was attired in top hat. During the Nazi years, when Jews did not wish to arouse any unnecessary attention by walking to the synagogue on a Friday evening or Saturday morning in a top hat, the men would keep their hats in leather boxes stacked in the foyer of the synagogue, changing into them from their street hats when they arrived.

Well-trained choirs—in Orthodox synagogues only male choirs, men's and boys' or both—enhanced the beauty of the liturgy. Contemporary Jewish liturgical composers borrowed freely and unabashedly from the classical masters: Brahms, Schubert, Beethoven and even Wagner. Many of the melodies of our Hebrew hymns, still used and cherished by Jews in American synagogues and temples and thought to be sacred tunes from ancient tradition, happen to be derived from German folk songs. Best known of these hymns are *ayn keloheinu* and *adon olam,* and others, sung at the dinner table on festive occasions. On one occasion celebrating the "Liberation" of the Rhine from French and British occupation after World War I, and long before the advent of Nazism, our cantor opened the Sabbath morning service with the hymn *shochen ad marom ve'kadosh she'mo* to the tune of *Deutschland, Deutschland, über Alles,* leaving not a dry eye in the congregation. In retrospect, this picture seems incomprehensible; yet the cantor achieved celebrity status wherever this story was circulated.

It was equally as important for the Jews during this period to maintain the highest standards of honesty and morality. With unspeakable slander constantly being hurled at us, the product largely of the obscene imagination of the architects of the new "racial science," the community was not about to loosen its high order of self-discipline. We were not about to give cause for such defamation, as though it would have made a difference.

While commuting to Frankfurt, I occasionally carried a letter from my father to deliver to a friend of his who was one of my teachers. It was sure to reach him within a couple of hours, sooner even than the most efficient postal service could do. Each time Father would tear up a stamp explaining that delivering mail is the prerogative of the government. As a private citizen I have no right, he reiterated, to deprive the government of its rightful due for this service, thus tearing up the stamp satisfies the government's claim on the citizen. This lesson in honesty was never lost on me. While I have not always been able to live up to this example, I have used it as an object-lesson for myself, our children and countless religious school students.

None of these passionate efforts to maintain Jewish standards, to maintain this symbiosis between Jews and Germans, saved the Jewish community from that terrible night which foreshadowed the *Shoah*. *Kristallnacht* on November 9, 1938, and the arrest of tens of thousands of Jewish men and their confinement to concentration camps, left little doubt in the minds of the German Jews that the oncoming catastrophe could not be prevented.

My father's synagogue was irreparably vandalized that night. He managed to rescue one damaged Torah scroll, which he took home for safekeeping. Mother, ever inventive and determined, had the idea that the safest place to be that night was on a train bound for anywhere. She took my father to the railroad station, sequestered him in the restroom and proceeded to buy two tickets on the next train leaving town. She then retrieved my father and rushed him to the train. On that short walk, my father, being the prominent and widely recognized citizen he was, was spotted by a Gestapo agent and arrested. A few days later, Mother was told he was incarcerated in Buchenwald and so she began a constant and fearless vigil in front of the Gestapo Headquarters in Wiesbaden. After some ten weeks he was released on condition that he leave the country within thirty days.

At the time, those prisoners with visas to leave Germany could easily obtain their freedom. Father later insisted that he left only so Mother would cease her harassment of the Gestapo hoodlums. By late February in 1939 my sister and I welcomed my parents to London. We hardly recognized our father. His head and beard had been shaved before his release and he had lost much weight, yet his spirit was undaunted. Although he made light of it, we heard of Father's heroic conduct in Buchenwald from fellow inmates whose lives he had saved. Among his most memorable stories is the one in which he told us that each night, after lights-out and the two hundred or so prisoners with whom he shared a barrack had been locked up, he would deliver a lecture from memory. "And what an audience," he said. "For the first time in my career nobody walked out in the middle."

He also told us how many Orthodox men in Buchenwald were concerned about the food, such as it was, and whether they could eat it since it was not kosher. In order to resolve the issue Father stood up at one mealtime and, before hundreds of fellow prisoners, ate a spoonful of this indefinable slop, thus giving permission, by example, to those who were as observant as was he. He never ate anything again in the camp except some raw vegetables when he could find them.

In England, my parents rented a large home, taking in boarders, feeding about ten and full-boarding six of them. British Jewry was most generous towards the refugees coming to England. They provided modest monthly grants of money, clothing and other essentials in kind. By 1939, most refugees were arriving penniless and, if lucky, with one or two suitcases. My parents were too proud to take advantage of this largesse, however, and felt compelled to open their home to others. Father used to say: "Those who do not have anything to eat give others to eat." We subsisted on our boarders' leftovers. It was quite a change from a rabbinic household. The chores in this enterprise were evenly divided. Mother did the cooking; with his modest English language skills, Father did the shopping. My sister cleaned the rooms. I went to school the better part of the day and, on late afternoons four days a week, worked in the repair shop of a furrier salon on Bond Street, earning one pound sterling a week for mind-numbing work. I also received a small stipend from the seminary.

In July 1940, after the tragic defeat of the British Army at Dunkirk, the British government decreed that all male German and Austrian immigrants, including the Jewish refugees, be arrested and interned. The fear of quislings planted among them by the Germans demanded caution. My father and I were sent to the Isle of Man and Huyton, near Liverpool, respectively. By then my father was 61 years old.

A few days later the British asked for volunteers to go to Canada, promising that their families would follow. As a German invasion of Great Britain appeared imminent, I felt that a sojourn in Canada seemed safe. When two thousand volunteers did not come forward despite this tempting offer, the authorities filled the complement from a list of the internees in alphabetical order. Thus I found myself among the passengers of the *Dunera* which wound up in Australia fifty-seven days later. Many of my shipmates had been concentration camp inmates in Germany. They insisted that the treatment meted out to the Jews by the British military personnel in charge of the prisoners was more cruel and sadistic than what they had experienced in the German camps. The issue of the identity of the "enemy" became blurred.

On our arrival in Sydney, exhausted and emaciated from the rigors of that long journey, we were sent by train to an internment camp in the middle of the Australian desert. Despite Britain's openly stated regret at this error, we remained confined to camp until after Pearl Harbor. The peril to Australia from a Japanese assault was now quite real. The manpower shortage in that underpopulated continent persuaded the Australian authorities to release us on condition that we join the Australian Armed Forces in a unit especially created for us. We found ourselves one day behind barbed wire guarded by armed Australian soldiers and the next day wearing the uniforms of Australian soldiers. In war, allies and adversaries are often and easily interchangeable.

My father was released from the Isle of Man a few months after his arrest and returned to London. In the meantime my mother and sister managed the boarding-house operation by themselves.

In 1943, my father was offered the position of Rabbi in a small newly formed synagogue in Northwest London. It was located in a private home converted into a House of Worship. Most of its members were German refugees. My father was expected to preach in German and English on alternate Sabbaths. My family could now close the boarding-house and move to smaller quarters. By a peculiar coincidence, on my first visit to England from Australia after the war in 1946 to introduce my bride Fae to my parents, we noted on a plaque in the entrance hall to the little synagogue that it was created in honor and memory of members of my wife's mother's family. Unbeknownst until that day of our discovery, her family had contributed to the rescue of ours.

In 1953 I visited England again on the occasion of Queen Elizabeth II's coronation. On the Sabbath prior to this event, churches and synagogues devoted their services to the celebration of this national as well as religious event. In my father's synagogue it came time for his inimitable, highly stylized German sermon. Waxing poetic, with British patriotism oozing from every sentence, he spoke of "our noble Queen" and England's role in the preservation of liberty and fairness.

He could not have been more eloquent had he been a signatory to the Magna Carta. A new patriotism had blossomed in my father's breast and intellect. When he received his British citizenship and passport a few months after I had received mine, he sent me a congratulatory letter: *"mazel tov.* You are now second-generation British!" It was a product of his extraordinary sense of humor but there was also a grain of seriousness and genuine pride at this accomplishment. I did not want to offend my father's sensibilities but the thought that patriotism, this time for the

Rabbi Jonah Ansbacher seated with wife Rosa and
son Joseph in the Ansbacher apartment in Golders Green,
London, 1953. The portrait of his spiritual mentor, Samson
Raphael Hirsch, hangs in the background.

British Empire, once again preoccupied his mind evoked in me a flash of
déjá vu.

Several years in England fashioned for my father as deep a sense of
loyalty to Britain as did centuries of living in Germany for his ancestors.
I do not know whether this is a German trait but it describes, perhaps in
the most elementary way, the Jews' fierce attachment to the world
around them. Their commitment to Western civilization has been second
only to their commitment to Jewish values.

IN MY FATHER'S HOUSE

Raphael Asher

I HAVE ALWAYS BEEN AWARE that my father's rabbinate and our home life were essentially influenced by his German-Jewish upbringing. My father's pulpit style, his blend of formality and humor with congregants and colleagues alike, the anecdotes which he transmitted to me and to my brother all conveyed that combination of dignity, wit, and keen discernment that was German Jewry.

In April 1965, when I was 15, I was more ambivalent about my father's staunch pride in his German background and the bold unconventional claims he would make as a survivor of the Nazi era. In that month he had a feature article published in *Look* magazine. The German government had invited him to speak with high school students in Hamburg and in his hometown, Wiesbaden. He was to consult on the first drafts of their Holocaust curriculum and advise on their education about Jewish faith and culture. The *Look* essay was the record of his return "home."

I remember reading the article with trepidation and wondering in the face of Jewish friends whose families would not even listen to German music how he could justify his discomforting proposition that some search for reconciliation with the German people was in order. I can also still recall how I felt having finished the last paragraph—that my father had demonstrated a compelling wisdom, that his argument surpassed the commonplace, albeit justifiable bitterness which pervaded post-Holocaust Jewry: How could we hold a younger generation in Germany responsible for the sins of their fathers?

Hundreds of letters in response to the *Look* essay registered the passions that this thesis aroused. Dad was gratified by those who agreed with him but also took note of the angry words of censure from a generation that had not yet begun to sort out its feelings about the Holocaust.

Dad's reflections on the implications of the Holocaust were shaped by three seminal experiences. Hearing his father's horror stories from Buchenwald demonstrated to him how misguided German-Jewish patriotism had been. His own mistreatment by sadistic Scottish Allied Forces on the ship Dunera from London to Australia was an indelible object lesson that Germans had no monopoly on cruelty and anti-Semitism. Thirdly, his assignment in 1947 as a chaplain in the British Army of Occupation gave him a grim perspective on how even the surviving Jewish spirit had been blunted by Nazi degradation and that there would be scant remnants of Jewish civilization.

At the suggestion of Lily Montagu whom Dad had befriended in London, Leo Baeck had asked Dad if he would serve the needs of the displaced persons of Bergen-Belsen. For two months he would act as liaison between the British Commander-in-Chief and the thousands of Jewish refugees who had yet to receive immigration papers. The tragic stories he heard there of the camp's atrocities and the hardened characters he met among the survivors made him mourn both the passing of German Jewry and the threadbare fate of its remnant. Like Baeck, who had declared in 1933 that "the thousand-year history of the German Jews" had come to an end, my father was always more intent on emphasizing the glories and legacy of German Jewry rather than the instruments of its destruction.

In American pulpits from Olean, New York to Sarasota, Florida to Tuscaloosa, Alabama to Greensboro, North Carolina and finally to San Francisco's Congregation Emanu-El, my father took special satisfaction in convictions that were quite different from most. His German background and Orthodox rabbinic lineage vested him with that noble pose which defies the trendy, abhors the cliché, and finds the morally complacent reprehensible. In his rabbinate my father had been quick to assume the prophetic mantle on moral issues and to lambaste the banal in society.

My father's manner was well-suited to the Jewry in the southern United States. When we were in Tuscaloosa and Greensboro, from 1956 to 1968, the two communities adored my father's European manner. My parents in turn appreciated the reserve and gentility of the Southern Jewish community, as well as its eccentricities. However, when the civil

THE WORLD UNION FOR PROGRESSIVE JUDAISM

Hon. Secretary: THE HON. LILY H. MONTAGU, O.B.E., J.P.

THE RED LODGE, 51, PALACE COURT, LONDON, W.2

Home Telephone: BAYswater 1124
Office   „   EUSton, 3836

23rd May 1947

We hereby state that the Rev. J. Asher, assistant
Minister to the Melbourne Liberal Synagogue, Australia,
has undertaken, under the auspices of The World Union for
Progressive Judaism, to make an investigation in Germany
into the religious conditions of Progressive Jews in order
to prepare the way for more permanent Progressive religious
work of rehabilitation.

President:

Chairman:

Hon. Secretary:

Letter of authorization from the World Union
for Progressive Judaism for "Rev. J. Asher."
(private collection)

41

rights movement challenged the social and political norms of the South, my father was ready to take the fight to his congregation and to the community at large. The Southern rabbi was one of the very few white clergy to support the first sit-ins in Greensboro, to point out racial injustice in the workplace, including those of Jewish employees, and to push for school integration and bussing. My father's own exposure to bigotry and ostracism as a teenager in Germany compelled him to forego his affection for Southern cultural norms for this important mission.

In San Francisco in the late sixties and seventies, Dad's cultural sensibilities were affronted by the strident tones of protest against the war in Vietnam. As a student at Berkeley I took my cue from him, shying away from mass public protests. I found it impossible to ridicule a national guardsman, a myopic governor, or a deluded president. Yet from the pulpit Dad would cite chapter and verse from the Torah or prophets as ample license to be a vociferous critic of our involvement in Southeast Asia and of our national leadership. He certainly admired the kind of peaceful protest inspired by his adored Reverend Martin Luther King, Jr., but placards and chants and mass anger offended his German-Jewish nature and perhaps frightened him at the same time.

Even more a social critic than a political one, my father was daily confronted in San Francisco with drug cultures, counter-cultures, new religions and charismatics of every stripe. It was not primarily his *yekkishe* decorum which took issue with these social changes; indeed, I think the vitality and inventiveness of the Bay Area was stimulating for him. Rather, he took affront on behalf of the pulpit which he felt was sacrosanct for he believed that a rabbi had infinitely deeper knowledge than any of the neo-Hasidic *rebbes*, that the synagogue stood on ground more fertile than any marijuana grove, and that Judaism should not stoop to compete for Jewish souls with EST, TM or Esalen.

Dad refused to sit on a podium with Jim Jones long before the mass suicide of Jones' People's Temple in 1978. He showed open disdain for the experimentation of a whole generation of post-confirmands with every sect imaginable. And although Emanu-El gave considerable financial support to Shlomo Carlebach's House of Love and Prayer, privately he was repulsed by Carlebach's pied-pipering.

Within the parlance of German-Jewish history my father, like my grandfather Jonah Ansbacher before him, could very well be termed a *"misnaged"* (a contrarian towards Hasidism). He himself might have rebelled against his father's Torah-true Judaism, but he was viscerally opposed to the slightest public affront to the Torah, the synagogue, and the office of rabbi. Later this *misnagdic* stance extended to those who took issue with him on his critical positions towards Israel.

Dad's alliance with Breira, the national voice of those who felt there was an alternative to Israel's hardened position during the Begin years, and his insistence that Israel should be held to a higher standard brought claims of disunity and even anti-Zionism to his office door. This challenge to his immaculate Zionist credentials brought Dad and the family much frustration through the last decade of his rabbinate. "Where were these Johnny-come-latelies to the Zionist bandwagon before it became the vogue?" This was the bitter tone of many dinner conversations which our mother could not appease.

On this subject there was a gulf between pulpit and laity that my father was not going to bridge. Only in the years after his retirement in 1986 did his views find greater resonance in the Jewish community. His criticism of Israel may indeed be viewed as a kind of prophetic elitism by which Jews should not be subject to the same flaws as other nations but it was also the product of a long "Love of Israel" which far surpassed the Zionist ambivalences of pre-Holocaust German Jewry.

The dinner table was often a sounding-board for Dad to vent his frustrations. My brother and I grew up with a skewed view of the foibles of the Jewish community, but we were also impressed by his conviction that the Jewish laity were fair-minded, well-intentioned, and eager to be informed. Dad's affectionate relationship with many of his congregants was not paternalistic but as one among equals. On many levels the American democratic ideal supplanted the elitist tendencies of the Ansbacher family line. In other areas that elitism still existed.

At rabbinical conferences a group of German-born rabbis would always get together and exchange jokes and stories. A number of them, my father included, had had difficulties acculturating to American life in the thirties and forties as well as additional problems with professional acceptance. Consequently, they took special pleasure in sharing their professional successes as a group. A number of this country's national leadership positions and important pulpits in the 1970s and 1980s were now occupied by those German-born rabbis who had been inspirited with the lofty stature of the pulpit in the German synagogue.

Dad always enjoyed his roles as pastor and teacher, but the pulpit and the sermon were his lifeblood. Certainly he was courageous with much of his political and social criticism, but especially satisfying to him was the turning of a phrase or the coining of an epithet. He had fashioned his style after Rabbi Hermann Sanger whom he had served as assistant in Melbourne, Australia in 1945-46. Sanger himself was from a distinguished German rabbinic family and had contributed much to the resettling of Jewish refugees in Australia. He had also successfully transplanted a Germanic dignity to the pulpit of Australia's largest Liberal congregation. Dad admired Sanger's classical education and emulated his eclectic, well-hewn sermons.

My father induced me to take four years of Latin in high school, but I could hardly have duplicated the type of German education he received at the *Gymnasium*. Neither did I get the rigorous Jewish education that my father acquired every day after school in Grandfather's synagogue in Wiesbaden. Nevertheless, in bits and pieces, my brother and I were exposed to some of the flavors of the traditional German household. The pace and melodies of the *birkat* were distinctively German. There was no dawdling over the body of the blessings after the Sabbath meal which we were told was Grandfather's style. Our melody for the opening psalm *"shir hamaalot"* was appropriated from some German folk song, and towards the end of December it would be punctuated, tongue-in-cheek, with a few measures of "A Partridge in a Pear Tree." The Seder as well included melodies I've never heard elsewhere, and we were sure to hide the *afikoman* in the correct German way with the children hiding and the parents searching.

We were exposed to "high culture" subtly through our mother's interest in music and the arts and through honored guests who came through our house. Over the years we were privileged to meet Arthur Goldberg, Balfour Brickner, Ellis Rivkin, Jacob Marcus, Bruno Bettelheim, J.L. Talmon, and Irving Howe around our dinner table. However, father and sons most enjoyed the "low culture" of baseball and choice TV sitcoms. "The Game of the Week" with Dizzy Dean was our regular Shabbos afternoon activity together, and "Hogan's Heroes," of all shows, was a time reserved for Dad to wail with laughter. Whereas many understandably found the program to trivialize the horrors perpetrated by the Third Reich, Dad would not be denied these moments to give comic caricature to the falsely portrayed ineptness of the German army.

Humor and laughter are the most precious heirlooms which have been handed down from Grandfather Jonah to my father and, in large measure, to my brother Daniel and myself. Stories and anecdotes ranging across three generations cannot be conveyed with the proper German cadence. The humor which comes from setting the sardonic, the sallying, or the off-color against that legendary German propriety cannot be reproduced on paper, and that is a loss.

One anecdote, however, does transmit in part the atmosphere of the German-Jewish community in the thirties. The episode reflects some of the tension between German Orthodoxy, Hasidism, and Reform Jewry, and hopefully preserves a little of that historic vitality which this Festschrift celebrates:

My father tells the story of how when he lived in Wiesbaden many rabbis would come to the town for the baths of that famous spa. Among these the Belzer Rebbe would come every year with his entourage of disciples, and it was only fitting that my grandfather, concealing his distaste for Hasidism, would pay his respects. On this occasion he took my father along, adding the warning to be polite but not to believe a word that their hosts said.

When they arrived for *seudah shlishit,* the Shabbos afternoon meal, the Rebbe started to test my father's Torah knowledge. So impressed was he by my father's learning that he included him in a special Hasidic blessing. Taking a banana and breaking it in two, he gave my father the second half and enacted the rite of *shrayim.* According to this foreign custom it would be a special honor for my father to partake of the Rebbe's leftovers with a *berakha* (blessing). Grandfather Jonah cringed at the sight.

When some twenty years later on a visit to London my father got up the courage to tell his father that he had become a Reform rabbi, my grandfather responded, "It was the *berakha* of the Belzer Rebbe!"

Although many blessings uttered on German soil were uprooted, and many others had tragic, ironic, and unanticipated consequences, the blessings of centuries of German-Jewish vitality should continue to find welcome habitation among the generations of our people.

45

A SINGULAR ELEGANCE

Robert Kirschner

ON THE HIGH HOLYDAYS OF 1849, at the height of the California gold rush, a small group of pioneers gathered in a tent for the first Jewish worship service to be held on the Pacific Coast. Many of these merchants and tradesmen who had chosen to settle in the far western frontier city of San Francisco were among the some 200,000 Jews who had emigrated to the United States between 1835 and 1880 from the German-speaking lands of Central Europe. Within the next year (the exact date is a matter of dispute), Congregation Emanu-El was founded. Its charter, filed in April 1851, was signed by sixteen Jews, most of them from Bavaria. The founders framed a constitution whose first article provided that "the mode of worship of this congregation shall be in conformity to the *Minhag Askenass* (Custom of the German Israelites)."

Virtually every rabbi of Congregation Emanu-El has felt the impress of German Jewry. Julius Eckman (rabbi, 1854-1855) and Elkan Cohn (1860-1889) earned doctorates from the University of Berlin and were students of Leopold Zunz, the father of *Wissenschaft des Judentums*. An immigrant from Holland, Jacob Voorsanger (1889-1908) was the outspoken ideological disciple of Kaufmann Kohler, whose teachers in Germany included Samson Raphael Hirsch and Abraham Geiger. Martin Meyer (1910-1923), Louis Newman (1924-1930), and Irving Reichert (1930-1948), the congregation's first American-born rabbis, were each descended from German-Jewish forebears. Among all of the Emanu-El rabbis, however, only one was actually born in Germany: Joseph Asher, the scion of a rabbinic succession dating back to the era of Mendelssohn.

Joseph Asher's tenure as Rabbi of Congregation Emanu-El (1968-1985) fulfilled, in its outer expression and its inner integrity, the synthesis of continuity and reform that Mendelssohn himself first sought. On the one hand, Rabbi Asher ardently defended the millennial principles of Jewish moral conduct and ethical probity, even when these collided with contemporary realities. He steadfastly preserved the formal and aesthetic dimensions of congregational worship, even at a time when they were not in fashion. He refused to dilute the prophetic message of Judaism with appeals to ethnicity or concessions to expediency. In all of these respects he was the guardian of Jewish tradition, yet he was not its slave. "When our sages urge us to look at the past," he once said, "they do not mean for us to stay there." While his father, Rabbi Jonah Ansbacher, inclined to a westernized Neo-Orthodoxy, Joseph Asher was the first in his line to break from Orthodox observance and embrace Reform Judaism. Ever respectful of Orthodoxy, he could not abide what he called "mindless traditionalism": practice divorced from purpose, religion devoid of intellect, form without content. Because of his traditional upbringing and familiarity with the *halakhic* regimen, he was never intimidated by Orthodox aspersions upon his piety. His piety, like his past, bridged two worlds.

The early years of Rabbi Asher's tenure at Emanu-El coincided with a period of social unrest in the United States. In San Francisco, the extremes of cultural experimentation were often evident. In this time of spiritual drift and estrangement from religious institutions, the challenges to rabbinic leadership were formidable. Recognizing that the synagogue could not be immune to the currents of change, Rabbi Asher chose, at times, to wade in. He introduced an education program on Jewish marriage for interfaith couples and was among the first rabbis to appoint a woman as Assistant Rabbi. Ever the enemy of excess and vulgarity, he was nonetheless open to innovation in educational programs, liturgical composition, and ecumenical initiative.

An emblematic example of his capacity for invention was his response to a quandary posed by the boycott of table grapes by migrant farmworkers in central California. It had always been the congregation's custom, during the *Sukkot* festival, to decorate its *sukkah* with lavish clusters of grapes. Those in sympathy with the boycott demanded that this practice cease. Those who decorated the *sukkah* each year liked it just the way it was. The dispute was brought before Rabbi Asher. While he sympathized with the plight of the farmworkers, he did not wish to polarize the congregation on a festival of rejoicing. His solution: plastic grapes. Both sides were mollified. Here was a case of innovation balancing tradition with contemporary reality.

If Mendelssohn was one spiritual forbear of Joseph Asher, Samson Raphael Hirsch was another. Hirsch's notion of *Torah im Derekh Eretz,* Jewish learning combined with secular education, was the ideal of rabbinic vocation that Rabbi Asher inherited from his own father and grandfather. Although the tribulations of the war years deprived him of the sterling education he might have had in Germany, Rabbi Asher was by aptitude and temperament a true intellectual. This was always evident at Temple Emanu-El, where the lectures he gave and the courses he offered were lessons in acuity, lucidity and wit. From the pulpit, Rabbi Asher never stooped to conquer: he sought the heart by way of the mind. His sermons were more thoughtful than theatrical, more akin to discourse than homily. His greatest delight was to discover a *hiddush*, a novel interpretation. One of my favorites was his explanation, which he attributed to his father, of the familiar phrase from the High Holyday liturgy: "Repentance, prayer and charity annul the severe decree." Commentators have long been troubled by the notion that a forgiving God would render a harsh verdict. But Rabbi Asher pointed out that such a conclusion proceeds from a faulty translation: the Hebrew for "severe" is inflected as a noun, not an adjective. The correct interpretation, therefore, is: "Repentance, prayer and charity annul the severity of judgment." God is sometimes only perceived as harsh; our own reflections and action can alter the perception. The facility and ingenuity of this exegesis were characteristic of Rabbi Asher's approach to rabbinic tradition. Whether teaching or preaching, his was a high intellectual standard. Occasionally he may have overestimated his audience; he never underestimated it.

This unfailing standard is evident, for example, in Rabbi Asher's reply to a query by one of his most learned congregants, the distinguished lawyer and member of an eminent California pioneer family, Frank H. Sloss. (This notable exchange later appeared in the *Journal of Reform Judaism,* 1983.) Sloss was particularly distressed by a passage in the High Holyday morning services of the new prayerbook, finding it to be "a doleful catalogue of foreordained dooms" that he did not associate with Judaism. Rabbi Asher responded as follows:

The *"unetaneh tokef"*…is indeed a most troublesome text [that] needs to be understood in the context of its origin….It should be seen as one of the few examples of martyrology in our liturgy. Thus, the gruesome tone of what may befall us. And, comparing the version in our prayerbook with that in the traditional *Machzor* (the holyday prayerbook), let it be said that quite a number of even the more gruesome prospects have been expurgated.

It is interesting that the preceding *Union Prayerbook* had eliminated the *"unetaneh tokef"* altogether. I would presume that its editors were motivated by the same sensibilities that strike you. It is my guess that the editors of this new prayerbook were induced by the Holocaust, and felt impelled to restore the prayer. In that context, I really cannot find fault with them for it.

Now, for your observation of what you understand to be the afterthought, "the tiny dab of *charoset* on the horseradish" (which is a delightful analogy): I enclose the text as it is printed in the German Machzor. This photocopy comes from the "Prayers for the New Year," published in Rödelheim in 1864. You will note that the phrase **"Penitence, Prayer and Charity"** is printed in outsize letters. Hardly an afterthought. Indeed, it is the very focus of the passage. It alone merits the inclusion of the entire passage in the Holyday liturgy.

Leo Baeck, spiritual leader of German Jewry during the Nazi persecution and colleague of Rabbi Asher's in postwar London, once wrote of the distinction between *leben* and *erleben,* the tasks of life and the flights of experience. The first, Baeck explains, is the classical concept of religion, the second the romantic. *Leben* describes the disposition that confronts reality, that sees the world without illusions, that demands ethical action and communal responsibility. *Erleben,* in contrast, seeks to transcend reality, strives for ecstasy, wants to be embraced by a flood of feeling. Of the two archetypes, Rabbi Asher preferred *leben* to *erleben,* the classical to the romantic. His tenure as Rabbi of Congregation Emanu-El was characterized by a scrupulous adherence to religious decorum, intellectual honesty and communal obligation. He recoiled from sentimentality, from inflated emotion, from claims to salvation or bliss. In his capacities as leader, teacher, pastor and preacher, Rabbi Asher embodied those attributes of German Jewry of which his generation was the last living witness: dignity, sobriety, erudition, and a singular elegance.

PART II

Judaism and the German Mind

Encounter with a Lost Era[*]

Peter von der Osten-Sacken

IN GERMAN-SPEAKING COUNTRIES throughout the modern era, there has never been such an intensive Jewish life as there once was in Berlin. Since its beginnings as a modern Jewish community in the late seventeenth century, Berlin's Jewish families lived in close proximity to the city's Christians and the Christian community had an incomparable opportunity to get to know Jews of all kinds. With the first writ of privileges of September 1671, the elector of Berlin extended its first residence permits to Jewish families, a gesture which held the promise of mutually beneficial social, cultural and commercial relations. Yet as we so well know, the relationship between Berlin's Christian Germans and Jewish Germans developed far differently than might have been anticipated.

At the end of the eighteenth century, when Jewish life in Berlin began to flourish, Lessing, in his landmark drama, *Nathan the Wise,* chided his fellow Germans to be zealously unerring in their love for truth and of their neighbors and to be free from all prejudices.[1] This prophetic admonition, however, was widely disregarded so that during the years of the Weimar Republic, when democracy was at stake, Christianity proved totally powerless to stem the tide of anti-Semitism that engulfed the country. With the decision at the Wannsee Villa on January 20, 1942 to pursue the "Final Solution," Berlin became the headquarters for a crime committed against the Jewish people whose horror passes understanding.

53

The crimes committed in Germany and in the occupied countries between 1933 and 1945 are all the more incomprehensible when contrasted with the perceptions and hopes of the preceding decades. No more revealing commentary on this historical paradox is to be found than in Selma Stern's introduction to the reprint of the first volume of her *The Prussian State and the Jews*. As Stern explains, she wrote the first two volumes of this magisterial work in an "optimistic mood" in the 1920s, when "one could believe in the regeneration of Judaism out of the spirit and resources of modern science and in a meaningful symbiosis of Germans and Jews, who respected and understood one another's character, religion and history as well as their own. It seemed possible that European culture could be enriched, renewed and deepened out of the synthesis of the scholarly, the artistic and the religious experience of both Germans and Jews."[2] By examining the relationship between Jews and Christians in Berlin before 1933, we will attempt to place Stern's perceptions in historical context.

THE SCIENCE OF JUDAISM

One of the most important events in Jewish life in Berlin was the establishment of the Science of Judaism in the second decade of the nineteenth century[3] by a group of young Jews who began exploring one question: What should be the basis and form of Judaism to address effectively the dilemma of civil and social emancipation, a fundamental change which would challenge but ought not extinguish the traditional forms of Judaism? On November 7, 1819, they founded the Association for the Culture and Science of the Jews *(Verein für Kultur und Wissenschaft der Juden)*, which found its literary voice in the *Journal for the Science of Judaism (Zeitschrift für die Wissenschaft des Judentums)* in 1823.

The organizers of the Association intended the new science to focus on the historical description of Judaism, the philosophical definition of its essence, and the philological examination of its literature. In this explication, which directly contrasted with the rabbinism of the preceding century, the new science was to provide an academic niche that would integrate Judaism into European life. In addition to such famous names as Eduard Gans and Heinrich Heine, most important certainly in the Berlin circle was Leopold Zunz, the founder and indefatigable promoter of the Science of Judaism for several decades.[4] In 1832, eight years after the Association had been dissolved, Zunz published *The Liturgical*

Lectures of the Jews from the Perspective of History, a contribution to the study of classical antiquity and biblical criticism, to literature and the history of religions, a pioneering work that finally elevated the Science of Judaism to the status of an academic discipline.[5]

Leopold Zunz (1794-1886) had grown up in a Jewish orphanage in Wolfenbüttel and had attended the local *Gymnasium,* the first Jewish student to do so. At the newly founded University of Berlin, he focussed on classical antiquity and the Hebrew Bible. From 1820 to 1822, in the years of the Association, Zunz had preached in the "New Israelite Synagogue," where the German sermon, introduced just a few years earlier, was in vogue.[6] Zunz was "the foremost representative"[7] in this "first phase of the modern Jewish sermon…which would soon spread out from Germany to the Jewry of all of Western Europe and America."[8] Within the context of the Science of Judaism he applied the methods of his studies of classical antiquity and biblical criticism to the traditional literature of Judaism. Similarly, in his elaboration of the new preaching methods, so completely different from the traditional style of other Jewish preachers before and after him, Zunz learned from Christian preachers.[9] An undated note, which Alexander Altmann discovered in the *Silesian Dictionary of Writers,* imparts to this whole context a special charm:

> It was interesting to see the most popular Christian preachers of this period, Hauenstein, Ritschel, Schleiermacher and others sometimes attending the German synagogues on the Sabbath and attentively listening to these young preachers, who ventured into the new area, until then untrodden by their fellow-believers; and interesting for the young men themselves to receive many tips and much advice from those great [Christian] preachers after worship.[10]

In his essay on Zunz, Solomon Schechter summed up the implications of the role of the Association for the Culture and Science of the Jews for Jewish learning:

> Thus we find the German Jews at the beginning of this century in the helpless transitory condition which only a man of the pure character and deeply religious mind of a Zunz could possibly survive. The old glorious yeshivot, in which Jewish learning had found a home for many centuries, were gone, but the seminaries had still to be founded. The old venerable rabbis who were at the head of those colleges were considered as an antiquated survival of an obscure time fit only for "intoning"

psalms for the salvation of departed souls; whilst the new Jewish professor with his rabbinical learning and scientific training had still to be born.[11]

THE GRADUATE SCHOOL FOR THE SCIENCE OF JUDAISM

Though the Association recognized the necessity for the establishment of new academic institutions, it could not make itself heard by the Jewish public. Decades of hard effort[12] were required before the first educational academic institutions could be founded. The first, the Jewish Theological Seminary in Breslau, was established in 1854 with a generous grant.[13]

The Graduate School for the Science of Judaism in Berlin *(Lehranstalt* or *Hochschule für die Wissenschaft des Judentums)* followed in 1872.[14] Its first president was Abraham Geiger (1810-1874), a scholar who is counted among the fathers of the Science of Judaism,[15] along with Zunz and Moritz Steinschneider.[16] The Graduate School, rising from modest beginnings, flourished in the first decades of the twentieth century, and like the Breslau seminary, took pride in its galaxy of distinguished scholars from Geiger to David Cassel, Israel Levy, Eugen Taeubler, and Eduard Baneth to Ismar Elbogen, Julius Guttmann, Abraham Joshua Heschel and Leo Baeck. The *Hochschule* continued to function under the most difficult circumstances and with an admirable richness of creativity and dedication far into the Nazi era,[17] until—in the end,[18] with a tiny circle of students around Leo Baeck—it was forced to dissolve in July 1942.[19]

The founding of the Graduate School had been the condition which Geiger, the pioneer of Reform Judaism, had stipulated for his acceptance of a Berlin pulpit in 1869. His tenure at the Berlin congregation was of enduring impact as it led eventually to the division of the Berlin Jewish community. In connection with the election of a new rabbi, the Conservatives had petitioned the board of directors of the community that "the necessary guarantees be offered, that institutions and schools in the community, which are dedicated to religious purposes, have to be led in the spirit of traditional Judaism, that the board appoints a rabbi, who besides sufficient academic education, has a profound Talmudic knowledge and who has proven in his life and work that he adheres to the traditional lore."[20] When the board responded by appointing Geiger, a great number of Jews separated themselves from the community. This movement led to the formation of a private religious association, the Law-observing Jewish religious association Adass Yisroel, which later acquired state recognition as the Israelite Synagogue Community Adass Yisroel of Berlin *(Israelitische Synagogengemeinde Adass Jisroel zu Berlin)*.

Subsequent to the separation of the Conservatives and Liberals, Esriel Hildesheimer (1820-1899), the newly elected rabbi of the secessionary congregation,[21] founded the Rabbinical Seminary for Orthodox Jews in Berlin, the Orthodox counterpart to the Liberals' Graduate School.[22] After the Liberals moved across the street at the beginning of the twentieth century, the two seminaries literally were counterpoised on the Artilleriestrasse.

CHRISTIAN BERLIN'S RESPONSE TO JUDAISM

The disturbances connected with the secession in Berlin had hardly calmed down when the Jews of Berlin were hit by an outpouring of hatred and animosity which had not appeared in such measure since the "Germanomanie" in the first decade of the nineteenth century.[23] The 1870s and 1880s became the decisive period in the development of modern anti-Semitism, which developed under the social, economic and political circumstances in the years after the foundation of the German Reich. Although Jews had experienced anti-Semitism at the beginning of the century, this new enmity was markedly different. The ideology of this anti-Semitism tended toward a worldview with totalitarian tendencies, striving to become a mass movement. It organized itself politically and tried to infiltrate the existing parties.

The Church and the universities were among the foremost representatives of this development. Adolf Stoecker, acting since 1874 as one of the four court chaplains and thus invested with an office "which belonged to the most reputable of his time,"[24] founded the Urban Mission of Berlin *(Berliner Stadtmission)* in 1877, to counter the secularization of the masses and step by step turned towards party politics. After the failure of his Christian-Social Worker's Party, he appealed to the Berlin public with a new slogan on September 19, 1879, directed against omnipotent liberalism and modern Jewry which Stoecker accused of being its pace-maker.[25]

"The Jews are and will be a people within the people, a state within the state, a class by itself among a foreign race. All immigrants in the end became merged into the people [*Volk*], among which they live; the Jews do not. They counter the Germanic nature with their unbroken Semitism, Christianity with their stiff legal cult or their Christ-hatred"[26]—therefore the motto is "strengthen the Christian-Germanic spirit,...return to the more Germanic legal and economic life, return to Christian faith."[27]

In the same year, in university circles, Berlin historian Heinrich von Treitschke's diatribe, "The Jews Are Our Misfortune," found a vigorous echo and set off the so-called Berlin Anti-Semitic Controversy *(Berliner Antisemitismusstreit)*.[28]

Stoecker was unexpectedly successful with his nebulous mixture of Christianity and Germanness so much so that at his entry into the *Reichstag* in 1881 he brazenly called out to the liberals: "Behind me I have millions!"[29] It is true in the long run that he failed as a politician and fell into such disgrace at the court that he had to relegate his activity entirely to the Urban Mission of Berlin; however, his influence on countless theologians and Christians was significant. His political thoughts became the ideological basis for the nationalist and anti-Semitic Association of German Students *(Verein deutscher Studenten)* which was founded in 1881 and "especially attracted theologians."[30]

THE SOCIETY FOR THE PROMOTION
OF CHRISTIANITY AMONG THE JEWS

It is particularly unfortunate that the Berlin Mission for Jews, founded on February 1, 1822 as the Society for the Promotion of Christianity Among the Jews, influenced from London and claiming to be motivated by love for Israel, did not resist the anti-Semitism provoked by Treitschke and by Stoecker's demagogic performances.[31] In the 1820s, when the Association for the Culture and Science the Jews had held its meetings, the Mission was known to the members of the Association.[32] Ideologically and practically supported by Berlin theologians such as C. Ritschel, Ph. K. Marheineke and A. Tholuck, and financially supported by Frederick William III, it had established branches in several cities in Prussia within a very short period of time.

When Stoecker embarked on his anti-Semitic activities, the Society should have been among his opponents. The claim that the Society "raised its voice vehemently against Jew-baiting"[33] is unfounded; in fact, the Society had itself started to disseminate anti-Semitic propaganda through its publication "Messenger of Peace."[34] Ten years later J. F. de le Roi, one of the leaders of the missionary movement among the Jews wrote in *Protestant Christianity and the Jews:*

> Protestant Christianity cannot turn backwards (that is, beyond the mission to the Jews) anymore; for the Jews in its midst leave it the choice either to win the Jews for Christ's service or to see them grow into a vast power of destruction, of material, social, national, religious and spiritual subversion in their own territory. The Jewish question has become a burning one for the Christian nations. For while the pagans live far away, this is different with the Jews: they became limbs of the body of the Christian nations and thus quite directly contribute to their health and their sickness. Our century has irrefutably shown this. Jews who have accepted the gospels in their heart are a great blessing for our people, the others an increasing danger. With the Jews there is in fact just the Either-Or. Either they are outwardly controlled by the power of the gospel and inwardly overcome, or they help destroy what we still have.[35]

This attitude summed up the Christian relationship to the Jews. It called for their conversion and total dissolution. In addition, given the necessary political circumstances, this attitude could be ignited into an extremely destructive response.[36]

THE INSTITUTUM JUDAICUM IN BERLIN

The three volumes by de le Roi appeared as the ninth work in the *Publications of the Institutum Judaicum in Berlin.* The title "Institutum Judaicum," from a contemporary viewpoint, is of course misleading. The name was coined in the eighteenth century to designate an institution for missionizing Jews. It had been founded in 1728 by the Franke disciple Johann Heinrich Callenberg in Halle and was "supposed to take care of the most necessary preparation of the missionaries as well as of their mission and their supervision and, at least in Halle, practiced proselytizing."[37]

In the 1880s, however, the term "Institutum Judaicum" referred to the "student associations for the cultivation of mission for Jews,"[38] which were founded at several universities with the initial purpose of learning about Judaism. These associations had a student member as president, but "a professor had to be responsible" for the "academic support."[39] Two of these "Instituta Judaica" had an especially long existence:

the oldest one in Leipzig (1880)[40]—the later *Institutum Judaicum Delitzschianum,* still in existence in Münster—and the *Institutum Judaicum Berlinense,* which was continued at the Humboldt University in Berlin/GDR until 1956.[41] In Berlin the study-group was established on November 13, 1883 on the initiative of an Old Testament associate professor Hermann Leberecht Strack, who in a series of public lectures early in his teaching career in the summer of 1878 had already started to teach Christian students about the literature, the history and the religion of Judaism. This instruction continued for almost forty years until Strack's death in 1922, in weekly sessions at the Institute and, further, through the *Publications of the Institutum Judaicum in Berlin* (published by Strack from 1886 onward) which were meant "to inform about Judaism and partially about the work of the Protestant Church with Israel."[42] It so happens that the journal *Nathanael* had a loose affiliation with the Institute. Strack edited the first issue in 1885 on behalf of the Society for the Promotion of Christianity Among the Jews. Afterwards, he edited it independently. *Nathanael* was "to strive most of all to mediate exact knowledge of Judaism and all that is required in discussions with Jews," and that in a generally intelligible way.[43]

When Leopold Zunz died in 1886, Strack wrote in his eulogy, "He was, in spite of being a democrat, a good German."[44]This fundamental conservatism, joined to a desire to do justice to his Jewish colleague, is characteristic of Strack's theological work. Thus his theological attitudes towards Israel, as expressed in Romans 10:2[45] ("To their zeal for God I can testify") merged with an immense knowledge of Judaism, also recognized by Jews.[46] This knowledge was not only presented in his "Introduction to the Talmud and Midrash,"[47] but was also used "in his argument directed against the widespread anti-Semitic defamatory campaigns which had the misrepresentation of the Talmud and the blood libels as their subject."[48]

ADOLF VON HARNACK AND LEO BAECK

The movement to missionize Jews was not successful in Berlin, nor did it gain many Christian followers. Its theology, however, was influential in the lecture-halls of teachers, for whom Judaism was no more than a dark background against which Christianity appeared all the brighter. No one represented this outlook more effectively than did Adolf von Harnack who gave lectures on "The Essence of Christianity" in the winter semester of 1899-1900 before 600 students from all departments. Published in 1900, *The Essence of Christianity* became one of the books with the most editions in the history of theology.[49]

Harnack's Jesus is free from all ties with Judaism and contemporary history,[50] and in his total opposition to the surrounding world reveals himself to be the "essence of Christianity."[51] In Harnack's view although "the pure well-spring of the holy...had long been disclosed," although Jesus found "a rich and deep ethic" rooted in his people,[52] and although Jewish religious history had been the "deepest and richest, which a people had ever experienced,"[53] that once-disclosed wellspring had long ago been obscured,[54] the ethic had been limited by its connection with "the external cult and technical religious exercises"[55] and the mission of Jewish religious history had been fulfilled with the bestowal upon Jesus of the title Messiah.[56] In addition, "everything had remained weak and therefore harmful. It is not words which become effective, but the power of the personality behind them."[57] According to Harnack:

> He (i.e. Jesus) immediately confronted the official leaders of the people, and in confronting them he confronted corrupted human nature in general. They imagined God as a despot, who supervises the ceremonies of His house rules, whereas he breathed in the presence of God. They only saw Him in his law, which they had turned into a labyrinth of abysses, of erroneous ways and secret escapes, he saw and felt Him everywhere. They had thousands of commandments from Him and therefore believed that they knew Him. They had turned religion into an earthly business—there has never been anything more disgusting—he proclaimed the living God and the nobleness of the soul.[58]

Harnack's printed lectures provoked among both Christians and Jews a wave of reactions,[59] which, surprisingly, overlapped, for both were moved by the absence of dogma in Harnack's "Essence of Christianity." While Christians complained about the deletion of the "redemptive elements" in the life of Jesus,[60] Jews proclaimed their satisfaction with Harnack for omitting precisely those elements which they found unacceptable.[61] Although Jews criticized the anti-Jewish implications of Harnack's work, it seemed that Harnack had unwittingly described "a religious form which is very close to Judaism":[62]

> Harnack against his own will arrived at a justification of Judaism and encouraged us in our loyalty and devotion to our religion, which he cannot replace with anything new or better. It is a special joy and

satisfaction for us to know that a man of such intellect, scholarship and religious depth as Harnack, is inwardly so close to us, and we will not allow ourselves to be misled by the fact that he often does injustice to Judaism...[63]

Among the many Jews who responded was young Leo Baeck, from the Silesian Oppeln,[64] who demands attention for two reasons. First, he was destined to become one of the leading Jewish personalities in Germany.[65] Second, his reaction differed significantly from other Jews. *Sine ira et studio,* Rabbi Baeck proved in his analysis, paragraph by paragraph, that the dark picture of ancient Judaism which Harnack developed or presumed on every page, was not based on any genuine knowledge of its cultural expressions. Harnack apparently did not respond to either the young rabbi or to other Jewish critics.[66] A few years later Baeck, without mentioning Harnack, wrote *The Essence of Judaism,* which was to be published in many editions.[67] After Baeck's striking summary "One has to know the Jews to understand the Gospel,"[68] there are two revealing passages:

> And this leads us to yet another aspect. Most of the (sc. Christian) portrayers of the life of Jesus omit to mention that Jesus in each of his traits is a genuine Jewish *character,* that a man like him could emerge only from the background of Judaism, only there and from no other. Jesus is a truly Jewish personality. All his efforts and actions, his bearing and feeling, his speaking and silence bear the mark of his Jewish personality and stance of Jewish idealism, of the best that there was and is in Judaism, but only in the Judaism of his time. He was a Jew among Jews....[69]

Baeck then explains what remains important and singular about Jesus:

> For paganism the day had finally come that it could begin to accept Israel's lore, and God has created His own for this. For the founder of Christianity, therefore, Jews can only entertain love and deference.[70]

It is certainly one thing for a Jewish scholar to turn to the historical Jesus of Nazareth and another for him to express his view of the Gospel, and even to do so in positive terms. It is just this which especially distinguishes Leo Baeck, who went farther in his historical and theological understanding of Jesus and the Gospel as Jewish phenomena than would have seemed possible without the renunciation of Judaism. Without being intimidated by the conditions of the time, in 1938 he published a book entitled *The Gospel as a Document of the History of the Jewish Faith,* in which he elaborated his earlier view in a more far-reaching way.[71] In the first part he characterizes the genre 'gospel' with its form—transition- and redaction-critical implications—and discusses which form the oldest Gospel might have had. In the second part he puts forward the text, reconstructed by him, beginning with John the Baptist and continuing to the discovery of the empty grave with its message of the resurrection. This analysis can only be valued properly if it is seen in relation to the ancient Aramaic pamplet *"Toledot Yeshu,"* which had prevailed for centuries. It is difficult to imagine that anybody in the times which the book reflects would have imagined that a Jew would ever, without giving up his Jewishness, write about Jesus and the Gospel of the early Christians based on no other sources than the texts of the New Testament which Baeck cites selectively but in full. Baeck's own summary at the beginning of his text may serve as an illustration:

> In the old Gospel which is thus opened before us, we encounter a man with noble features who lived in the land of the Jews in tense and excited times and helped and labored and suffered and died: a man out of the Jewish people who walked on Jewish paths with Jewish faith and hopes. His spirit was at home in the Holy Scriptures, and his imagination and thought were anchored there; and he proclaimed and taught the word of God because God had given it to him to hear and to preach. We are confronted with a man who won his disciples among his people: men who had been looking for the messiah, the son of David, who had been promised; men who then found him and clung to him and believed in him until he finally began to believe in himself and thus entered into the mission and destiny of his age and indeed into the history of mankind. These disciples he found here, among his people, and they believed in him even after his death, until there was nothing of which they felt more certain than that he had been, according to the words of the prophet, "on the third day raised from the dead."[72]

"Behold a man," writes Baeck of Jesus,

> who is Jewish in every feature and trait of his character, manifesting in every particular what is pure and good in Judaism. This man could have developed as he came to be only on the soil of Judaism; and only on this soil, too, could he find his disciples and followers as they were. Here alone, in this Jewish sphere, in this Jewish atmosphere of trust and longing, could this man live his life and meet his death—a Jew among Jews. Jewish history and Jewish reflection may not pass him by nor

ignore him. Since he was, no time has been without him; nor has there been a time which was not challenged by the epoch that would consider him its starting point.[73]

When this old tradition confronts us in this manner, then the Gospel, which was originally something Jewish, becomes a book—and certainly not a minor work—within Jewish literature. This is not because, or not only because, it contains sentences which also appear in the same or a similar form in the Jewish works of that time. Nor is it such—in fact, it is even less so—because the Hebrew or Aramaic breaks again and again through the word forms and sentence formations of the Greek translation…It is a Jewish book because—by all means and entirely because—the pure air of which it is full and which it breathes is that of the Holy Scriptures; because a Jewish spirit, and none other, lives in it; because Jewish faith and Jewish hope, Jewish suffering and Jewish distress, Jewish knowledge and Jewish expectations, and these alone, resound through it—a Jewish book in the midst of Jewish books. Judaism may not pass it by, nor mistake it, nor wish to give up all claims here. Here, too, Judaism should comprehend and take note of what is its own.[74]

The controversy between Leo Baeck and Adolf von Harnack is instructive in many ways. Harnack's "Essence of Christianity" demonstrates that an orientation towards the so-called historical Jesus and the resultant claim of an undogmatic Christianity is by no means any healthier for Christian-Jewish relations. One can obviously—and for this there are many examples—play off the historical Jesus no less than the dogmatic Christ against the Jewish people. One can also appropriate both in a way that does not nurture but helps to overcome anti-Judaism. More important, it seems, is to resume Leo Baeck's appraisal of the Gospel and to carry out the cross-checking. Thus, Rabbinic literature too breathes the spirit of the Holy Scripture, to use the language Baeck had chosen for the Gospel. Rabbinic literature too is permeated with biblical confidence, hope and action. But have Christians developed an appreciation of the Written and Oral Torah, which would have, if only faintly, resembled Baeck's appreciation of the old Gospel?

AT THE UNIVERSITY OF BERLIN

In the 1920s, the relationship between Jews and Christians in Berlin seemed to be taking an even more positive turn. After Strack's death in October 1922, the Institutum Judaicum, under the leadership of Hugo

Gressmann, ceased to view its work as a preparation for the conversion of Jews. Gressmann's presidency came after failed attempts to change Strack's Chair for Old Testament into one for post-biblical Judaism with special emphasis on its relations to the New Testament.[75] Integrated into the theology department at the University of Berlin, the Institute itself became a "seminar for post-biblical Judaism" to address the central question of how Christianity emerged from the Judaism of the Hellenistic-Roman period, a period of prime importance for Christians.[76] Citing "the unusual vitality of this religion,"[77] Gressmann invited Leo Baeck and four other teachers from the Graduate School for the Science of Judaism to give lectures on subjects in their areas of scholarship in the fall semester of 1925-26.[78] The series of lectures was to acquaint Christian students at the University of Berlin with the religious and spiritual world of Judaism through the study of primary sources.[79] At the same time, it was to represent the integration of the Science of Judaism into the *universitas litterarum,* from which it had been excluded since its emergence despite the efforts of both Jews and Christians.[80]

Gressmann's step provoked opposition, leading the *Messenger of the Messiah (Messiasbote)* to declare that the "Protestant institute for the scholarship of post-biblical Judaism...had turned into a Jewish-theological seminary,"[81] the author insisting that Jewish scholars lecturing on Judaism within a Protestant theological department were an "anomaly" which should make a Protestant theologian cringe.[82] At the inauguration of the lecture series, Gressmann explained his program, to which the former friends of the institute objected:

> Precisely today when a strong wave of anti-Semitism is sweeping over our people, and when the image of Judaism is distorted...we need to present the historical facts in the most objective...way possible.
>
> Furthermore, this appraisal can be done best when Judaism speaks for itself. For genuine objectivity always presumes love, and therefore the Jewish scholar is always at an advantage in relation to the Jewish religion and necessarily has to know it better than the Christian scholar. Therefore he can more easily deepen our historical understanding, for it is not essential that one agree with all claims and evaluations. On the contrary, the academic judgement can only be formed through criticism and critical argument with the views of others, the assumption being that all of us honestly strive for the same goal of truth.[83]

These memorable words, also included in the printed lecture series, seem to have been unheeded after Gressmann's death in 1927; a National

Socialist Old Testament scholar, Johannes Hempel, took the presidency of the Institute in 1936.[84] It does not seem that many of today's Christian theologians possess Gressmann's attitude towards Judaism.

At about the time Leo Baeck lectured on the "origin and beginnings of Jewish mysticism" at the Institutum Judaicum, he concluded: "All in all Judaism today is deepened, invigorated and more certain about itself and the future than it was a century ago."[85] Only a few years later, Baeck would admit: "The thousand-year history of German Jews has come to an end."[86]

BERLIN TODAY

The question remains to be answered: Do Christians and Jews in Berlin have a future together? Leo Baeck, a survivor of Theresienstadt, did not live in Germany again after his liberation, though he had spent most of his life there. And yet when invited, he came bearing witness to the "essence of Judaism," as it had been expressed in Germany.[87] His return, however brief, his demeanor and his very presence in Germany can be encouraging to those of us who, years later, still search for a new beginning.

In that new beginning there are scant ties to the lost era. In the first decades of this century about half a million Jews lived in Germany, a third of them in Berlin. Today, however, there is perhaps one Jewish German for over a thousand Christians while extensive Jewish life exists only in a few larger cities, and even there the Jewish communities are small.[88] Given the dearth of German Jews, often lecturers from abroad have had to serve as dialogue partners or conference participants. Yet depite these limitations, the encounters of Christians with Jews in Germany remain encouraging.[89]

In Germany today Jewish life lives on beyond the small pockets of existing communities. Still palpable are the extraordinarily rich contributions made by Jewish men and women in all walks of German life over the last two hundred years.[90] We have to remember the millions of persecuted, expelled and murdered Jews for their sake, but for our own sake as well, so that our memory may not be subverted by an ugly historian's quarrel about the uniqueness of the crimes against the Jews. The challenge that older and younger Germans face in the encounter with the "lost era" has been formulated from the Jewish perspective by H.G. Adler:

Only for the best [personalities] of the fifth generation after the Enlightenment, who were born after 1870—the sixth already came too late to be able to fully unfold—was the symbiosis complete....We think, in particular, of the achievements of Leo Baeck and Martin Buber, in whose work Jewish character attained German form. Their works belong to the Jews as much as to the world: for the German people they present a legacy, an inheritance that has outlasted the catastrophe. It is up to the Germans if, with the help of those mediators, they want to get to know Judaism as a whole, as one of the great historical realizations of human existence, and the Jewish reality itself, as it was lived in the world and particularly in Germany, and thus make up for what most of them missed for 150-200 years when this symbiosis was in process.[91]

Once again Jews and Judaism are present in the Church in a special way for from time immemorial no one has been as concerned about the Jews as have been Christians, even if completely subconsciously so most of the time. For whenever Christians, be it lay people or theologians, read, interpret, teach or preach the Bible, they have to face the Jewish people on every page of the Hebrew Scriptures and the New Testament. And whenever they pick up the Bible and pass on its stories, its conflicts and hopes, German Christians create to a considerable degree an image of present-day Jews and Judaism. Here Jews are present and absent everywhere at the same time—present insofar as their name is often mentioned as one talks about and sometimes against them; absent insofar as the Jews cannot speak for themselves, cannot reveal the richness of their tradition, cannot in their own words explain Judaism's divergence from Christianity. Due to their absence Jews are still, in certain critical situations, at the complete mercy of those who teach in theological seminaries and churches.

The harm that an unchallenged prejudice-laden Christian lore on Jews and Judaism has inflicted up to the present time is well-documented. The task that the German churches, theologians and Christians now face is as inescapable as our history. It might best be defined as representative talking and acting, a process and behavior that would not exploit the absence of Jews, but rather make it imperative to listen to the Jewish tradition, to recognize Jewish life and, within the context of scriptural exegesis, recount both as if it were the Jewish voice itself. This demanding daily task is probably the most important thing that Christians can do in the context of the renewal of Christian-Jewish relations. Moreover, this will be the best preparation for answering the question as to whether

Christians and Jews have a future in Berlin and make manifest how Christians, in their hope for such a future, can "hold out [their] hand towards the miracle as if to a bird."[92]

NOTES

*In its original form, this essay, "Christen und Juden in Berlin Begegnung," was published in the Festschrift *450 Jahre Christliche Theologie in Berlin* (Vandenhoeck and Ruprecht, Göttingen, 1989). Adapted and abridged, it has been translated by Charlotte Fonrobert.

A list of abbreviations for these notes appears at the end, on page 72.

1. Lessings Werke, Bd. III (Stuttgart, 1869), 105.

2. Selma Stern, *Der preußische Staat und die Juden,* Bd. I/1 (Berlin, 1925; repr. Tübingen, 1962), XII (Bd. II-III: Tübingen 1962-1971; Bd. IV: Gesamtregister, hg. v. M. Kreutzberger, 1975).

3. Hierzu K. Wilhelm (Hg.), *Wissenschaft des Judentums im deutschen Sprachbereich,* Bd. I-II (Tübingen, 1967), darin bes. Ders., *Zur Einführung in die Wissenschaft des Judentums,* Bd. I, 3-58; ferner G. Scholem, "Wissenschaft vom Judentum einst und jetzt," in: Ders., *Judaica,* Bd. I (Frankfurt-am-Main, 1963), 147-64.

4. Zu Zunz s.S. Schechter, Leopold Zunz (1889), in: Ders., *Studies in Judaism,* Bd. III (Philadelphia, 1924), 84-142, 279-91 (279f: ältere Lit.).

5. G. Scholem, a.a.O. (Anm. 4), 155. Zu den "Vorträgen" wie zu den nachfolgenden Werken s. von allem deren Charakteristik bei S. Schechter, a.a.O. (Anm. 4), Bd. III, 118ff.

6. S. hierzu A. Altmann, "Zur Frühgeschichte der jüdischen Predigt in Deutschland: Leopold Zunz als Prediger," in: YLBI 6 (1961), 3-59, hier: 5. S. auch unten, Anm. 10.

7. A.a.O., 5.

8. A.a.O., 4.

9. S. außer dem genannten Beitrag von A. Altmann (bes. 9ff) auch seine Weiterführung des Nachweises in: "The New Style of Preaching in Nineteenth-Century German Jewry," in: Ders. (Hg.), *Studies in Nineteenth-Century Jewish Intellectual History* (Cambridge, Mass., 1964), 65-116.

10. A. Altmann, Prediger, a.a.O. (Anm. 7), 11.

11. S. Schechter, a.a.O. (Anm. 5), Bd. III, 90.

12. S. hierzu K. Wilhelm, Einführung, a.a.O (Anm. 4), 19f.

13. S. zum Seminar G. Kisch (Hg.), *Das Breslauer Seminar. Jüdisch-theologisches Seminar* (Fraenckelscher Stiftung) in Breslau 1854-1938. Gedächtnisschrift (Tübingen, 1963).

14. I. Elbogen, "Die Hochschule, ihre Entstehung und Entwicklung," in: *Lehranstalt für die Wissenschaft des Judentums: Festschrift zur Einweihung des eigenen Heims* (Berlin, 1907), 1-98; Ders., "Die Wissenschaft des Judentums: Festrede," in: *42. Bericht der Hochschule für die Wissenschaft des Judentums* (Berlin, 1925).

15. Zu Geiger s. L. Geiger (Hg.), *Abraham Geiger: Leben und Lebenswerk* (Berlin, 1910); S. Schechter, Abraham Geiger, in: Ders., *Studies in Judaism,* Bd. III, a.a.O. (Anm. 4), 11ff.

16. S. zu ihm, dem "Begründer der jüdischen Literaturwissenschaft," K. Wilhelm, Moritz Steinschneider, in: *Bulletin des Leo-Baeck-Instituts,* Nr. 1 (1957), 35-47, hier: 40.30; Ders., Einführung, a.a.O. (Anm. 4), 14ff.

17. R. Fuchs, "The *Hochschule für die Wissenschaft des Judentums* in the Period of

the Nazi-Rule," in YLBI 12 (1967), 3-31.

18. Vg. a.a.O., 30.

19. Text nach M.L. Munk, "Austrittsbewegung und Berliner Adass Jisroel-Gemeinde 1869-1939," in: H.A. Strauss/K.R. Großmann (Hgg.), *Gegenwart im Rückblick, Festgabe für die jüdische Gemeinde in Berlin 25 Jahre nach Neubeginn* (Heidelberg, 1970), 130-49; weitere Lit.

20. a.a.O. (Anm. 24); siek ferner M. Offenberg (Hg.), *Adass Jisroel: Die jüdische Gemeinde in Berlin (1869-1942). Vernichtet und vergessen* (Berlin, 1986).

21. S. die Artikel über ihn (Vorname auch: Asriel, Azriel, Israel) von I. Marlon, in: EJ 8, 34-36; N. Eliav, in: EJ Jenis 8, 476-78 (je Lit.).

22. S. die Artikel von E. Pessen, in: JL 4/1 (1930), 1208f, u. von L. Jung, in: EJ Jenis 13, 1459 (je Lit.), sodann I.J. Eisner, "Reminiscences of the Berlin Rabbinical Seminary," in: YLBI 12 (1967), 32-52.

23. "Germanomanie" is the term used by Saul Ascher (1767-1822) in his attack on German chauvinism, published in 1890. See E. Peonore Sterling, *Judenhaß: Die Anfänge des politischen Antisemitismus in Deutschland (1815-1850)* (Frankfurt-am-Main, 1969).

24. S. etwa P.W. Massing, *Vorgeschichte des politischen Antisemitismus* (engl. 1949) (Frankfurt-am-Main, 1959); U. Tal, *Christians and Jews in Germany: Religion, Politics, and Ideology in the Second Reich, 1870-1914* (Ithaca/London, 1975); H. Engelmann, *Kirche am Abgrund: Adolf Stoecker und seine antijüdische Bewegung* (Berlin, 1984), 7ff.

25. Vgl. H. Engelmann, a.a.O. (Anm. 25), 62.

26. K. Kupisch, Die antisemitische Speer spitze, in: P.v.d. Osten-Sacken (Hg.), *Judenfeindschaft im 19. Jahrhundert* (Berlin, 1982), 51-54, hier: 51.

27. A. Stoecker, *Das moderne Judentum in Deutschland, besonders in Berlin: Zwei Reden* (Berlin, 1880), 17.

28. S. hierzu W. Boehlich (Hg.), *Der Berliner Antisemitismusstreit* (Frankfurt-am-Main, 1965); H. Engelmann, a.a.O. (Anm. 25), 91ff.

29. Vgl. K. Kupisch, a.a.O. (Anm. 31), 54. For clerical support of Stoecker, see H. Engelmann, a.a.O. (Anm. 25), 102ff; for clerical opposition, a.a.O., 111ff.

30. K. Kupisch, a.a.O. (Anm. 27), 54. Vgl. auch H. Engelmann, a.a.O. (Anm. 25), 168. Zur Reaktion jüdischerseits s. S. Ragins, *Jewish Responses to Anti-Semitism in Germany, 1870-1914* (Cincinnati, 1980), 23ff.

31. Zur Geschichte der "Gesellschaft," d.h. der organisierten Berliner Judenmission, s.m.a. J.F.A. de le Roi, *Die evangelische Christenheit und die Juden,* Bd. II (Berlin, 1891), repr. Leipzing 1974, 142-57; P.G. Aring, Christliche Judenmission, Neukirchen-Vluyn 1980, 154-70, 214-25.

32. Heine, above all, made note of it.

33. So G. Aring, Judenmission, a.a.O. (Anm. 37), 216, unter Verweis auf "Friedensbote 1880, 49ff.169.193.222 uam." - die Stellen belegen jedoch das genaue Gegenteil.

34. Vg. Friedensbote 10 (1878), 182ff.

35. J.F.A. de le Roi, *Die evangelische Christenheit und die Juden,* Bd. III (Berlin, 1892; repr. Leipzig, 1974), 406.

36. One could also put it like this: The mission to the Jews wanted to have the Jews on its own terms, i.e. as converts, something that one could not say for most Protestants, who, for anti-Semitic reasons, were against missionizing to the Jews altogether.

37. G.H. Dalman, *Kurzgefaßtes Handbuch der Mission unter Israel* (Berlin, 1893), 15f.

38. H.L. Strack, "Das Institutum Judaicum in Berlin," in: *Nathanael* 4 (1888), 56-62, hier: 57.

39. Ders., Das Institutum Judaicum Berlinense in den ersten 30 Jahren seines Bestehens, in: a.a.O. 30 (1914), 1-16, hier: 2.

40. A.a.O., 1, Anm. Stemchen.

41. Zur Geschichte des Instituts s. außer dem Bericht H.L. Stracks (a.a.O. [Anm. 40]) vor allem R. Golling, Das Institutum Judaicum, in: WZ(B) GS 34 (1985), 533-38.

42. H.L. Strack, a.a.O. (Anm. 40), 5.

43. Ders., An die Leser des 'Nathanael', in: *Nathanael 1* (1885), 161

44. Ders., Leopold Zunz, in: a.a.O. 2 (1886), 91.

45. S. seinen Beitrag: "Sie eifern um Gott, aber mit Unverstand" in: a.a.O., 129-49.

46. S. z.B. den Art. über ihn von B. Kirschner, in: JL 4/2 (1930), 735ff.

47. 1921; 1982 (in völliger Neubearbeitung von G. Stemberger).

48. R. Golling, a.a.O. (Anm. 42), 534.

49. A.v. Harnack, *Das Wesen des Christentums* (1900). Mit einem Vorwort von R. Bultmann (Gütersloh, 1964).

50. For further details see my essay, "Anti-Judaism in Christian Theology," in: *Christian Attitudes on Jews and Judaism 55* (1977), 1-6.

51. A.v. Harnack, a.a.O. (Anm. 50), 40.

52. A.a.O., 53.

53. A.a.O., 91.

54. Vg. a.a.O., 40.

55. A.a.O., 53.

56. A.a.O., 53.

57. Vg. a.a.O., 91.

58. A.a.O., 40f.

59. See here especially U.Tal, "Theologische Debatte um das 'Wesen' des Judentums," in: W.E. Mosse and G. Paucker (Hgg.), *Juden im Wilhelminischen Deutschland 1890-1914* (Tübingen, 1976), 599-632 (dort besonders 599 Anm. 1 u. 603 Anm. 7, weitere Lit.).

60. As put by P. Billerbeck in a glossary of a Jewish discussion of the text by F. Perles "Was lehrt uns Harnack?" (1902) in the "Popular-wissenschaftlichen Blättern zur Belehrung über das Judentum" (1902, 162ff) that was published in 'Nathanael' (19[1903], 93-95) zum Abdruck brachte. For Perles, also see references in U. Tal, a.a.O. (Anm. 60), 603 Anm. 7. F. Perles' response to Harnack was reprinted in his subsequent collection of essays, *Jüdische Skizzen* (Leipzig, 1912), 208-36.

61. A.a.O., 212f.

62. A.a.O., 228.

63. Ebd.

64. L. Baeck, "Harnack's Vorlesung über das Wesen des Christentums," in: MGWJ 45 (1901), 97-120 (erweiterter separater Nachdruck 1902). Die Zitate werden nach der Erstfassung gegeben.

65. Siehe A.H. Friedländer, *Leo Baeck: Leben und Lehre* (engl., 1968) (Stuttgart, 1973), 47ff, bes. 55: "Baeck was more than a symbol. He was the centerpiece of German Jewry."

66. Wie z.B. die bedeutsame Entgegnung von J. Eschelbacher, *Das Judentum und das Wesen des Christentums* (Berlin, 1905).

67. Berlin, 1905; Frankfurt-am-Main, 1922; Wiesbaden o.J.

68. L. Baeck, "Harnacks Vorlesungen," a.a.O. (Anm. 65), 118.

69. A.a.O., 119.

70. Ebda.

71. For a contribution to the rooting of the church in Judaism in these years, see

"Judaism in the Church," in: HUCA 2 (1925), 125-44; and for the postwar period, "The Faith of Paul," in: JJS 3 (1952), 93-110.

72. L. Baeck, *Das Evangelium als Urkunde der jüdischen Glaubensgeschichte* (Berlin, 1938), repr. in: Ders., *Paulus,* 99-196, die Pharisa'er und das Neue Testament (Frankfurt-am-Main, 1961). See Walter Kaufmann, trans., *Judaism and Christianity: Essays by Leo Baeck* (Philadelphia, 1958), 100-01 for translation.

73. *Judaism and Christianity,* 101.

74. *Judaism and Christianity,* 102.

75. R. Golling, a.a.O. (Anm. 42), 536.

76. H. Greßmann, "Die Aufgaben der Wissenschaft des nachbiblischen Judentums," in: ZAW 43 (1925), 1-32, hier: 1; R. Golling (a.a.O. [Anm. 42], 536) deutet den Aufsatz sicher zutreffend als "Konzeption" für die Instituts-Ausarbeit.

77. H. Greßmann, a.a.O. (Anm. 77).

78. The others were Judah Bergmann, Ismar Elbogen, Julius and Michael Guttmann.

79. H. Greßmann, Einführung, in: L. Baeck u.a., *Entwicklungsstufen der jüdischen Religion* (Gießen, 1927), 2f.

80. S. zur Geschichte dieser Bemühungen, die kein Ruhmesblatt deutscher Universitätsgeschichte sind, A. Jospe, "The Study of Judaism in German Universities before 1933," in YLBI 17 (1982), 295-319.

81. Messiabote 21/1 (1926), 16.

82. H. Keßler, Ein evangelischer Geistlicher wider die Judenmission, in: a.a.O. 24/1 (1929), 3-12, hier: 8.

83. H. Greßmann, a.a.O. (Anm. 80), 2f. Vgl./U. Kusche, *Die unterlegene Religion: Das Judentum im Urteil deutscher Alt-Testamentler* (Berlin, 1991), 144f. Zur Würdigung s. auch R. Golling, a.a.O. (Anm. 42), 536f; zur Würdigung von jüdischer Seite s. E.I.J. Rosenthal, "Ismar Elbogen and the New Learning," in: *Semitic Studies,* Bd. I (Cambridge, Mass., 1971), 327-52, hier: 338f.

84. Vgl. R. Golling, a.a.O. (Anm. 42), 537.

85. L. Baeck, Art.: Judentum III, in: RGG II, 491.

86. Berichtet von R. Weltsch, "Das Leo Baeck Institut," in: Ders., *An der Wende des modernen Judentums* (Tübingen, 1972), 67. Vgl. G. Stern, "German-Jewish and German-Christian Writers: Cooperation in Exile," in: J. Reinhartz and W. Schatzberg (Hgg.), *The Jewish Response to German Culture* (Hanover/London, 1985), 150-63, hier: 150 Anm. 1. Zur Situation der Juden in Berlin in den nachfolgenden Jahren der Naziherrschaft, d.h. zu Diskriminierung und Verdrängung, zu Verfolgung, Widerstand und Deportation, s. C. Engeli and W. Ribbe, Berlin in der NS-Zeit (1933-1945), in: W. Ribbe (Hg.), *Geschichte Berlins,* Bd. II (München, 1987), 952ff. 1001ff.

87. S. hierzu K. H. *Rengstorf, Leo Baeck: Eine geistige Gestalt unserer Zeit* (o.O.), 1958, 13f.

88. Zur Situation von Juden und jüdischen Gemeinden s. H.M. Broder and M.R. Lang (Hgg.), *Fremd im eigenen Land* (Frankfurt-am-Main, 1979); M. Brumlik u.a. (Hgg.), *Jüdisches Leben in Deutschland seit 1945* (Frankfurt-am-Main, 1986). *Zu Berlin (Ost und West) s. Wegweiser durch das jüdische Berlin* (Berlin, 1987).

89. For the present-day association and collaboration with the Jewish Council in Berlin, the works of "Gesellschaft für christlich-jüdische Zusammenarbeit" and "Ständige Arbeitskreis Juden und Christen" must be cited.

90. Cp. a.o. B. Engelmann, *Deutschland ohne Juden* (Germany without Jews) (München, 1970; repr. München, 1974); also the survey in E. G. Loewenthal, *Juden in Preussen: Ein biographisches Verzeichnis* (Jews in Prussia: A Biographical Listing) (Berlin, 1982). We also must include in this remembrance those contemporaries—such as

Dietrich Bonhoeffer, again closely connected to Berlin—who raised their voices on behalf of the Jews and were drawn closer to them as a consequence of their own persecution.

91. H.G. Adler, *Die Juden in Deutschland: Von der Aufklärung bis zum Nationalsozialismus* (München, 1960), 160f.

92. This phrase is taken from lines by the German-Jewish writer, Hilde Domin, in which she responds to the question about the possibility of a German-Jewish encounter in the future: "Do not tire / but towards the miracle / softly / as if to a bird / hold out your hand." (Hilde Domin, in *Mein Judentum* (My Judaism), ed. H. J. Schulz (Stuttgart, 1978), 104-17, here p. 117.) Guy Stern also closed his informative and moving "German-Jewish and German-Christian Writers: Cooperation in Exile" with these lines. In J. Reinharz and W. Schatzberg, eds., *The Jewish Response to German Culture* (Hanover/London, 1985), 150-63, here p. 150, n. 1.

ABBREVIATIONS

EJ   Encyclopaedia Judaica (Berlin)

HUCA   Hebrew Union College Annual

JL   Jüdisches Lexikon

JJS   Journal of Jewish Studies

MGWJ   Monatsschrift für Geschichte und Wissenschaft des Judentums

RGG   Die Religion in Geschichte und Gegenwart

WZ(B)GS Wissenschaftliche Zeitschrift der Humboldt–Universität Berlin/DDR, Gesellschaftswiss.

YLBI   Year Book of the Leo Baeck Institute

ZAW   Zeitschrift für die alttestamentliche Wissenschaft IXX

GERMAN ORTHODOXY, JEWISH LAW, AND THE USES OF KANT

David Ellenson

MORE THAN ANY OTHER MODERN PHILOSOPHER, Immanuel Kant has entered into Jewish religious thought. Five major articles appearing in the twentieth century have highlighted this relationship. In the first two, Julius Guttmann and Hermann Cohen attempted to demonstrate the affinity between Judaism, as they defined it, and Kantian moral philosophy.[1] Neither of them, however, was particularly interested in what Kant actually said about Judaism. On the other hand, Nathan Rotenstreich, in his article, "The Image of Judaism in Kant," concerned himself exclusively with what Kant said about Judaism.[2] H.M. Graupe, in "Kant und das Judentum," focused both on Kant's description of Judaism and on his influence on Jewish intellectual circles after his own time.[3] And, finally, Jacob Katz's "Kant and Judaism" analyzes Kant's influence on his Jewish contemporaries.[4]

None of these scholars, however, have dealt with the impact of Kant's thought upon German-Jewish Orthodoxy. This is not surprising, inasmuch as Kant, in speaking of Judaism in his 1794 work, *Religion Within the Limits of Reason Alone,* characterized Judaism negatively as *"statutarisches Gesetz,"* an externally imposed system of heteronomous legislation.[5] Indeed, even when Kant acknowledged that Judaism contained moral elements that were accessible through reason alone, the legal character of Judaism "perverted" these pure moral sentiments and transformed them into binding statutes which one obeyed only because of the threat of external compulsion. For example, Kant wrote that even had the Ten Commandments not been revealed publicly, they would still have been arrived at through reason. However, in Judaism these laws were obeyed not in response to an internal autonomous sense of morality, but because they were externally imposed by a lawgiver upon people who feared to disobey.[6]

Given Kant's pejorative description of Judaism as an inferior system of heteronomous legislation, it is not surprising, as Katz shows, that Kant's attacks were enthusiastically welcomed into Jewish circles hostile to halakhic Judaism. Nor is it astonishing, as others have shown, that philosophical advocates of Liberal Judaism, with their rejection of the divine, immutable nature of the totality of the Oral Law, would have employed aspects of Kantian thought to aid them in constructing their own understanding of Judaism as well as in their struggles for emancipation.

What remains to be analyzed, though, is how and why Kant's thought was eventually transformed and adopted so that it could be employed even within German Orthodox circles. As very little research has been devoted to this issue, this essay proposes to expand our knowledge in this area by examining selected works of three major representative figures within the German Orthodox community at the beginning of the twentieth century—Joseph Wohlgemuth (1862-1932), Nehemia Anton Nobel (1871-1922), and Isaac Breuer (1882-1946)—to describe and analyze how they utilized aspects of Kant's teachings to augment their own ideas.

From the moment that Rabbi S.R. Hirsch published his *Nineteen Letters* in 1836, the leaders of German-Jewish Orthodoxy, as well as the community they served, were thoroughly imbued with a philosophy that held Judaism and German culture as complementary. These leaders and their lay constituency were as comfortable with Kant, Schleiermacher, Hegel, and Goethe as were their non-Orthodox contemporaries. Cultural integration, as numerous scholars have observed, was the hallmark of German Judaism and the thought of interpreting Judaism in contemporary philosophical language and concepts was as natural to the German Orthodox as it was to the Liberals.

Such cultural uniformity on the part of German Jewry should not obscure the doctrinal differences that still distinguished the Orthodox from the other German-Jewish groups. As rabbis Esriel Hildesheimer (1820-1899) and S.R. Hirsch (1808-1888)—the leaders of German Orthodoxy during the 1800s—observed, the theological differences separating Orthodox Judaism from Reform or Positive-Historical trends were as great or greater than those which separated various Christian denominations from one another.[7] This doctrinal difference centered on the notion of God's revelation of Jewish Law. From an Orthodox perspective, "The Law both Written and Oral," in the words of Rabbi Hirsch, "was closed with Moses at Sinai."[8] This belief, which denied the possibility that the Law had developed over time, touched off a major controversy between the Orthodox and Positive-Historical camps in Germany between 1859 and 1861. Zacharias Frankel, father of Positive-Historical Judaism and head of the Jewish Theological Seminary in Breslau, had maintained in his *Darkhe HaMishnah* (1859) that elements of the Oral Law had evolved through history.

Particularly galling to the Orthodox was Frankel's contention that talmudic laws subsumed under the category *"halakhah l'Moshe mi'Sinai"* were not, as a literal translation would have it, laws given orally by God to Moses at Sinai. Instead, these laws, Frankel claimed, were of such great antiquity and so firmly established that it were *as if* they had been revealed to Moses. Frankel, in effect, was asserting that these laws were essentially the enactments of later generations.[9] Hirsch and others recognized that Frankel's position threatened the Orthodox belief that the Law was eternal and above the ravages of time. In a series of articles published by Hirsch in *Jeschurun,* Hirsch and Rabbi Gottlieb Fischer accused Frankel of heresy.[10] Hildesheimer even labeled Frankel as a *meshumad* (apostate) because of this book.[11]

Interestingly, Hermann Cohen, who was then a young student at the Theological Seminary, wrote a private letter to Hirsch after these articles appeared describing Frankel as an observant Jew who conducted himself in all respects in a strict rabbinical manner, "standing in the synagogue with the prayer shawl over his head, singing *zemirot* (hymns)...on holiday evenings, and also on occasion in his talmudic lectures zealously commenting, 'A God-fearing person must here be stringent.'" Hirsch printed part of this letter in the pages of *Jeschurun* along with his own reply. Frankel's practice, Hirsch charged, was unimportant if it was not accompanied by proper beliefs. In fact, Hirsch stated, affirmation of the divine origins of the Oral Law was as much the *sine qua non* of an authentic Orthodox Judaism as belief in the Mosaic revelation of the Written Law.[12] A philosophical system which could explain and defend this notion, as well as supporting their relationship to contemporary German culture and thought, became of paramount importance to the

Orthodox. It was this need which may well explain how and why the Orthodox leadership of German Judaism at the turn of the century appropriated Kant in the way they did.

Joseph Wohlgemuth, a faculty member at the Rabbinerseminar, continued this Orthodox emphasis upon the belief in an immutable divine law as constituting the foundation of Judaism. In an important 1914 essay, "Etwas über die Termini 'Orthodoxes und gesetzestreues Judentum,'" Wohlgemuth traced the development of the term "Orthodox" as applied to the traditionalist party within Judaism. He concluded that "Orthodoxy" was a *"Relationsbegriff,"* a "concept of relation" borrowed, obviously, from a non-Jewish religious vocabulary. It was the relativism of the term that disturbed Wohlgemuth, for such relativism failed to capture the essence, the absolute sense, of Judaism. Rather, the label "Orthodoxy" defined Judaism only in relation to other doctrines.[13] Consequently, Wohlgemuth preferred the term *"gesetzestreues Judentum,"* for it was this faithfulness to a Law that was both divine and impervious to history that marked for Wohlgemuth, as it had for Hirsch, the essential feature of Judaism. As he wrote, "Faithfulness to the law,...a revealed law from God, [is]...the characteristic essence of Judaism."[14]

This view of Judaism as "divine law" is parallel to the definition offered by Kant in his *Religion Within the Limits of Reason Alone,* where he wrote, "Religion is the recognition of all duties as divine commands, not as sanctions, i.e., arbitrary and contingent notions and ordinances of a foreign will, but as essential laws of any free will as such."[15] It is true that Wohlgemuth does not explicitly cite this Kantian passage. However, it is certain that Kant's views were known to Wohlgemuth, a teacher of philosophy, as well as to the German intellectual audience for which he wrote. As a result, Wohlgemuth, in his article, was able to continue the line of argument initiated by Hirsch and others in the previous century that *Gesetz,* understood as divinely commanded Law impervious to the exigencies of history, constituted the essence of Judaism. More significantly, because of the affinity between Kant's view of religion as "the recognition of all duties as divine commands" and the Orthodox emphasis upon Judaism as *"Gesetz,"* Orthodoxy was able to gain a significant contemporary intellectual warrant for its doctrinal system. For an Orthodox community informed by and concerned with German culture, Kant lent an important aura of respectability to their system of belief.

The influence of Kant and his appeal to Orthodox Jewish thinkers is evident as well in the writings of Nehemia Anton Nobel, *orthodoxer*

Gemeinderabbiner in Frankfurt from 1910 until his death in 1922. Nobel, a graduate of the Orthodox Rabbinerseminar who studied for his doctorate with Hermann Cohen, stood unsurpassed, in Alexander Altmann's view, "as the only true philosopher amongst German-Jewish Orthodoxy."[16] He was as concerned as Wohlgemuth to respond to the Liberal Jewish claim that the law was a result of historical development and, as such, could be amended or abrogated in light of academic research or the needs of the time. Nobel was particularly concerned to respond to *Die Richtlinien zu einem Programm für das liberale Judentum (Guidelines of a Program for Liberal Judaism)*, issued by a group of sixty-one German rabbis for adoption as a statement of principles and beliefs by a conference of the Union for Liberal Judaism held in Posen in 1912. The *Guidelines* received a great deal of publicity and Nobel, as a spokesman for Orthodoxy, felt obligated to respond to them in both sermons and pamphlets.

Of particular concern to Nobel were those statements in the *Guidelines* which asserted that Jewish law had developed in history. The Liberals claimed that "every generation adopted the faith of the fathers through its own particular religious concepts and expressed it in its own particular forms." The *Guidelines* continued:

> Liberal Judaism therefore recognizes the validity of evolution, which gives Judaism in every age the right and duty to abandon certain historically conditioned beliefs and forms, or to develop them, or to create new ones, while safeguarding its own essential content. This duty speaks with special urgency to our time. Through the entrance of Jews into the...community of this age,...many traditional concepts, institutions and customs have evaporated and disappeared and thereby lost both content and significance.[17]

Some ordinances, the Liberal rabbis contended, remained obligatory for modern Jews, while others could simply be abandoned. For example, in addressing the issue of the Sabbath, these rabbis held that whatever "disturbs [the] solemnity [of the Sabbath] must be avoided, and, conversely, whatever does not disturb it cannot be considered as prohibited." Liberal Judaism, the rabbis concluded, "recognizes as worthwhile only that which for the individual has the power to elicit pious sentiment, to advance moral action, and to recall religious truths and experiences vividly."[18] Such teachings clearly foreshadow the sentiments expressed by Franz Rosenzweig (1886-1929), the great teacher of modern Liberal Judaism, who spoke of the necessity for the Jew to transform a static and impersonal Law (*Gesetz*) into an address of personal commandment (*Gevot*).[19]

It was this emphasis upon the law as historically conditioned and subject to the will of the individual that so disturbed Nobel and his Orthodox contemporaries. While Nobel acknowledged the purity and sincerity of their intentions, he attacked the sentiments contained in the *Guidelines* as springing from the soil of a "Protestant communal consciousness." They literally constituted a "war against the halakhah," against the system of "statutes and judgments" that lay at the heart of authentic Judaism.[20] Rather, the halakhah permitted the moral values of Judaism to become manifest in life. For Judaism, as Nobel had asserted in an article in *Die Jüdische Presse* years before, "could never have become a universal religion had it confined itself to a system of abstract thought."[21]

Nobel further demonstrated that the biblical prophets themselves, whom the Liberals loved to cite in support of their antinomian posture, never opposed the law. They only opposed its rote performance by those who observed it as something "superficial and external." Like his teacher Cohen, Nobel asserted that there could be no authentic "religion without morality." However, the Liberals failed to realize that genuine Jewish observance of the Law sprung from an internal state of freedom that permitted the Jew to appropriate God's commandments autonomously. Law and ethics were not opposed in Judaism; on the contrary, they were its identity. The Law, as Nobel put it, did not constitute a "yoke." The Jew observed it "with joy and celebration."[22] It was not transitory but eternal and anyone who struck at it diminished and threatened "the existence of Judaism itself."[23] Nobel's claims that Law constituted the "essence of Judaism" and that any attack upon the binding quality of the law was tantamount to an attempt to destroy Judaism were not novel. Indeed, Nobel was simply one of many Orthodox rabbis to express such sentiments. What is significant is that Nobel defended his arguments about the Law in a framework derived from Kant.

In a 1918 essay on the "Sabbath," Nobel argued that the Sabbath was testimony to the existence of freedom in the world. God created Nature and established an order within it. God was not, as Spinoza would have it, an extension of Nature. Like his teacher Hermann Cohen, who had attacked Spinoza, Nobel explicitly rejected the "pantheistic-mythological" imagination that advanced such a belief.[24] Such a doctrine, from a Kantian perspective, made no distinction between the sensible and intelligible worlds, between the realm of deterministic nature and the realm of moral freedom. In short, if God and Nature were one, as pantheism maintained, then freedom and hence morality were illusory. Judaism, like Kantian thought, denied this. Nobel wrote that Sabbath and its laws were the signs and symbols of both "human freedom" and the ability of humanity to transform the world in accord with God's will and desire. The Sabbath shows humanity's ability to transform nature and impose divine purpose and meaning upon life. The Sabbath, for Nobel, symbolized the link between the realm of nature and the realm of freedom: "Ethics and socialism established a covenant at the hour of creation. The Jewish religion sanctified it. This covenant gave birth to the Sabbath."[25]

Nobel's vocabulary and the ethical intent he ascribed to the Sabbath are remarkably akin to sentiments expressed by Cohen[26] and clearly derived from arguments put forth by Kant. Kant, in his *The Critique of Judgment,* had written:

> Now even if an immeasurable gulf is fixed between the sensible realm of the concept of nature and the supersensible realm of the concept of freedom, so that no transition is possible from the first to the second (by means of the theoretical use of reason),...yet the second is *meant* to have an influence upon the first. The concept of freedom is meant to actualize in the world of sense the purpose proposed by its laws....There must, therefore, be a ground of the *unity* of the supersensible, which lies at the basis of nature, with that which the concept of freedom practically contains.[27]

In other words, the realm of the intelligible, which is the moral realm of freedom, must be capable of informing the sensible realm of nature if moral purpose is ultimately to be realized. Thus, Kant posits that "in order to be able to project a final purpose consistent with the moral law, we must assume a moral world cause..., i.e., we must admit that there is a God." However, Kant admitted that this argument was not "an objectively valid proof of the existence of God" but only a "subjective argument sufficient for moral beings."[28] The notion of final purpose belonged, strictly speaking, to the realm of reason alone and could not genuinely be inferred from nature. However, this notion did possess the practical benefit of enabling humanity to see its duties "as divine commandments."

It is interesting that Nobel employed this Kantian insight to frame his argument about the Sabbath, the goals of human freedom, and unity with the divine that such purposive transformation could bring. However, for Nobel, the Sabbath and the divine legislation that accompanied it were not, as religion was for Kant, an "as if" solution to the philosophical problem of the division between the realm of nature and the realm of freedom. The Sabbath, for Nobel, was a metaphysical bridge that united the realm of freedom with the realm of nature. It allowed the former to infuse the latter with purpose and meaning. Jewish law, stemming as it did from God, allowed the human being, blessed by God with freedom, to invest the physical world with moral significance. Thus Nobel not only explicated the symbolic significance of the Sabbath but also, by extension, defended the ethical integrity and wholeness of a Law that mandated such observance from its would-be detractors. The debt Nobel owed Kant for such a rendering is readily apparent.

The appropriation of Kant by German Orthodox Jewry reaches its zenith in the writings of Isaac Breuer, grandson of Rabbi Samson Raphael Hirsch and one of the leading members of Agudat Yisrael. Kant's significance for Breuer is revealed in his autobiography, where he wrote:

> It is my deep conviction that the God and King of Israel sends enlightened men among the nations from time to time, called and destined to play a part in Jewish 'Meta-History.'…And when the hour…broke…in which Israel…had to protect herself against the pressures of the outside world…,God caused to rise among the nations the exceptional man Kant, who, on the basis of the Socratic and Cartesian skepticism, brought about that "Copernican Turn," whereby the whole of man's reasoning was set in steel limits within which alone perception is legitimized. Blessed be God, who in His wisdom created Kant! Every real Jew who seriously and honestly studies the "Critique of Pure Reason" is bound to pronounce his "Amen" on it.[29]

Kant, for Breuer, became a weapon to protect Judaism and the Orthodox view of revelation from the presumptions "of the *Kundschafter* (adventurers) of our times."

As Zvi Kurzweil has explained, Breuer employed Kant's well-known distinction between the phenomenal and noumenal worlds to demonstrate that human knowledge was limited exclusively to the realm of appearances. Humans were unable to penetrate into the world of the noumena—the world-in-itself to use Kant's term—which remained unknown to human intelligence and hidden from human perception.[30]

Breuer then used this distinction to defend the notion that the Torah records the literal word of God, as well as to affirm the inerrancy of Scripture against attacks launched by biblical critics. In his *Der neue Kusari: Ein Weg zum Judentum,* he criticizes both literary and philological attempts to cast doubt upon the accuracy of the Masoretic text of the Bible and maintains the historical accuracy of certain biblical narratives. Drawing upon the Kantian distinction between phenomena and noumena, Breuer claims that Torah was something noumenal, a miraculous appearance of the "meta-historical" in time.[31] Academic inquiry into Scripture, he concedes, might have validity in the sphere of phenomena. However it is irrelevant to the noumenal reality of Torah. Scripture, written in Hebrew and endowed with holiness, is both phenomena and noumena, creation and nature. Breuer articulates the significance of this distinction when he writes, "Philologists, using their methods, view [the Bible] as merely something that has evolved...and relate it to a specific language group. Its role as the mouthpiece and the Word of God...remains totally concealed from them."[32]

Critical methods of inquiry are unable to penetrate the deepest layers and ultimate meaning of the noumenal content of the Bible, Breuer felt. Instead, it is only the guiding interpretation of the Oral Law, itself divine in origin, which can rescue us from this dilemma and allow us to unlock the hidden and true meaning of Scripture. As Kurzweil has pointed out, when the Bible narrates human situations, "The Torah speaks in human language." However, when the Torah makes statements of a metaphysical nature, i.e., pertaining to acts of creation, revelation, and redemption, we can never be sure of grasping their ultimate meaning. Therefore, Breuer said, the Oral Law, as well as Kabbalah, must be studied assiduously so as to uncover the noumenal character of Scripture. It was this appropriation of Kant's distinction between the phenomenal and noumenal worlds which provided the epistemoligial basis for Breuer's immersion into the realm of Kabbalah, as Gershom Scholem noted over fifty years ago.[33] Kant allowed Breuer to answer the challenges of biblical criticism and the notion of an evolving Jewish law to his own satisfaction.

Breuer was thus able to describe Judaism, as did his grandfather S.R. Hirsch, Wohlgemuth, and many others before him, as *Gesetzesreligion.* However, Breuer felt, the law of Torah is not, as Kant characterized it, a heteronomous one. Rather, it is *Naturrecht,* a "Law of nature," and there exists a natural harmony between the law of Torah and the Jewish people. This relationship between God, Torah, and the Jewish people is thus defined by autonomy, as Nobel had argued, rather than heteronomy.

As Breuer phrased it, "The way of Judaism…starts out with the heteronomy of God's Law and…leads to an autonomy…which embodies God's will completely in the will of self."[34] Kant himself correctly perceived, wrote Breuer, "that the world as conceived conforms to law…." Kant's one deficiency, according to Breuer, was that he was unable to identify this law, the content of this law, because he lacked revelation.[35]

Breuer thus went further than Kant in his own application of Kantian principles to an understanding of Judaism and Torah. As an acculturated German, Breuer had internalized Kant and understood his own world in light of Kantian teachings. However, he also had a need to defend and explain Judaism in contemporary cultural and philosophical terms. Kant gave him the language to do so. Thus, he was able to write, in words reminiscent of Hermann Cohen, "In Judaism law and ethics are in essence absolutely identical. Our highest goal is to fulfill God's royal law out of love for the Torah. The path leads…from man in the multiplicity of his phenomena to man-in-himself; from the Torah of the spoken word to the Torah of the written word—to Torah-in-itself."[36] The words of *Pirke Avot,* "Make God's Will your own," bespeaks for Breuer the moral task incumbent upon every Jew.

In sum, it is clear that German Orthodox thinkers, as represented by Wohlgemuth, Nobel, and Breuer, were as anxious as their Liberal colleagues to articulate a philosophy of Judaism in modern philosophical terms. They were themselves acculturated members of German society who had internalized the values and teachings of *Bildung* and who were addressing their works to a comparably acculturated audience. Because of their background, they saw nothing alien or artificial in explaining and defending Judaism in contemporary philosophical—in this case Kantian—language. This does not mean that other philosophers such as Hegel did not have a significant impact elsewhere in their writings.[37] However, they felt that their commitment to the doctrine of an immutable, divinely revealed Law residing at the heart of Judaism could best be explained in terms of Kant's teachings on ethics and on the distinction Kant drew between the phenomenal and noumenal worlds.

Kant's writings, insofar as they focused on the nature of both obligation and the reality of a meta-historical realm—and not on the subtleties of religious development and change—were seen as particularly amicable to the doctrines of Orthodox Judaism. His emphasis upon an "ethics of duty" gave the Orthodox a culturally respectable warrant to shift away from a developmentally oriented "history of religions" approach to Judaism to one that was more philosophically informed. In this way, the challenge of the Historical School to an Orthodox notion of Jewish Law and to the unitary authorship of the Torah could be circumvented.

Michael Meyer has observed that "there is no modern philosopher who influenced Jewish thinkers more than did Immanuel Kant. From Solomon Ludwig Steinheim...through Hermann Cohen and Leo Baeck..., the Kantian imperative was equated with the call to moral responsibility..."[38] This does not mean that Kant became the arbiter of what was essential in Judaism. It is to assert that the Orthodox philosophers, as much as their Liberal peers, saw an affinity between the nature of Jewish doctrine as they understood it and the teachings of Immanuel Kant. The Orthodox philosophers truly employed a new language—a Kantian one—to awaken and defend an ancient faith.

NOTES

1. H. Cohen, "Innere Beziehungen der Kantischen Philosophie zum Judentum, " *Jüdische Schriften,* 3 vols. (Berlin, 1924), 1:284-305; and J. Guttmann, "Kant und das Judentum," *Schrifte* (Leipzig, 1908), 42-62.

2. N. Rotenstreich, "D'mut hayehadut eitzel Kant" (The Image of Judaism in Kant), *Tarbitz* 27 (1957-1958), 388-405. Also see, N. Rotenstreich, *Jews and German Philosophy* (New York, 1984).

3. H.M. Graupe, "Kant und das Judentum," *Zeitschrift für Religions – und Geistesgeschichte* 13 (1961), 308-33.

4. Jacob Katz, "Kant v'hayehadut" (Kant and Judaism), *Tarbitz* 41 (1971-1972), 219-37.

5. Immanuel Kant, *Religion Within the Limits of Reason Alone* (New York: Harper and Row, 1960), 116.

6. Ibid.

7. *Rabbiner Esriel Hildesheimer Briefe,* ed. Mordechai Eliav (Jerusalem: Verlag Rubin Mass, 1965), Letter 29.

8. S.R. Hirsch, *Horeb,* 2 vols. (London, 1962), 1:20.

9. Z. Frankel, *Darkhe Hamishnah* (1859), 20.

10. S.R. Hirsch, "Schriften betreffend Dr. Z. Frankels 'Darke hamischna,'" *Gesammelte Schriften,* 6 vols. (Frankfurt, 1873), 6:322-434. See especially pp. 339ff.

11. *Hildesheimer Responsa, Yoreh Deah,* no. 238.

12. *Jeschurun* 7 (1861), 297-98.

13. J. Wohlgemuth, "Etwas über die Termini 'Orthodoxes und gesetzestreues Judentum,'" *Festschrift zum siebzigsten Geburstag David Hoffmann,* ed. Simon Eppenstein, Meier Hildesheimer, and Joseph Wohlgemuth (Berlin, 1914), 446.

14. Ibid., 449.

15. Kant, *Religion Within the Limits of Reason Alone,* 142.

16. Alexander Altmann, "Theology in Twentieth Century Germany," *Leo Baeck Institute Year Book* 1:211.

17. Ibid.

18. W. Gunther Plaut, *The Growth of Reform Judaism* (New York: World Union for Progressive Judaism, 1965), 69-71. Emphasis mine.

19. Quoted in *Contemporary Jewish Thought,* ed. Simon Noveck (Clinton, Mass.: B'nai B'rith Department of Adult Jewish Education, 1963), 232.

20. Nehemia Anton Nobel, *Hagut va'halakhah* (Meditations and Halakhah) (Jerusalem: Mossad Harav Kuk, 1969), 66-70 and 89.

21. Quoted in Eugen Eliahu Mayer, "Nehemia Anton Nobel," in *Guardians of Our Heritage,* ed. L. Jung (New York: Bloch 1958), 567.

22. Nobel, *Meditations and Halakhah,* 90.

23. Ibid.

24. Ibid., 93.

25. Ibid., 99.

26. See Cohen's suggestive essay, "Spinoza über Staat und Religion, Judentum und Christentum," in his *Jüdische Schriften* 3:290-372 as well as his "Der Sabbat in Seiner Kulturgeschichtlichen Bedeutung," in his *Jüdishe Schriften* 2:45-72.

27. Immanuel Kant, *Critique of Judgment* (New York: Hafner, 1951), 12.

28. Ibid. (1968 translation), 301.

29. Quoted in Salomon Ehrmann, "Isaac Breuer," in *Guardians of Our Heritage,* 624-25.

30. See Zvi Kurzweil, *The Modern Impulse of Traditional Judaism* (Hoboken, N.J.: Ktav, 1985), 36.

31. Isaac Breuer, *Der neue Kusari* (Frankfurt-am-Main, 1934), 341-42.

32. Ibid., 393.

33. See Kurzweil, *The Modern Impulse of Traditional Judaism,* 37. Scholem's essay on Breuer appears in English translation as "The Politics of Mysticism: Isaac Breuer's *New Kuzari,*" in G. Scholem, *The Messianic Idea in Judaism* (New York: Schocken, 1971), 325-34.

34. Quoted in Ehrmann, "Isaac Breuer," 627.

35. Isaac Breuer, *Concepts of Judaism,* ed. Jacob S. Levinger (Jerusalem: Israel Universities Press, 1974), 277.

36. Ibid., 280.

37. For Hegel's impact on Hirsch, for example, see Noah Rosenbloom, *Tradition in an Age of Reform* (Philadelphia Jewish Publication Society, 1976), *passim.* Also, Alan L. Mittelman, in his insightful study of the philosophical teachings of Breuer, *Between Kant and Kabbalah* (Albany, N.Y., 1990), 158-60, elucidates Hegel's impact on Breuer's views of the relationship between law, ethics, and society.

38. Michael Meyer, "Modernity as a Crisis for the Jews," *Modern Judaism* 9:2 (May 1989), 150.

84

PART III

Historical Judaism

THE END OF THE SCIENCE
OF JUDAISM IN GERMANY*

Herbert Strauss

BETWEEN HITLER'S SEIZURE OF POWER in January 1933 and the last mass-deportation of Berlin's Jews in February 1943, German Jewry in its classical form came to an end. A study of history shows that precisely because German Jewry had been emancipated in a century when the national unity of Germany had been transformed into a substitute religion and German nationalism had become the definitive form of collective self-affirmation, Jewish self-understanding could be expressed only in those forms that the spiritual life of the time could provide. The epoch of German-Jewish history, destroyed by violence and murder, proved to be the test-case for the modernization of Judaism.

It was during the period of Emancipation, beginning just toward the end of the Napoleonic era, that Judaism acquired as its form the Science of Judaism. The concept of science prevalent at that time was impregnated by classical philology and its methods. The Science of Judaism, mirroring this concept, remained philological in its methods through its entire development: for example, some three or four generations of rabbis, who produced numerous dissertations, were dedicated to editing texts of the oral tradition or to Semitic languages and philology. The work of Leopold Zunz or Moritz Steinschneider reflects this predominance of philology.

An awareness that from then on historicism would inform scholarship accompanied this concept of science modeled on the classical studies of the Greco-Roman world. Certainly Judaism had developed a

87

particular historical conscience of its own since its origin. Great events in Judaism's past became the archetypical models by which all later events would be understood: the exodus from Egypt, for instance, served as a model for the perception of all later wanderings and persecutions. The *new* European concept of history was influenced by the models of the organic development of Romanticism and its search for origins, which were regarded as "purer" than any later developments. The roots of a historical event were believed to determine the subsequent events. The study of the "essence" of an event, of its sources—a part of Renaissance, Reformation and Humanist thought—served to separate the authentic from the inauthentic. Historicism, as it was later quite ambiguously labeled, was still free of the taint of relativism.

Thus for Judaism, philology and history became central models of thought. The Science of Judaism, which by 1817 had acquired its name through the well-known Association for the Culture and Science of Judaism *(Verein für Kultur und Wissenschaft des Judentums)*, did not intend at all to dissolve Judaism. Thoroughly impregnated by the Enlightenment throughout its development, it wanted to restore Judaism to its original purity, to prove scientifically and rationally which beliefs were valid and which invalid. Interestingly, the critical rationality of conservative Deism, as developed earlier in English Protestant thought, shows many similarities with the structure of this Science of Judaism.

The Science of Judaism has created an impressive roster of institutions and scientific accomplishments, enabling generations of Jewish functionaries to attain an intellectual identity. Supported by a German-Jewish bourgeoisie that was not only successful but also educated, this science presented patterns of life to the Jewish petite-bourgeoisie who constituted the majority of German Jews at that time, pointing the way to Jewish self-respect to their children and grandchildren, as far as they remained Jewish—only a few converted to Christianity—and interested in Judaism. Emerging at the same time as the emancipation and secularization of European Jewry, this science was also motivated by the desire to gain support for political and social equality.

The core function, however, of the Science of Judaism was to respond to a spiritual void in the Judaism of the time which had nothing to counter the attractions of the surrounding culture, nothing but a tradition that had stiffened into formalism. By affirming Judaism in a world of mounting secularization and conditioned by the intellectual and political exclusiveness of German nationalism, Jews in Germany attempted to defend themselves against disregard and discrimination. In spite of their outstanding scholarly achievements, however, academic recognition remained elusive: Judaic scholars did not succeed in establishing a single professorial chair for the Science of Judaism at a German university in almost 100 years. Even the professorship held by Martin Buber at the University of Frankfurt, established in 1923 and the only one of its kind in Germany before the founding of the Federal Republic, was a chair for Jewish philosophy of religion and ethics, and not for the Science of Judaism.

To generate academic recognition, five institutions for Jewish studies were founded as private institutions by German Jews, two of them as teachers' training colleges and three as graduate studies centers on the highest levels of research and teaching. The first scientific institution, the Jewish Theological Seminary in Breslau, was established in 1854 by Zacharias Frankel, its leader until his death in 1875; the second, the Graduate School for the Science of Judaism, was founded in 1872 in Berlin; the third, the Orthodox rabbinical seminary, the so-called Hildesheimer Seminary, named after its first and academically brilliant director Esriel Hildesheimer, followed one year later.

Although each institution had a similar dependence on modern concepts of science, they differed in their social and spiritual outlooks. The seminary in Breslau, primarily training rabbis and academic teachers of religion, matched the fundamental traditionalism of the Jewish communities in Germany: even if a congregation were less Orthodox, observing fewer rituals, the rabbi still had to be educated as well as observant. Thus Breslau received sufficient financial support from its community, at least until the inflation of 1920-1923. By contrast, the Hildesheimer Seminary's constituents were made up of the separatist wing of German Orthodoxy.

Both institutions attracted students predominantly from Eastern Europe. The fact that Northern German Jewry for centuries remained open to the influence of East European Jewish learning was of considerable importance for its institutions, particularly in the Talmudic disciplines, where the East European Jewish spirit remained an integral part of Jewish scholarship. In addition to financial support, the graduate schools in Breslau and Berlin offered East European students social advancement, and in return the immigrants infused German Jewry—especially in north and west German cities—with a vitality which went deeper than did the differences that divided West and East.

Yet despite the petit-bourgeois origin of many students, the Science of Judaism never affected the broader strata of German Jewry. Unlike the Breslau Seminary, the Graduate School for the Science of Judaism experienced financial difficulties throughout its entire existence, especially during and after the inflation of the early 1920s. Science was not accepted at its true value—though only through science could one have countered the pseudo-scientific arguments of modern anti-Semitism. Nor did the Graduate School affiliate itself with any one denomination. It wanted to be open to all scientific influences, in contrast to the sometimes narrow self-understanding of its sister institution in Breslau. What seemed to be an intellectual strength, however, turned out to be an institutional weakness. When financial support from communities ceased, the congregational representations refused financial support, insisting that the acceptance of Christian students was diluting the character of a rabbinical academy—as they understood it. Thus the Science of Judaism in Germany, in its entire history, suffered from missed opportunities, unfinished plans, and lack of basic research and continuity. It was typical that even a high-level but popular intellectual journal like *Der Morgen* (The Morning) never had more than 1,000 subscribers.

Both splendor and misery characterized the institutional development of the Science of Judaism in Germany. Without the important influences which German-Jewish life received from East European Jewry, it would have lacked the dynamic tension which had infused the golden epoch of Jewish scholarship in the Hellenistic age and in medieval Spain. In retrospect, the era of *Wissenschaft* may be called the golden time of modern Jewish scholarship and two scholars in particular, Ismar Elbogen and Eugen Taeubler, made exemplary contributions at the end of this historic epoch.

Ismar Elbogen and Eugen Taeubler had fundamentally different perceptions of Judaism, as I learned thanks to my personal relationship with each of them. I came to know Elbogen when I was 18, in my first semester as a senior at the Graduate School for the Science of Judaism in Berlin in the summer of 1937. My report book records a colloquium with Elbogen on the modern period, 1599-1750. Elbogen also was one of my examiners when on June 21, 1938 I stood for the entrance examination to Beth Hakerem, the Jerusalem teacher's college, with an office in Berlin to facilitate immigration to Palestine. It was to be the last time I saw him.

As for Eugen Taeubler, who was born in 1879 and died in Cincinnati in 1953, I heard his lecture in 1938 on "Judaism as Tragic Existence"[1] and I attended his seven-lecture series on History and Old Testament from the spring semester of 1939 until his emigration in the spring of 1940. I met Taeubler again in New York in early 1947. Our personal contact in Berlin during the first years of the war, and in New York until the end of the forties, had grown into a close intellectual friendship.

Elbogen, as well as Taeubler, came from small towns in the province of Posen. For both of them that meant a childhood conditioned by the folk-piety of the East European Jewish tradition. Elbogen's father was a teacher of religion and as long as Elbogen lived he remained faithful to his Jewish roots. In his intellectual development he embraced a religiosity that, as far as we knew, he never questioned. His rabbinical studies at the Jewish Theological Seminary in Breslau did not mean a spiritual break with his past and his first extensive scientific work was a philological-historical analysis of the *amidah* of the *Achtzehngebet,* which he later developed into his main work in Judaica. From 1902 on, he was a teacher at the Lehranstalt. During the eras of the German Empire and the Weimar Republic, through war and inflation, and finally during the Nazi years until his emigration shortly before *Kristallnacht,* Elbogen, more than any other individual, remains that school's epitome of scholarship.

Ismar Elbogen had a gracious and humble personality, gifted with humor and irony, which, as he used to say, was never without love. He conveyed that East European Jewish ability to reduce the absurd and pompous aspects of Jewish as well as non-Jewish life to their human measure; he possessed something of the Yiddish folk-humor, of the wholesome, even if defensive and ultimately powerless petit-bourgeois morality of the Midrash, which in the religious life of the small town perhaps had been the strongest force for shaping Jewish personality. I do not think it pure chance that Elbogen, in his Festschrift for the 25th anniversary of Leo Baeck's professorship, contributed an essay on Hillel explaining his sayings and the many legends about the gentle Hillel in deepest sympathy, celebrating him as a historical figure who had reno-vated Jewish teachings and made them accessible to the people.

Many aspects of Elbogen's activities matched Hillel's. Elbogen's scientific prestige rests on a rich productivity in many different areas: the classical-talmudic tradition (he also taught Talmud at the Graduate School), the history of the Jews in the Middle Ages and modern times, and an apparently inexhaustible knowledge of scientific literature and its sources. Vast learning characterized his pedagogy as well as his publications: his method was source-criticism, and he did not allow any of his students to get away with generalizations without asking them the source of their theories, the small eyes in his big, somewhat puckish face smiling in ironic friendliness. Method and man seemed to be in harmony, the sobriety of Elbogen's science matching his common sense. This kept him from regressing into sermonizing and sentimentality, as would have been in character considering his origin.

The introduction Elbogen wrote for the first volume of the *Germania Judaica*[2] in 1934 was a model case for the intellectual resistance still possible to German Jewry in the early years of Nazism. In this volume, Elbogen emphasized the integration of German Jews into the social and legal order of the early Middle Ages to about 1240. He showed that the history of medieval Jews was not just a history of martyrs but also of coexistences richly documented for centuries—with secured, if inferior, rights from the first mention in Roman Cologne in the year 321 to the customs decree of Raffelstett in 906 and the great imperial documents of the thirteenth century.

Much of his presentation seems to us in our day a direct answer to the politics of the Nazis. Yet even in this apologetic context it was a history of the *community* in its social as well as economic aspects. It has been this "inside" view of Jewish history which had turned Elbogen into an internationally recognized personage by 1933, linking German-Jewish science with Jewish scholarship abroad. Already in the twenties, he had been appointed guest professor at the new Jewish Institute of Religion in New York, and was acting as consultant to other American-Jewish institutions.

His concentration on the internal history of the Jews gave his works a special significance after the Holocaust. Jewish Studies programs in the postwar period, although approaching the discipline from their own historical stances, adopted Elbogen's view. A non-Zionist, Elbogen, recognizing limits in Dubnow's territorialism in method and contents, could draw on his experience with the folk-culture of Eastern Europe to serve as a bridge to the ethnic self-understanding of the present.

Elbogen does appear as a traditional representative of the Science of Judaism rather than as a harbinger of the future. In a warmly appreciative article on the twentieth anniversary of Elbogen's death, the elderly Semitist and Orientalist, Erwin Rosenthal, living in his advanced years in Cambridge, England, understood Elbogen ultimately as a theologian and his Science of Judaism as a historical-philological expression of his religiosity, if erring when he relates Elbogen to the early nineteenth-century Protestant theologian Schleiermacher.

Essentially Elbogen's religiosity was rooted in the popular survivals of the Enlightenment, as Alexander Altmann has shown for the sermon literature of the nineteenth century. Elbogen's concept of science was rationalistic and pragmatic, maintaining that Judaism and humanism were identical, and that science must serve faith as well as life. He saw the Science of Judaism as a path to Jewish self-assertion. As evident in his compilation "The Doctrines of Judaism" *(Die Lehren des Judentums)*, he expected that scientific knowledge would end anti-Semitic prejudices and generate in the wider society a just appreciation of Judaism. Though time and time again he criticizes the decline of the philological method for lapsing into irresponsible detailism, he remained ironically inspired by the "and yet" of faith. As a religious Jew, as a German citizen of Jewish faith, as an anti-Zionist, and as an opponent of Dubnow's thought and historical terminology, Elbogen lived his faith, trusting the vitality of the Jewish people in its religiosity.

He died before the full truth about the end of European Jewry permeated the conscience of his time.

Eugen Taeubler's origins were in Posen too, and there is no doubt that his close friendship with Leo Baeck during World War II and his good relationship with Ismar Elbogen which lasted until Elbogen's death were rooted in their common origin and shared folk experience. Taeubler knew, as did Elbogen, that the history of the Jews cannot be understood unless it is related to the intellectual trends of their environment. Yet Taeubler, in contrast to Elbogen, was an extremely complex person, constantly calling himself into question. His humble origins seemed never to let go of him. From his grandfather, a Talmud scholar, he absorbed lasting impressions, yet both he and his widow remained silent about his parents, which is indeed ironic for a man who co-founded Jewish family research.

At 10 years of age, he left his family to receive a humanist education at the Comenius high school in Lissa, the birthplace of Leo Baeck, Akiba Eger, and Hirsch Kalisher, a town vibrant with Jewish intellect and religion. His humanism, unlike Elbogen's midrashic morality, was influenced by the Protestant tradition of the great Czech pedagogue whose name had been given to the school he attended. The Latin-Greek methodology of classical philology attracted Taeubler, who chose

Classical Philology and Ancient History as his majors at the University of Berlin, which, in the late 1800s, boasted such famous scholars as Theodor Mommsen, Ulrich von Wilamowitz-Moellendorf, Otto Hirschfeld, Hermann Diels, and Eduard Norden. He became Mommsen's research assistant, while studying Talmud at the Hildesheimer Seminary and at the Graduate School for the Science of Judaism. In 1906, at the age of 27, he interrupted his study of classical antiquity, for reasons we will examine later, and took over the directorship of a newly founded General Archives for German Jews, a position which he occupied for 13 years, interrupted by military service in the Prussian army at the Eastern front.

His most important achievement for the Science of Judaism came in 1919, when he was appointed the first director of the newly founded Academy for the Science of Judaism in Berlin. With half a dozen colleagues he turned the Academy into a climactic center for the development of the discipline. He had been qualified in 1918 (or perhaps as early as 1910) as a university lecturer in Ancient History at the University of Berlin, and though he continued to lecture, he gave up the chair of Jewish history which he had occupied at the Graduate School for the Science of Judaism in 1912. Professorships in Ancient (Roman) History at Zurich (1922) and at Heidelberg (1928-1933) followed. When the Nazis came to power in January 1933, and dismissed Jewish civil servants forthwith (Law of April 7, 1933), Taeubler resigned his position of his own free will, although as a veteran of World War I he was exempted from the law's provisions. In 1936, he returned to the Graduate School for the Science of Judaism as a lecturer and in 1941 migrated to the U.S. where he was appointed Research Professor in Biblical and Hellenistic Literature at the Hebrew Union College in Cincinnati.

This constantly shifting focus of activity, evident even in this compressed sketch, in contrast to Elbogen's steadiness, appears to be reflective of the encounter between German-Jewish life and social reality in the province of Posen. Taeubler, like Buber, was not religious in the traditional or orthopractic sense. His concept of religion stemmed from Wilhelm Dilthey's philosophy of life which he had studied at the University of Berlin and had been even more personalized through the existentialist philosophy he encountered at Heidelberg. He was aware of the contradictions occurring in the social fabric around him, and since his high school days had been a Zionist, again and again working out immigration and university plans for a Jewish Palestine. Yet it seems his Zionism was shaped by the German nationalism of a Jew from the

Eastern border provinces and was more enthusiastic and self-conscious than the Jewish identity of more balanced South German Jews living as Jews in a Catholic milieu.

Under Mommsen's tutelage Taeubler studied Roman history from the perspective of the old constitutional law of the nineteenth century (*Staatsrecht*). As Ungern-Sternberg has rightly noted in a reissue of Taeubler's "Roman State" in 1985, it would be a mistake to define him solely as a follower of Mommsen, for he advanced beyond Mommsen's history of constitutional law, giving due weight to factors that condition law and state. Taeubler had likewise absorbed a great deal from Otto Hintze, German pioneer in social history whose importance has been rediscovered only recently, and from Ratzel's historical geography. Against this background one should examine his inaugural lecture of 1910 about the international geo-political role of the Jewish state in Hellenistic times, or his embedding of the Maccabean state, which he admired, into the Roman politics of border defense.

Taeubler's criticism of Mommsen pointed towards the new social and economic history and went beyond the mere documentation of constitutions as practiced during the nineteenth century. His intellectual break with Mommsen mirrored the cultural tensions in Taeubler's personal psychology. In a letter to Julian Morgenstern, President of the Hebrew Union College, Cincinnati, in 1942, Taeubler regarded his commitment to Judaism as responsible for his sudden shift from classical antiquity to the Science of Judaism. His subsequent return to classical studies between 1918 and 1933 attains greater significance when one recognizes his manic-depressive tendencies when periods of intensive and diverse activity alternated with periods of desperation and deep depression. In such periods, according to his student and wife Selma Stern, he withdrew into contemplation and poetic creativity. Wrote Taeubler to a friend:

> It is hardly believable that I delay letters for weeks and months. What is the reason for this? Dissatisfaction with myself more than with the circumstances. All my life I have been in a state of waiting....I have always something ahead of me to which I want to get, but at a distance of ten steps. I have had enough of it and I look for something else.[3]

All this made difficult his relations with his colleagues, for he was very easily hurt and at the same time aggressive as is often the case with people who question themselves. Perhaps Taeubler's quest for the origins of

Roman as well as Israelite history stemmed from the fact that he did not feel at home anywhere.

However that may be, Taeubler's contributions to the Science of Judaism remain outstanding and innovative and contrast with Elbogen's traditionalism and adherence to sources. In 1908, as director of the General Archives for German Jews he set forth his scholarly credo:

> The conditions which have determined the integration and...gradual fusion of the Jews with the German people and that have influenced the inner development of the Jewish people...emerge from the legal, economic, religious and general-cultural circumstances of the German people....
>
> Besides this there is the even more complex inner history of the communities, their mutual relations, religious development, literature and folklore. These areas as well are influenced in their development from the outside. But in their inner essence they are Jewish.

It is difficult today to appreciate the revolutionary impact of Taeubler's conception on subsequent historical scholarship in that it has long become commonplace in Jewish studies the world over. Yet, Taeubler's Jewish history "from inside" has been largely ignored in German historiography where general history has instead functioned as background, whether for the history of Christianity, or for economic, persecution, or legal history. With this concept, however, Taeubler pointed to historic processes which reveal the interdependence of Jewish and general history, their unstable tensions and alternating balances. Taeubler was lucky to find colleagues when he took charge of the Academy for the Science of Judaism in 1918 who could develop his concept in their own disciplines. Yitzhak Baer wrote the history of the Jews in Spain during the Middle Ages as an interaction of Islamic and Jewish culture. Julius Guttmann, Taeubler's successor at the Academy, wrote the history of Jewish philosophy in the context of the history of philosophy. Hanoch Albeck, David Baneth and Arthur Spanier worked in the Talmudic area or studied medieval archives, and Taeubler's future wife, Selma Stern, researched the documents of the Secret State Archive *(Geheimes Staatsarchiv)* on Prussian government policies regarding the Jews. Like Yitzhak Baer, she had found the balance between inner and outer history, between action and interaction, which in the end had perhaps been denied her husband. His biblical essays in which he tried to develop his ideas within the history of the Old Orient have failed to gain acceptance and his "Essays on the Problem of Jewish Historiography 1908-1950" no longer are thought to address contemporary problems of Jewish historiography (1977).

Thus Taeubler's essential accomplishment was as a great organizer and initiator. In a different manner than Elbogen, he had represented the last stage in the historical consciousness of the Science of Judaism and introduced a conception which has prevailed until today. The destruction of the German-Jewish roots, on which Eugen and Selma had staked their existence, deeply wounded both of them. In 1962 Selma Stern depicted the catastrophe in its human dimension in the introduction to the reprint of her magnum opus, *The Prussian State and the Jews:*

> I started [this] work in 1920 under the auspices of the research-institute of the Academy for the Science of Judaism in Berlin....A small staff of young scholars was required by the director (Eugen Taeubler) to reach the average level of related disciplines through new methods and principles, adjusted to the Science of Judaism....That is, the essence of Judaism was no longer to be explained through an adjustment to and a fusion with the philosophical or religious systems of the European environment, but its specific peculiarity and its particular fate were to be made intelligible out of the roots of its own...as well as the change of its form with the help of historical self-examination, a change which it has experienced in the diaspora through the connectedness with a manifoldly unified culture in the assimilation to the emotional and spiritual forms of life in Europe....
>
> ...In this expectant atmosphere...I have written...volumes I/1 and I/2. The third was composed in the years 1935-1941 in a different political and cultural atmosphere....Until then I had lived in a country where for centuries my ancestors worshipped their God and found their wisdom in commandment and prayer, Torah and Talmud....But now the communities...had vanished. Until then I had believed that Emancipation could no more be impeded than could the realization of justice, law and the constitution of the state....But now "actual history" proved that my work had lost all meaning.
>
> ...Thus I now experienced something that has influenced Jewish fate nearly as much as the changing forms of state and society: The genius of the Jewish people, forever renewing itself in suffering and death, has become aware of itself, its origins, and its mission.
>
> If I have continued the work in spite of everything, with no hope of seeing it published and almost certain of its destruction, I did so because I felt compelled...to search for those forces that had brought us from the old lore to new perceptions, returned us from knowledge to faith, and remained alive in us as a creative element until this very day....

In his inaugural address at the Graduate School for the Science of Judaism in Berlin, Eugen Taeubler, standing in front of colleagues and students and hardly able to control the excitement in his somewhat high-pitched lecturing voice, had emphasized the historical role of the Jewish community as tragic existence. He died in 1953 before he could see that the contradictions and hopes which had formed his vision of history still illumine the glory and tragedy of the Jewish fate in the new epoch of Jewish history.

NOTES

*Translated by Charlotte Fonrobert.
1. Published by his widow in 1977.
2. Which appeared in 1934 and was reprinted in 1963.
3. Taeubler to S. Guggeneim, April 6, 1936 in the archive of the Leo Baeck Institute in New York. This text has been made available by Dr. Christhard Hoffmann.

AMERICA-BOUND:
WISSENSCHAFT IN ENGLAND

David G. Dalin

IN 1908, AFTER TWENTY YEARS IN ENGLAND, the *Jewish Quarterly Review* *(JQR)*, the first English language forum in the world for *Wissenschaft des Judentums,* ceased publication. Two years later, under the auspices of the new Dropsie College for Hebrew and Cognate Learning (the Annenberg Research Institute since 1987), the first Anglo-Jewish learned journal resumed publication in Philadelphia where it became the premier organ of Jewish scholarship in America. An examination of the *JQR's* first twenty years in England will reveal how vital was its pre-American sojourn.

The *Jewish Quarterly Review* was founded in 1888 by two public-spirited Anglo-Jewish scholars, Israel Abrahams and Claude G. Montefiore, and was published in England under their co-editorship for the next twenty years. Clearly the *JQR* found its model in the *Monatsschrift für Geschichte und Wissenschaft des Judentums,* which had been founded a half century earlier by Zacharias Frankel, the Rabbi of Dresden. Under Frankel's editorship, which continued until his death in 1868, the *Monatsschrift* became the Jewish world's leading serious jour-nal, the one whose scholarly standards Abrahams and Montefiore sought consciously to emulate.

In June 1887, when Abrahams and Montefiore were busily engaged in launching their *JQR,* Heinrich Graetz, Frankel's successor who had just turned seventy and had retired from editing the *Monatsschrift,* accepted the invitation from the Anglo-Jewish Exhibition to visit London that summer and deliver the keynote address. Although Graetz's visit to England during the summer of 1887 coincided with the temporary cessation of publication of the *Monatsschrift,*[1] he himself suggested "that the continuity was not long broken, for the *Jewish Quarterly Review* would take its place."[2] While Abrahams and Montefiore presumably never aspired for the *JQR* to replace the *Monatsschrift,* which resumed publication in 1892, Graetz's enthusiastic approval and "his promise of active cooperation" were strong factors in encouraging them to proceed with the *JQR*'s publication.[3] The founding and editing of the *Jewish Quarterly Review* was then "much more than a passing episode" in the development of *Wissenschaft* in England:[4] The twenty volumes of the *JQR* provided a forum for scientific Jewish scholarship, and "gave a home to Jewish learning" in England and subsequently in America.

The launching of the *JQR* was thus given a more than symbolic "shot-in-the-arm" by Graetz's visit, for, as Ismar Schorsch has suggested, Graetz was "the most energetic, versatile and durable practitioner of *Wissenschaft des Judentums* in the nineteenth century."[5] As much as any man of his generation, Graetz represented the spirit and potential of the *Wissenschaft* for Abrahams, Montefiore, Solomon Schechter and their circle of associates who were seeking to introduce the modern scientific study of Judaism in England. Graetz's pioneering work, characterized as it was by an almost all-embracing knowledge of Jewish studies and a skillful devotion to the scientific method, set the standards of critical scholarship that the editors and early contributors to the *JQR* sought to emulate. Graetz's well-received paper on "Historic Parallels in Jewish History," delivered before an enthusiastic audience at the London Anglo-Jewish Exhibition,[6] served as a compelling example of what a thorough command of traditional Jewish sources coupled with a modern critical approach to Jewish historical study could achieve. For Graetz, as for the emerging *Wissenschaft* circle in England, the scientific study of Judaism was an all-encompassing concept which included not only a mastery of the entire range of Jewish literature—Rabbinic through modern—but also an awareness of its historical development and a knowledge of the circumstances which had led to that development. Indeed, Heinrich Graetz's last major essays were written "for England" and, at the urging of Abrahams and Montefiore, published in the earliest volumes of the new *JQR.*

ANGLO-JEWISH SCHOLARSHIP DURING THE 1800s

The *JQR* was an attempt to create a forum for Jewish learning and scientific scholarship which, prior to the 1800s, was almost nonexistent in England. In the words which Leopold Zunz used to characterize German Jewry half a century before, Anglo-Jewry had ceased, or not yet begun, to think. Until the very late 1800s, the Anglo-Jewish community was culturally backward when compared with German Jewry, which counted amongst its men of learning such scholars as Zunz, Moritz Steinschneider, Abraham Geiger, Moritz Lazarus, Zacharias Frankel and Graetz, who had done so much to pioneer and further the scientific study of Judaism in previous decades. Anglo-Jewry, on the other hand, as Norman Bentwich has pointed out, had until this time produced "scarcely any books" of serious Jewish historical or rabbinic scholarship.[7] There did not yet exist a Jewish Historical Society of England and the critical study of Anglo-Jewish history—as of Jewish history generally—had been sadly neglected. Until well after the turn-of-the-century, moreover, Israel Abrahams would remain the only native-born professional Jewish scholar in England. In addition, the English rabbinate had not been known for its contributions to Anglo-Jewish learning and scholarship: "No English Rabbi," the historian Isaak Markus Jost had reported after a visit to England in 1841, "has a place in the Jewish learned annals. Everybody was too busy to study, and no honour lured and confirmed those thirsting for knowledge,"[8] a characterization that would be applicable several decades later as well. Although Jews' College, the Orthodox seminary founded in 1856 for the training of Anglo-Jewish ministers and teachers and headed since 1865 by Michael Friedlander, had on its staff (by the 1880s) some scholars of stature, including Abrahams and Solomon Schechter, the English rabbinate was, for the most part, not known for its interest in or contributions to the scientific study of Judaism.[9]

At its inception, the *JQR*'s editors had doubts about the need for such a publication in England. They felt that there was only a "feeble interest" amongst English Jewry in the scholarly investigation of the history and literature of the Jewish people.[10] In their introduction to the first volume of the *JQR*, they noted that the Jewish community of England seemed sadly indifferent to the lack of a scholarly periodical devoted to the history of Judaism. They particularly stressed the "mournful fact of the neglect which modern Jewish scholarship has shown to that greatest and most vital of all works of Jewish literature, the Bible. If we want instruction on Isaiah or Job, or Proverbs, it is not from recent Jewish scholars that we can get it."[11] Abrahams and Montefiore felt "this lack of interest and care" to be "both discreditable and dangerous."[12] They also recognized that there were young scholars, like themselves, who were interested in Jewish learning, but who had no English-language forum in which to express their thoughts and publish the results of their scholarly research. The lack of such a scholarly forum, they believed, was responsible for the low status of Jewish learning in the English-speaking world.

There were, however, a few Jewish scholars in England in the late 1800s, such as Adolph Neubauer and Solomon Schechter.[13] Neubauer, a native of Hungary, immigrated to England during the 1860s to become librarian of the Bodleian Library at Oxford University. As a young man Neubauer had studied in Prague with Solomon Judah Rapoport, from whom he had first learned to employ the scientific method to shed light on the development of Judaism.[14] Neubauer, who was appointed Reader in Rabbinic Hebrew at Oxford in 1884, was an exact and prolific *Wissenschaft* scholar and bibliographer who would contribute no less than forty-two articles to the *JQR* between 1889 and 1899.[15] Neubauer was one of the very small number of Jewish scholars who had immigrated to England before Solomon Schechter.

The date of Solomon Schechter's arrival in England in 1882 should be marked as "epoch-making" for Jewish learning and critical scholarship in the country, according to Adolph Jellinek of Vienna.[16] Indeed, the arrival of Schechter, who exerted a profound influence on the direction and standards of Anglo-Jewish scholarship during the 1880s and 1890s, can be viewed as the real beginning of a *Wissenschaft* movement in England.

When Schechter arrived in London in 1882, he did not come directly from his native Romania, but from Berlin, where he had been both studying and teaching at the *Hochschule für die Wissenschaft des Judentums* since 1879. Schechter, who could read Hebrew at the age of three and knew the Pentateuch at five, had received a traditional yeshivah education in Romania, where he had studied with one of the greatest Talmudic authorities of the time, Rabbi Joseph Saul Nathanson of Lemberg.[17] In 1875, he had gone to Vienna to study at the Beth ha-Midrash, "a modernized Talmudical high school" which, as Alexander Marx has noted, showed a happy blending "of old-time Talmudic scholarship" and the modern scientific method, stressing the historical development of halakhah.[18] After receiving rabbinical ordination, Schechter moved to Berlin, to study and teach at the *Hochschule*.[19]

In particular, it was from his studies with Moritz Steinschneider at the *Hochschule* that Schechter acquired the scientific perspective which would later shape his own approach to Jewish scholarship in England. While in Berlin, Schechter learned from Steinschneider "to pass from bibliography to history," from the cataloging of books to their interpretation.[20] The bibliographer is the forerunner of the historian," Schechter would later write, "for it is only when you know the sources of your subject and their sequence that you can form a notion of the genesis and development of thought; and this was the great gift which Steinschneider bestowed on every one of us..."[21]

One of Schechter's pupils in Rabbinics during his last two years in Berlin was Claude Goldsmid Montefiore, nephew of Sir Moses and scion of two of Anglo-Jewry's most prominent families, who had come to the *Hochschule* to study after graduating from Balliol College, Oxford.[22] Montefiore had hoped to continue his Jewish studies in England and, in 1882, had persuaded Schechter to accompany him to London to continue as his tutor in Rabbinics. This tutorial relationship, which lasted well over a decade, left "a permanent imprint" on Montefiore's scholarly endeavors.[23] It was largely through Schechter's influence that Montefiore came to appreciate the importance of Rabbinic Judaism and its centrality to Jewish life. His lifelong preoccupation with Rabbinic literature— including several *JQR* articles on the subject—and his decision to launch and help finance Anglo-Jewry's first scholarly publication could be attributed in large part to Schechter's teaching and inspiration.[24]

Inspired also by Schechter, who was a lecturer in Talmud at Jews' College from 1883 to 1890, was an informal group called the "Wanderers" formed in London, "partly of English-born amateur scholars"[25] and "partly of foreign-born professional scholars" to discuss serious questions of Judaism, ancient and modern. This unique group, whose members shared an intense commitment to Anglo-Jewish cultural development as well as to the scientific study and critical discussion of Jewish history and literature, played a part in the development of Judaism and Jewish scholarship in England comparable with that which the *Kulturverein* of Zunz, Gans and Heine had played in the Judaism of Germany fifty years earlier.[26] This group, of which Schechter became the "acknowledged leader" and which first met at Schechter's home, included in addition to Schechter and Montefiore, Dr. Moses Gaster, the

Romanian-born *haham* of London's Sephardic synagogue and a Jewish scholar and folklorist of note, the Anglo-Jewish historian Lucien Wolf; the novelist Israel Zangwill; Asher Myers, the talented editor of the *Jewish Chronicle;* and Joseph Jacobs who, like Schechter, had studied with Steinschneider at the *Hochschule* in Berlin.[27]

One of the pillars of the group, soon to become Schechter's protégé and Montefiore's scholarly associate, was Israel Abrahams who, since 1881, had been a Lecturer in Homiletics at Jews' College, and who for several decades would remain the most distinguished Hebrew and Rabbinics scholar among English-born Jews.[28] Born in 1858, Abrahams would remain "intimately connected" with Jews' College, the foremost institution of higher Jewish learning and rabbinical training in England, throughout the first forty-four years of his life.[29] The son of Barnett Abrahams, who had served as both headmaster and principal of the college, Abrahams received his early Jewish education at the Jews' College secondary school while simultaneously continuing his studies at the University of London where, in 1881, he received his M.A. degree, the first graduate of Jews' College to do so. Named in 1899 to the newly created position of senior tutor, a post second in importance only to that of principal, Abrahams continued to teach at Jews' College until 1902, when Solomon Schechter left England to assume the presidency of the Jewish Theological Seminary in New York and when Abrahams was appointed to succeed him as Reader in Talmudic and Rabbinic literature at Cambridge University.[30]

Throughout the 1880s, the members of the "Wanderers" also participated in the Jews' College Literary Society, the recognized public forum in London for Jewish lectures and scholarly discussion, that Abrahams had been instrumental in founding.[31] Jacobs and Wolf played key roles in organizing the Anglo-Jewish Exhibition of 1887, and in the formation of the Jewish Historical Society of England in 1893;[32] they were joined by Abrahams, Montefiore, and Zangwill, who would each serve as president of the new Society. As Norman Bentwich has noted, moreover, many of the scholarly books and essays published by Abrahams, Wolf, Jacobs and Montefiore during the 1880s and 1890s were stimulated "by the free talk and exchange of ideas" through participation in this informal discussion circle of which Schechter was the central figure.[33] Out of this group, and created largely for its benefit, came the *Jewish Quarterly Review,* to which Schechter, Abrahams, Montefiore and Jacobs would contribute 126 articles during its twenty years of publication in England.[34]

ANGLO-JEWISH *WISSENSCHAFT* AND THE STUDY OF RABBINICS

The history and critical study of Rabbinic Judaism was of particular significance to the contributors to the *JQR* during the first two decades of its publication. The many articles written for the journal in the areas of Talmud, Mishnah, Midrash, Rabbinic prayer and theology, and Talmudic history, represent the accumulated effort of turn-of-the-century *Wissenschaft* scholarship—especially in England—to deal critically with the origin, history and development of Pharisaic Judaism. With their mastery of the history of the Graeco-Roman period, Hellenistic papyrology, Roman Law and New Testament literature, coupled with their complete familiarity with Rabbinic sources, the *Wissenschaft* scholars were able to understand the Rabbinic texts historically, relate them to their background, and see in them a mirror of actual Jewish life and theological concerns during the Pharisaic period. Jewish *Wissenschaft* scholars, such as Schechter and Louis Ginzberg, were able also to utilize the newly discovered manuscripts of the Cairo Genizah to make important scholarly contributions to the scientific study of Rabbinics, in the areas of Midrash, geonic responsa, and Rabbinic halakhah.[35]

The scientific study and analysis of Rabbinic theology and prayer, in particular, was one area where Schechter and Abrahams contributed significantly.[36] Throughout his *JQR* writings, Schechter was very concerned with the study and explication of aspects of Rabbinic theology, the major concepts and ideas which formed the basis of the religious consciousness or worldview of Pharisaic Judaism. One such concept, that of holiness, an idea that is prevalent in Rabbinic literature, is critically discussed by both Schechter and Abrahams in the *JQR*. The rabbinic notion of holiness, which Schechter equates with the notion of *Imitatio Dei,* or the "Imitation of God," is a religious duty originating "in Israel's consciousness of its intimate relation to God," which is, as Schechter endeavors to show, "the central idea of Rabbinic theology."[37]

Schechter and Abrahams' analysis identifies the idea of holiness as the "highest achievement" of Rabbinic law, an achievement that had been completely ignored by Christian critics of Rabbinic Judaism such as Emil Schurer. In accusing the ancient Rabbis of excessive legalism, notes Abrahams, "Schurer says nothing of the spiritualizing effect of the idea of the *"Imitatio Dei"* theme which "pervades the Rabbinic theology,"[38] and which is the very basis of "the forgiving spirit" that is found throughout Rabbinic literature.[39]

This critical response to Schurer held profound significance for the scientific and "objective" study of Rabbinic Judaism that was so central to *Wissenschaft* scholarship in turn-of-the-century England. The scholarly enterprise of *Wissenschaft,* as it developed in nineteenth-century Germany, had been shaped by the desire to recover the Jewish historical past "coupled with a powerful need to right the commissions and perversions of Christian scholarship."[40] The same can be said about the Jewish *Wissenschaft* movement emerging in late-nineteenth-century England, reflected in some of the contributions to the *JQR* between 1888 and 1908 by Jewish scholars who were incensed by what they considered to be the distortion and misuse of Rabbinic literature by contemporary Christian scholars. Some of the most important essays on Rabbinic Judaism published by Schechter and Abrahams in the *JQR* during this period, were written, in part, in response to the viciously anti-rabbinic writings being published by some Christian New Testament scholars. In so doing, they hoped to offer liberal Christians a more sympathetic and accurately informed account of the ancient Rabbis than the one offered by the leading Christian studies of the subject.

While at the Berlin *Hochschule* between 1879 and 1882, Schechter had become all too familiar with the German Christian scholarship of Rabbinics which was so bitterly hostile to ancient Judaism. Already, while still in Berlin, Schechter had recognized "that this was a form of academic anti-Semitism,"[41] based on an imperfect knowledge and blatant distortion of Rabbinic literature, an argument that he would make on the pages of the *JQR* in 1900. "Matters have indeed come to such a pass," Schechter noted, "that the principle has been laid down that it is not necessary to have a thorough knowledge of Rabbinic literature in order to express an opinion about its merits or demerits."[42]

Through their *JQR* essays, Schechter and Israel Abrahams were, at the turn of the century and afterwards, among a handful of British and American scholars who sought to respond to, and correct, the polemical and implicitly anti-Jewish assertions of nineteenth-century German scholarship concerning the nature of Judaism during the first Christian century. The influential writings of Schurer, Wilhelm Bousset and Ferdinand Weber,[43] among others, all developed essentially the same anti-rabbinic theme: the Judaism of Jesus' day had become synonymous with rigid and uncompromising legalism and Rabbinic Pharisaism synonymous with hypocrisy. Bousset, for example, had stressed in his earliest writings the "fundamental cleavage" between Jesus and the Rabbinic Judaism of the Pharisees, to which Jesus allegedly stood in uncompromising protest.[44] For Bousset, as for Schurer and Weber, Judaism was the antithesis of Christianity, a legalistic religion in which God was remote and inaccessible. The moral maxims of the Pharisaic sages, they argued, were only "external ornamentation," while the essence of their purported piety consisted in their unbending conformity with the precept of the Rabbinic law.

The "tendentious accounts" of Rabbinic Judaism presented by these New Testament scholars, whose interest in the study of ancient Judaism was not for its own sake, "but for the light it might throw on the beginnings of Christianity,"[45] contributed immeasurably, as Abrahams recognized, to Christian misunderstanding and to prejudicial notions about Rabbinic Judaism. The "crude and fanatic charges" of the earlier German Christian writer Eisenmenger who, as George Foot Moore correctly noted, was the "notorious source of almost everything that has been written since his time in defamation of the Talmud,"[46] were for the most part "absent or greatly modified"[47] in the writings of Bousset and Schurer; their anti-Rabbinic diatribes nonetheless might well be considered representative of what Schechter so aptly called the "Higher Anti-Semitism," of which the Higher Criticism of Wellhausen was the most blatant example.[48]

The most systematic and comprehensive critique of Schurer is contained in Abrahams' essay "Professor Schurer on Life Under Jewish Law," published in the *JQR* in 1899. The methodology utilized by Schurer, argues Abrahams, "is the method not of the historian but of one determined to formulate an indictment. Schurer does not criticize the Law, he condemns it. He passes the severest sentence without any recommendation of mercy."[49] Underlying Professor Schurer's "whole case against the Pharisaic religion," claims Abrahams, is the "assumption that a life of the spirit is incompatible with very fully developed ritual."[50] In his thoughtful critique of Schurer's writings, Abrahams suggests that his one-sided and distorted portrayal of Rabbinic Judaism was attributable in part to his dismal ignorance of Rabbinic literature, a compelling criticism of the Weber-Schurer German Christian school that was later made by George Foot Moore as well.[51] The Rabbinic sources which Abrahams, as well as Schechter, correctly viewed as "indispensable tools" for the understanding and interpretation of Pharisaic Judaism, were largely ignored by "Christian critics of Rabbinism" from Eisenmenger to Weber and Schurer. Schurer, suggested Abrahams, was a "dilettante" who was not at home in the field of Rabbinics, relying primarily on mistranslations of the Mishnah and second-hand sources to interpret Judaism in the age of Jesus.[52]

In their Rabbinic scholarship published in the *JQR*, Schechter, Abrahams and especially Montefiore sought also to illuminate Christian origins in their relation to their Rabbinic background through a careful discussion and analysis of parallels between Rabbinic literature and the Gospels. This comparative approach to the study of Rabbinic literature, as evidenced for example in Schechter's seminal *JQR* essay on "Some Rabbinic Parallels to the New Testament," reflected the newly discovered importance of Rabbinic literature for understanding the New Testament for some practitioners of *Wissenschaft*. The significance of Rabbinic materials and their exegesis for the study of the New Testament had been clearly recognized by Abraham Geiger, who together with Zunz, Frankel and Graetz had helped to establish the foundation for the scientific study of Judaism in Germany. Geiger had been one of the first Jewish scholars to insist that Rabbinic literature was fully as important as, if not more important than, the Apocrypha, Pseudepigrapha, and various Hellenistic writings in understanding the background of the New Testament, a scholarly insistence that was to be reiterated within the pages of the *JQR* as well. "If the Rabbis have nothing to tell us about the personality of Jesus," wrote Schechter, "Rabbinic literature has a good deal to teach us about the times in which he lived and laboured. And what is more important is that a thorough study of this literature might, with due discretion, help us towards a better understanding of the writings attributed to Jesus by his disciples."[53]

In seeking to interpret the Christian Gospels in light of Rabbinic thought, Schechter, Abrahams and Montefiore hoped to establish a better understanding between liberal Christians and Jews. As Schechter noted, his essay on "Some Rabbinic Parallels to the New Testament" was "intended as an invitation to fellow students to devote more attention to a branch of literature, from the study of which Christian divines might derive as much profit as the Jewish Rabbi."[54]

Schechter's desire to establish a better intellectual understanding between liberal Christians and Jews derived, it seems, from his experiences at Cambridge University, where he was the only professing Jewish "don" during the greater part of his twelve years (1890-1902) as Reader in Rabbinics.[55] As a teacher at Cambridge, as Alexander Marx has noted, Schechter would introduce Christian theologians and students for the ministry to the mysteries of Rabbinic literature,[56] a task continued by

Israel Abrahams when he succeeded Schechter in 1902. Throughout their distinguished academic careers at Cambridge, Schechter and Abrahams thus inspired and helped shape the perspective of liberal Christian scholars such as the Unitarian minister H. Travers Herford and Charles Taylor, the Master of St. John's College, who were interested in the study of Rabbinic Judaism, and who also published articles in the *JQR* during this period. In thus examining the relationship between Pharisaic Judaism and the Gospels, and rescuing Pharisaism from the stereotyping and anti-rabbinic bias it received in the Gospel narratives, Schechter, Abrahams and Montefiore made major contributions to the scientific study and evaluation of Rabbinic Judaism.

GENIZAH SCHOLARSHIP AND
THE SCIENTIFIC STUDY OF JEWISH LITURGY

Solomon Schechter's 1896 discovery of the fabulous fragments of the Cairo Genizah manuscript has aptly been described as the most significant Jewish manuscript discovery of modern times, prior to the discovery of the Dead Sea Scrolls in the 1940s. The arduous task of sifting, classifying, analyzing and comparing, editing and then publishing, the thousands of fragments from the Cairo Genizah, which were deposited in the Cambridge Library, the Bodleian Library at Oxford and the British Museum, was one of the singular achievements of Jewish *Wissenschaft* scholars in England and America at the turn of the century and thereafter. No less than 39 studies based on the newly discovered Genizah fragments were published in the *JQR* prior to 1908 and their publication signaled a new phase in the modern scientific study of Judaism, a development that was accorded recognition by the entry of a new section, "Genizah (Cairo) MSS" in the table of contents of volume 10 of the *JQR*.[57]

While Schechter's own first publications of Genizah material consisted of fragments of lost classical texts, such as *Ben Sira,* his Genizah research shed light on Jewish history in the Middle Ages as well. His "Genizah Specimens: A Letter of Chushiel," did the same for an understanding of Jewish learning in North Africa at the turn of the first millennium.[58] Schechter's writings raised the possibility that a "thorough examination" of the Genizah material would open up "totally unanticipated vistas" of Jewish history, especially relating to the scientific study of the Geonic period, that subsequent *JQR* publications would confirm.

Jewish *Wissenschaft* scholars also utilized the Genizah documents to make extremely vital contributions to the study and analysis of Geonic Responsa and Rabbinic Halakhah, that shed new light on all aspects of Jewish life during the Geonic period. The Genizah documents analyzed in the *Jewish Quarterly Review* revealed the intimate and consistent relations between the Talmudic academies of Babylonia and those of North Africa and Spain. The Geonic Responsa, so carefully edited by Louis Ginzberg, were heretofore a lost corpus of primary halakhic source material that reflected the religious-communal life and concerns of the period.[59]

More than any other single development, however, it was Schechter's discovery of the Genizah material that stimulated scholarly research in the area of Jewish liturgy in England. It was only with the beginning of *Wissenschaft* in nineteenth-century Germany, that an historical approach was applied to the development of Jewish literature, in general, and to the evolution of Jewish literature in particular. In his monumental study, *Die gottesdienstlichen Vorträge der Juden,* published in 1832, Leopold Zunz had been the first modern scholar to stress the gradual, evolutionary development of the *siddur* and of all of the individual prayers contained therein.[60] This scholarly interest in demonstrating historical development in the Jewish liturgy, pioneered by Zunz, was later continued by *Wissenschaft* scholars, Schechter, Abrahams, Buechler and Elbogen, who published the findings of their research in the *JQR* between 1888 and 1908.[61]

As Jakob J. Petuchowski has noted: "If the detailed comparative study of the diverse editions of the Jewish prayerbook, both in manuscript and in print, of which the activity of Zunz is the prototype, led to a new understanding of how the prayerbook evolved, the field available for comparative study became vastly extended towards the end of the nineteenth century, with...the publication of ancient manuscript fragments which had been preserved in the Cairo Genizah."[62] Much of Schechter's eight studies of the Genizah fragments published in the *JQR* between 1898 and 1904 had direct relevance for modern liturgical scholarship. In his "Genizah Specimens," which appeared in 1898, Schechter published liturgical fragments of a distinct Palestinian character—portions of the Jewish liturgy in their oldest extant form—known heretofore only from scattered and random quotations in later Rabbinic literature and by inferences based on those quotations.[63] On the basis of these quotations, Schechter recognized general portions of the daily

Palestinian *Amidah* among the fragments of the Genizah, the transcription and publication of which may be said "to have revolutionized the scientific study of Jewish Literature,"[64] and to have influenced the direction of scholarship in this area for decades to come.

Adolph Buechler, like Schechter, one of the most prolific representatives of *Wissenschaft* of this era and later principal of Jews' College, published a seminal and lengthy *JQR* study, "The Reading of the Law and Prophets in a Triennial Cycle," that was also inspired by a manuscript from the Genizah material that Buechler's uncle, Adolph Neubauer, had acquired for the Bodleian Library.[65] Buechler's study not only placed the "Triennial Cycle" on the agenda of modern critical scholarly concern, but also gave rise "to a whole literature which connects studies in Jewish liturgy with modern New Testament scholarship."[66]

CONCLUSION

In 1908, Israel Abrahams and Claude Montefiore announced their intention to cease publishing the *Jewish Quarterly Review*. Their decision was at least partially financial for it was generally assumed that, after twenty years, Claude Montefiore had "tired of footing the bills."[67] There were, however, other factors as well, for by 1908 Abrahams was finding his editorial responsibilities increasingly onerous.[68] He confided to Cyrus Adler, president of the Dropsie College of Hebrew and Cognate Learning in Philadelphia, that a "deciding factor" in his decision to give up editorship of the journal was his ongoing difficulties with authors, "all of whom wanted their articles printed in the 'next number' and persisted in rewriting these articles in proof." As a result, complained Abrahams, "he had not a friend left in Europe."[69] Adler, after consulting with the Board of Governors of Dropsie College, who were ready to provide "a substantial subvention toward upkeep of the journal,"[70] proceeded to transfer the *JQR* to Philadelphia. Soon thereafter, at Adler's invitation,[71] Solomon Schechter agreed to serve as its co-editor and, in July 1910, the *JQR* resumed publication in America.

The Genizah discoveries and subsequent publications in the *JQR* expanded so many new avenues of Jewish scientific research that they have essentially "revolutionized" entire areas of Jewish scholarship—a "revolution" begun by Schechter, Abrahams, Neubauer and other turn-of-the-century *Wissenschaft* scholars working in England. Publication of Geonic material from the Cairo Genizah provided the primary source material, for example, for a new chapter of Jewish history during the period of the Geonim in Spain and North Africa from the ninth through eleventh centuries. By providing a tremendous quantity of previously unknown material on the daily life, both private and communal, of the Jews around the Mediterranean during these centuries, *JQR* supported the Genizah scholarship begun in England in the 1890s, which radically transformed Jewish historiography on Geonic civilization.[72] Between 1888 and 1908, the *Jewish Quarterly Review,* under the editorship of Israel Abrahams and Claude Montefiore, served as the primary vehicle for establishing and furthering the scientific study of Judaism in England and subsequently opened the way for the transplantation of *Wissenschaft* onto American soil. Providentially, Solomon Schechter, the most celebrated contributor to the *JQR* and the preeminent Jewish scholar of his generation, had come to America in 1901 to serve as president of the newly reconstructed Jewish Theological Seminary. Schechter's acceptance of Adler's invitation to serve with him as co-editor reaped the fruits of the Anglo-American connection to the full and in July 1910 ensured an auspicious beginning for the *JQR* when it resumed publication.

NOTES

1. See the article on the *Monatsschrift für Geschichte und Wissenschaft des Judentums* in the *Encyclopedia Judaica,* vol. 12, col. 240.

2. Israel Abrahams, "H. Graetz, the Jewish Historian," *JQR* 4 (1892), 192.

3. Ibid.

4. Stephen S. Wise, Foreword to *Jewish Studies in Memory of Israel Abrahams* (New York: Jewish Institute of Religion Press, 1927), xii.

5. Ismar Schorsch, "Ideology and History in the Age of Emancipation," in *The Structure of Jewish History and Other Essays,* by Heinrich Graetz, translated, edited, and introduced by Ismar Schorsch (New York, 1975), 1.

6. Heinrich Graetz, "Historic Parallels in Jewish History," translated by Joseph Jacobs in *Papers Read at the Anglo-Jewish Historical Exhibition* (London: Publications of the Anglo-Jewish Historical Exhibition, no. 1, 1887), 1-19.

7. Norman Bentwich, "The Wanderers and Other Jewish Scholars of My Youth," *Transactions of the Jewish Historical Society of England* 20 (1959-1961), 52.

8. C. C. Aronsfeld, "German Jews in Victorian England," *Year Book of the Leo Baeck Institute* 7 (1962), 323.

9. Solomon Schechter, for example, "deplored" Chief Rabbi Hermann Adler's "neglect of Jewish scholarship." Bentwich, *Solomon Schechter: A Biography* (New York, 1964), 52.

10. Israel Abrahams and Claude Montefiore, *JQR* 1 (Oct. 1888), 2.

11. Ibid.

12. Ibid.

13. For biographical material on Adolph Neubauer, see: "Adolph Neubauer," in *Encyclopedia Judaica,* vol. 12, cols. 1003-5.

14. Ibid.

15. Isaiah Berger, ed., *Analytic Index to The Jewish Quarterly Review* (New York: KTAV Publishing House, Inc., 1966), 18-19.

16. Alexander Marx, *Essays in Jewish Biography* (Philadelphia, 1947), 229.

17. Ibid.

18. Ibid., 230-31.

19. Ibid., 232.

20. Bentwich, *Solomon Schechter: A Biography,* 43.

21. Ibid.

22. Ibid., 47-48; on Montefiore, see also: Chaim Bermant, *Cousinhood: The Anglo-Jewry Gentry* (London, 1971), 313-28.

23. Eugene Mihaly, "Prolegomenon" to Claude G. Montefiore, *Rabbinic Literature and Gospel Teachings* (New York: KTAV Publishing House, Inc., 1970), XIII.

24. Ibid.

25. Bentwich, "The Wanderers and Other Jewish Scholars of My Youth, op. cit., 52.

26. Bentwich, *Solomon Schechter: Biography, 59.*

27. Ibid., 62.

28. For biographical material on Abrahams, see: Herbert Loewe, *Israel Abrahams: Biographical Sketch* (London: Arthur Davis Memorial Trust, 1944); and David G. Dalin, "Israel Abrahams: Leader of Liturgical Reform in England," *The Journal of Reform Judaism* 32 (Winter 1985), 68-83.

29. Loewe, ibid., 3; and Dalin, ibid., 68-69.

30. Dalin, ibid., 70.

31. For a discussion of the activities of, and the participants in the Jews' College Literary Society, see: *Jews' College Jubilee Volume* (London: Luzac & Co., 1906), LXIX-LXXVI.

32. On the formation of the Jewish Historical Society of England, see: Lucien Wolf, "Origin of the Jewish Historical Society of England," *Transactions of the Jewish Historical Society of England* 7 (1911-1914), 206-21.

33. Bentwich, *Solomon Schechter: A Biography,* 52.

34. Isaiah Berger, ed., *Analytical Index to Jewish Quarterly Review,* 2-3, 13, 17-18, and 20-21.

35. On the contributions of Ginzberg, see: Louis Finkelstein, "Necrology: Louis Ginzberg," *Proceedings of the American Academy Jewish Research* 23 (1954), xliv-liii.

36. Solomon Schechter: "The Doctrine of Divine Retribution in the Rabbinical Literature," *JQR* 3 (1891); "The Rabbinical Conception of Holiness, *JQR* 10 (1898); and "Some Aspects of Rabbinic Theology," *JQR,* vol. 6 (1894), vol. 7 (1895) and vol. 8 (1896). Israel Abrahams: "Some Rabbinic Ideas on Prayer," *JQR* 20 (1908).

37. Schechter, "The Rabbinical Conception of Holiness," ibid., 1.

38. Israel Abrahams, "Professor Schürer on Life Under Jewish Law," *JQR* 11 (1899), 635.

39. Israel Abrahams, *Studies in Pharisaism and the Gospels,* First Series, p. 166.

40. Ismar Schorsch, "Historical Consciousness in Modern Judaism," *Year Book of the Leo Baeck Institute,* 28 (1983), 431

41. Norman Bentwich, "Solomon Schechter," in *Great Jewish Personalities in Modern Times,* ed. Simon Noveck (B'nai B'rit Department of Adult Education, 1960), 138.

42. Solomon Schechter, "Some Rabbinic Parallels to the New Testament," *JQR* 12 (1900), 418.

43. Perhaps the most thorough discussion and critique of the writings of Schurer, Weber and Bousset can be found in George Foot Moore, "Christian Writers on Judaism,"

Harvard Theological Review 14 (1921), 197-254.

44. Morton S. Enslin, *Prolegomenon* to Israel Abrahams. *Studies in Pharisaism and the Gospels* (New York: KTAV Publishing House, Inc., 1967), viii-lx.

45. Moore, "Christian Writers on Judaism," 241.

46. Ibid., 214.

47. Enslin, op. cit., viii.

48. Solomon Schechter, "Higher Criticism – Higher Anti-Semitism," in *Seminary Addresses and Other Papers* (Cincinnati: Ark Publishing Co., 1915), 35-39.

49. Abrahams, "Professor Schürer on Life under Jewish Law," 626-42.

50. Ibid., 632.

51. E.g., Moore, "Christian Writers on Judaism," op. cit.

52. Abrahams, "Professor Schürer on Life Under Jewish Law," 628 and 630.

53. Schechter, "Some Rabbinic Parallels to the New Testament," 415.

54. Ibid., 415-16.

55. Bentwich, "Solomon Schechter," 140.

56. Marx, *Essays in Jewish Biography*, 240.

57. A review of Genizah scholarship since 1896 can be found in: Norman Golb, "Sixty Years of Genizah Research," *Judaism* 6 (1957).

58. Gerson D. Cohen, "The Reconstruction of Geonic History," in *Texts and Studies in Jewish History,* ed. Jacob Mann (New York, Inc., 1972), xxxiii.

59. Ginzberg, "Geonic Responsa," *JQR,* vol. 16 (1904), vol. 17 (1905), vol. 18 (1906), vol. 19 (1907) and vol. 20 (1908); see, also: Finkelstein, "Necrology: Louis Ginzberg," op. cit., xlix.

60. Richard S. Sarason, "The Modern Study of Jewish Liturgy," in *The Study Ancient Judaism: I,* ed. Jacob Neusner (New York, 1981), 110.

61. Jakob J. Petuchowski, *Contributions to the Scientific Study of Jewish Liturgy* (New York, 1970), xiii.

62. Ibid., xxiv.

63. Ibid.

64. E.g., Louis Finkelstein, "Development of the Amidah, *JQR,* vol. 16 (New Series) (1925-1926).

65. Adolph Buechler, "The Reading of the Law and Prophets in a Triennial Cycle," *JQR,* vol. 5 (1893) and vol. 6 (1894).

66. Petuchowski, *Contributions to the Scientific Study of Jewish Liturgy,* xix-xx.

67. Gold, "Sixty Years of Genizah Research," op. cit.; and Shelomo Dov Goitein, "What Would Jewish and General History Benefit by a Systematic Publication of the Documentary Genizah Papers?" *Proceedings of the American Academy of Jewish Research* 23 (1955).

68. Cyrus Adler, *I Have Considered the Days* (Philadelphia, 1941), 279.

69. "Jewish Quarterly Review," *Encyclopedia Judaica,* vol. 10, cols. 88-89.

70. Cyrus Adler, *I Have Considered the Days,* 279-80.

71. Ibid., 279.

72. Adler letter to Solomon Schechter, May 3, 1909, reprinted in: *Cyrus Adler: Selected Letters,* ed. Ira Robinson (Philadelphia, 1985), 155-57.

PART IV

The People

THE COMMON FOLK IN MENDELSSOHN'S DAYS

W. Gunther Plaut

THE HISTORY OF EIGHTEENTH-CENTURY GERMAN JEWRY is dominated by the towering figure of Moses Mendelssohn who is properly regarded as a major influence in advancing and directing the emancipation of his fellow Jews. But it is well to remember that Mendelssohn and his Berlin followers moved in rarefied strata—a number of them even attaining an advanced education and considerable wealth—while the vast majority of German Jews lived in an entirely different universe which for many years was hardly touched by the famous savant. Their life had a character all its own, and it is this, more than Mendelssohn's model, that defined the nature of a community which a few decades after Emancipation would become the seedbed of enormous changes and the birthplace of modern Judaism in all its varieties.

Yet we have heard little about those Jews who were dispersed over Germany's villages and towns. Some Hebrew sources are available, among them Hayyim Joseph David Azulai's travel impressions[1] and Jacob Emden's responsa reflecting social and religious conditions.[2] There is, however, another and in most respects far richer source at our disposal in published form which so far has not been sufficiently exploited—a series of some seventy-odd volumes of reports by Christian missionaries who traveled the land attempting to bring the Gospel to the Jews.

These emissaries were sent out by the Institutum Judaicum, founded and directed in Halle by the Reverend Johann Heinrich Callenberg,[3] a Protestant divine who mounted a life-long effort to convert the Jews by

117

spreading the faith through full-time missionaries who would meet Jews face to face, even in the smallest villages, in order to bring them the Good News. Though the success of these missionary efforts was modest when measured in actual conversions, the enterprise unwittingly created rich historical materials, for the missionaries faithfully sent reports back to their employer who in turn printed them in order to justify the Institute's existence to its financial backers.[4] No less a personage than Mendelssohn himself was a subject for the Institute's conversionary efforts.[5]

Of course the missionaries' observations were colored by their goal of conversion and the optimistic notes which the emissaries frequently entered into their correspondence must be seen in that light. After all, it would not do merely to report failure and only a very occasional success.[6] Despite the missionaries' bias, we can learn much from these reports, for the writers had no reason to be less than accurate when they related how Jews lived. Their reports cover all aspects of Jewish life, from people's occupations to housing and business practices; from family affairs and charities to language, education and religious practices. Drawing upon these reports, this study will concentrate on the social conditions of ordinary Jews in various parts of Germany,[7] a subject until now fairly inaccessible to the student of history.[8]

Even though the Callenberg volumes span more than sixty years, from 1730 to 1790, they reflect remarkably little social change. The intellectual and social ferment of the outside world apparently did not touch the vast majority of German Jews. With few exceptions, poverty and isolation were their common lot, especially in the small communities where they lived in a world apart. Most cities had identifiable Jewish quarters and streets. Only if the number of Jews was small did they live interspersed among the Gentiles, though usually as close to one another as possible and always in easy reach of their synagogue.[9]

Their language has been characterized as "Western Yiddish" by some, and "Judeo-German" (*jüdisch-deutsch*) by others. It was closer to High German than Eastern Yiddish (today referred to simply as "Yiddish"), which became a separate language with its own identifiable grammar and lexicon. German Jews, unlike those in Eastern Europe, lived among German-speaking people and therefore were reasonably acquainted with their language and understood and spoke it, however imperfectly, in its various dialects—while at the same time expanding it with a vocabulary and grammatical variances of their own. The intermingling of these two linguistic streams was precisely what Mendelssohn's Biblical translation tried to resolve, and therefore he wrote High German in Hebrew characters. His intention was not, as has often been misstated, to teach German Jews the German language *de novo,* but to teach them *proper* German, a language with which they, who knew street German and spoke Judeo-German, were less familiar.

West German Yiddish was not as distinct a tongue as was (Eastern) Yiddish and possessed an additional feature: a kind of "secret" speech which Jews used among themselves when dealing with Gentiles in a commercial relationship. These linguistic idioms, easily understood by other Jews in the trade, in time became outmoded, though not entirely forgotten, because the Gentile parties learned to understand them.

Elements of Judeo-German itself persisted into the twentieth century as a kind of familial seasoning to Jewish speech, especially in the western reaches of the country. Every Jew whom I knew in my youth in Germany spoke High German but would also understand expressions like *ausgebackene lecho-daudis, schmontzes barjontzes* or *emes bajazzo.*[10]

How did the missionaries view these Jews who spoke a different language and lived a different life? One missionary's judgment was reflected throughout the collection: most Jews were "poor and humble and would be repressed in the presence of a well-groomed man," he wrote.[11] Life was hard for them. The outside world was unfriendly, often inimical, and business relations were governed by mutual caution. A continual refrain runs throughout the missionaries' chronicles of the Jew's response to their fate: Times are bad, and we can't remember when they were good.

Despite this response, the missionaries found that Gentiles believed that Jews had money. Though the number of wealthy Jews was very small, these few exceptions were taken to represent the whole.[12] In reality Jewish hardship was intensified by the high cost of living, not only because Jewish ritual needs required special foods and clothes,[13] but because Gentiles would charge Jews higher prices. One writer estimates that the Jewish cost of living was twice that of their neighbors, an exaggeration perhaps, but apparently a common perception among Jews.[14]

As for the Jews' occupations, the missionaries noted a number of craftsmen and professionals, but the majority made their living in petty trade; they were storekeepers, peddlers, and cattle dealers.[15] Agriculture was generally closed to them as were those crafts that required guild membership. Where Jews were restricted from owning land they occasionally got around the law by arrangements with Gentile farmers who were made to appear as the owners. The missionaries rarely saw the peddlers or those working outside the towns, but interacted mostly with Jews who awaited customers in their shops and loan establishments. All too often they found them alone, waiting, and therefore concluded that "all Jews were lazy" and unfit for physical labor or even "regular work."[16] One report even quoted a Jew as having said: "If I really could get an apprentice, and even if I would offer to teach him for nothing, I wouldn't get anyone, for they are too lazy."[17]

The missionaries found tailors, silver and goldsmiths, book binders, glaziers, barbers, shoemakers, bakers, dealers in old clothes, an occasional farmer, and entertainers such as musicians, magicians, and acrobats. Traveling preachers would receive pay for their sermons and itinerant book sellers would purvey works which they or others had written. In Halberstadt a Jewish numismatist specialized in old Roman coins[18] and in the Meissen district another bought defective pennies.[19] Other occupations encountered were brewing and distilling of spirits, wine growing, tobacco, and leather works. The reports also noted that Jews dealt with Christian items in business life. A Jewish seal maker filled an order which specified the image of Jesus on the seal,[20] and another even was found selling missionary literature.[21]

Among the professionals, the *melammed* (teacher) was most frequently mentioned; he would either teach a group of children or serve as a private tutor for some wealthy family—the kind of work that gave Mendelssohn his start in Berlin. Teachers were often poorly trained; it was deemed sufficient if they could read, write and had a reasonable knowledge of prayerbook and Torah. Larger communities were able to support full-fledged rabbis, but cantors often needing an additional occupation might be ritual slaughterers or circumcisers as well.

The missionaries did discover a few Jewish physicians with academic training and mentioned this as extraordinary, for instance when they identified one doctor who studied at the universities of Giessen and Leiden.[22] Occasionally the local rabbi would function as a physician, as Maimonides had in his day.

Women too worked when they could and when their assistance was required. The missionaries noted that women minded the store while their husbands were asleep, buying supplies, attending to religious duties, or away on other business.[23] This might indicate that such care-taking was not a regular occupation for Jewish women, as it frequently was in Eastern Europe. One reference to Jewish cottage industry notes that lace making was "the commonest work" of the women.[24]

In Germany, as in Eastern Europe, Jews were innkeepers, and the missionaries found that the lower-class Gentiles who most often frequented these places could be a source of friction. One amusing report describes some drunks who late in the evening asked for more alcohol and were refused. As tensions rose the innkeeper's wife began to recite the evening prayers, inducing the raucous guests to depart.[25]

The Jews sometimes used these local inns as a place for assembly or prayer services, especially when they had no synagogue building, a practice which confused the missionaries, one reporter believing that this practice made the innkeeper into the "rabbi" of the village.[26]

We also learn about money-lending from the missionaries. One report quotes interest charged at one kreutzer a week for every gulden, which would amount to a yearly rate of 52%. Another speaks of a rabbi who earned his living loaning funds but enjoyed little standing among his fellow Jews because he lent to Gentiles as well as to Jews.[27] But the reportage is not altogether trustworthy because the missionaries would often not know who was or was not a rabbi. Any literate and bearded man might mistakenly be believed to fit the role.

The majority of Jews whom the missionaries encountered, or chose to encounter, were poor. The disadvantaged have historically been the first target of conversionary efforts and therefore the reports should not be taken as the basis for statistical data. Still, they do convey the impression that these poor whom the roving reporters found were not a discrete economic underclass but a substantial portion of the Jewish population who complained incessantly about their wretched condition.

In addition, a "professional" class of beggars, the *schnorrer*,[28] created problems. Begging was widespread, with children often panhandling for the elderly.[29] A number of communities felt so beset by itinerant beggars that they tried to hustle them out of town before they became a public charge. In Wasserbüdingen there was a Jewish poorhouse outside the town where wandering charity seekers would be accommodated, and in Dessau, Mendelssohn's birthplace, a special poorhouse existed inside the city's gates.[30] The itinerants traveled considerable distances, some of them wandering through Bohemia, Moravia and on to southern Germany and Holland. In some localities Jews were advised not to give alms to such "traveling Jews," as they were known.[31]

However, many Jews faced the constant threat of being reduced to beggary. If one could not pay the annual head tax one might be forced to leave the community, and join the "travelers," a constant fear at the lower end of the economic scale. In contrast, the few rich assumed the role of princes, the famous court Jews kindling the imagination of many a Jew who naïvely likened their influence to that of the Emperor himself.[32]

But the famous "Jud Suess"—Joseph Suess Oppenheimer, a powerful court Jew who was hanged in 1738—was not their favorite, for his disastrous fate demonstrated the fragility of Jewish life. Besides, he was said to be a quasi-renegade who did not even observe Yom Kippur. All of this did not prevent him from being a constant topic of discussion, even arguing whether he had a share in the world-to-come.[33]

The rich guarded their shaky position jealously, causing the missionaries to draw some unflattering parallels between them and similarly placed persons in the Christian community.[34] Wealthy Jews would often imitate the habits of their rich Gentile townsmen by ostentatious displays and thereby attract the envy of both Jew and Gentile.[35]

Riches also became a pathway toward assimilation. Of one rich Jew it was said that his major occupation consisted of eating, drinking and gambling with his non-Jewish associates.[36] It need hardly be added that if such a person eventually "converted," it was likely not from conviction but simply an outflow of his social ambitions and the desire to escape the severe restrictions still placed on Jews in most German areas.

Though Jews tried to live as close to one another as possible they were not generally ghettoized but dwelled among their Christian neighbors which made missionary work among them more difficult and which also made for greater caution among Jews. They would not leave their doors open. Even during the day a visitor might pull the bell cord several times before he was answered and might then be asked for an identification before being admitted.[37]

Since in most places in Germany Jews were not allowed to own real estate, they generally inhabited rented and, more often than not, over-crowded and unsanitary dwellings. There were exceptions,[38] but typically the missionaries found Jewish families living in one room where they would eat, sleep and also do business. In Leipheim a visitor even encountered people selling meat in a room where a sick man was bedded on straw in the corner. In addition, one single room might be the site of sundry occupations, such as two tailors working in the barber shop.[39]

Usually more than one family lived in each house, and in the larger cities, with space restricted and expensive, Jews would enlarge the building by adding stories, if permitted to do so, one report relating that five stories were not uncommon. Altogether, Jewish living conditions reflected the economically and socially depressed status of the Jews.[40]

Not surprisingly, it required all their wits to make a living. Even meager success would lead Gentiles to accuse them of sharp dealing. The missionaries also were quick to point out Jewish shortcomings and note their unethical business practices, to which Jews would reply that Christians generally cheated them and thus forced them to adopt survival tactics. One such report has a frustrated Jew explain his poverty by saying that he could do much better "if he would cheat like other Jews."[41]

Jewish criminals were also part of this society, especially among the *schutzlose Juden,* Jews with no state protection who were, by definition, extra-legal persons. For some reason forced to leave their original homes, they roamed the countryside, being refused admission everywhere and having no way of earning a decent livelihood. They might join bands of thieves, as they did in southern Germany.[42] In Jena two Jewish thieves, Emanuel Heinemann and Hoymer (Hayim) Moses, whose Gentile sobriquets were Carbe and Ingolstädter, were executed for their misdeeds and a special booklet was issued describing their low life and their end.[43] In Frankfurt-am-Main two Jews were accused of having murdered for revenge and a man was broken on the wheel for having slain one Mayer Gabel of Heidelberg.[44] One report tells of a Jew seeking conversion to lighten his punishment and another of a Jew being kept in jail because he had stolen from his *shul.*[45]

Yet, we know from other sources that for the most part Jewish ethical teaching permeated Jewish life, despite the marginal conditions under which these people lived; given the opportunity in the New World, their exemplary ethics attracted special praise from their Gentile neighbors.[46]

These fragments about Jewish existence in eighteenth-century Germany reveal nothing about the success and failure of the conversionary efforts of our reporters, a subject addressed in some of the later, less accessible volumes. The missionaries' reports do provide, however, a glimpse into Jewish life not readily available elsewhere—a small contribution to an understanding of the background of a people who, a hundred years later, would attain middle-class standards, higher education, and widespread integration into German economic and cultural life.

NOTES

1. *Sefer Ma'agal Tov,* first published from 1753 to 1778, and edited by Aron Freimann (Jerusalem, 1934).

2. *She'elat yavets,* first published from 1738 to 1759; a later edition appeared in Lemberg, 1884, in 2 vols. See also Boas Cohen, *Kuntres Ha-Teshuvot* (Budapest, 1930).

3. Callenberg was born in 1694 and died in 1760. In 1791 the Institute merged with the Franckesche Stiftung.

4. The series has a variety of names. Originally it was called *Bericht an einige christliche Freunde von einem Versuch das arme jüdische Volck zur Erkenntnis und Annehmung der christlichen Wahrheit anzuleiten,* 2d ed. (Halle, 1730) (noted as Ber.). Subsequent volumes of this series entitled *Fortsetzung* are noted as F, F1, F2, etc. In 1738 the series appeared under a changed title: *Relation von einer weiteren Bemühung...* and are noted as R, R1, R2, etc.; in 1752 the title changed to *Fortwährende Bemühung...,* and its nine volumes are noted as FB, FB1, FB2, etc.; in 1754 the series was called *Christliche Bereisung...* (noted as CB). From 1760 on, after Callenberg's death, the editors were Stephan Schultz and after him, Justus Israel Beyer. The new volumes were entitled *Fernere Nachricht...* (noted as JA1, JA2, etc.). An index appeared in 1744 which makes the earlier volumes easier to analyze, but no index appeared thereafter.

5. I published this particular interview in *Commentary* 25, no. 5 (1958), 428-30. Mendelssohn politely demolished his visitor's missionary arguments.

6. Reporting to one's superiors was then, as always, somewhat inflated, a practice to which this writer confesses with some embarrassment concerning his own military reports on his chaplaincy work during the Second World War. I am quite sure that I visited fewer soldiers in hospitals and had smaller synagogue attendances than my official memoranda reported.

7. "Germany" here is used as a broad term meaning the lands which were in 1871 unified into the German Reich. A century before, the principal states were Saxony (whose King Augustus served also as king of Poland), Bavaria, and Prussia, which was fast rising to preeminence. The rest of Germany consisted of numerous independent dukedoms, free cities and other principalities. Only occasionally would the missionaries roam as far as Hungary.

8. One should note, however, the highly useful study by Herman Pollack, *Jewish Folkways in Germanic Lands (1648-1806)* (Cambridge, Mass., 1971). Even though the author did not utilize the Callenberg reports, he explored much other material which enabled him to portray the general physical condition of their habitats, including descriptions of the interior of their homes and the extent of their libraries. Pollack's sources also describe areas such as Moravia, Bohemia and Austria proper.

9. See Pollack, ibid., 1-3.

10. Freely translated: "As far-fetched as baked Sabbath prayers," "silly nonsense," "really true." See Werner Weinberg's collection and analysis of this material in *Die Reste des Jüdischdeutschen* (Stuttgart, 1971). The renowned linguist Uriel Weinreich, however, treats Judeo-German as a part of Yiddish; see his article in *Encyclopaedia Judaica* 16:790

et seq. See also Rudolf Glanz, *Geschichte des niederen jüdischen Volkes in Deutschland* (New York, 1968).

11. CB 365.

12. Ber 20.

13. In clothing, the prohibition of *sha'atnes,* the mixture of wool and flax.

14. F4:93.

15. Especially among the cattle dealers of Westfalen and Hessen, the Jewish "trade lingo" was common.

16. F4:31.

17. JA1:154.

18. FB2:3.

19. FB3:76.

20. F9:311.

21. F7:199.

22. 45.

23. F12:18; F8:336.

24. F6:29 et seq.

25. F5:89; R24.

26. F16:228.

27. R15:69, 78; F11, vol. 2:32.

28. The word in time entered High German parlance as well. It is a corruption of the Hebrew *she-nodar[lo]* someone [to whom] one has pledged [a gift].

29. R4:17.

30. See Azulai, 15 and JA13:177.

31. R15:68.

32. R14:115.

33. R5:162; R10:6 et seq.

34. F3, vol. 2:116.

35. F8:115.

36. F9:217.

37. F8:330; F6:17.

38. Such as recorded in F9:217.

39. JA15:144; F6:42.

40. See R14:112, and note that what the report calls "first story" is referred to as "second story" in North America; see also Azulai's comment on housing conditions in a place called Buttenwiesen (p. 13).

41. F9:178; F7:119; R21:62; R23:21.

42. R79.

43. R2:59 et seq.; see also R15:93 which describes a Jewish band in the Rhineland which stole 12,00 florins from a nobleman and burned down his house.

44. R6:61 et seq. and R7:2; R15:93.

45. F16:4; F11:33.

46. See Leon Huehner, "The Jews in Georgia in Colonial Times," *Publications of the Jewish Historical Society* 10:65 et seq.

THE REMNANTS
OF JUDEO-GERMAN*
Werner Weinberg

JUDEO-GERMAN HAS BEEN A VITAL ELEMENT of the German-Jewish experience. A full-fledged idiom of Jews for Jews, its beginnings reach back a thousand years. Only in the eighteenth century in the time of the Enlightenment did more and more Jews shed the idiom in favor of High German. But remnants of the idiom—single words, short phrases, expressions, proverbs, and the like—were still alive, especially in rural parts of Germany in the 1930s, when German Jewry itself came to an abrupt end.

In this study, the author attempts to identify these remnants and show that they had not lost their vitality even at this late date.[1] Our focus will be primarily on those Judeo-German words derived from the Hebrew, although Romance and other language origins will be considered as well.

Most of the Judeo-German words and expressions presented here stem from the author's own memory. Others have been gathered from numerous reliable informants predominantly in Westphalia, but also in the Rhineland and the Palatinate as well as Bavaria, Baden, Württemberg, Hesse and Lower Saxony. Often social and geographical factors determined the distribution of the vocabulary in each region. In religiously conservative areas, such as Lower Franconia or in East Frisia, the vocabulary was the largest; but there were also people with an extensive vocabulary in the liberal provinces, such as the Rhineland or Westphalia.

NAME AND CHARACTER

The term "Judeo-German" has appeared in the literature since the sixteenth century (first in its Latin form: *Judaeo-Germanice*). But it saw its culmination in the philological writings of the scholars of the *Wissenschaft des Judentums* in the nineteenth century, coming down to us from writers such as Zunz, Steinschneider, Graetz, etc.[2] But we used the term itself only rarely. Some Jews in the first third of the twentieth century applied it to the writing of regular German with Hebrew characters, found for instance in many prayerbooks. Instead of a name we would refer to someone with an active knowledge of these remnants as: "He uses Jewish expressions," or simply: "He speaks Jewish." Some would use the designation *loshen kodesh*, literally "holy tongue," which, however, could also refer to Hebrew. The word *mauscheln* was used derogatively by both Jews and Christians.

In print, Judeo-German was often referred to as *Judensprache* ("Jew language"). This expression had an anti-Semitic connotation, and furthermore was misleading since not all Jews used Judeo-German words or even knew them. The derogatory designation *Judendeutsch* ("Jew German") used by German writers was also erroneous, as "Jew German" was not at all the German of the Jews. In the beginning of the twentieth century, the designation *ivretaitsh* (Hebrew-German) could still be heard, but most often one encountered the expression "Jewish dialect" in print as well as in conversation. This too is incorrect, for Judeo-German cannot be compared to one of the German dialects, as that of Berlin, of Bavaria, Saxony, etc. In phonetics and intonation the remnants of Judeo-German incorporate the German dialect of the respective area; the differences between Judeo-German and normative German were predominantly lexical.

The designation "Jewish jargon," sometimes used by both German and Jewish intellectuals, described a partial function of the idiom: Jewish cattle-dealers would use Judeo-German words specific to their trade, making it a sort of trading or even secret language.[3] Yet the vestigial Judeo-German cannot truly be designated a jargon for its vocabulary was not extensive enough and its morphology and syntax not distinguishable enough to serve as an independent vehicle of communication, nor did it exclusively serve internal Jewish use.

The designation "West Yiddish," which is used by most linguists today instead of "Judeo-German," was unknown to those German Jews from whom this material was collected, including the author. We knew the designation "Yiddish" exclusively as the language of the East European Jewish community. Acquisitions from Yiddish probably originate in the Polish-Jewish emigration following the Chmelniecki pogroms in the seventeenth century. Also the Prussian Eastern provinces and the city of Berlin served as a permanent bridge to the home of Yiddish. During the First World War Polish Jews, while passing through and settling in Germany, brought new influences to bear on Jewish-German. Finally, the influence of modern Hebrew on the language of the Jews living in Germany can easily be discerned in the conversations of German Jews returning from Israel. "Judeo-German" will here refer to the residues of the old idiom of the German Jews, that still were heard when the author grew up in Westphalia.

SPEAKERS AND UTILIZATION

The Jews who knew Judeo-German, of course, also spoke regular German. Judeo-German words, expressions or proverbs were reserved for use in one's own milieu or in certain contacts with non-Jews. The upper social stratum of the Jewish community—doctors, lawyers, manufacturers, merchants—had almost completely abandoned the use of Judeo-German. The members of this stratum distanced themselves from the idiom, forbade their children to use *"Jüdische Ausdrücke,"* and often denied any knowledge of the vocabulary. Thus Judeo-German was predominantly spoken by the middle and lower classes, that is wine and hop mongers, furriers, cattle-dealers, shop-owners, traveling salesmen in the textile trade, craftsmen and peddlers. Within those circles the Judeo-German idiom was preserved, and even cultivated, as the tradition of the fathers, distinguishing Jews from non-Jews, as a source of fun and jokes and sometimes also as a "code language."

Within these social groups it was predominantly the cattle- and horse-dealers who not only preserved the greater vocabulary, but even creatively expanded it, disseminating Judeo-German through their frequent journeys to different cattle-markets. At the weekly cattle-market in Westphalian, Hessian or Lower Franconian towns, Judeo-German could almost serve as a professional language. In their interaction with Christian farmers and butchers, Jewish dealers and middlemen used Judeo-German, particularly the numeric values of the Hebrew alphabet, as a secret code. However, quite a few Christian farmers and butchers

129

commanded a considerable portion of the vocabulary. For Jewish listeners it was always amusing to hear a dialogue such as the following:

The Jewish merchant: "I give *beis meis shivvem shuk* for the *beheime*." (I give 270 marks for the cow.)

The Christian farmer: "Do you want to *beseibeln* (cheat) me? *Mei ratt* or no *massematten!*" (Hundred taler [1 taler = 3 marks] or no business.)

Attempts to use Judeo-German to communicate secretly in the home often failed as well. The non-Jewish housemaids, for example, soon mastered bits of the vocabulary: *"Stieke,* the *shikse!"* (Quiet, the housemaid!) was the well-known warning when the maid entered the room. If the conversation was unfit for the ears of children, the adults would alert each other by saying: *"Stieke, 'skotenche"* (Quiet, the little one) or *"Stieke, 's yeled"* (Quiet, the child).

One favorite technique of jest translation was to dissect German words into several parts and to translate them syllable-by-syllable into the "Jewish" idiom. Thus the words *Menuche meshugge beheime* were the "translation" for the name Rudolphi (Ruh-doll-Vieh, or rest - mad - cattle). This game was especially played with geographic names: Aschaffenburg became *toches meloches ziyaun* (Arsch-schaffen-Burg, or ass - work - Zion); Schweinfurt (hog-ford) became *chassermokem;* Würzburg (spice-castle) turned into *besomenmokem.*

In conversations with one another, Jews constantly and quite unconsciously used Judeo-German words for a number of reasons, not the least of which was habit. In addition, the Judeo-German terms often were more graphic or were more apt than their German equivalents, or had no such equivalent.

In the 1930s, Judeo-German produced no real literature, yet in many homes one could still find humorous booklets such as joke anthologies.[4] Parodies of classical German literary works were particularly popular. For example, the Judeo-German version of Schiller's *Die Glocke* (The Bell) replaced the casting of the bell with the baking of Jewish dishes, the *kugel* or *shalet.* Schiller's philosophical reflections were parodied with descriptions of Jewish family life, holidays, the synagogue and the shop. The author of such works usually disguised himself with a "Jewish" comic pseudonym such as Yankev Medinegeier (peddler), Gumpel Assesponim (cheeky fellow), or Chochem of the Manishtanne (the wise son from the Passover Haggadah). The language of those booklets is, however, misleading: Many words and expressions stem from the East Yiddish and the phonetic, morphological and syntactic distortions of the German were either imitations of East Yiddish or were arbitrary corruptions of normative German.

WORD FORMATION

Judeo-German did not have a syntactical structure of its own. The word order was German and German words were used for pronouns, prepositions, and conjunctions. The few exceptions to this rule include the occasional use of *ani* for "I," *sheli* for "mine," and the prefix form *be-* and *ve-*, meaning respectively "in" and "and." There were only a few Judeo-German adverbs, namely, compounds with *be* such as *bekan* (here); *benakhes* (quiet); or *beshtike* (silent). However, not everybody was familiar with them and in most cases German adverbs were used. The Judeo-German morphology as well was essentially German.[5] Most of the time there existed a harmonic symbiosis between Hebrew stem and German structure in the use of prefixes and suffixes, forms of conjugation and declension.

Judeo-German words of a non-Hebraic origin represent only a small fraction of the vocabulary in the 1930s. A number of words had Romance origins, probably via French and Italian. For example, *benshen* meant to bless (from the Latin *benedicere*), *dormen* to sleep (from the French *dormir*), or *memmerbuch* book with the names of the dead (French *memoir*). *Peiaz*, or fool (see e.g., the novel *The Poyaz* by K. E. Franzos) derives from *pagliacci,* either directly or indirectly via the German *Bayazzo* or the Polish *pajacs*. *Chotsce* (already, finally, even, perhaps) and *lokshen* (a noodle dish) both seem to have a Slavic or Hungarian origin. *Almemor,* the lectern in the synagogue, derives from Arabic.

The etymology of *nebbich*, an expression of compassion, pity or contempt, remains uncertain in spite of many theories. The same is true for *minnig*, which designates dishes that are neither *"milchding"* nor *"fleishding."* Some words of German origin were almost completely restricted to Judeo-German, for instance *yitshen* (*"juedishen"*), to circumcise (humorously used for shortening the horns of a cow to make it appear younger); *kugel,* a Sabbath dish; *shul,* synagogue; and *trendel* (East-Yiddish: *dreidel*), a Chanukkah toy. Other words of Germanic origin were perceived as exclusively "Jewish" by Jews, for example *gasht* (pl. *gaesht*) meaning riffraff or beggars; *ruddeln* to spread gossip; or *shnorrer* beggar; however, it is difficult to determine to what extent those words also belonged to German dialects or to colloquial German.

Certain German words and expressions were predominantly, perhaps even exclusively, used by Jews. Some colorful examples: *"Alles boese weit aweg!"* the wish that after a bad event things from now on may be better; *"anbeissen,"* breaking the fast; *"beshreien,"* to do evil to somebody by praising something; *"er weiss viel von seinem Gesund,"* someone who does not know what it is all about; *"nit gestoge(n) und nit geflogen,"* without rhyme or reason, neither hand nor tail, nothing of this is true; and finally *"unsere Leut,"* our people, which referred to the Jews.

The following entries have been selected from the original glossary which focuses on words and expressions that are derived from the Hebrew.

GLOSSARY

acheln, achelen, achlen, vt. & i. To eat. From stem *akhal* אכל.

achelei, f.; pl. -en. Meal.

achelpeter, m. Glutton.

achler, Eater, glutton. (*Kinnemachler,* lice-eater, curse)

achiele, also *chiele.* Meal, dinner.

ackschen, m. Stubborn or obstinate person. From akshan עקשן.

amche, subst. or adj. The Jewish people; Jewish, e.g. "bist du *amche?*" "are you amche?" or simply "amche?" a code-word among Jews. From עמך (lit. your people), probably from the liturgy for shabbat: ומי כעמך ישראל. The ending was regarded by some of the speakers as a diminutive.

amoretz, m.; pl. *amoratzen.* An uneducated person, a block-head. From עם הארץ.

ascherjozerpapier, n. (m.). Toilet-paper. From אשר יצר (lit. who has created), the beginning of a blessing about body-functions.

assesponem, n. Insolent person. From עזות (insolence) and פנים (lit. face).

ausbaldowern, vt. To find out. From בעל דבר (lit. Lord of the word).

ause sholaum bimraumov, He absconded. From עושה שלום במרומיו (lit. he who creates peace up on high), the concluding phrase of the Kaddish and the *shmone-esreh* prayer, during which one takes three steps backwards.

bechinnem, adv. Gratis, free of charge. From בחינם. Also *choze bechinnem* or "half for free," i.e. dirt-cheap. "*Bechinnem* ist der Tod," or "only death is for free."

betucht, also *betuch, betuach*, adj. Well-off, respected. From בטוח (lit. safe). "Er ist schwer *betucht*" (very wealthy), "ein *betuchter sege*" (a wealthy man).

bilbel, m.; pl. *bilbulem, belbulem, balbolem, also bambulem, bebulem, mebulem, mebules, mabulem, mabules*. Dispute, squabble, most often used in the plural, from בלבול(ים) (lit. confusions); "mach keine *bibulem*" (don't cause difficulties; don't start an argument); "sie haben *bilbulem*" (they are breaking up); "er sucht *bilbulem*" (he seeks a quarrel).

chaddeschemone, kaddeschemone, f. coll. Protestants, Protestant religion, from חדש (new) and אמונה (faith).

choge, chogge, choche, chocke, f.; pl. -n or -s, also *chago-em*. Christian holiday; sometimes also just Christmas. From חגא .

chonte, f.; pl. -n. Prostitute. Etym. uncertain. Among the proposed derivations one can find: חנה (to lie), חנות (shop), חנט (to mature) and חנן (to give favors). "Aus der Kammer lief die *chonte*, weil der *chammer* nicht mehr konnte" (the prostitute ran out of the room, because the fool was exhausted).

chontebajes, n. Brothel (lit. house of whores).

dalfen, m.; pl. *dalfonem*. Poor man. Probably from the folk-etymological connection of דל (poor) and דלפון , one of the sons of Haman (Esther 9:7). "Der *dalfen* hat vorne nix und hinten nix," (he does not have anything.) This phrase derives from folklore: Dalfon, among all sons of Haman, is the only one who has neither in the beginning nor in the end a letter 'א'.

dibbern, dabbern, also *medibbern, medabbern*, vi. and t. To speak. From stem דבר; perhaps from both forms דִּבֵּר and מדבר . "*Lau dibbern; lau medibbern; dibber lau*" (don't speak; don't say anything!).

eisew, (1) Non-Jew from עשו (lit. Esau). (2) n. Cigar, tobacco, from עשב , through the translation "herb."

gallach, m.; pl. *galochem*. Christian cleric, usually Catholic, from גלח .

gannew, also *ganowe*, f. *gannewte*; pl. *ganowem*. Thief; also shrewd person. From גנב . "So ein gannew!" (such a shrewd person) "dem gannew brennt der Hut," (that is, the thief does not have a minute of relaxation) (lit. the thief's hat is burning). Also to interpret

G.m.b. H. (German abbreviation for Incorporation) as *Gannew mit beide Haend* (steals with both hands). "Der *gannewt* die *schul* mitsamt dem *almemor*" (he steals the synagogue together with the lectern), meaning he is a dyed-in-the-wool swindler.

hawelawolem, hewelawulem, also *heflefulem,* pl. Vain words, from הבל הבלים (vanity of vanities).

jankew, nom. pr. Jakob, from יעקב. "Wer *Jankew* nicht gibt, muss Esau geben" (lit. whoever does not give to *Jankew,* has to give to Esau), that is whoever does not do charity to his Jewish brothers, will in the end have to give his money to non-Jews.

jascher kausch, jejascher kausch, also *schekauach, schkauch.* Thank you, thank you very much, from יישר כוח or יישר כוחך (lit. May God sustain your strength!). Most often said in the synagogue after the priestly blessing, but also in secular contexts. *Schkauch sagen,* vi. to say thank you.

kapore, kapores, adj. and subs. f. Broken, wiped out; destruction, doom. From כפרה (lit. atonement, sacrifice of atonement). "Er geht *kapores*" (he dies). Also in colloquial German "meine *kapore!*" (I don't care). *Kaporehinkel, -haehndel,* n. (chicken for atonement.) From the tradition of slaughtering a chicken on the day before Yom Kippur, onto which chicken all sins are transferred, meaning: scapegoat, also Schlemiel.

kille, f.; pl. -s. Jewish community, from קהילה. *Kille kedausche* (also *kaudesch*), such as in "die ganze *kille kedausche*" (the whole community). Sometimes also with a local name: "die ganze *kille kedausche* Rheda" (the community of Rheda). From קהילה קדושה (lit. holy congregation), which traditionally accompanies the name of a Jewish community.

lecho daudi, as in the expression "gebackene or eingemachte *lecho daudis*" (baked, preserved *lecho daudis*). Sometimes added: "mit Spinnwebenmayonnaise" (with cobweb-mayonnaise). The language is meaningless. Used as an angry, elusive or mocking answer to the question "what is there to eat?" from לכה דודי (lit. go, my friend) from the Friday night liturgy. Perhaps stemming from an anecdote.

macke, f.; pl. -s or -n. Hit; mishap; mistake, handicap; expensive ware. The pl. with -s was predominantly used as "hits," the one with -n as "mistakes"; from מכה. "Die *beheime* hat 'ne *miese macke*" (the cow has a bad handicap). "er hat mackes gekriegt" (was beaten up).

mauscheln, vi. To speak Judeo-German; also: to use Jewish gestures or intonation; to mumble. The word took on a derogatory sense when applied to Jews as well as to non-Jews. Grimm's Wörterbuch also relates it to Jewish ways of doing business: "wie ein Schacherjude verfahren" (to behave like a Jew sharper). Perhaps from משה (Moses), or Mausche in Ashkenazic pronunciation, where the name collectively represented the Jews.

meschugge, adj. Crazy, from משוגע. "Wenn einer meschugge wird, faengt's im Kopf an" (when someone becomes crazy, it starts in the head). "Meschugge ist Trumpf" (meschugge is trumps), meaning "totally crazy." "Meschuggener Fisch" (lit. crazy fish or crazy person); from the anecdote: Asked what a דוכיפז (hoopoe) is, the teacher answers with embarrassment: "a meschuggener Fisch." When the student protested: "But it can fly" (as it is listed among the birds), the teacher answered: "Das ist doch seine meschugas" (that is exactly its craziness).

mos, mo-es, also *mei-es,* n. Money. From מעות.

mummer lehaches, m. Mean person; "Jewish anti-Semite." From מומר להכעיס (lit. segregate—from Judaism—in order to cause anger).

nabbeln, vt. (1) To slaughter an animal in an unkosher way: "die *pore* ist *genabbelt*" (the cow has been slaughtered unritually). (2) To make an animal appear worse to lower the price.

nefieche, f.; pl. Fart, wind. From נפיחה. "*Nefieche* im Schnupftuch" (lit. a fart in your handkerchief) meaning worthless, unimportant, bagatelle. "*Nefieche* soll dir am Kopf zerplatzen," a curse which was supposed to sound worse than its meaning implied.

ratt, m. Coin. From ר"ט, abbreviated from Reichstaler, an imperial coin.

risches, m. Anti-Semitism. From רשעות (lit. wickedness, naughtiness). "Er hat *risches*," (he is anti-Semitic); "Bei risches Bier," a wordplay (bei-risch = bayrisch = Bavarian) on Bavarian beer in view of the proverbial Bavarian anti-Semitism. *Risches machen,* vi. to cause anti-Semitism; "Mach keinen *risches*" (lit. don't make risches) meaning don't behave in a conspicuous way. *Rischesmacher,* a Jew who is accused of causing anti-Semitism.

schajerokes, m. Mess; worthless stuff. From שאר ירקות (lit. various green stuff) from the Pesach Haggadah.

schegez, scheigez, also *scheijez,* m.; f. *schickse;* pl. *schkozem,* and *schickses,* -n. Christian boy, and Christian girl, especially house-maid; sometimes *schegez* was also the friend of the housemaid or an abusive word for a Jewish boy; the plural, *schkozem,* was especially used for children (lit. crawling animal); from שקץ. Also in colloquial German, esp. *schickse,* which was used for Jewish girls.

schicker, adj. and subst. m.; pl. *schikorem.* Drunk; drunkard, from שבור. "*Schicker* wie Lot" (as drunk as Lot), meaning totally drunk. "Das ganze Jahr *schicker* und nüchtern zu Purim" (lit. drunk the whole year and sober for Purim) meaning somebody who goes against tradition.

stuss, m.; pl. -em, -en. Nonsense; stupid talk; senseless joke. From שטות.

tack, m. pl. -en. Penny, ten-pfennig coin. From ט"ג, abbreviated from *Teutscher Groschen* (German penny).

temune, f., Christian religion, probably from אמונה (faith).

tiffle, f.; pl. -s. Church; probably conscious inversion of the word תפלה prayer with the connotation of תִּפְלָה, or something offensive (Jeremiah 23:13).

tippel, m. Fall; epilepsy. Either from the verb *tippeln* or directly from תפול. *Tippeln,* vi. to fall, from תפול (lit. you will fall), probably from a well-known Bible quote, such as Exodus 15:16 in the daily morning-prayer.

toches, m. The butt, from תחת (lit. below). "*Toches* muss man haben" or "One needs *toches,*" meaning, ironically, one needs to have brains. "Mit einem *toches* auf zwei Kirmessen" (lit. with one *toches* on two fairs), meaning one cannot be at two places at the same time. "Dein *toches* feiert Kirmes" (lit. your *toches* celebrates a fair), meaning you get beaten on your butt. "Er hat den *toches* voller Flöhe" (lit. he has the butt full of fleas), meaning he cannot sit still. "Er hat kein Hemd am *toches*" (lit. he has no shirt on his butt), meaning he is terribly poor. "Zu 'nem grossen *toches* gehört 'ne grosse Hose" (lit. a big butt needs large pants), meaning a grand appearance needs the corresponding means.

tofel, adj.: old. "a *tofle beheime*" (old cow); "the *tofele*" (the old guy); also the jack of clubs in card games (*toufflete:* old woman; *tofel mokem:* old city; *malbusch toufel:* old dress). However, neither one of the two possible Hebrew root-words mean "old"; תפל is tasteless and טפל irrelevant. These meanings partially intermingle.

The meaning "old" for *tofel* could have developed from *tofelemone*.

tofelemone, toflemone, f. Catholic, Catholic faith, Catholic church. The second part of the word stems from אמונה (faith). The first part was understood as "old," thus the older (Christian) the Catholic faith. However, *tofel* did not mean "old" originally, but rather "tasteless" (from תפל) or of "secondary" importance (from טפל). Probably the meaning "old" originally emerged in juxtaposition to חדש *chaddeschemone* Protestantism ("new faith") and then was generally used for "old."

NOTES

*This essay and glossary were derived from the author's, *Die Reste des Jüdisch-deutschen* (W. Kohlhammer, 1969) and translated by Charlotte Fonrobert.

1. The extensive religious vocabulary of Judeo-German has been omitted, because its extent depended entirely on the Jewish education of the individual.

2. See W. Weinberg, "Die Bezeichnung Jüdischdeutsch," *Zeitschrift für deutsche Philologie* 100 (1981), 253-90.

3. Early authors—invariably anti-Semitic—emphasize the secretive character of Judeo-German. Thus Tirsch in his *Kleines jüdisch-deutsches Wörterbuch* described the use of the idiom: "...so that they could all the better deceive, take advantage of, curse without shame and bewitch Christians...." Seligone asks: "Is it not right and proper to learn the language of people who live among us...and thus to prevent a lot of damage?"

4. Judeo-German words and expressions can be found in the works of Jewish writers such as Berthold Auerbach, Jakob Loewenberg or Karl Emil Franzos and in the satires of Sammy Gronemann.

5. The predominance of German morphology and syntactical structure in Judeo-German is not symptomatic of the decline of the idiom. Rather, it is typical of the idiom even in its prime, as some examples of early authors indicate: Lutke (1733): *"es houlicht mir tof"* or "I am doing well" (*halakh, tov*); Chrysander (1750): *"am Shabbes achle ich gern tofle dogim"* or "on Shabbat I like to eat good fish" (*akhal, tov, dagim*).

BETWEEN EXPULSION AND INTEGRATION: EAST EUROPEAN JEWS IN WEIMAR GERMANY*

Trude Maurer

DURING A HEATED DEBATE in the Prussian Diet on the immigration of East European Jews in 1922, the Social Democratic Minister of the Interior, Carl Severing, reminded the deputies of the example of Lessing. According to Severing, the poet had demonstrated in his famous play *Nathan der Weise* "that we are not born first and foremost as Christians nor as Jews nor as Moslems, but rather as human beings."

The record of the proceedings records the response "Hear! Hear! Very good!" from the left side of the chamber, and laughter from the ranks of the German National People's Party. Severing then continued:

> If we remind ourselves of this statement during the discussion of the problem [of the immigration of East European Jews] without becoming sentimental, then, I believe we will be able to prevent anti-Semitic excesses, avoid ill-will toward our Jewish fellow-citizens and yet do justice to German interests.[1]

Was this the "ethical reorientation of German politics" which the Zionist organ *Jüdische Rundschau* had noted as being a sincere desire expressed by people from various walks of life? For it was precisely in the treatment of Jewish immigrants that, according to the *Rundschau,* such reorientation should be manifested. The author implied that giving asylum to these refugees was not only a moral opportunity but a moral obligation as well.[2]

The topic of East European Jews is of central importance for the history of Jews and anti-Semitism in Germany—both in respect to the internal development of the Jewish community and the status of Jews in Germany. For—apart perhaps from the official recognition of Judaism as a religion entitled to equal rights with the various Christian denominations—this was the only area in which state agencies had to formulate a policy toward the Jews.

In approaching the history of East European Jews in Germany, the historian is confronted with a complex relationship among three groups: (a) German society, and the various governments of the Reich and the constituent states which determined official policy toward the *Ostjuden*, (b) German Jewry which formed a separate group within German society—both in terms of self-perception and from the perspective of the German public—and which was directly affected by the immigration of Jews from the East; and (c) the *Ostjuden* themselves.

There is substantial source material only for the first two groups. The East European Jews themselves have left us precious little in the way of historically utilizable material for Germany was, by and large, a country of transmigration and transient residence for Jews, rather than one of immigration. In Germany the *Ostjuden* did not form a community with separate institutions, such as a Yiddish press, as they had, for example, in the United States and elsewhere. Consequently, if we wish to examine them, it must be principally through the eyes of the two other groups, for they do not appear as the subject of their own history; rather, *Ostjuden* remain the object of the considerations and endeavors of German Jewry on the one hand and German policymakers on the other.

I intend to concentrate on official German government policy toward Jews from Eastern Europe and the reactions of German Jewry to their immigration. The development of the Eastern European Jewish population itself will only be treated insofar as it is important in this connection. In regard to official policy, I will focus mainly on (a) the national level (*Reich*) and (b) the state of Prussia, where more than 70% of the *Ostjuden* lived.

Before World War I,[3] some two million East European Jews passed through Germany on their way to America, while only a small number chose to remain in Germany. There were some 70,000 *Ostjuden* living in the German Reich in 1910. During World War I, Germany—in contrast with the earlier policy which the country had of restricting residence privileges and expelling large numbers of *Ostjuden*—recruited Jews for work in German industry and even imported about 30,000 forcibly from Eastern Europe. At the end of the war, a special decree (*Grenzsperre*) specifically and exclusively prohibited Eastern Jewish workers from setting foot on German soil.[4] However, Jewish refugees had entered Germany during the war and continued to do so after its end, although the borders then were closed to all immigrants from the East and not to Jews alone. Jews first came west fleeing from the Russian armies, later from the Russian Revolution, and finally from the fury of the pogroms in the newly established Polish state and of those in the Ukraine during the Russian Civil War.

The Jewish influx, including deported workers, between the years 1914 and 1921 is estimated at 100,000, some 40% of whom had already moved further west by 1921 or returned home, as immigration was often followed by further migration.

In the year 1925, when the only general census in the Weimar Republic was taken, there were nearly 108,000 Jewish foreigners living in Germany, of whom at least 80% were *Ostjuden*. However, these census data do not supply any information about dates of immigration. In 1930, Heinrich Silbergleit's published occupational data on the Jews, dividing them into local and immigrant communities,[5] does not correlate occupation and citizenship. Consequently, we can conclude only that 57% of gainfully employed foreign Jews in Prussia (including *Ostjuden*) were engaged in trade or commerce, 32% in industry (including craftsmen), 1% in agriculture, while the rest were employed in private households, Jewish community institutions or in the professions. On the basis of these data, we are not able to distinguish between recent immigrants and long-time residents. In the years following the war, there had been a considerable influx of *Ostjuden* into heavy industry and mining, although I have certain doubts about the contemporary figure of 12,000-15,000.[6] This concentration may be due to the exemption of mining and agriculture from the so-called economic demobilization measures which enabled employers to dismiss non-local employees, including, of course, foreigners, in order to create vacancies for returning soldiers. Such demobilization measures, along with the introduction of a special licensing procedure for the employment of foreigners in 1923, encouraged Jews to turn or return to trade and peddling as sources of livelihood. That trend was then further reinforced by the crisis in the Ruhr, when large numbers of workers—Jews included—lost their jobs.

German policy toward Jewish immigration from Eastern Europe must be viewed within the context of the public debate on *Ostjuden* both in the press and in the various parliaments of the Reich and the constituent states.[7] Anti-Semites tended to portray the *Ostjude* as the polar opposite of the honest and upright German. He was usually seen as an unproductive dealer who wedged himself between producer and consumer thereby gaining high and unwarranted profits from the hard work of others. He was supposedly infested with lice, a carrier of disease and a sexual molester, exploiting German women not only for his personal pleasure but again for business and profit in the form of "white slavery" (*Mädchenhandel*). He was alleged to be a criminal who was harmful to the lives of honest Germans; above all, he was seen as belonging to a foreign race, one which posed a threat to the racial purity of the German people and that would degrade the level of German culture. Anti-Semitic propaganda linked all these stereotypes and even coined such expressions as "hygienic Bolshevism"[8] or spoke about "lousy and morally mangy *Ostjuden*."[9] All these characteristics were illustrated and portrayed in connection with the welter of problems which beset postwar Germany, such as inflation, inadequate housing and food shortages.

More significantly, it was during and through the discussion of these contemporary problems that anti-Semitic views pertaining to Jews from Eastern Europe spread beyond the confines of the right wing into the liberal and socialist camps, although these groups were opposed to anti-Semitism in principle, and indeed continued to defend *Ostjuden* against anti-Semitic attacks. The Prussian Minister of Trade and Industry, Otto Fischbeck (*Deutsche Demokratische Partei*), who prided himself on being a member of the mixed Jewish-Gentile League against Anti-Semitism, is a case in point.[10] Indicative of this spread of anti-Semitism, although not representative of the Social Democrats as a whole, was the fact that their theoretical party journal *Neue Zeit* published an article in two installments, long passages of which were copied verbatim from a wartime pan-German pamphlet on *Ostjuden*.[11] This indicates that the views held by non-anti-Semites, or even by declared opponents of anti-Semitism, were in fact not so firm, and could be made to waver when it came to a specific group of Jews, such as those migrating into Germany from the East.

However, in regard to concrete motions in parliament, it was the right-wing parties which attempted to restrict the rights of Eastern Jews.

In the early 1920s, it was usually the *Deutschnationale Volkspartei* which introduced such motions, followed later in the decade by the *Völkisch* and National Socialist parties. In addition to the traditional calls for the restriction of Jewish immigration and the expulsion of immigrants, these motions included the call for the internment of immigrant Jews in special camps. The National Socialists gave such motions a more radical twist by adding calls for denaturalization and dispossession of *Ostjuden,* i.e., for cancellation of their constitutional rights. When grievances became known, the left-wing parties in turn introduced motions calling for an end to internment.

Turning to the decision-making bodies, we also occasionally find that considerations were indeed influenced by anti-Semitic notions. Apart from a few instances of the use of current stereotypes (such as blaming revolutionary agitation on foreign Jews), such notions cropped up chiefly when it came to questions like the estimated number of immigrants, though official estimates never even approximated the fanciful figures given by anti-Semitic agitators. The distressing economic situation was usually the point of departure for discussion. There is no doubt that the situation was serious: there were difficulties in the supply of basic products and a lingering shortage in housing which had not been eliminated even by the end of the 1920s.

Thus, to most Germans, *any* immigration whatsoever was undesirable. Politicians and leading government officials repeatedly made declarations to this effect in regard to immigrants from the West and non-Jewish foreigners as well. Indeed, the principal aim and objective of the official policy on *Ostjuden* was to prevent their immigration. However, this was enforced more strictly along the eastern border than on Germany's western borders. The policy of *Grenzsperre* meant that a visa was required for entry into Germany and this was granted only after the reasons given by visa applicants for wanting to visit Germany had been carefully examined. Normally, the visa was valid for only a limited amount of time. If a foreigner wished to take up residence in Germany, he had to prove that he had both a job and a place to reside. Under the existing regulations on housing and employment, this entailed numerous difficulties for the foreigner. Along with preventing further immigration, the need to promote emigration was repeatedly mentioned as an important objective of governmental policy, though it was seldom acted upon. Aside from reducing the fee for obtaining an exit visa, the government took no other concrete steps. It is difficult to establish whether measures in the early

1920s such as police raids, expulsions and deportations achieved their intended purpose.

The official treatment of *Ostjuden* thus had to be decided on within the legal framework of general police measures dealing with aliens (*Fremdenpolizei*); the guiding principle here, as it had been formulated in particular by the Prussian Interior Ministry, was that equal treatment was to be accorded all foreigners in Germany. Enforcement of regulations in accordance with this principle can be investigated by examining (a) the nature of the protection given by the police to immigrants, (b) measures taken against foreigners and (c) the procedure of naturalization, i.e., the attempt by the foreigner to shed his alien status in order to achieve equal rights with German citizens in all spheres of life. I will begin with an examination of the naturalization process.

The Reich and State Citizenship Law of 1913, which was still in effect during the Weimar Republic, stipulated that a foreigner should be naturalized by one of the constituent states and that citizenship in the Reich was then obtained indirectly. This corresponded with the fact that every German was, in legal terms, first a citizen of a specific *Land* and only by dint of this did he or she hold citizenship in the Reich as well. Naturalization, moreover, could only be approved after the Reich Minister of the Interior had established that none of the other federal states in the Reich objected.

Bavaria led all states in its attempts to prevent naturalization in other parts of the Reich. The 1913 law did not lay down a minimal period of residence prior to naturalization. However, such stipulations did exist in the constituent *Länder*. Bavaria required 20 years, Lübeck 25, and Saxony a full 30 years of residence as a prerequisite. In Prussia, requirements varied between 10 and 20 years during the Weimar Republic. In general, these provisions enabled only those individuals who had come to Germany before or during World War I to obtain German citizenship. When an option for shortening the period of minimal required residency was finally introduced, as in Prussia in the late 1920s, many officials were reluctant to make use of it.

Nevertheless, a total of some 12,500 *Ostjuden* were naturalized during the Weimar period. It is debatable whether this figure is relatively low or high in comparative terms. This can only be decided definitively after examining all applications by foreigners and establishing the ratio between unsuccessful applications by Jews and by non-Jews. One would then still have to take into due consideration the fact that a large number of foreign aliens chose not to apply for German citizenship at all and that the number of naturalizations was thus also dependent on this factor.

When it comes to the behavior of the police, one can find examples where the general regulations were applied with excessive ardor and spite, as in the *Scheunenviertel,* for example, a Berlin quarter where many *Ostjuden* were concentrated. Police raids searching for racketeers seem to have been carried out more frequently there than in other quarters. In November 1923, when there were protracted anti-Semitic disturbances in the *Scheunenviertel,* the police protected the Jews only on the evening of the first day and during the second day of the events; yet when the trouble broke out they initially had not only neglected their duty but in some cases had even arrested and maltreated Jews who had been the victims of anti-Semitic attacks, or were members of a self-defense group sent to the scene by the Association of Jewish War Veterans (*Reichsbund jüdischer Frontsoldaten*). There were, however, a number of cases in which people who were tried because of protesting self-defense against anti-Semitic attacks or arbitrary measures by the police were subsequently acquitted by the courts.

Expulsions came under the jurisdiction of the *Länder.* In Prussia, a series of decrees pertaining to expulsion listed an increasing number of reasons for the measure. However, the objective of giving an exhaustive enumeration of possible reasons for deportation implied that the number of potential reasons was limited. To be sure, the officials were left with considerable discretion, and the "burdensomeness" (*Lästigkeit*) of the foreigners was, in terms of international law, always regarded as a sufficient reason for initiating deportation procedures.

Considering the prevailing atmosphere, it can be assumed that regulations pertaining to aliens were applied with greater rigor and strictness when it came to Jews from Eastern Europe. However, it is difficult to prove this conclusively in the absence of comparable research on other groups of foreigners, in particular on non-Jews of the same nationality. Yet it is clear that the perception of what *Ostjuden* were and what they did, especially in regard to their conduct of business, was significantly influenced—if not indeed shaped—by prevailing anti-Semitic views.

On the other hand, when trying to properly evaluate the practice of deportation, we should bear in mind that the actual deportation was often postponed repeatedly or not carried out at all, thus enabling those marked for expulsion to stay on in the country for years. Such delays were granted in particular out of consideration for local members of the family. Furthermore, individuals threatened with deportation often had recourse to judicial appeal, and were frequently successful in having the orders of the lower authorities overruled by the decision of a higher-placed authority, especially the Prussian Interior Ministry. Compared to the imperial period, when in the 1880s alone more than 10,000 foreign Jews were expelled from Prussia, the number of actual deportations during the Weimar years remained low. Of the 26,000 individuals expelled from Prussia, at least 3,900, or some 15%, can he identified as Jews. It should be noted that in 1925, 12.7% of all foreigners in Prussia were Jewish. Unlike the situation in Wilhelminian Germany, there were no mass deportations during the Weimar period. Certain constituent states, such as Bavaria and Thuringia, did attempt to expel large numbers of Jews, but such deportations were forbidden by international law.

Assembling all available evidence, let us return to the initial question: was there indeed a reorientation of German policy toward *Ostjuden* in the Weimar era? I think it is necessary in this connection to distinguish between the individual states. When it came to the Reich and the government of Prussia, the answer appears to be in the affirmative, but I have doubts about other German states which I have not examined in detail. The political parties which significantly framed policy toward *Ostjuden* in the Reich and Prussia in the early and decisive years were the Social Democrats and the German Democrats. They were not only traditional defenders of Jewish equality but also saw in anti-Semitism an instrument of their political opponents. Although they always affirmed and safeguarded the priority of German interests, these parties were committed (a) to the moral obligation of giving asylum to refugees and (b) to the equal treatment of all foreigners. Indicative of this reorientation is the decree issued by the Prussian Interior Ministry in November 1919 which stated that *Ostjuden* could not be sent back to Eastern Europe, since such an act might endanger their lives.[12] Even in Prussia, however, the implementation of the official maxim of equal treatment left much to be desired.

Nationalists and anti-Semites opposed immigration not so much for practical reasons—such as difficulties in the provision of basic commodities and the competition for housing and jobs—but rather for ideological reasons alone. In their view, immigration and toleration of Eastern Jews could only lead, in the long run, to an increase in the number of Jewish citizens in the Reich. The anti-Semites reproached the government with showing favor toward East European Jews and even went so far as to identify the Weimar Republic itself with these Jews. As a result, they succeeded in intimidating the government and placing it on the defensive. The immigration of East European Jews into Germany was thus part of two interlocking problems: (a) the presence and treatment of foreigners in general and (b) the Jewish question as it was posed by the anti-Semites.

Let us now turn to the response of German Jews to the influx of Jews from the East. They were confronted with this problem both as Germans whose *Deutschtum* was frequently being called into question and as Jews. As Germans, they acknowledged the general undesirability of any immigration; in addition, they also harbored fears that immigration might endanger their own position in Germany. Certainly this was not the only danger they feared since anti-Semitism had a long tradition and was not merely based on reactions to the immigration of Eastern Jews. Rather, it was aimed at Jews as German citizens enjoying equal rights under the law. However, immigration reaffirmed and recreated the image of the Jew as alien. In the eyes of the anti-Semites, the Berlin *Scheunenviertel* was the breeding ground of future German citizens of the Jewish faith.[13]

The danger for German Jews, as they saw it, resulted from the attempt of anti-Semites to equate German Jews with Eastern Jews. Thus, anti-Semitic attacks against *Ostjuden* were clearly the starting point for the public response of German Jewry to immigration. They realized that the anti-Semites simply singled out the Eastern Jews as the weakest and most vulnerable segment within Jewry. Therefore, with the exception of the marginal group of German Nationalist Jews (*Verband nationaldeutscher Juden*), the spokesmen for all other organizations within German Jewry persistently defended the Eastern Jews, at least in public. This was a question of Jewish self-respect and was at the same time a matter of anticipatory self-defense by the Jewish citizens of the German Reich. Felix Goldmann, a Liberal rabbi and a leading member of the largest Jewish organization at the time, the *Centralverein deutscher Staatsbürger jüdischen Glaubens,* had made this point as early as 1915 when he rejected any plans to close the border specifically against the influx of Eastern Jews.

> Those smart people who think one should muzzle anti-Semitism and sacrifice the East European Jews to it are sorely mistaken if they expect repose or even tranquility from this concession. It would only intensify the hatred of Jews. Heretofore anti-Semitism had to put up with the

reproach of breaching the law, regardless of the form in which it appeared. Thereby, however, it would suddenly gain firm ground and [i.e. by closing the border] support, from which it could easily go further. Today it would be directed against the Polish Jews, tomorrow against the naturalized, the day after tomorrow against the old-established German citizens. Today it would be a matter of economic questions, tomorrow political rights and the day after tomorrow of the freedom of religion.[14]

This statement is representative of the motives that moved German Jews to come to the defense of Eastern Jews during the Weimar Republic. However, the leaders of the German-Jewish community not only rejected the introduction of special legislation aimed at *Ostjuden* or their unequal treatment, but they also created an extensive network of relief organizations. On the one hand, this was regarded as a moral obligation of the community—indeed, even as a religious obligation. On the other hand, however, these organizations were also established in order to counter anti-Semitic criticism and reproaches. The main objective of such relief work was, first of all, to help send new immigrants on to the West or back to their home countries; secondly, relief work aided in integrating Eastern Jewish immigrants into the German economy, especially within the so-called "productive" occupations, as opposed to the traditional Jewish occupations in trade and commerce. These activities were supplemented by providing welfare and legal protection, particularly in matters pertaining to deportation.

Yet one would misjudge the situation if one were to view the attempt to send immigrants on to other destinations as being nothing but an attempt by German Jews to get rid of the burdensome *Ostjuden*. This approach was also based on a realistic reading of the situation at the time, namely, the judgment that living conditions for new immigrants in postwar Germany were unfavorable and that there was indeed hardly any possibility for economic survival at all.

Jewish relief organizations were in close contact with the German authorities responsible for immigration and could even influence their plans. This is another indication of the reorientation of German policy discussed above. There was also some reorientation in the relief work organized by German Jewry. This was evident, first of all, in the emphasis placed on social policy, particularly occupational retraining, rather than philanthropy. Secondly, it could be seen in the attempt to co-opt representatives of Eastern Jewish organizations and include them in the central relief organization. Thirdly, it was reflected in cooperation by ideological opponents within German Jewry, particularly the Zionists and the *Centralverein*, in respect to relief for *Ostjuden*.

From the outset, attitudes toward Eastern Jews within the Jewish community in Germany varied. The Zionists and Orthodox welcomed the immigrants for they believed that the *Ostjuden* embodied Jewish values that German Jews were lacking. The Orthodox appreciated in particular the piety of the Eastern Jews and their generally strong adherence to the precepts of religious law. To the Zionists, who wished to reaffirm the existence of a Jewish nation, the Eastern Jews were "the people" par excellence, the foundation of the national rebirth of the Jewish people, since they had preserved their own culture and had avoided assimilating into their non-Jewish environment. Furthermore, both the Orthodox and the Zionists hoped to win new supporters among the immigrants in order to strengthen their own minority position within the Jewish community.

The traditional life of the *Ostjuden* as well as their interpretation of religious law were alien to those who were liberal in a religious sense. Nevertheless, they appreciated the piety of the Eastern Jews. For the members of the *Centralverein*—who were predominantly religious liberals and who, in contrast to the nationalist view held by the Zionists, believed in a synthesis of *Deutschtum* and *Judentum*—the defense of the Eastern Jews constituted an integral part of their efforts to combat anti-Semitism. It was their duty "as Jews, as Germans and as human beings"[15] to help the Jews from the East. Liberals and members of the *Centralverein* may not have welcomed immigration, but they accepted it as a fact and reality. Since Eastern Jews and German Jews differed in large measure socially, culturally and religiously, it is not surprising that those segments of the German-Jewish community that were in favor of religious liberalism and emphasized the importance of German culture disliked the prospect of *Ostjuden* being able to determine and shape conditions in the local Jewish communities. Above all, these liberals rejected the concept of a *Volksgemeinde* as opposed to a *Kultusgemeinde* ("ethnic community" vs. "religious congregation"). As postulated by the Zionists and most of the Eastern Jews, the *Volksgemeinde* was intended to provide for *all* the needs of its members, including social and cultural affairs and was not focussed only on religious matters. The liberals held that this could only lead to the isolation of the Jews from German society, to the refashioning of a kind of voluntary ghetto.

These apprehensions induced a segment of the liberals to deny to the

Eastern Jews the right to vote within the communities (*Gemeinden*), and to oppose their religious demands insofar as they concerned the congregation as a whole. It should be pointed out, however, that the idea that *Ostjuden* and Zionists could ever succeed in actually "taking over" the local Jewish communities was unrealistic—with the exception perhaps of the communities in Saxony, where up to two-thirds of their members were Jews from the East. The same is true when it comes to the claim of "self-ghettoization." The disputes over the voting rights of Eastern Jews in some extreme cases provided a kind of mirror image of the public debate on Eastern Jews, with one party discrediting the other by arguments which were usually employed by anti-Semites in their attacks on Jews. It should be emphasized that such disputes were engaged in almost exclusively by German Jews. The Eastern Jews hardly participated at all, even though it was their rights which were at stake.

The conceptions which the majority of German Jews and the majority of *Ostjuden* held in regard to religious services and religious practice in general differed so greatly that the *Ostjuden* usually had synagogues or prayer-halls of their own. The rules for proper conduct laid down by the Jewish communities for Eastern Jewish groups wishing to use their premises reflect the internalization of German patterns of behavior by German Jews. They were unable to view any deviation from it other than disapprovingly. Furthermore, they wished to prevent the *Ostjuden* from arousing the suspicion of non-Jews. However, this reflected a lack of a sense of confidence and security, of not being fully accepted themselves among Germans. Compared to the situation in Wilhelminian Germany, the social gulf separating German and Eastern Jews widened, for now the social disparity was even greater. Such distance—and, in some cases, conscious aloofness—could even be found among the Zionists and the Orthodox.

At the same time, it is possible to note a growing interest in the culture of the East European Jews among German Jews. Its achievements were acknowledged even by the liberals. This interest, reflected in the journals published by organizations which otherwise differed considerably, extends far beyond mere apologetic statements or defense against anti-Semitism. Indeed, both the newfound interest in Eastern Jews and the necessity to confront and combat anti-Semitism encouraged further reflections on the nature of *Judentum*. The Jewish component in the identity of German Jews was strengthened, since Eastern Jewish piety was emphasized and the existence of an Eastern Jewish, though not "pan-

Jewish," nationhood was generally acknowledged, and because *Judentum* was now defined by the *Centralverein* not solely as a religious community, but rather as a community of origin and fate (*Abstammungs- und Schicksalsgemeinschaft*).

Unlike the situation in the Wilhelminian period, the Eastern Jews themselves developed their own network of associations during the Weimar Republic. In addition to the existing Eastern Jewish congregations (*Synagogen-Vereine*) and several mutual-aid societies that had been created in the years leading up to World War I, now youth clubs, *Arbeiterkulturvereine* and *Landsmannschaften* began to spring up. Their initial and main purpose was likewise mutual aid. Yet they also served to enrich social life by organizating cultural activities, charity balls and festivities on Jewish holidays. In addition to these local associations, Jews from Eastern Europe also organized on a regional and national level. However, the Jewish immigrants formed neither a socially nor a culturally homogeneous group. The Russian Jews came predominantly from the professions and in part from the wealthy commercial class and had received a Russian education; the Polish Jews, on the other hand, were largely Yiddish-speaking and working-class. This was also reflected in the institutional life of the immigrants, who created *two* central associations.

The tiny League of Russian Jews was an institution for self-help without any political objectives. Its specific focus was in giving effective aid to individuals who had been financially well off but had fallen on bad times and were now living in poverty and to do this without offending their sense of self-respect. It is worth noting that this organization was immediately successful in carving out a niche for itself within the organizational framework of Russian immigration although it also forged bonds of cooperation with the other organization of Eastern Jewish immigrants in Germany, the *Verband der Ostjuden*. The organizational separation between various groups of Jews from Eastern Europe did not in any way imply disapproval of one by the other.

The *Verband der Ostjuden* was established in 1919 with the support—and possibly at the initiative of—the Zionists, who were interested in recruiting new members to their ranks. Individuals could, of course, join the League of Eastern Jews, but from the mid-1920s on its basic aim was to unite the existing associations under an organizational umbrella. By 1930, some 100 associations had joined the League, which had a total membership of 20,000. One of its founders summarized the objective of the League as "defense and enlightenment outwards [i.e. for the general public] and education, strengthening of responsibility and strictest self-control inwards." Yet the League also had to counteract tendencies toward disintegration resulting from the adoption of anti-Semitic stereotypes by Eastern Jews themselves and from the attempt by the successful to abandon and flee the immigrant community. Apart from cultivating everything Jewish this also required "closest affiliation with the national hopes of the Jewish people."[16] Although the concept of *Judentum* that was implied in the last part of this statement differed from the conceptions held by the majority of German Jews, this program in many ways resembled German-Jewish liberal strategies. In regard to practical activities, the League of Eastern Jews in the beginning provided aid for refugees arriving in Germany. Later on, its program concentrated on activities for the resident *Ostjuden* who had stayed in the country. The Eastern Jews were not to be "objects of philanthropic charity" but were supposed to become the masters of their own affairs.[17] In the late 1920s, the *Ostjudenverband* cultivated an Eastern Jewish identity within a Jewish national orientation and attempted to safeguard the interests of Eastern Jews in the Jewish communities. The cooperation with the Zionist organization in this field resulted in tensions between the two organizations, since the Zionists demanded allegiance, while the League of Eastern Jews claimed to be an equal and independent partner.

This new self-awareness among Eastern Jews is documented by the League's statements on its policy in respect to the *Gemeinden*. It aimed not only at removing special regulations for foreigners but also wanted to work constructively in the communities and even to reconcile differences—this in the interest of Jewry as a whole. It not only emphasized cooperation with German Jews but even wanted "to take in and assimilate the positively Jewish creations of German Jewry especially in the field of Jewish science" without being fully absorbed by it or losing its own distinctive cultural identity. Rather, it was thought that Eastern and Western Jews, working together, could lead Jewry toward a brighter and better future, overcoming all difficulties of cultural assimilation and economic hardship.[18] The League summarized the aim of all its endeavors as follows:

> Not the continuation of Jewish life in the East, the "perpetuation of East European Jewry in West Europe," ought to be our slogan, but rather the construction of a new Jewish life in the Western countries. Foremost

was and is the striving for a synthesis between the old-Jewish life, the spirit of the new milieu and the demands of contemporary economic and cultural life.[19]

Several thousand members of the League had obtained German citizenship. This not only reflects the fact of their extended residence in Germany, probably true of non-naturalized members of the League as well, but also indicates a level of adjustment to and familiarity with German language and culture in line with the requirements of naturalization procedures at the time. On the one hand, the activities of the League of Eastern Jews reflect a strong sense of Jewish and Eastern Jewish awareness and identity which can also be shown in the remembrances of those who were not members of the League. On the other hand, the fact that many members were German citizens—and that parallels can be found between the League's program and the objectives and strategies of German-Jewish organizations—points to the reality of a long-term integration of those Eastern Jews who did not choose to move on immediately to the West.

In sum, Eastern Jews in Germany lived under the threat of expulsion. This was especially true of recent immigrants. But they also lived with the prospect of gradual—though by no means unimpeded—integration into the German-Jewish community, leading eventually toward the attainment of German citizenship.

NOTES

*Reprinted with additional translations and slight revisions from *Tel Aviver Jahrbuch für deutsche Geschichte XVII*, 1988. A comprehensive account can be found in Trude Maurer, *Ostjuden in Deutschland 1918-1933* (Hamburg, 1986).

1. "Sitzungsberichte des Preußischen Landtags, 1." *Wahlperiode*, vol. 10, col. 13574 (November 29, 1922).

2. F. L., Neuorientierung, in: *Jüdische Rundschau* 24, no. 90 (December 12, 1919), 703.

3. Two important works on the prewar period and somewhat after are Steven Aschheim, *Brothers and Strangers: East European Jews in German and German-Jewish Consciousness, 1800-1923* (Madison, 1982) and Jack Wertheimer, *Unwelcome Strangers: East European Jews in Imperial Germany* (New York and Oxford, 1987).

4. On the closing of the border, see Trude Maurer, "Medizinalpolizei und Antisemitismus: Die deutsche Politik der Grenzsperre gegen Ostjuden im Ersten Weltkrieg," in: *Jahrbücher für Geschichte Osteuropas* 33 (1985), 2, 205-230.

5. Heinrich Silbergleit, *Bevölkerungs- und Berufsverhältnisse der Juden im Deutschen Reich: Aufgrund von amtlichen Materialien bearbeitet*. Band I: Freistaat Preußen (Berlin,

1930) *(Veröffentlichungen der Akademie für die Wissenschaft des Judentums: Sektion für Stastik und Wirtschaftskunde 1).*

6. On Eastern Jewish workers in the Ruhr, see Ludger Heid, "'Mehr Intelligenz als körperliche Kraft': Zur Sozialgeschichte ostjüdischer Proletarier an Rhein und Ruhr 1914-1923," in: *Jahrbuch des Instituts für Deutsche Geschichte* 15 (1986), 337-62. This article is an abridged version (but more detailed regarding the contemporary charge of Jewish involvement in revolutionary activities) of Ludger Heid, "East European Jewish Workers in the Ruhr, 1915-1922," in: *Leo Baeck Institute, Year Book* 30 (1985), 141-68.

7. For a brief outline of this debate in English, see Trude Maurer, "Stereotype and Attempted Rebuttal," in: *Studies in Contemporary Jewry I,* ed. Jonathan Frankel, (Bloomington, 1984), 176-98.

8. This term was quoted from an unidentified newspaper and approved by a deputy of the Deutsche Volkspartei, Siegfried von Kardorff, at a meeting of the Reichstag. "Verhandlungen des Reichstags 1: Wahlperiode 1920," *Stenographische Berichte* 354 (April 5, 1922), 6857.

9. Th. F. [Theodor Fritsch], "Zur Scheidung in der deutsch-nationalen Volkspartei," in: Hammer, *Zeitschrift für nationales Leben* 21, no. 484 (August, 15, 1922), 313-16, quotation 314.

10. See his speech in the Prussian Diet and his letter to the Minister of the Interior, Wolfgang Heine, "Sitzungsberichte des Preußischen Landtags, 1," *Wahlperiode* 10, cols. 13588-93 (November 29, 1922). Letter to Heine, August 3, 1920, in: *Bundesarchiv Koblenz, Nachlaß Georg Gothein,* no. 20.

11. Theodor Müller, "Die Einwanderung der Ostjuden," in: *Neue Zeit* 39 (part 2), no. 13 (June 24, 1921), 293-98; and no. 14 (July 1, 1921), 325-30. Müller copied from pages 23, 29-32, 34, 39-43 of Georg Fritz, *Die Ostjudenfrage: Zionismus & Grenzschluß* (München, 1915).

12. I would suggest, however, that the importance of this decree was exaggerated by Adler-Rudel because he did not mention criticism of it within the government itself, nor did he take future and somewhat harsher decrees into consideration. Cf. S[halom] Adler-Rudel, *Ostjuden in Deutschland 1880-1940: Zugleich eine Geschichte der Organisationen, die sie betreuten* (Tübingen, 1959) (Schriftenreihe wissenschaftlicher Abhandlungen des Leo Baeck Institute of Jews from Germany 1).

13. Hammer, *Blätter für deutschen Sinn* 26, no. 593 (March 1, 1927), 136.

14. Felix Goldmann, "Deutschland und die Ostjudenfrage," in: *Im deutschen [!] Reich* 21, nos. 10-11 (Oct.-Nov. 1915), 195-213, quotation 200-01.

15. "Hauptversammlung des Centralvereins am 20. und 21. November 1921," in: *Im deutschen Reich* 28, nos. 1-2 (Jan.-Feb. 1922), 1-28, quotation 24 (the speaker was Kurt Alexander).

16. Jakob Reich, "Der Verband der Ostjuden," in: *Neue Jüdische Monatshefte* 4, no. 11/12 (March 10/25, 1920), 266-68, quotations 266, 267.

17. "Zusammenschluß der Ostjuden in Deutschland," in: *Jüdische Rundschau* 24, no. 33 (May 9, 1919), 256-57, quotation 257 (from a proclamation of the League of Eastern Jews). Cf. Ostjüdische Konferenz, in: *Israelitisches Familienblatt* 22, no. 22 (May 27, 1920), 3 (summarizing a speech by Jakob Reich).

18. H. Koretz, "Hat das Judentum im Westen ein Programm?" in: *Jüdische Welt, Zentral-Organ des Verbandes ostjüdischer Organisationen in Deutschland* 3, no. 13 (July 1, 1930), 1-2.

19. H. Koretz, *Die Grundlagen unserer Arbeit,* in: *Jüdische Welt* 4, no. 1 (January 1, 1931), 1-2, quotation 2.

PART V

A Diversity of Legacies

TORAH IM DEREKH ERETZ

Immanuel Jakobovits

THERE IS PROBABLY NO SINGLE INDIVIDUAL who contributed more to the image of modern Orthodoxy than did Samson Raphael Hirsch (1808-1888) who already at the age of 28 anonymously published his *Nineteen Letters* outlining his life's program for making observant Jews respectable in Western society. In tracing the remarkable story of Hirsch's influence on the progress of traditional Jewish life since his death, as well as the limits of that influence, let me deal at some length with what I can only describe as an exceedingly strange phenomenon.

Before World War II there were in Europe three major dynamics or movements which maintained and reinvigorated Orthodoxy in the face of considerable attacks—from the Reform on the one side and from the Haskalah and the secularists in pursuit of secularist Jewish scholarship on the other. Facing these forces on the prewar European scene and, by extension, in the United States, Palestine and in other parts of the modern world were two East European movements: Hasidism, with an enormous number of adherents and the power of its teachings emanating from the heartland of Poland and Galicia and extending to Hungary and Russia; and the yeshivot together with the musar movement of R. Israel Salanter, galvanizing the enormous institutions of Talmudic learning maintained by the *mitnagdim,* the opponents of Hasidism—an exceedingly vibrant force which sustained Jewish life before the war, and not only in Eastern Europe.

In Western Europe, meanwhile, there was *Torah im Derekh Eretz,* Hirsch's synthesis of Judaism with Western secular culture. Further, Hirsch's philosophy, like the philosophy of Reform Judaism, albeit along very different lines, held that the ultimate Jewish national purpose is the mission to the nations.

Then came the destruction of East European Jewry by the Holocaust leaving only tiny remnants of the Hasidic and the yeshiva worlds. The Western world and culture to some extent survived and with it the Jewish communities of the Anglo-Saxon countries mainly in Britain and in the United States.

Since the Holocaust hit the Eastern world far more devastatingly than it did the Western world, one might have expected that after the war the two Eastern movements would be impotent and that the Western brand of Orthodoxy as represented by Hirsch's *Torah im Derekh Eretz* would strike root in the Western world and survive. And yet the opposite has happened: wherever there are Jewish communities, the Hasidic and yeshivot movements are both dynamic and prolific.

On the other hand, *Torah im Derekh Eretz,* the philosophy of synthesis, of some relationship linking religions with secular values, studies and pursuits—the humanism of Samson Raphael Hirsch—is extinct. No longer is there a single institution of higher Jewish learning in the world that can truly claim to be guided by the teachings and philosophy of Hirsch. There are *ersatz* institutions which claim to be in the tradition of *Torah im Derekh Eretz* but not as Hirsch understood it.

This is a phenomenon that requires explanation. Why should Hirsch's teachings as embodied in a movement have suffered such an eclipse, notwithstanding the renewed interest aroused in his writings and in many of his concepts? I believe the principal answers are to be found in the two cataclysmic events of recent Jewish history. Firstly, Germany's betrayal of civilization, culminating in the Holocaust, produced a terrible disillusionment with all Western culture and science. Our generation can no longer accept the inevitability of civilization's progress and of man's enlightenment, as assumed by Hirsch. Secondly, and equally unforeseen by Hirsch, the rise of Israel as a political reality and primary focus of Jewish life and thought has not only seriously compromised Hirsch's *Weltanschauung* with its acclamation of the *galut* but has divested it of his dynamic concept of Israel's mission to humanity. The emphasis today is on self-preservation and on the reclamation of Jews. All our energies are fully engaged in the mission to the Jews, not to mankind. By contrast, the yeshivot and Hasidic movements have gained momentum for the very reason that they are inward-looking, unconcerned with the outside world and the Jewish role in it, even though both these movements, too, have yet to come to terms fully with the Jewish State.

To examine the place of *Torah im Derekh Eretz* in contemporary society, let us first focus on its authenticity. To what extent does what we commonly attribute to Hirsch—some form of synthesis—represent his actual teaching?

The notion that it absolutely embodies Hirsch's philosophy is indeed being widely contested and challenged. There are many who claim that Hirsch's true belief did not lie in what we commonly call today *Torah im Derekh Eretz* but that he merely applied it as a *Hora'at Sha'ah*. This means a temporary and exceptional measure taken to meet an emergency situation such as he encountered in nineteenth-century Germany with the onslaught of Reform—the need to find a response to the inroads made by Reform theology and Reform teachings, by the eagerness of the Reform Jews to come to terms with the culture in which they lived. Hirsch, it is argued, gave this response an Orthodox form, leading to the formulation of *Torah im Derekh Eretz*. But this was not meant as a genuine ideal *per se*: it was merely an expedient to meet an exceptional situation such as confronted him in Frankfurt at the time when he took on his tiny little community, the remnant of Orthodox traditional people left as a little island in the sea of assimilation and Reform that engulfed German Jewry at that time.

Hirsch was far too great a master of Rabbinic Judaism—a *gaon*, a *lamdan* of the highest rank—and he was far too zealous a fighter for unadulterated Orthodoxy to be directly attacked for his views. As one of the great sages of his time, he was safe from any frontal attack denouncing him for holding "heretical" or otherwise unacceptable opinions. He was, after all, also a disciple of leading Torah scholars of his generation, rabbis Jacob Ettlinger and Isaac Bernays, who were universally recognized. Therefore no one could question his rabbinic credentials or his expertise in Torah learning.

Hence, those who quarreled with his philosophy did not denounce his teachings but argued that he did not really mean them. He was not himself convinced—so it was rationalized—that these teachings were ideals but merely adopted them under the pressure of outside circumstances.

In fact, contemporary records indicate that the great East European Torah sages of the day always regarded Hirsch with the highest respect. Indeed, some wrote endorsements and recommendations for his published works, such as the enthusiastic acclaim of Rabbi Yitzchak Elchanan Spector of Kovno. And yet these scholars completely rejected his philosophy. They were uncompromisingly opposed to his idea of *Torah im Derekh Eretz*. What they argued was that his views were fine for German Jews—unlearned people who lived in an environment of rampant assimilation. So a Samson Raphael Hirsch was needed to speak in highfalutin modern terms, use all the humanistic language of his day, as a concession to the times and to local conditions. But this was not real Torah. If you want the genuine Torah teaching, these sages felt, go to the yeshivot in the East and drink at the wells of pure Jewish learning.

Therefore there was this dichotomy. On the one hand these scholars endorsed the personality of Hirsch, and on the other they disengaged themselves from his teachings. This attitude already was fairly widespread in his lifetime. Thus were his views ascribed to force of circumstances rather than to genuine conviction.

The charge, then, is that *Torah im Derekh Eretz* was not really his sincere commitment but was used only as a means to preserve and build up Orthodox teaching in a Western and therefore highly adulterated environment. This charge takes two forms. One attacks the validity of the synthesis itself, that the fusion with Western culture cannot genuinely be called an authentically Jewish teaching. The other attacks the application of scientific or modern scholarly methods to the study of Judaism.

The two objections are not quite identical. In the first, *Torah im Derekh Eretz* was interpreted to mean there are Torah teachings and there are secular teachings and somehow a bridge must be built between them. That synthesis was refuted as unauthentic. In the second argument, what was rejected as not genuine in *Torah im Derekh Eretz* were the modern methods of scholarship used in the study of Judaism, methods all the more exceptionable for being the tool provided by *Wissenschaft* and the Haskalah in order to promote the understanding of Jewish sources and Jewish teachings. Both charges have been rejected not only in the postwar era but in earlier times as well.

One of the greatest scholars recognized unreservedly in the Torah world and yet a product of Western European Orthodoxy was Rabbi David Hoffmann, the Rector of the Rabbinical Seminary in Berlin, who succeeded its founder Rabbi Ezriel Hildesheimer. Hoffmann was the author of the well-known responsa *Melamed Leho'il,* widely used to this day whose authenticity as a source of reliable Torah judgments will not be questioned by any rabbinic authority. In a contribution dated 1920 to the seventh volume of *Jeschurun,* under the heading *"Torah und Wissenschaft"* (Torah and Scholarship), after quoting Hildesheimer, Hoffmann wrote on the affirmation of the pursuit of *Wissenschaft,* such as exegesis and history, as follows:

> With love and scientific seriousness, are these [namely exegesis, history] to be pursued....This view decidedly protests against the opinion which, even if it recommends concern with *Wissenschaft* to contemporary rabbis, still regards it only as a necessary evil, since—as is erroneously assumed—it disturbs the study of the Torah....In fact this is not so. Through earnest scholarship, scholarly research, in honour of God (*Leshem Shamayim*), the study of Torah can only be promoted and enriched.[1]

Similarly, in the same volume of *Jeschurun,* Dr. Joseph Wohlgemuth, the editor, records the following conversation between Hoffmann and Hirsch forty years earlier. Evidently Hoffmann had mentioned several novel interpretations contained in his famous exegetical commentary *Leviticus,* and Hirsch asked him "Do you consider modern research in your lectures?" (quoting Wohlgemuth's report). And Hoffmann answers: "As far as lies in my weak powers. I am here well served by the contributions of Dr. Guggenheimer in your *Jeschurun*"[2] (the earlier magazine published by Hirsch). To which Hirsch answered: "That is very essential. Future rabbis must be informed on this," in other words, on modern methods of research.

In the postwar years as well, these objections to Hirsch's synthesis have been analyzed and discussed. After the war, Hirsch's whole world was uprooted, with the destruction of Frankfurt—site of Hirsch's school which is a prototype of our day schools—and the Adass communities built in its image. Subsequently the main exponent of *Torah im Derekh Eretz* was Rabbi Dr. Joseph Breuer who became the rabbi of the newly founded Adass type of community in Washington Heights, New York. In an article entitled *"Torah im Derekh Eretz – a Hora'at Sha'ah?"*—which was originally published in *Mitteilungen* in 1965 and reprinted in the *Jewish Tribune* in London—no greater expert on Hirsch than his own grandson, successor, and the principal heir to the whole tradition of Samson Raphael Hirsch wrote:

Certain circles which found it difficult to remain unaware of the greatness of Rabbi Hirsch maintain that his demand of *Torah im Derekh Eretz* was but a *Hora'at Sha'ah* essentially prohibited for the Torah-true Jew and only found necessary for the salvation and strengthening of Torah. It is claimed that its validity, as that of every *Hora'at Sha'ah,* is limited to the conditions of life prevailing in the time of Rabbi Hirsch.

Anyone who has but a fleeting insight into the life and work of Rabbi Hirsch will realize that this *Torah im Derekh Eretz* formula was never intended by him to be a *Hora'at Sha'ah*.[3]

Then Breuer quotes from Hirsch: "Our school [with the title deeds of the school he founded in Frankfurt] must be governed by the spirit of *Torah im Derekh Eretz*; at no time and circumstances may it give up these principles (of *Torah im Derekh Eretz* education)."[4] Thus he states firmly in a draft of bylaws for his Kehilla.

Breuer then quotes from Hirsch's polemic against the Breslau Seminary, the historical school of Judaism:

For if there were no alternative and we had only the choice between Judaism and Science (meaning *Wissenschaft*—modern scholarship), then there simply would be no choice and every Jew would unhesitatingly make his decision...rather to be a Jew without science than science without Judaism. *But thank God this is not the case...*[5]

affirms Breuer quoting his grandfather. Then he asks,

Does this Hirschian demand for *Torah im Derekh Eretz* bear the slightest resemblance to a *Hora'at Sha'ah*?

Let us for a moment assume that the *Torah im Derekh Eretz* precept was indeed a *Hora'at Sha'ah* (which it decidedly was not): there is a type of *Hora'at Sha'ah* which remains valid for an infinite period of time if the conditions which brought it about last for many centuries. This is borne out by the following: it is common knowledge that the Torah prohibited the written documentation of the *Torah Shebe'al Peh* (II 34.27; *Gittin* 60) [one was not allowed to write down the Oral Law]. Pressing circumstances and the increasing dispersion of our people, posing a severe threat to the survival of the "Oral Teaching" led to the writing down of *Mishna* and Talmud, a *Hora'at Sha'ah*. As the conditions which resulted in this emergency measure continued to prevail throughout the ensuing centuries until our own time, this *Hora'at Sha'ah* became a permanent institution—and thus was born our immense Torah literature.

We ask: are the conditions which led Rabbi Hirsch and the

rabbinical leaders to the supposed *Hora'at sha'ah* of *Torah im Derekh Eretz* any less valid in our time? Are they not rather more acute and far more pressing?[6]

Breuer had no doubt that *Torah im Derekh Eretz* was no "necessary evil," but the genuine teachings of Hirsch in which he fully believed.

It is also critical to examine the authenticity of Hirsch's teachings as perceived at another stage. His leading exponent in Great Britain, the late Dayan I. Grunfeld, not only pioneered the classic translations of Hirsch's writings but also interpreted his teachings to our generation.[7]

> The usual conception of the slogan as the combination of Torah and secular education touches only the surface of the problem. What Samson Raphael Hirsch meant by *Torah im Derekh Eretz* is, as has been pointed out correctly by the late Dr. Isaac Breuer [brother of Joseph Breuer], the relationship between Torah and civilization of a given epoch. The application of the values of the Torah to a given *Derekh Eretz*—i.e. a given civilization—has ever been the historic Jewish task. But great dangers have always arisen for the survival of the Torah at epochs of transition, at moments of crisis of civilization, when one civilization has decayed and a new one has arisen. That was exactly what happened in the days of Hirsch—and that is exactly what is happening again in our own day. And because our position in history is so similar to that of the time of Rabbi Hirsch, it is so important to understand his life and time so that he can be a guide in our own perplexed days.

Grunfeld continues his explication of Hirsch:

> Here was the great danger to the continuation of historic Judaism, a situation which S.R. Hirsch recognized with the eye of a genius. He was not afraid of meeting the onslaught of the new civilization, the new *Derekh Eretz*. He was convinced that the Torah could and would rise above it, as it had risen above other civilizations before. A deep study of both Torah and the manifestations of humanism had created in Samson Raphael Hirsch the flaming conviction of the eternal newness and applicability of the Torah to any situation which might arise. And so the young author of the *Nineteen Letters on Judaism* embarked on his life-task of putting into practice for his generation the maxim *Torah im Derekh Eretz* as he understood it. *The proclamation of the sovereignty of the Torah within any given civilization.*[8]

Grunfeld's definition differs from the one given by Joseph Breuer. But six years later, in Grunfeld's translation of Hirsch's monumental volume *Horeb,* which has a lengthy introduction to Hirsch's philosophy and teachings, Grunfeld makes only a passing reference to *Torah im Derekh Eretz* and makes no reference at all to the attacks on it.

Writes Grunfeld on Hirsch's "Torah and Humanism":

> What is necessary is not to reform the law, but to reform ourselves...in accordance with the religious and human ideal of the Torah. This true reform of ourselves we can only achieve by listening to the two existing revelations: the natural revelation and the moral consciousness within us, and the supernatural revelation at Sinai, both of which will lead us to a "God-rooted religious humanism" and its program of *Torah im Derekh Eretz.*[9]

Comparing what he wrote in 1956 and in 1962, Grunfeld clearly became less concerned with pointing to *Torah im Derekh Eretz* as the focal teaching of Hirsch. With the passing years and presumably under pressure from a growingly influential East European Judaism, he came to view it increasingly through Hasidic and yeshiva eyes.

In our time, I believe the greatest living authority on Hirsch is no doubt his great-grandson Professor Mordechai Breuer of Bar Ilan University. Professor Breuer contributed a very well documented article on *Torah im Derekh Eretz* to the Israeli journal *Hama'ayan* (Tishri 1968), based on sources readily available only to a specialist in this field. In referring to Hirsch's commentary on Genesis 3:24, he quotes a Midrash on the verse and remarks, "To guard the way of the Tree of Life"; he then adds the following: *"Die Kultur beginnt das Erziehungswerk des Menschengeschlechts und die Torah vollendet es."* (Culture begins the educational process of raising a human being and the Torah completes it.) For Hirsch, this concept was the meaning of *Derekh Eretz Kodmah Le-Torah*—"*Derekh Eretz* is the precondition for Torah." And in fact Breuer draws the parallel that, just as the Six Days of Creation precede the Sabbath which is their ultimate aim and therefore sanctified, so does *Derekh Eretz* anticipate the Torah. The two are both necessary, and the former is a condition for the latter; yet only the Torah is sacred. This view, as based on Hirsch's own words, certainly does not ascribe to *Derekh Eretz* the merely temporary or "necessary evil" role of *Hora'at Sha'ah.*

In this essay Mordechai Breuer also mentions that the use of the term *Derekh Eretz* for secular culture and secular pursuits preceded Hirsch. He cites for example Rabbi Naftali Herz Weisel who came from Hamburg, Germany, in the eighteenth century, 100 years before Hirsch.

Indeed, Breuer makes it plain that in his view, derived from his study of the sources, this *Torah im Derekh Eretz* principle was certainly not just a compromise or an expedient but an ideal in itself. Indeed Hirsch had enshrined it in the foundation scroll of his community when he included in it the exhortation, "Let us raise our children for *Torah im Derekh Eretz* together, as our fathers and mothers taught us in truth."

Mordechai Breuer acknowledges in his essay that Hirsch's earlier works, notably the *Nineteen Letters on Judaism* and later his *Horeb*, contained no reference to *Torah im Derekh Eretz*. However, that the idea was already with him is shown in the first sermon he ever delivered. At that time he was still Chief Rabbi of Moravia, seated in Oldenburg, and had not assumed his position in Frankfurt. Preaching in Oldenburg on Rosh Hashanah in 1830, he included the following significant statement: "Out of nature and out of history, the Lord speaks to you."

Hirsch was recognizing that there is a revelation of God to us through nature and through history—the two words we have previously come across in the analysis of Hirsch's teachings. Therefore Mordechai Breuer comes to the conclusion that when Hirsch speaks of *Torah im Derekh Eretz,* he does not intend a physical mixing of Torah and *Derekh Eretz,* but a chemical synthesis, where two elements fuse together and in which each constituent enriches the other. In other words, Torah is enriched by the application of modern methods of scholarship and research; and modern scholarship is enhanced by applying the insights and commitment of Torah.

For a while the debate remained relatively quiescent. But it flared up again on the death of Joseph Breuer in 1980 when there appeared in the *Jewish Observer,* published in America by the Agudah, an obituary jointly written by Ernst Bodenheimer, a leader of the Agudah, and Rabbi Nosson Scherman, editor of the *Artscroll* publications. In it they write that Breuer "lost no opportunity to refute the frequently heard argument that the philosophy of Rabbi Hirsch was a compromise, a temporary response to the problems of his time, a solution that was valid only in a Torah community under fire. Rabbi Breuer insisted that *Torah im Derekh Eretz* was a timeless credo." As we have seen before, that certainly was Breuer's conviction, but it was acknowledged even after his death by those who paid tribute to him.

On the other hand, the well-known Rabbi Shlomo Wolbe in Israel, in a tribute published in *Hama'ayan* (Teveth 1981) shortly after the passing of Rabbi Breuer, argues that Hirsch did not adopt the *Torah im Derekh*

Eretz principle before he came to Frankfurt. Wolbe also contends that Hirsch had refused to endorse a plea that made representations to Jerusalem for the introduction of some secular education. Wolbe uses these two instances to indicate that synthesis was not really Hirsch's own conviction, that under different circumstances, while in Oldenburg, he did not subscribe to *Torah im Derekh Eretz.*

Professor Mordechai Breuer disputes Rabbi Wolbe's assertion in a subsequent issue of *Hama'ayan* (Nissan 1981) and demonstrates instead that while Hirsch was still in Oldenburg he did advocate *Torah im Derekh Eretz,* as is evident in a plan he had published while there to establish a rabbinical seminary where he would combine modern scholarly teaching in secular subjects with rabbinic teaching. In fact, it was because of local opposition by rabbis who would not tolerate this combination that he had to leave Oldenburg, moving eventually to Frankfurt to further develop this idea. And likewise he argues that the refusal to intervene in Jerusalem was not because he did not believe in it, but simply because he recognized the sovereignty and the jurisdiction of the rabbinate in Jerusalem in its opposition to the innovation. Mordechai Breuer concludes his refutation of Wolbe's charges by asserting that Hirsch indeed followed the trail blazed by Solomon ibn Gabirol and by the Rambam who had influenced the whole of Jewish philosophy. Breuer then mentions that even R. Israel Salanter, who was a contemporary of Hirsch, engaged in secular pursuits both in Berlin and in Paris. Hirsch therefore was not all that much out of step with some of his own contemporaries.

How, then, is all this relevant today? Was *Torah im Derekh Eretz* genuine, or was it a compromise, a *Hora'at Sha'ah,* an emergency measure? To understand its relevance, if any, we must pose two questions. First, what would Hirsch have said to our generation were he to have lived a hundred years later? What would be his teachings now? And second, how timely is *Torah im Derekh Eretz* at the present time? Compromise or no compromise, under existing conditions, how relevant is this whole philosophy as we have now established it?

As to what Hirsch would have said to our generation, I suppose it is always purely speculative, if not altogether futile, to project a towering personality into another age and ask what he would have said or have done in a time in which he did not live. We are all children of our time— we are all largely the product of the age and circumstances in which we live. There is no telling how any of us would think and act were we to live in a different age.

Perhaps this is the literal meaning of our Sages when they tell us that we should seek judgment by going "to the judge who will be in those days." You can only act on the guidance of someone who lives in your time and knows the conditions that obtain in your age. A rabbi's authority extends only over his generation and his jurisdiction ends with his contemporaries. Therefore it is meaningless to ask whether the Rambam would be a Rosh yeshiva at Ponevez or in a yeshivat Heser, or perhaps a rabbi teaching at the Einstein Medical School at Yeshiva University were he alive today.

There is more justification in the second question. What are we to absorb from his teachings comparable to what we absorb from the Rambam and countless others who have preceded us and from whose fount of wisdom we drink to this day?

Here the Rambam does yield an instructive example. The Rambam's teachings are of course immortal. What he laid down as halakhah remains permanently valid. Yet the Aristotelian formulations of his philosophy as given in the *Guide for the Perplexed* are dated. The efforts the Rambam made to bring Jewish teachings in line with Aristotelian principles—the accepted philosophy of the Judeo-Arabic world in which he lived—is completely obsolete. But the orientation itself, the example of his effort to come to terms with the culture around him, is timeless.

Nor did the Rambam's teachings in terms of philosophy stand for a movement and for an ideology applicable anywhere or everywhere. They were adjusted to meet the needs of his environment, originally in Spain, and later in North Africa (Morocco and Egypt), where he faced a highly cultured secular environment to which he had to respond. For Franco-German Jewry of the twelfth century, however, the culture of their environment was so underdeveloped that they did not have to come to terms with it. In the Rambam, then, we have an illustration of some elements within his philosophy transcending time, while other more specific features relating to challenges of a bygone age have become obsolete.

Likewise, Hirsch's postulates were predicated on certain assumptions no longer valid and in some instances perhaps never valid. He assumed the inevitability of human progress—hence the humanism to which he subscribed. He was convinced, as a great German patriot, that he lived in a society and in an age that was moving towards the promised millennium of universal enlightenment and ultimately of human brotherhood. He believed in the mission of the Jews and their message to the

167

non-Jews around them. Wishful thinking or not, he and most of his contemporaries shared all these assumptions.

However, if some of these assumptions are tragically out of date, the balanced critique of Hirsch and his teachings by my late father-in-law, Rabbi Elie Munk, are still applicable today. In his critique, Munk emphasized the following:

1. Presently we are aware that Hirsch overestimated the value of Western civilization. Surely this overestimation was definitely understandable in the period in which he lived, for that civilization was as yet saturated with the ideas of the classic German humanists such as Kant, Beethoven, Goethe, Schiller. The philosophy of humanism represented traditional Torah....Unfortunately, the passing of time taught us that this philosophy was not able to resist historic and political change. One single century was enough to destroy our inspiration in the brilliant culture of humanism;

2. A second objection to Hirsch's system is that by definition it is a hybrid. It has been argued that these two respective cultures could never mix fully due to the fact that they are diametrically opposed. Accordingly people shaped by this double ideal carry within themselves a residue of internal contradictions, despite their outward appearance of harmonious unity. The end result consequently lowered the degree of culture. Therefore personalities who were the product of *Torah im Derekh Eretz* did not become outstanding spokesmen either for Western civilization or famous *Talmidei Chachamim* with very rare exceptions. This hybrid program did lead to a lowering in the knowledge of Torah in contrast to those students who attended the yeshivot;

3. Finally the entire system has been questioned at its core. For if the Torah represents for us the totality of all truth, then is it conceivable that it must have recourse to a culture outside of it?

Judaism is not only a religion but the expression of a total culture, rich enough to dispense with the need to borrow outside of itself.

This last argument however does not necessarily militate against *Torah im Derekh Eretz* as a possible way of life but rather strips it of its idealistic structure and interpretation. It is still conceivable to approve a method of synthesis of Jewish culture and positive elements of Western civilization that would enrich Judaism.

It is this practical attitude that has been accepted today by those committed to *Torah im Derekh Eretz*. They estimate that under the present conditions of life, it is necessary to combine the knowledge of science and other elements of the general culture with those of the Torah in order to create persons basically religious and capable at the same time of practicing the modern professions, especially in Eretz Yisrael where the need for these professions is so great.[10]

Whatever the reverses suffered by the *Torah im Derekh Eretz* movement, Hirsch is far from being a spent force. In many ways, his impact has reached a new peak. But his influence no longer lies in providing an ideological banner around which Orthodox Jews and their congregations can rally as a movement, any more than the *Guide* of Maimonides provides such guidance today. The value of Hirsch's immortal contributions as a thinker and supreme interpreter is to be found rather in providing unique insights into the Written and Oral Laws and the harmony between them and as a philosophical pathfinder showing the timeless capacity of Judaism to be applicable in every age and within all cultures, however advanced. His artistry in portraying the incomparable beauty of holiness remains as unsurpassed as his pedagogical skill and his powers of persuasion in teaching the discipline of Judaism in an age distracted by dazzling strides in science and technology, by the agony of the "*Weltschmerz,*" and by the allurements of religious nihilism, moral permissiveness and materialistic hedonism. Hirsch may yet prove a mighty factor in the inevitable regeneration of Israel's spiritual glory.

NOTES

*This essay is based on two of the author's earlier treatments of Hirsch's philosophy and influence, "Samson Raphael Hirsch: A Reappraisal of His Teachings and Influence in the Light of Our Times" (1971) and *"Torah im Derekh Eretz* Today" (1985).

1. The statement clearly dissents from the view of those who hold that this pursuit is to be condoned only, as he puts it, as a necessary evil, whereas Hirsch's intention really was to promote scholarly research out of genuine love for the advancement of the proper study of Torah and its enrichment.

2. Joseph Wohlgemuth, Editorial Note on "Thora und Wissenschaft," in *Jeschurun* 7 (1920), 511

3. Joseph Breuer, in *Mitteilungen* (New York, 1965).

4. Ibid.

5. Ibid.

6. Ibid. For these quotations, see also my *"Torah im Derekh Eretz* Today," in *L'Eylah* (London, New York Issue 5746), 38ff.

7. His first volume entitled *Judaism Eternal* (1956), that includes extracts from Hirsch's *Gesammelte Schriften,* collected writings, *Torah im Derekh Eretz* in the introductory essay, "Samson Raphael Hirsch: The Man and His Mission."

8. I. Grunfeld, *Judaism Eternal* (London, 1956), vol. 1, pp. xv, xviii.

9. I. Grunfeld, ed., *Horeb* (London, 1962), vol. 1, pp. xcv-xcvi.

10. See Munk's article in the French Jewish journal, *Traite-d'Union* (December 1956), which was translated by his children.

THE DEVELOPMENT AND DESIGN OF
A GERMAN-JEWISH PRAYERBOOK
Jakob J. Petuchowski

IN THE HISTORY OF LIBERAL OR REFORM JUDAISM, there have been three different types of prayerbook of which one or more may be in use at the same time in different kinds of congregations. One type is a modified form of the traditional *siddur*. It follows the rubrics of the traditional liturgy. It is meant for a worship service conducted primarily in Hebrew. It more often than not opens from right to left, the way a Hebrew book opens, and it includes the three traditional paragraphs of the *Shema' Yisrael*. Its departures from tradition consist primarily in the omission of the repetition of one and the same prayer or psalm within the same service, which is so frequent in the traditional liturgy, and the omission of the more recondite type of *piyyut* and of such Rabbinic passages as deal with the location within the Jerusalem Temple of different kinds of sacrifices, or with the fuels and wicks suitable for the Sabbath light. Other departures from tradition may take the form of abbreviations of traditional prayer texts by the omission of heaped-up synonyms, and by minor alterations of the wording of traditional prayer texts, dictated by theological considerations. Thus most prayerbooks of this type do not voice the longing for the Return to Zion, the Ingathering of the Exiles, and the restoration of the sacrificial cult—although there are exceptions to that rule. The twelfth of the Eighteen Benedictions, which in its present form calls for the destruction of the wicked, is either totally omitted or changed in wording so as to envisage the cessation of wickedness and arrogance, rather than the destruction of wicked and arrogant people. Prayers like the first paragraph of the *'Alenu,* in which the Election of Israel is expressed in negative terms ("who has not made us like other nations"), tend to be reworded positively ("who has chosen us for His service"). References to angels are liable to be reduced in European prayerbooks of this type, and to be totally expurgated in their American and British counterparts. And while American prayerbooks change the *go-el* ("redeemer") of the first of the Eighteen Benedictions to *ge-ullah* ("redemption"), and the reference to the Resurrection of the Dead in the second benediction to a reference to spiritual immortality, the majority of the European prayerbooks kept the Hebrew text of those two benedictions intact, even while many of them referred to spiritual immortality in the vernacular translation or paraphrase, and a few even rendered *go-el* as "redemption."

For it is one of the characteristics of this type of prayerbook that it contains a vernacular translation or paraphrase. The service itself may be primarily in Hebrew, but it is also taken for granted that the worshipper's knowledge of Hebrew is such that a vernacular translation cannot be dispensed with—except in the case of "school editions" of the prayerbook, in which a "pony" is intentionally withheld from the student.[1] Prayerbooks of this type usually also contain vernacular prayers for private meditation as well as vernacular prayers to be spoken by the rabbi at the beginning and end of services, prayers for the government and for the congregation, and prayers upon removing and replacing the Torah Scrolls, as well as introductions to the reminiscences of the Atonement rites in the Jerusalem Temple, and Memorial Services. Some prayerbooks also contain the vernacular texts of some hymns and of anthems to be sung before and after the sermon.

Representative of that type of "modified traditional *siddur*" are the *Hamburg Temple Prayerbook* of 1819 (and subsequent editions), the prayerbooks of 1854 and 1870, edited by Abraham Geiger, the liturgy of the West London Synagogue in England, published in the 1840s, Isaac Mayer Wise's *Minhag America* of 1857 (and subsequent editions), and the prayerbooks adopted by most major Jewish congregations in Germany—like Berlin, Munich, Leipzig, Nuremberg, Frankfurt, Königsberg, etc., where the main synagogue had opted for a "modernized" form of worship with organ accompaniment, while separate provisions were made for the Orthodox minorities to continue worshipping in their accustomed ways.

The second type of Liberal or Reform prayerbooks is anything but a

172

"modified traditional *siddur*." On the contrary, it is a prayer and meditation manual specifically composed for the "edification" and religious inspiration of the "modern" Jew. Here and there, a segment of the traditional liturgy might make an appearance, sometimes even in Hebrew, but the overall impression created by that type of prayerbook is that it does not want to be a museum of Jewish liturgical antiquities. This type of liturgy consciously departs from tradition not only in the ideas expressed, but also in the patterns of prayer and in the sequence of the rubrics. It is meant for a worship service primarily, if not indeed exclusively, conducted in the vernacular.

Representative of that type of prayerbook is the liturgy of the Berlin *Reformgemeinde,* which, from 1845 on, constantly underwent revisions—until, in the early 1930s, it had been reduced to a leaflet of no more than 64 pages. Those sixty-four pages contained the liturgy for the entire year, including the weekly services, the services for the three Pilgrim Festivals, for *two* days of Rosh Hashanah (!), Yom Kippur, Hanukkah, and Confirmation. Brevity, however, is not necessarily a characteristic of this type of prayerbook. The *Liberal Jewish Prayer Book,* edited by Israel I. Mattuck in London, culminating in the edition of 1957, is much more extensive. Mattuck seems to have subscribed to the notion that "variety is the spice of prayer," and his 1957 prayerbook contains no fewer than twenty-six different services for weekdays and Sabbaths. Unlike traditional prayerbooks, this volume contains selections from the Apocrypha, and, in a "Supplement," offers poems by Sir Philip Sidney, Emily Brontë, Browning, Wordsworth, Shelley, Tennyson, Milton, Coleridge, Keats, and others. It also contains a goodly amount of traditional Jewish liturgical material, often in Hebrew, although the services were meant to be conducted mainly in the vernacular. But, in order to provide the desired variety, and, possibly, to demonstrate his freedom from traditional mandates, Mattuck was very careful not to let the traditional prayers appear in their traditional sequence. Thus, in the Ninth Service, the first paragraph of the *Shema'* precedes, and the first two benedictions of the *'Amidah* follow the Reading of the Torah. (There is no *Qedushath* in that particular service.) In the Fifteenth Service, the *Qedushath Hashem* follows (!) the *Qedushath Hayyom*; and the Nineteenth Service actually begins (!) with an English version of the *'Alenu.*

Containing much less traditional material than Mattuck's liturgy, and approximating in brevity the prayer leaflet of the Berlin *Reformgemeinde,* are the "service manuals," primarily meant for Sunday

Morning Services, of a number of American Reform rabbis. *The Service Ritual* (Philadelphia, 1888) and *The Service Manual* (Philadelphia, 1892), both edited by Joseph Krauskopf, may here be mentioned as representative examples.

If the first type of Reform or Liberal prayerbook can be said to be primarily concerned with the *qebha'*, the fixed and traditional aspect of the Jewish liturgy, and if the second type can best be described as sacrificing the *qebha'* of the past to the *kawwanah,* the spontaneity, of the present, then, to those familiar with Hegel's thought, it should not come as a surprise that yet a third type of Reform prayerbook was brought into existence, one in which the demands of both *qebha'* and *kawwanah* were given equal consideration. The pioneer of that type of liturgy was David Einhorn, who published his prayerbook, *'Olath Tamid* in Baltimore in 1856-58.

'Olath Tamid contained many new prayers, composed by Einhorn himself, which expressed the *kawwanah* of the nineteenth-century Reform Jew. But those prayers were placed within the framework provided by the Jewish liturgical tradition. The (abbreviated) *Shema'* and its surrounding benedictions as well as the first and last three benedictions of the *'Amidah* were given in Hebrew, emended in accordance with Einhorn's Reform beliefs and in the form which the nascent *Wissenschaft des Judentums,* under the guidance of Leopold Zunz, had postulated them to have had in the early Rabbinic period. That constituted the *qebha'* element of *'Olath Tamid,* while Einhorn's own liturgical effusions, often enough incorporating biblical and Rabbinic components, represented the *kawwanah* element—which, for Einhorn and his Baltimore congregation, as well as for the other American congregations adopting *'Olath Tamid,* was meant to be recited in German.

It was Einhorn's *'Olath Tamid,* rather than Wise's *Minhag America,* which served the Central Conference of American Rabbis, an organization which Wise had founded, as the model on which the *Union Prayer Book,* published in 1894-95, was based. Wise thereupon withdrew his own *Minhag America.* That *Union Prayer Book,* undergoing several subsequent revisions, in its turn influenced, in a greater or lesser degree, the creation of Reform and Liberal liturgies in other parts of the world. The influence of the *Union Prayer Book* can be seen, although only in part, in Mattuck's London *Liberal Jewish Prayer Book,* first published in 1926, and, as far as form is concerned, to an even larger extent, in the 1925 *Rituel des Prières Journalières* of the Paris *Union Libérale Israélite,* and in Caesar Seligmann's 1910 Frankfurt *Israelitisches Gebetbuch* and its second edition in 1928.

The type of prayerbook which is of primary concern to us here is the first type we have described, i.e., the modified form of the traditional *siddur*. German Liberal Jewry had a large number of them.[2] As early as 1855, Rabbi M. Präger wrote in the Preface to the first edition of *Seder Ha'abbodah—Israelitisches Gebetbuch für…die israelitische Gemeinde in Mannheim*:

> Even those who desire to combine the venerable past with the living present, who neither want to remove all of the Hebrew nor retain it in its entirety,…even they might indignantly proclaim with the Prophet: "Your gods have become as many as your towns, O Judah!" (Jeremiah 11:13) As many prayerbooks as there are towns! There should be unity among the new Israel, just as there had been in the old. And there should not be different worship services in Frankfurt, in Mayence, in Coblenz, in Aachen, in Breslau, and in Hamburg!

Präger sympathized with the sentiment, but argued that, before there could be a common liturgy, there would have to be different experiments in different places. There were indeed to be many more experiments with a modernized liturgy than could have been dreamt of by Präger in 1855. But, as a result of those experimentations, no common Liberal prayerbook seemed to be forthcoming. As late as 1926, Heinrich Stern complained that there were five Liberal synagogues in Berlin, using three different prayerbooks![3]

Caesar Seligmann, who, as we shall see, was to become the moving spirit behind the common prayerbook once such a liturgy was ultimately to appear in 1929, blamed that state of affairs on "the Liberal conservatism of the communities or the vigorous opposition of Orthodoxy and Zionism."[4] To understand the full implications of Seligmann's accusation, one has to bear in mind that most major Jewish communities in Germany catered to *all* of the local Jews. The main synagogue in town was not a "denominational" Orthodox or Liberal synagogue, but the main *local* synagogue. Its rabbi might have Orthodox or Liberal leanings, but he was primarily employed as the *local* rabbi. If reforms were to be introduced into the local synagogue (an abbreviated liturgy, for example, or a mixed choir and organ accompaniment), or if a rabbi of Liberal tendencies was to be appointed, then the decision rested with the board of the entire Jewish community; and those of more traditionalist inclinations had to be convinced or outvoted. Ultimately there was indeed to be a Union of Liberal Rabbis, and a Union for Liberal Judaism for the laity. But the majority of German Jews, non-Orthodox though they may have been in practice, did not have the feeling of belonging to a different Jewish "denomination," the way in which American Jews think of themselves as Orthodox, Reform, Conservative, or Reconstructionist. Under the circumstances, even Liberal prayerbooks, to have any chance of adoption by a major Jewish community, had to take into consideration the religious susceptibilities of local Jews who, without being Orthodox in any technical sense, were more traditionally inclined.

Seligmann's reference to "the vigorous opposition of Orthodoxy or Zionism" had a specific application to the attempt at introducing a modernized prayerbook—really of a rather conservative character—in the State of Baden, in 1905, an attempt which led to a protracted controversy, in which the Zionists (who resented the rewording of the messianic prayers) joined forces with the Orthodox (who objected to any changes at all); and the two groups together succeeded in blocking the adoption of the new prayerbook.[5]

But in a way the Liberal Jews of Germany shared in the general conservatism in matters liturgical, common to all German Jews. Not only did two different Orthodox liturgies coexist on German soil: *minhag ashkenaz* (the German Rite) in West and South Germany, and *minhag polin* (the Polish Rite) in North and East Germany, but even within one and the same rite there might be local variations. Those variations might be slight, concerning the sequence in which certain *piyyutim* (poetic embellishments of the standard prayers) were to be recited, and sometimes even the sequence of words in one and the same prayer. Thus, while the *Abhinu Malkenu* litany in both the German and the Polish Rite contains the petition, "Our Father, our King, inscribe us in the book of pardon and forgiveness (*besepher selihah umehilah*)," prayerbooks of the German Rite will note that "in Frankfurt on the Main one says: 'book of forgiveness and pardon (*besepher mehilah uselihah*).'"[6]

Whether those local variants had any intrinsic significance or not, German Jews were very proud of their local *minhagim* (liturgical customs). Those *minhagim,* in a way, were an expression of local *kawwanah* (spontaneity) within the overall *qebha'* (routine). They were also a memorial to those local forebears who had introduced them in the first place, pious ancestors to whom one was connected by ties of family, rather than the prescriptions of some more general, amorphous body of

176

"Sages of Israel"—even though some pious country folk may not have been above believing that their particular local variant was part and parcel of the Sinaitic Revelation itself.

German Liberal Jews shared that religious "local patriotism" with their Orthodox coreligionists. When Abraham Geiger revised his 1854 prayerbook in 1870, he not only gave it a more pronounced "Reform" character, but he also meant for this revised edition to make its way into a number of different Jewish communities. The 1854 edition had been intended specifically for the Breslau community, which Geiger had served at that particular time. Consequently Geiger's 1870 prayerbook was published in two different editions: one for *minhag ashkenaz,* and one for *minhag polin.* And, to anticipate a little, when German Liberal Jewry finally did get around, in 1929, to the publication of its *Einheitsgebetbuch* ("Union Prayer Book"), that prayerbook appeared in three different editions: one for Frankfurt, one for Berlin, and one for Breslau!

The first steps taken in the direction of issuing a common prayerbook for all the Liberal Jews of Germany were not so much motivated by ideological considerations as they were forced upon German Liberal Jews by economic conditions. That is openly admitted by Caesar Seligmann, who took the initiative in getting such a common prayerbook published. In his autobiographical memoirs, Seligmann wrote:

> The question of an *Einheitsgebetbuch* became acute again in Germany when the economic distress of the postwar period made it impossible for the communities to publish new editions of their out-of-print prayerbooks. At my urging, the Union for Liberal Judaism, in 1922, appointed a Prayerbook Commission, which laid down the outlines of the *Einheitsgebetbuch* in accordance with my suggestions. At the main assembly of the Liberal rabbis in Cologne, in 1925, I spoke about "Principal Questions and Principles of the Liberal *Einheitsgebetbuch.*" In order to assure a positive outcome, I propagated the idea that, to begin with, the three large communities of Berlin, Frankfort, and Breslau, all of which had adopted Geiger's prayerbook,—each one, to be sure, with its own local variations,—should unite for the purpose of adopting a common prayerbook. Prior to that, I had spoken with the leading personalities of those three communities. My suggestion then found the lively support of Baeck-Berlin and Vogelstein-Breslau. After the Liberal Worship Commission of the Prussian Union of Jewish Communities, over which I presided, had been constituted, that Worship Commission undertook the further preparatory work. I took on the

main task: Editor-in-Chief, drawing up the first draft and preparing the German translation of the Hebrew prayers. Elbogen worked particularly on the Hebrew text; and Elbogen and Vogelstein undertook, each one for himself, the painstaking reading and correction of the manuscript pages and the galley proofs. A large number of outstanding experts was brought in for a further reading of the galleys.[7]

To appreciate fully what Seligmann here condensed into a few lines, the modern American reader might find it helpful to have more detailed information about the persons and institutions mentioned by Seligmann:

There is, first of all, Seligmann himself. Caesar Seligmann (1860-1950), a graduate of the Conservative Jewish Theological Seminary in Breslau, was, at first, a rabbi of the famous Hamburg Temple, and then, for many years, he served as a rabbi of the Frankfurt Jewish community, officiating at the Liberal Westend Synagogue. He also became prominent as an ideologue of German Liberal Judaism, both through his organizational work and through his writings and his editorship of journals championing the Liberal Jewish cause. In 1910, Seligmann produced a prayerbook in two volumes, of which a second edition, with the Hebrew components greatly expanded, appeared in 1928. He was also the editor of a widely used Passover Haggadah, published in 1914. His liturgical productions showed Seligmann's flair for language, his aesthetic sense, and his unique ability to blend tradition with modernity. At that, Seligmann's liturgical works come closest, on the European continent, to that kind of blend of tradition with modernity, which, in the United States, was exemplified by Einhorn's 'Olath Tamid and by the Union Prayer Book—although Seligmann stayed closer to the traditional rubrics and wording than the American liturgies did.[8]

Leo Baeck (1873-1956) was, of course, the most representative figure of German Judaism in the twentieth century. Although liberal in his religious outlook and ultimately serving as the President of the World Union for Progressive Judaism, Baeck was traditional in his personal religious practice, recognized the duality inherent in Judaism (universalism *and* particularism; immanence *and* transcendence; prophet *and* priest; mystery *and* commandment; etc.), and rated the noun "Judaism" higher than the adjectives "Orthodox," "Liberal," and "Conservative." Thus he managed at one and the same time to serve as a member of the executive of the Central Union of German Citizens of the Jewish Faith, as a vice president of the German pro-Zionist *Keren Hayesod* and also as a non-Zionist member of the Jewish Agency. No wonder that, at the hour

178

of its supreme crisis, German Jewry of all shades of religious belief chose Leo Baeck to head its representative body.[9]

Ismar Elbogen (1874-1943) was, in his time, *the* internationally recognized expert in the field of Jewish Liturgy. His book, *Der jüdische Gottesdienst in seiner geschichtlichen Entwicklung* (Jewish Worship in Its Historical Development), first published in 1913, appeared in several editions, and an updated Hebrew translation of the work appeared in 1972. In addition to liturgy, Elbogen taught history and Talmud at the Berlin *Hochschule für die Wissenschaft des Judentums,* the Liberal rabbinical seminary of Germany. He also took an active part in the institutional and organizational life of the German-Jewish community. Like his colleague Leo Baeck, Elbogen, too, was active in the World Union for Progressive Judaism, and tended to be traditional in his personal religious practice. His ability to transcend the "denominational" divisions within Judaism is dramatized by the fact that, in 1938, he was brought to the United States by the joint efforts of the Hebrew Union College, the Jewish Institute of Religion (then still separate institutions), the Jewish Theological Seminary of America, and Dropsie College.[10]

Hermann Vogelstein (1870-1942), rabbi in Oppeln, Königsberg, and Breslau, was one of the leading Liberal rabbis of Germany, as his father, Heinemann Vogelstein, was before him. In 1894, Heinemann Vogelstein had produced an edition of Geiger's 1870 prayerbook for use by the Westphalian congregations, applying the Reform principle even more rigorously than Geiger himself had done. His son, Hermann, also took a somewhat more radical Liberal position than most of his colleagues in the Liberal rabbinate. Nevertheless he was able to say in 1928:

> If, in the early period of Liberalism, it was a question of fighting against the preponderance of forms, which threatened to kill the soul of religion, and to make room for development, today we are able to face with complete freedom the problem of the religious language of forms. The unconditional and uncritical submission to the form is unfree. But equally unfree is its unconditional rejection.[11]

The Union for Liberal Judaism (*Vereinigung für das liberale Judentum*) had been founded in 1908. It was primarily an organization of the Liberal Jewish laity to promote the concerns of Liberal Judaism within the German-Jewish communities. In 1912, it "shelved," rather than accepted a set of "Guiding Principles" (*Richtlinien*) of Liberal Jewish belief and

179

practice, which had been proposed by the Union of Liberal Rabbis, and urged particularly by Seligmann. In 1919, the Union for Liberal Judaism had 47 local chapters with about 4,000 members. By 1930, the number of chapters had gone down to 42, but the number of members had increased to about 10,000.[12]

If we bear in mind that, in 1925, there were 564,379 Jews in Germany,[13] and that, at that time, the majority of the German Jews did not consider themselves to be Orthodox, the 10,000 members of the Union for Liberal Judaism must have been particularly self-conscious champions of ideological purity, but hardly representative of the typical German Liberal Jew. That may have been at least a partial reason for the rather "conservative" character of the *Einheitsgebetbuch* upon its appearance in 1929.

The Prussian Union of Jewish Communities (*Preussischer Landesverband jüdischer Gemeinden*) was founded in 1921, with the aim of uniting all synagogal congregations in Prussia for the pursuit of common interests—particularly in raising the level of religious life, and, while preserving the independence of the individual congregations, in creating and maintaining common institutions, in representing the Prussian Jewish community in all common concerns, and in supporting the financially weak congregations. It was governed by a council consisting of 35 members, of whom six had to be rabbis, and two had to be teachers. For matters relating to worship and education, two separate commissions were provided, corresponding to the two religious wings, Orthodox and Liberal, of the Prussian Jewish community.[14] It was, therefore, through the Liberal Worship Commission of the Prussian Union of Jewish Communities, over which he presided, that Caesar Seligmann had to steer his *Einheitsgebetbuch*.

The *Einheitsgebetbuch,* officially called *Tephilloth lekhol hashanah—Gebetbuch für das ganze Jahr* (Prayerbook for the Whole Year), consists of two volumes: volume I containing the prayers for weekdays, Sabbaths and festivals, and volume II containing the prayers for New Year and the Day of Atonement. The title-page of each volume bears the seal of Wolf Heidenheim, just as the most widely used prayerbook of German Orthodox Jewry did, the famous "Roedelheim Siddur." Heidenheim (1757-1832) had, of course, nothing to do with the *Einheitsgebetbuch*. His seal on the title-page indicated, on one level, nothing more than the fact that the printer and publisher of the *Einheitsgebetbuch* was the one who had purchased the printing and publishing establishment founded by Heidenheim, which, in 1806, had published Heidenheim's edition of the Orthodox prayerbook, *Siddur Sephath Emeth,* and which had continued publishing it through the generations.[15] But much more is conveyed, on other levels, by Heidenheim's seal on the title-page of the *Einheitsgebetbuch.* Heidenheim's prayerbooks were cherished for the correctness of their grammar and the satisfying aesthetics of their typography. Moreover, Heidenheim's seal on the title-page of the *Einheitsgebetbuch* also indicated very clearly that the prayerbook was to be perceived as an authentic Jewish prayerbook, and not as the mere worship manual of some sectarian group.

That impression was quite justified, and we recall in this connection that Ismar Elbogen, the universally recognized expert in the field of Jewish Liturgy, had been put in charge of producing the Hebrew text. Volume I begins with the weekday morning service, which, as a matter of course, contains the benedictions for donning the *tallith* and the *tephillin.* The two volumes between them provide all the worship services of the year, mandated by the Jewish liturgical tradition, including the second days of New Year and the three Pilgrim Festivals, services for Hanukkah, Purim, and the Ninth of Abh, the *musaph* for Sabbaths, festivals, the High Holydays, and New Moon, the special inserts for fast days and the Ten Days of Repentance, and even the *minhah* services for the Eve of New Year and the Eve of the Day of Atonement. Moreover, while a few German prayers do figure within parts of the High Holyday liturgy, the prayerbook is obviously usable for services conducted almost entirely in Hebrew. What is more, the German translation accompanying the Hebrew text is not a paraphrase of the kind used by many other Liberal and Reform prayerbooks, including Seligmann's own *Israelitisches Gebetbuch,* but a real translation, which does not shrink from translating *go-el* in the first of the Eighteen Benedictions as *Erlöser* ("redeemer"), or from translating *mehayyeh hamethim* in the second of the Eighteen Benedictions as *der die Toten belebt* ("who revives the dead"). No wonder that many an American Reform Jew, when shown the *Einheitsgebetbuch,* tends to classify it at once as "Conservative," if not indeed as "Orthodox."

But that turns out to be a wrong classification. Not only does each volume contain an Appendix with new German prayers, which can be used either to supplement or to replace some of the Hebrew prayers, as well as German anthems to be sung before and after the sermon, but the editors, in their Introduction, also suggest that some congregations might choose to substitute, in some instances, the German translation for the Hebrew original. There is also a quite recognizable abbreviation of the various worship services—some traditional prayers being entirely omitted, while in others the number of synonyms used in one and the same prayer is heavily cut. Above all, changes based on theological considerations have been consistently introduced throughout the prayerbook, even though the attempt has been made to make the new versions *sound* as much as possible like the old ones for which they have been substituted.

The American Reform Jew may regard the substitution of "redemption" for "redeemer" and of spiritual immortality for physical resurrection as shibboleths for the true "Reform" character of a liturgy, whereas the German Liberal Jew managed to understand those traditional images as metaphors. But apart from those two instances, the *Einheitsgebetbuch* is theologically just as "Reform" as the *Union Prayer Book* in America used to be in Reform Judaism's "classical" phase. That is to say that, while the *Einheitsgebetbuch* has not removed all liturgical references to Jerusalem, as some other Reform and Liberal prayerbooks have done, it contains no petitions for the Return to Zion, the Ingathering of the Exiles, the reinstatement of the Davidic dynasty, and the restoration of the sacrificial cult. With the exception of the Day of Atonement, when the Temple service of the ancient High Priest is recalled in the *musaph* prayer (the 'Abhodah), even the *Musaph* Services do not contain as much as a historical reminiscence of the ancient sacrificial cult. The angelology of the traditional prayerbook has been considerably reduced, and particularly crass expressions of particularism have been softened or omitted. The new Hebrew version of *Kol Nidré,* instead of asking God, as the traditional version does, for an annulment of vows, actually pleads with God to *accept* the vows which people are making on the Day of Atonement.[16]

Comparing the individual prayers in the *Einheitsgebetbuch* with those of the traditional Ashkenazi prayerbook would be very instructive, but, alas, it would also go far beyond scope of the present study. However, equally indicative of the spirit of the *Einheitsgebetbuch* are the Scripture readings provided by this prayerbook, both in the Hebrew original and in the German translation, when seen in terms of their agreements with the traditional readings, and in terms of their divergences. It should here be pointed out that the *Einheitsgebetbuch* maintains the custom of reading from *two* Torah Scrolls on festivals and High Holydays, and from *three* Torah Scrolls on *Simhath Torah*. Also the number of people "called" to the Torah on the various occasions corresponds to that stipulated by tradition. Three illustrations should help to clarify what has been said:

(a) On the first day of Passover, the traditional reading from the first Torah Scroll is Exodus 12:21-51, that is to say, the law about smearing the blood of the Paschal lamb on the lintels of the door, and the story of the Exodus itself. The *Einheitsgebetbuch* provides for the reading of Exodus 12:29-51, a reading which, in essence, is identical with that of the tradition, but shorter, and omitting the law about the smearing of the blood.

The traditional reading from the second Torah Scroll is Numbers 28:15-25, which commands the observance of Passover, the eating of unleavened bread, and the abstention from work, and which ordains the special sacrifices to be brought on Passover. The *Einheitsgebetbuch* provides for the reading of Numbers 28:16-18, again a reading which is *partially* identical with the traditional one, but which omits the laws about the special sacrifices.

The traditional *Haphtarah* for the first day of Passover is Joshua 5:2-6:1, the story of the mass circumcision which occurred at the time of Israel's entry into the Promised Land, so that all the male Israelites could participate in the Passover sacrifice. The *Einheitsgebetbuch* provides instead for the reading of Isaiah 43:1-21, a passage in which Israel is told not to be afraid, for God will redeem Israel from Babylonian exile as He had done from Egyptian slavery.

(b) On the eighth day of Passover, the traditional reading from the first Torah Scroll is Deuteronomy 14:22-16:17, which deals with the giving of the tithe, with the sabbatical year, with the dedication of the firstborn, and with the festival calendar. The *Einheitsgebetbuch* provides for the reading of Deuteronomy 15:12-16:17, that is to say, basically the traditional reading in a slightly abbreviated form.

The traditional reading from the second Torah Scroll is Numbers 28:19-25, which deals with the special sacrifices for Passover. The *Einheitsgebetbuch* here departs from the traditional reading, and instead provides for the reading of Exodus 23:14-17, a brief festival calendar, in which Passover is also mentioned.

The traditional *Haphtarah* is Isaiah 10:32-12:6, a messianic prophecy. The *Einheitsgebetbuch* has Isaiah 11:1-10; 12:1-16, that is to say, an abbreviated form of the traditional reading.

(c) On the first day of Shabhu'oth, the traditional reading from the first Torah Scroll is Exodus 19:1-20:23, describing the Sinaitic Revelation. The *Einheitsgebetbuch* reading is Exodus 19:1-20:22, i.e., just one verse less than the traditional reading. The omitted verse reads: "Do not ascend My altar by steps, that your nakedness may not be exposed upon it."

The traditional reading from the second Torah Scroll is Numbers 28:26-31, dealing with the special sacrifices to be offered on Pentecost. The *Einheitsgebetbuch* calls for the reading of Deuteronomy 16:9-12, i.e., the verses dealing with the Festival of Shabhu'oth in the festival calendar of Deuteronomy.

The traditional *Haphtarah* is Ezekiel 1:1-28; 3:12, a description of Ezekiel's vision, obviously chosen in order to carry on the Revelation theme of the reading from the first Torah Scroll. The *Einheitsgebetbuch* provides for the reading of Isaiah 6:1-13, that is to say, Isaiah's description of his vision. In this connection, it should be recalled that, according to the fourth-century Babylonian Amora, Rabha, Ezekiel and Isaiah had really been the recipients of the identical vision, but that Isaiah had a more urbane manner of reporting it.[17] Altogether, the traditional reading of Ezekiel's vision is somewhat problematic, and many traditionalist rabbis forbade translating it, because, as Rabbi S. Bamberger put it, "the sublime character of this *Haphtarah* cannot be expressed in a translation."[18] Of course, even a translation would be rather hard for a modern Jew to understand. But no such problems beset the sixth chapter of the Book of Isaiah, and it is easy to see why the editors of the *Einheitsgebetbuch* preferred it to the traditional *Haphtarah*.

What emerges from the above comparisons is not only the *Einheitsgebetbuch*'s tendency to abbreviate lengthy traditional readings, and to confine itself to readings which are relevant to both occasion and worshipper, but also its avoidance of passages dealing with the sacrificial cult, as well as its endeavor to substitute more easily comprehensible passages for some of the more recondite traditional ones. Yet it is all done with a sensitivity to the spirit of the Jewish liturgical tradition, and, notwithstanding the espousal of a liberal theology, with as little rejection of traditional practice as possible. And what we have said about the *Einheitsgebetbuch*'s Scripture readings can also be said about the *Einheitsgebetbuch* as a whole. That is, in fact, that prayerbook's distinguishing feature, particularly when we compare it with the liturgical works of the second and the third type, which we have described in our introductory section, above.

When Liberal Jews accustomed to the *Einheitsgebetbuch* had occasion to visit an Orthodox service, they might have felt that the service was too long, but they did not feel like strangers in some exotic place. If perchance Orthodox Jews ventured into a service where the *Einheitsgebetbuch* was used, they might have objected to the organ accompaniment, the mixed choir, the omission of certain prayers and the verbal changes in others; but they would have known and recognized the major rubrics of the service and the individual components of each rubric. Unlike many another prayerbook which has been produced by Reform or Liberal liturgists, the *Einheitsgebetbuch* did not contribute to the alienation of Jew from Jew.

The *Einheitsgebetbuch* appeared in 1929. Nine years later, most German synagogues were destroyed, and the National Socialist persecution, which had begun in 1933, was moving towards its horrible climax. It is thus impossible to judge the full effect, positive or negative, which the *Einheitsgebetbuch* had on the devotional life of German Liberal Jewry. The prayerbook was widely, but not universally used. Even in congregations where the cantor conducted services according to the *Einheitsgebetbuch,* and where the rabbi recited some of the *Einheitsgebetbuch*'s German prayers, the congregants could still follow the service by making judicious use of the traditional *siddur.*

It is also known that Ismar Elbogen, the liturgist who was responsible for the Hebrew text of the *Einheitsgebetbuch,* and who was active in the World Union for Progressive Judaism, attended, for his own devotional needs, the services of a private Orthodox synagogue founded by members of the Jewish *intelligentsia* in Berlin's Lessingstrasse, a synagogue of which Elbogen continued to be a member.[19] And it has been reported to this writer by an eye-witness that, when the students of the Berlin *Hochschule* visited Leo Baeck during the *shibhe'ah* for his wife, Natalie, in 1937, they were surprised to see that Baeck used the traditional *siddur* at the *minyan* in his home, rather than the *Einheitsgebetbuch,* the publication of which he had encouraged.

But then it is not altogether unheard of that Liberal and Reform rabbis publish, or encourage the publication of, prayerbooks to meet what they perceive to be the needs of the laity, while they themselves find their own devotional needs quite adequately met by the traditional liturgy. That is a subject which still remains to be investigated further.

On the other hand, German-Jewish refugees carried the

Einheitsgebetbuch with them in their emigration. In 1960, the *Verbond van Liberaal Religieuze Joden in Nederland* issued a photo-offset edition of volume II of the *Einheitsgebetbuch,* while, in 1962, an English trans-lation of that same volume by Jakob J. Kokotek was published in England.[20] And the liturgy edited by Fritz Pinkuss and Henrique Lemle for the Liberal Jewish congregations in São Paulo and Rio de Janeiro, Brazil, published in the 1960s, acknowledges the *"influência decisiva"* of the German *Einheitsgebetbuch.*[21] The influence of the *Einheitsgebetbuch* is also evident in the Liberal Jewish prayerbook published in the Nether-lands in 1964.[22]

Jews accustomed to the American *Union Prayer Book* might prefer, as did Abraham Z. Idelsohn, the prayerbook published by Seligmann in 1910, and revised in 1928, because it facilitates a more compact worship service, although hardly a more "traditional" one, as Idelsohn claims.[23] And the criticisms which Idelsohn levels against some of the Hebrew texts of the *Einheitsgebetbuch* should more appropriately have been levelled by him against Abraham Geiger and the prayerbook of the Neue Synagoge in Berlin, where those particular texts originated. Seligmann's 1910 prayerbook, it will be recalled, has been described by us as that European Liberal prayerbook which most closely approximated in structure and form the American *Union Prayer Book.* Yet the fact re-mains that it was Seligmann himself who withdrew his own prayerbook in favor of the *Einheitsgebetbuch.* Since a revised version of Seligmann's prayerbook appeared in 1928, that is, one year before the publication of the *Einheitsgebetbuch,* Seligmann must have been engaged, at one and the same time, in the revision work on his own prayerbook and in the editing of the *Einheitsgebetbuch,* which, within a year, was to displace it!

That act of self-abnegation calls to mind a similar act on the part of Isaac M. Wise, who withdrew his own *Minhag America* in favor of the *Union Prayer Book.* The difference between Wise and Seligmann is that Wise withdrew a prayerbook of the first type in favor of a prayerbook of the third type, while Seligmann withdrew a prayerbook of the third type in favor of a prayerbook of the first type. But both Wise and Seligmann, separated though they were in time and in place, acted out of the same deeply felt concern for unity in the devotional life of Reform and Liberal Jewry.

NOTES

1. An example is Heinemann Vogelstein, ed., *Israelitisches Gebetbuch für Schule und Haus* (Bielefeld, 1896).

2. Cf. the chronological bibliography in Jakob J. Petuchowski, *Prayerbook Reform in Europe* (New York, 1968), 1-21.

3. Heinrich Stern in: *International Conference of Liberal Jews* (London, 1926), 46.

4. Caesar Seligmann, *Erinnerungen* (Frankfurt-am-Main: Waldemar Kramer, 1975), 169.

5. Cf. Petuchowski, op. cit., 39-42.

6. Cf., e.g., *Siddur Saphah Berurah* (Basel: Victor Goldschmidt, 1964), 235.

7. Seligmann, op. cit., 169f. See also the English translation of the Introduction to the *Einheitsgebetbuch* in: Petuchowski, op. cit., 206-13.

8. On Seligmann, see Seligmann, op. cit., and Michael A. Meyer, "Caesar Seligmann and the Development of Liberal Judaism in Germany at the Beginning of the Twentieth Century," in *HUCA* 40-41 (1969-70), 529-54.

9. On Baeck, see Albert H. Friedlander, *Leo Baeck—Teacher of Theresienstadt* (New York, 1968).

10. On Elbogen, see Alexander Marx, "Ismar Elbogen: An Appreciation," in: Ismar Elbogen, *A Century of Jewish Life* (Philadelphia, 1946), xi-xx; and Erwin Rosenthal, "Ismar Elbogen and the New Jewish Learning," in: *LBIYB* 8 (1963), 3-28.

11. Hermann Vogelstein, "Der gegenwärtige Stand des Liberalismus in Deutschland," in: *First Conference of the World Union for Liberal Judaism* (Berlin, 1928), 29f.

12. Cf. Max Joseph, "Vereinigung für das Liberale Judentum," in: *Jüdisches Lexikon*, vol. 5, cols. 1175-77.

13. See the statistical table in: *Jüdisches Lexikon*, vol. 2, cols. 147-48.

14. Cf. Ismar Freund, "Preussischer Landesverband jüdischer Gemeinden," in *Jüdisches Lexikon*, vol. 4, cols. 1117-19.

15. This writer has in his possession the edition of 1931, which proudly identifies itself on the title-page as the 154th edition of *Siddur Sephath Emeth!*

16. For the textual changes within the Eighteen Benedictions, see Petuchowski, op. cit., 214-39. For the new version of *Kol Nidré*, see *idem*, op. cit., 346.

17. B. *Hagigah* 13b.

18. Quoted in: Jenny Marmorstein, trans., *Prayerbook for the Feast of Weeks* (Basel: Victor Goldschmidt, A.M. 5727), 88.

19. Cf. Max M. Sinasohn, *Die Berliner Privatsynagogen und ihre Rabbiner* (Jerusalem, 1971), 72.

20. Jakob J. Kokotek, ed. and trans., *Tephilloth lekhol hashanah—Prayer Book for Jewish Worship throughout the Year*, rev. ed. Part II: New Year and Day of Atonement (London: New Liberal Jewish Congregation, 1962).

21. F. Pinkuss and H. Lemle, eds., *Sidur—Livro de Rezas para todo o Ano Israelita*, 2d ed. (São Paulo/Rio de Janeiro, 1966); H. Lemle and Fr. Pinkuss, eds., *Machsor—Livro de Rezas para os Dias Sagrados de Rosh-Hashana—Yom Kippur*, 3d ed. (Rio de Janeiro/São Paulo, 1966).

22. *Seder Tobh Lehodoth*, 2 vols. (Amsterdam: Verbond van Liberaal Religieuze Joden in Nederland, 1964).

23. Cf. Abraham Z. Idelsohn, *Jewish Liturgy and Its Development* (New York, 1932), 298-300.

ZIONISM AND ZIONISTS IN GERMANY BEFORE WORLD WAR I

Simcha Kling

THERE IS A WIDESPREAD MISCONCEPTION that the rebirth of Jewish nationalism and culture in the late nineteenth and early twentieth centuries stemmed almost exclusively from the Jews of Eastern Europe. True, they were foremost in reviving the Hebrew language and Hebraic culture just as they were in advocating and engaging in the actual settlement of *Eretz Yisrael*. However, the role of Jews reared in German culture was also crucial to the founding and progress of Zionism. These German Jews, albeit a minority, saw the folly of assimilation and, though comfortable with German *Kultur,* recognized the national character of the Jewish people.[1]

The majority of German Jews yearned for integration into the larger community and were prepared to discard their Jewish heritage in order to be accepted as true Germans. Although few actually converted to Christianity, the majority simply gave up distinctive Jewish practices. Their efforts, however, were largely in vain, for, as the historian Walter Laqueur has observed, "By and large, a love affair between Jews and Germans remained one-sided and unreciprocated..."[2] A small group of German Jews were sensitive to the national character of the Jewish people and were convinced that the Jews needed a homeland of their own. Some of their leaders are the subject of this essay.

Max Bodenheimer (1865-1940) was a Zionist long before the appearance of Theodor Herzl. Upon his death, the *Palestine Post* spoke of him as "the practical talent without whom Herzl's dream might never have become a reality" and went on to say: "Neither the Congress nor its programme could have come about without the skill, devotion and organizing genius of Dr. Max Bodenheimer, probably Herzl's most loyal and efficient champion." When he was in his early thirties, Bodenheimer wrote to the revered Professor Hermann Schapira of Heidelberg University:

> I remember as if it happened today, how the Zionist idea overtook me with such force that I was unable to think of anything else for weeks. I came to realize that even if *Eretz Yisrael* was sandy desolation and any settlement activity scorned, it would be necessary to create the national center there.[3]

In 1890 Bodenheimer settled in the city of Cologne where he practiced law, but his concern for the precariousness of Jewish life in the Diaspora led him to use most of his time and talents to advance the Zionist cause. Years later in his memoirs Bodenheimer wrote:

> Since Jew-hatred is rooted in Jews being scattered among the nations, the evil can be removed only by creating a new breed of the people through gathering many Jews in their own land. But where is the land that can serve as a refuge? That can only be *Eretz Yisrael,* the ancient home of the Jewish people.[4]

In 1891, Bodenheimer wrote a pamplet to voice his conviction that his people was sick and needed healing and restoration to a national life. Called *Wohin mit den russischen Juden?* (Whither Russian Jews?), it led to some writers to classify Bodenheimer as a nationalist in the tradition of Moses Hess and Leo Pinsker. Bodenheimer called for a gathering of all Zionist organizations, the creation of a bank to finance agriculture and industry, the establishment of settlements on the shores of the Kinneret, the utilization of the Dead Sea for potash and table salt, and the financing of the new settlements through a joint stock company.

Soon after the publication of the pamphlet, Bodenheimer and his Cologne friend, David Wolffsohn, established a Zionist society, *Die Nationaljüdische Vereinigung,* which warmly responded to Herzl's call for a Zionist Congress in 1897. Bodenheimer hoped that others would also respond. One of those whom he persuaded to accept Herzl's call was Professor Hermann Schapira (1840-1898), a teacher of mathematics at Heidelberg University. Schapira had come from Eastern Europe, was an ordained rabbi at the age of 20 who received his doctorate at the age of forty and remained on the faculty as an observant Jew. A founder of

Hibbat Zion, he deeply believed that Jews should rebuild the Promised Land, but did not see the need for a Jewish state.

Bodenheimer carried on an extensive correspondence with the learned professor and convinced him that diplomatic efforts to establish a Jewish state would not endanger the efforts of the colonists already settled in the land nor erase the need for a spiritual center for the Jewish people in Palestine. The two men decided to meet, but before they were able to do so Herzl issued his call for his Congress which required a formal organization of Zionists in Germany. A call was issued for all Zionists to convene and they decided that they should participate in the First Congress and establish a German Zionist organization, praying "that the Congress may usher in a new era in the history of our people on its way to freedom." Dr. Bodenheimer was able to persuade Professor Schapira to attend the Zionist Congress in Basle where the venerated scholar put forth his suggestions for a Jewish National Fund and a Hebrew University.

Appointed to draft the by-laws and create the Jewish National Fund, Dr. Bodenheimer was named the Fund's first director, a post he held from 1907 to 1914. His responsibilities were formidable: organizing and raising funds, attending meetings and promoting public relations, traveling and speaking, advising and being involved in settlement projects. He did this without a salary, insisting on earning his living solely as an attorney.

It was in his capacity as Jewish National Fund director that Bodenheimer was able in 1909 to secure the loans necessary for 600 families to purchase the land that became the city of Tel Aviv. He also arranged the financing of the land bought on Mt. Scopus in 1908 for the Hebrew University.

In these years Bodenheimer's approach and that of the Zionist leadership in Germany was attacked by another more radical group of German Zionists as being patronizing and philanthropic. Kurt Blumenfeld, a student leader of the Zionist movement and from 1910 to 1914 director of the Department of Information of the World Zionist Organization Executive, proclaimed the necessity for a heightened Zionist consciousness, including a commitment to *aliyah* as part of a post-assimilationist German Zionism. Bodenheimer and the mainstream Zionist leadership were, by their own admission, more limited in their goals, ever-insisting that their brand of Zionism did not compromise their German convictions. Bodenheimer went so far as to discount Blumenfeld's radicalism as "rhetorical twaddle and drivel."[5] Although in

1933 Blumenfeld did settle in Palestine, the modest emigration to Palestine from Germany indicates the limits of his influence among German Jews. Meanwhile Bodenheimer could point to the accomplishments of the Jewish National Fund as ample proof that his "philanthropic Zionism" was not misguided or without substance.

When World War I broke out, Dr. Bodenheimer was most concerned about keeping the Jewish National Fund from falling apart, for contact with its many branches throughout Europe could not continue in the midst of war. Bodenheimer decided to transfer the offices to a neutral country, which was no simple task. Just one hour before the Dutch-German border closed, he managed to send all of the Fund's papers to Holland in two railroad cars. As a result of his actions, the office could be reconstructed and the Jewish National Fund was able to continue its work throughout the war.

Bodenheimer admired his colleague, David Wolffsohn, but recognized that he lacked the charismatic leadership qualities of Herzl. Nevertheless, when Herzl died in 1904 and Wolffsohn was persuaded to succeed him as president of the World Zionist Organization, Bodenheimer pledged him complete loyalty. Under Wolffsohn, the Zionist headquarters were moved to Cologne which allowed Bodenheimer an active role. In addition to his duties as head of the National Fund he also served as president of the German Zionist Organization.

Wolffsohn adhered strictly to his predecessor's policy of pursuing the development of a Jewish state by diplomatic, rather than pragmatic, means. That meant paying little heed to the settlements in Palestine or the encouragement of cultural activities. The "Practical Zionists" opposed him vigorously because they believed that the World Zionist Organization should place its priorities on settling Jews on the land and fostering the Jewish cultural renascence. After protracted struggle, they succeeded in deposing Wolffsohn from the presidency and in moving the Zionist headquarters from Cologne to Berlin. Bodenheimer was not prepared to uproot himself and therefore resigned his offices. He continued to write on Zionist matters but, after World War I, his influence was more limited. It was not until 1935 that he moved to Jerusalem where he continued to write and to participate in meetings, although no longer playing a central role in the Zionist leadership.

Unlike Bodenheimer, David Wolffsohn (1856-1914) was not a native German. He was born in Lithuania and grew up in an Orthodox, Yiddish-speaking home. He moved to Germany as a teenager and eventually settled in Cologne where he became a successful businessman. Wolffsohn became active in the local Jewish Literary Society where he first met Dr. Max Bodenheimer. Together they established the Cologne Association for the Furthering of Agriculture and Handicrafts in Palestine. His deep faith in the Zionist cause is expressed in this address presented to the Literary Society:

> Why have we struggled and fought for centuries, for thousands of years, why did we go to the stake, why have we endured all this hardship and oppression if not because we cherished the hope of happier days in Zion? Zionism is nothing new. It is old, as old as Judaism itself. The patriarchs were the first Zionists....The idea of the restoration of a Jewish state is too great, too noble for any one individual to carry out....But if the idea is taken up by the great mass of people it must and it will succeed.[6]

When Wolffsohn first heard about Herzl in 1896 with the publication of *Der Jüdenstaat,* he went to Vienna and was immediately impressed by his genius. From that moment, Wolffsohn became Herzl's most trusted confidant and loyal assistant, complementing Herzl's leadership with his own business acumen and knowledge of Judaism. It was Wolffsohn who chose blue and white, the colors of the *talit,* for the Zionist flag. When Herzl died, Wolffsohn took an oath at his open grave:

> You wanted no speeches at your grave, but we want to swear that we shall continue the work you began with all our strength; we want to swear that we shall always keep your name holy and never forget you so long as there is a single Jew living on this earth. In this heavy hour we want to repeat our oath: "If I forget thee, O Jerusalem, may my right hand lose its cunning."[7]

Wolffsohn did not seek the mantle of leadership and agreed to succeed Herzl only with great reluctance. As pointed out, he remained faithful to Herzl's principles, emphasizing large-scale diplomacy over small settlement projects. In striving for political success and not yielding to his opponents who advocated "Practical Zionism" (i.e. buying parcels of land when possible, encouraging colonists to settle where they could, and fostering Hebraic education and youth work), Wolffsohn faced strong opposition even from many of his closest collaborators. Finally, in 1911, at the Tenth Zionist Congress, he resigned as president of the World Zionist Organization. A new chapter in the history of Zionism, written by the "Practicals," then began:

The old guard accused the new leadership of embarking on risky and unprofitable economic ventures, of reducing the movement to a coloniz- ing agency, and of throwing diplomacy to the winds. However, there was more rhetoric than substance in these charges. Pioneering experi- ments could not be measured by a business yardstick and, as events showed, it was colonization that saved Zionism from stagnation.[8]

Wolffsohn's successor was Professor Otto Warburg (1859-1938), scion of a distinguished and assimilated wealthy family. Warburg, a famous botanist who had published extensively in his field and had traveled considerably in the Far East, taught tropical botany and agricul- ture at the University of Berlin. Warburg came to Zionism through his father-in-law, a committed Lover of Zion. Learning of the sufferings of East European Jews and their yearnings for Zion, he wanted to lend his talents to develop agriculture in Palestine. And subsequently, after meeting Theodor Herzl, he became a convinced Zionist.

Warburg visited *Eretz Yisrael* and devised a number of settlement plans, some of which were utopian and failed to reckon with financial realities. Herzl appointed Professor Warburg chairman of the commis- sion to investigate Uganda as an alternative site for settling refugees from Russian pogroms, a task Warburg accepted out of loyalty to Herzl but with reservations; he was more concerned with agricultural projects in Palestine.

A modest, generous man, without opponents or enemies, Warburg proved a natural balance wheel to his predecessor. Although he was more a man of science than a diplomat and lacked charisma, his expertise in settlement issues made him the appropriate candidate of the hour. The Zionist historian Mordecai Eliav has written:

> Warburg took upon himself the central role in directing the primary undertakings in the Land. As time passed, everything fell under his supervision and his name became a symbol of "Practical Zionism." There was no one in the upper circles of the movement who was a comparable expert in settlement matters and one must say that an important part of the dynamic development of Palestine settlement in the first decade of the twentieth century is due to him.[9]

Unfortunately, Professor Warburg was neither a fundraiser nor an orator who could inspire the masses. Working diligently, he enabled the "Practicals" to further their program but was not able to advance the political agenda of Zionism. During World War I, Warburg used his connections with the German government to try to influence the Ottoman authorities not to harass the Jews of Palestine, but the war prevented him and his colleagues from accomplishing much. After the war, the Zionist leadership was transferred to Chaim Weizmann.

When the actual running of the Zionist headquarters became too much for Professor Warburg, the responsibility was taken over by Arthur Hantke (1874-1953), a graduate of the universities of Berlin and Freiburg and a prominent lawyer. Hantke came from a very wealthy family but he rejected the life of a businessman, instead devoting his long life to the Zionist cause. In 1893, he joined a pre-Zionist group, *Jüdische Humanitätsgesellschaft* (Jewish Humanist Society), an association dedicated to fighting assimilation. When Theodor Herzl issued his call for a Zionist Congress, Hantke responded immediately and won over many people to the Zionist flag, first serving as president of the Zionist group in Berlin and later as president of the Zionist Organization of Germany. What his family was able to do in commerce and industry, Hantke was able to do for Zionist institutions and projects. Respectful of others and efficient, he possessed an enormous talent for organizing and executing programs and policy. Quiet, not interested in personal publicity, he always saw the cause as paramount. Zalman Shazar wrote of him: "I would say that he was never young. He seems to have been born mature. From the beginning of his appearance on the Zionist stage, he was deliberate in thought, moderate in outlook and clear in his decisions."[10]

In the controversy between those Zionists who stressed diplomacy and those who advocated settlements and schools, Hantke sided with the latter. He became a member of the Zionist Executive in 1911, in charge of administrative matters, and, through his connections with the German government, was able to influence those with close ties to Turkey to ease the treatment of Palestinian Jews.

After World War I, Hantke moved first to London and then to Jerusalem where he headed the *Keren Hayesod* from 1926 to 1955. He understood Zionism to include all of Judaism and, upon becoming a Zionist, Hantke began to live a completely Jewish life and was one of the few pre-Herzlian Zionists privileged to witness the establishment of the State of Israel.

Both Warburg and Hantke were influenced by the East European Zionists coming to Germany in increasing numbers at the turn of the century. It has been estimated that there were 41,000 East European Jews in Germany in 1900; by 1910, over 78,000.

In 1899, a group of brilliant students in Berlin founded the *Russisch-Jüdisch Wissenschaftlicher Verein* (Jewish-Russian Scientific Society), a study club dedicated to Jewish nationalism. Among the group's leaders were such East European Jews as Nahman Syrkin, Leo Motzkin, Shmarya Levin and, later, Chaim Weizmann. There were even a few German Jews among them, such as Heinrich Lowe. The *Verein* became a center of Jewish activity, an arena where the adherents of Zionism fought the adherents of Marxism with heat and passion. In his autobiography, Levin writes:

> Our Society was founded by and for the Jewish Nationalists: it turned into a rallying center for the Socialists and the anti-Nationalists who came there to sharpen their arguments on us. They attended every debate, and whatever it began with it always ended up with Socialism versus Nationalism....Our debates became famous, and the number of students frequently ran into several hundred. Then it was less a debate than a genuine battle between two philosophies in the presence of eager and passionate spectators.[11]

The members of the *Verein* were not the only contributors to the rebirth of Jewish activity in Berlin. Several of the famous men of Hebrew letters lived there: Agnon, Tschernichovsky, David Frishman and others. These leaders were open to all the cultural advantages of the great German metropolis—opera, theatre, university, cafes—and they, in turn, impressed others with their knowledge of Judaism and with their creative talents. Nevertheless, most of German Jewry outside of Berlin regarded these East European Jews as foreigners whose ideas might threaten their status in Germany.

It was during the Wolffsohn administration that the services of a young sociologist, Dr. Arthur Ruppin (1876-1943), were sought for a new Zionist project: the establishment of a Palestine Office. Though not deeply rooted in traditional Judaism, Ruppin was interested in Jewish affairs. After receiving his law degree, he went to work in the Jewish Statistical Institute in Berlin where he edited the *Journal of Jewish Demography and Statistics* and became the first to study the sociology of the Jews.

In 1907, the World Zionist Organization decided to look into the possibility of increasing agricultural settlement in Palestine. This project called for a preliminary study which Arthur Ruppin was asked to conduct. Ruppin's findings were positive but prescriptive. He found that the colonies were models of good farming but that their economic basis was not sound in that they limited cultivation to one product (grapes or oranges) which made them vulnerable to market uncertainties as well as dependent on Arab labor. Ruppin also advised eliminating the charity system (known as *halukah*) and introducing light industry and crafts instead. His prime concern, however, was with land settlement and the need to direct young people to the soil.

As a result of this report, the Zionist Organization concluded that it should proceed to open a permanent office in Palestine to represent its work there with Dr. Ruppin serving as its director. Indeed, such a move was radical for one immersed in the culture of German Jewry, for Ruppin would have to learn the ways and thinking of the Levant. Yet he overcame these obstacles and, in the ensuing three and a half decades, became the brain and the heart of Jewish agricultural settlement in *Eretz Yisrael*.

In 1904, Ruppin published his first book, *The Jews Today,* in which he criticized the Zionist policy of stressing diplomatic efforts at the expense of practical work. In the second edition published seven years later, he was able to report the accomplishments already achieved and to point to the possibilities of Jewish settlement.

Ruppin was not affiliated with any political party but had a keen political sense and followed all events, alert to any political activity that would help the work of settlement. A pragmatist, he cared more about helping settlers in Palestine than adhering to some abstract, limiting ideology.

When Ruppin began his work, he did not have a strong, prospering organization behind him. Indeed, Zionism was in poor shape. Herzl had died, the Uganda fiasco had led to increased factionalism, the Young Turk revolution in Turkey caused political changes, and the Zionist Organization was financially strapped. Dr. Ruppin recognized these problems but was not deterred. He recommended that colonists be trained, that industry should be encouraged, and that municipal neighborhoods should be developed in Jaffa and Jerusalem, a proposal which led to the founding of Tel Aviv.

Dr. Ruppin's recommendations were always based on fact or scientific study. Chaim Weizmann, in his autobiography, wrote about his impressions of Arthur Ruppin, whom he had met soon after Ruppin had accepted the directorship of the Palestine Office.

> I saw before me a young German—I would almost have said Prussian—correct, reserved, very formal, seemingly remote from Jewish and Zionist problems....All that one perceived on first meeting Ruppin was a German statistician and student of economics, but beneath that cool

exterior there was a passionate attachment to his people and to the upbuilding of Palestine....In all disputes he used to disarm opposition by his imperturbability, and in a movement which had its very excited moments, he would never let himself be provoked into anger or abuse. He would answer quietly, with a kindness that killed opposition.[12]

When Ruppin came to Palestine, he found a disparate Jewish community. There were the Orthodox, not all of them tolerant, who wanted to live in the Holy Land but did little to support themselves. There were those who rebelled against their bourgeois lives in Europe but had few social principles, their sole aim being to build farms, using Arab labor where necessary. And there were the *halutzim*, the primarily young pioneers who believed in socialism (Marxist and non-Marxist) and were convinced that physical labor would redeem their souls.

Ruppin knew how to get along with people of all kinds without taking sides. But he was particularly drawn to the *halutzim*, those young people who spurned material goods in order to create a new world order in which all Jews would be free and equal. Thanks to Ruppin, they were able to establish the first *kevutzah*, a settlement managed by the workers themselves without a manager or a boss. Ruppin, although not a socialist himself, was deeply impressed by the social ideals of the pioneers and his breadth of vision won him the well-deserved title of "Father of Jewish Colonization."

When needed, Ruppin created new institutions, such as the Palestine Land Development Company which collaborated with the Jewish National Fund in purchasing land and preparing it for settlement. In proposing the establishment of the PLDC, Ruppin wrote that the company was not to engage in philanthropy but to create the means whereby Jewish workers could become self-sufficient. They would be employed as day-laborers on the company's training ground where they would learn to farm, become accustomed to the soil and climate of Palestine, and share in the farm's profits and thus acquire funds to buy livestock and seed. Later, the PLDC would lease plots of land which the workers could gradually acquire by long-term payments. Ruppin also created the Agricultural Experimental Station to collect data on agriculture and to propose agricultural projects and initiated the Herzl Forest, the first experiment in large-scale afforestation.

Ruppin had very definite ideas of his own but he realized that he could not impose them on others. He understood the dignity and spirit of independence that characterized the nearly penniless but highly idealistic settlers and nurtured a sense of partnership and cooperation between them and the institutions aiming to assist them.

Ruppin also came into contact with Yemenite Jews. Struck by their sterling character, in 1910 he sent Shmuel Yavneli to Yemen to encourage Jews to come to the Holy Land. Yavneli aroused such enthusiasm that he had to convince them that he was not the Messiah! As a result, about 2,000 Yemenite Jews came to Palestine before World War I.

During World War I, Arthur Ruppin was the political head of the Jewish community in Palestine. He constantly attempted to prevail upon the Turks not to suppress the Jews, until finally they ordered him to leave the country. Exiled to Damascus, he then moved to Constantinople where he succeeded in securing funds from American Jews interested in the economic potential of Palestine.

When the war was over, Ruppin returned to Palestine and resumed his active direction of the World Zionist Organization's settlement work. He later wrote two monumental works, *The Jews in the Modern World* and *The Jewish Fate and Future,* and as Professor of Sociology at the Hebrew University continued to serve as one of the principal Zionist leaders following the Great War.

One of the key figures in the development of Palestine's cooperatives was Dr. Franz Oppenheimer (1864-1943) who had been removed from Jewish concerns until he met Herzl and Warburg. A physician whose study of medicine led him to study society and its problems, he became one of the outstanding economists and sociologists in Germany. Believing that the cause of social evil was to be found in the monopolization of land by the upper classes, he urged members of the lower classes to purchase land in agrarian cooperatives, leading to the highest form of human association, the cooperative settlement. Moreover, while Oppenheimer had not been involved in Jewish politics, he was enthusiastically devoted to the Jewish people. Wrote Oppenheimer in 1902:

> If Jewish capital and the Jewish heart were to carry out that which Jewish intelligence has devised, they will fulfill the promise of the Old Testament regarding the Messianic mission of Israel. They will heap burning coals upon the heads of their foes and cut down anti-Semitism at its roots.[13]

In 1903 Herzl invited Professor Oppenheimer to address the Sixth Zionist Congress. Oppenheimer impressed the delegates and was appointed to a committee of experts assigned to conduct a scientific investigation into the potential of Palestine. Oppenheimer became convinced of the need to establish cooperative villages and, in several eloquent addresses, he aroused Zionists to the point where they agreed to experiment. At the Ninth Congress, the Jewish National Fund was charged with providing the land for such villages and a fund was established to finance the project. By creating a large cooperative village, Oppenheimer hoped to combine the advantages of a large farm—modern methods of agriculture and smaller outlay on buildings—with those of a small holding so as to preserve the interests of the individual. Workers, as they succeeded, could live in communal dwellings or move into their own houses. If the latter, they could obtain building loans or become private farmers leasing parcels rather than remaining in the cooperative.

In the spring of 1911, Dr. Oppenheimer visited Germany and Austria to raise funds for his project. This time, thanks to Dr. Ruppin's help, the PLDC secured land and the settlement of Merhavia was founded in the Valley of Jezreel. A cooperative rather than a collective, Merhavia was unable to develop as envisioned by Oppenheimer but it did influence other settlements. In comparing this kind of settlement with a collective at Degania, Alex Bein notes:

> While Oppenheimer did not go so far as to believe that unfettered competition would lead to economic harmony, he thought that self-interest was the most powerful incentive, which he therefore wished to harness. With the aid of sensible organisation, this motive could be utilized to promote the co-operative venture. For the members of Degania, however, self-interest was not the incentive; they were impelled by the aim of working for the nation and building Palestine on the foundation of social justice....Instead of self-interest, they relied on the incentive of faith in the accomplishment of a common task.[14]

A number of young men occupied important positions in the German-Jewish community even before World War I and rose to prominence in the years following. Martin Buber (1878-1965), for example, became one of the world's foremost thinkers and one of the preeminent expositors of Hasidism from the 1920s onward. But his attachment to Zion began in his youth when he worked under Herzl and served as editor of the Zionist German-language newspaper, *Die Welt*. He accepted the need for a political movement but was closer to the "Father of Cultural Zionism," Ahad Haam, and joined Chaim Weizmann in forming an opposition group within the World Zionist Organization, "The Democratic Faction." The young people who associated with this group were offended not only by Herzl's authoritarianism but also by his indifference to the just demands of Cultural Zionists who wanted greater support for Hebrew literature as well as for other cultural undertakings. Buber also was bothered by the Zionists' lack of concern for spiritual matters. As he later wrote:

> Zion is "the city of the great King" (Psalm 48:3), that is, of God as the King of Israel. The name has retained this sacred character ever since. In their prayers and songs the mourning and yearning of the people in exile were bound up with it, the holiness of the land was concentrated in it, and in the Kabbala Zion was equated with an emanation of God Himself. When the Jewish people adopted this name for their national concept, all these associations were contained in it.[15]

Other German Jews, such as Kurt Blumenfeld, Pinhas Rosenbluth, Nahum Goldmann and Chaim Arlozorov, became the foremost leaders of the Zionist enterprise after World War I. Together with Ruppin, Warburg, and the others, they not only had to carry the Zionist word to their fellow German Jews and perform exhaustive organizational duties, but they also had to combat their Jewish antagonists who insisted that a person could be either a German nationalist or a Jewish nationalist but not both. For example, Herzl had to confront student opposition to his ideas of Jewish nationalism as soon as he became involved in his people's fate. After he issued a call for a convocation of Jewish nationalists, for what would become the first Zionist Congress, he was confronted with bitter opposition, forcing him to move the Congress from Munich to Basle.

German rabbis and laymen, outraged by the very concept of Zionism, quickly proclaimed their sole loyalty to Germany. In July of 1897, the executive of the Federation of German Rabbis published a statement in the *Berliner Tageblatt* and other leading newspapers protesting the "nonsensical distortion of the meaning of Judaism and of the ideas of the confessors of the Jewish faith." The aims of Zionism, they contended, contradicted "the prophetic message of Jewry and the duty of every Jew to belong without reservation to the fatherland in which he lives."[16]

Prominent Jews all over Germany joined these rabbis in disassociating themselves from Herzl and his colleagues, fearing the public discussion of Jewish affairs and agonizing over the possible questioning of their

German patriotism. Herzl, however, was not affected by their warnings, threats and denouncements. He wrote a stinging reply to the rabbis, dubbing the authors of the statement "*Protest Rabbiner.*"

Those who believed in Jewish nationalism and who supported Zionism may have been a minority within German Jewry, but they were convinced that Zionism was the answer to assimilation and that German anti-Semitism would increase rather than decrease. The Zionists, as historian Isaiah Friedman observes, "pointed out the danger of Jews assimilating themselves out of existence. They called upon their co-religionists to take pride in their national heritage" and insisted that "Jewish nationalism was not incompatible with German patriotism, nor did it conflict with the ethics of Judaism."[18]

Although the number of pre-World War I German Zionists was not large, their activities, influence and importance were crucial. Whether by formulating principles and ideologies, organizing and administrating, or responding to diplomatic negotiations or cultural demands, German Jews stood in the forefront of the Zionist movement. They were among the builders and architects of the World Zionist Organization and thereby became lasting partners in creating and sustaining the State of Israel.

NOTES

1. Jehuda Reinharz, *Fatherland or Promised Land: The Dilemma of the German Jew, 1893-1914* (Ann Arbor, 1975).

2. Walter Laqueur, *A History of Zionism* (New York, 1972), 34.

3. Hannah Bodenheimer, *Toldot Tokhnit Basle* (Jerusalem, 1947), 58.

4. Shalom Ben-Horin, *Hamishim Shnot Tziyonut* (Jerusalem: Rubin Mass, 1946), 38.

5. Stephen M. Poppel, *Zionism in Germany, 1897-1933* (Philadelphia, 1976), 57.

6. Emil Bernhard Cohn, *David Wolffsohn* (The Zionist Organization of America, 1944), 37-38.

7. Ibid., 134.

8. Isaiah Friedman, *Germany, Turkey and Zionism: 1897-1918* (Oxford, 1977), 125.

9. Mordecai Eliav, *David Wolffsohn: Ha-ish Uzmano* (Jerusalem: Tel Aviv University and National Library, 1977), 59.

10. Zalman Shazar, *Or Ishim* (Jerusalem: National Library), 1:110.

11. Maurice Samuel, trans., *Forward From Exile: The Autobiography of Shmarya Levin* (Philadelphia, 1967), 276.

12. Chaim Weizmann, *Trial and Error* (Philadelphia, 1949), 129.

13. Alex Bein, "Franz Oppenheimer and Theodor Herzl," *Herzl Yearbook,* ed. Raphael Patai (New York: Herzl Press, 1971), 7:75.

14. Alex Bein, *The Return to the Soil* (Jerusalem: The Youth and Hechalutz Department of the Zionist Organization, 1952), 85.

15. Simon Noveck, ed., "Zion and the Other National Concepts," Martin Buber in *Contemporary Jewish Thought: A Reader* (B'nai B'rith Department of Adult Jewish Education, 1963), 266-67.

16. Ben Halpern, *The Idea of the Jewish State* (Cambridge, Mass., 1961), 144.

17. Friedman, op. cit., 128.

A Refugee Rabbinate

Karl Richter

RABBIS WHO CAME TO AMERICA and other countries as refugees from Nazi persecution had an impact upon the Jewish communities they served. It is difficult, of course, to assess the complete influence of this diverse group of several hundred men, with great variations in age, religious philosophy and practice, personal experience and approach to their rabbinic vocation. Rabbis who came to this country between 1935 and 1941 have officiated in Orthodox, Conservative and Reform congregations. Some have spent their active years in the service of local or national Jewish organizations, as directors of Hillel Foundations, or as military and civilian chaplains. Renowned scholars who had made their mark in the academies of Central Europe were able to contribute their rich gifts to the deepening of Jewish scholarship in America. Some of them who had found refuge in this country as children and some who grew up as children of refugee rabbis devoted their lives to Jewish studies and acquired prominence in the American community.

To understand the intellectual and emotional roots of this special group one would have to study each individual biography. Unfortunately, interviews with these individuals are no longer possible, because many men who arrived during those critical few years before the Holocaust enveloped the Jewish communities of the Old World, are no longer alive. Secondary source material in the form of books or articles is also scarce. I am most grateful to my cherished colleagues and other friends who have directed my attention to a number of available sources.[1]

In order to circumscribe the area of this study, then, I have limited myself to students and graduates of several of the foremost rabbinic seminaries of Central Europe: the Jewish Theological Seminary of Breslau, founded in 1854;[2] the *Lehranstalt für die Wissenschaft des Judentums*, founded in 1870 in Berlin;[3] the Hildesheimer Seminary in Berlin, a Neo-Orthodox school established by Rabbi Ezriel Hildesheimer in 1873; and the *Landesrabbinerschule* in Budapest, founded in 1877,[4] which throughout its existence maintained close ties to its sister institutions in Germany.

Interestingly, because of the dearth of rabbinic candidates from Germany after the First World War, the administration of the Breslau Seminary advertised in Jewish newspapers in Poland, Czechoslovakia, Hungary, Romania, Yugoslavia and the Baltic states, inviting aspiring students to come to Germany. During my own years at the seminary (1928-1935) more than half the student body consisted of men from Eastern Europe. Most had studied in *yeshivot* or Hebrew *Gymnasia*, were thoroughly grounded in Talmud and the commentaries, and had acquired fluency in modern Hebrew. They came with strong Zionist convictions and in their interchange with faculty and members of the student body who had received their education in Germany contributed greatly to the dynamics of our intellectual growth. After ordination most of these men returned to congregations in their native countries. With the coming of World War II, those unable to escape to Palestine, then under the British Mandate, or other countries became victims of the *Shoah* along with their congregations.

For a few years after Hitler's assumption of dictatorial powers in 1933, the Jews of Germany believed that despite the constantly increasing pressure and the anti-Jewish policies of the government their congregations could maintain schools and other institutions separate from the general culture, attend to the religious and intellectual needs of the shrinking Jewish population, and prepare the very young and the very old for inevitable emigration. In these years, the seminaries continued to educate rabbis to serve in the congregations of Central Europe. While some of the older rabbis left the country between 1933 and 1938 and their places were taken by younger, newly ordained men, disaster did not descend upon the Jewish community until the infamous *Kristallnacht* of November 9, 1938. The destruction of hundreds of synagogues and most other institutions inflicted a final blow on the illusion that Jewish life could be continued with some semblance of dignity. Many rabbis were deported with other men of their congregations to the concentration camps of Dachau, Buchenwald and Oranienburg-Sachsenhausen. Proof of intended emigration was required for liberation from the horror of the camps.

In the ensuing months the exodus of rabbis from Germany grew to a veritable flood. *"Sauve qui peut"* became the rallying cry for congregations and their leaders. This process led to much soul-searching and anxiety. Did rabbis have the moral right to leave their congregations? As a young rabbi in Mannheim (1938-1939) I addressed this question to Rabbi Leo Baeck, who, in a memorable exchange of letters, assured me that, whereas he as a widower in his sixties would remain to share the destiny of his people, rabbis with young families had the same obligation to save their lives as did the members of their congregations. Thus the exodus began which catapulted German-trained rabbis to the four corners of the earth.

One cannot discuss rabbis who survived the *Shoah* without remembering those who, of their own volition or inability to escape the Nazi trap, went heroically to their death with their congregations. To the end they were aware of the "Yoke of the Torah" imposed upon them as spiritual leaders and the legacy of the *Kedoshim* who had added their names through the ages to the martyrdom of our people. Of the 123 students who had attended the Breslau Seminary between 1904 and 1939, thirty-two are among the known victims of the Nazi horror; twenty-seven of them were ordained in Breslau, five studied there and reached their ordination at the seminary in Budapest.[5]

We may assume that comparable numbers of the graduates of the Berlin seminaries must also be added to the list of these martyrs. We think of Rabbi Reinhold Lewin of Breslau, Rabbi Hans Andorn of Nuremberg and The Hague, and, tragically, Rabbi Israel Finkelscherer who died in Theresienstadt, and his sons, Rabbi Bruno Finkelscherer of Goettingen and Herbert Finkelscherer of Stettin who were deported with their congregations to the death camps of Poland. Most of the graduates who served congregations in Czechoslovakia and Poland perished with their people.

After *Kristallnacht* the British government was more generous in accepting refugee rabbis than U.S. authorities who had strict orders to enforce the rigid immigration quotas. Some rabbis who later came to America sojourned in England, while others were able to settle there and establish congregations of refugees. Rabbi Georg Salzberger of Frankfurt, for example, together with his emeritus, Caesar Seligmann, organized a flourishing congregation of mostly Central European immigrants. Other rabbis trained in Germany, such as Hermann Schreiber and Paul Holzer, were able to secure positions in British congregations, mostly in the London area.[6] Jacob Kokotek served in Dublin, Ireland and at the New Liberal Jewish Congregation in London. Bruno Italicener and Werner van den Eyl served at the West End Synagogue. The outstanding scholar Alexander Altmann occupied a pulpit in Manchester. German rabbis were instrumental in founding the Leo Baeck College for Jewish Studies in London in 1956, which is devoted to the education of rabbis and teachers. Albert Friedlander, a German-born graduate of the Hebrew Union College and rabbi of the Westminster Synagogue, is one of the leading spirits of the College.

Whether under the auspices of the World Union for Progressive Judaism or individually, other German rabbis founded congregations in Latin America, among whom were Henrique (Heinrich) Lemle in Rio de Janeiro and Frederico (Fritz) Pinkuss in São Paulo. Congregations were established by Hermann Sanger in Melbourne and Rudolph Brasch in Sydney, Australia. Joseph Schwarz and his wife Amelia served the congregation in Manila during the Japanese occupation and the American siege.[7] A special group of rabbis ministered to refugees in Shanghai, among whom were George Kantorowsky, Joseph Zeitin and Wilhelm Teichner. Curtis Cassell served in Bulawaya, Zimbabwe. Lothar Rothschild of St. Gallen was the standard bearer of Liberal Judaism in Switzerland.[8] Many of these rabbis, particularly those who were able to found large new congregations, had a profound influence upon the Jewish communities in their various adopted countries.

The Yishuv in Palestine during the British Mandate was not a fertile field for German-trained rabbis. Only a few graduates of the Central European seminaries were able to continue their rabbinic careers in Palestine, most of them taking positions as teachers or administrators. Rabbi Meir Elk of Stettin founded the Leo Baeck School in Haifa and served as its first headmaster. Among the prominent scholars who came to Palestine were Julius Guttmann, Professor of Jewish Philosophy; Ephraim Urbach, Professor of Talmud at the Hebrew University and President of the Israel Academy of the Sciences and Humanities; and

Zeev ben Hayyim (Wolf Goldman), Professor of Hebrew Philology. A few rabbis returned from Israel to Germany after the war to minister to the small surviving congregations, most notably Nathan Levinson, a graduate of the HUC-JIR, who devoted his professional life to the rebuilding of a Liberal Jewish community in West Germany.

What were some of the difficulties in America which rabbis with a European education had to overcome? American Reform Judaism required the greatest adjustment by the refugee rabbis. There was only one Reform congregation in Germany which followed the American pattern, the Reform Temple in Berlin, where to the wonder of German Jews most of the prayers were recited in German.

For the most part, even Liberal German congregations relegated women to the gallery or to one side of the sanctuary. Despite organ music and a mixed choir the services were traditional, with almost all prayers chanted by the cantor in Hebrew. Rabbis preached in German but never announced pages in the prayerbook assuming that everybody was familiar with the sequence of the liturgy. The traditionalism of the German synagogue was due to the role of the *Einheitsgemeinde*[9] which maintained both Liberal and Orthodox houses of worship and therefore depended on a centrist position in liturgy and custom.

The informality of the American service, with announcements of social activities and rabbis chatting from the pulpit or kissing women on the cheek during and after the service, would have been considered scandalous in Germany. The German synagogue did not foster sociability. The Oneg Shabbat was unknown, as was with a few exceptions, the late Friday evening service. The main service was held on Shabbat morning where men worshipped with their heads covered, most of them wearing the formal silk hat. The *kippah* (skull cap) of the Conservative service would have been considered inappropriate.[10] *Kippot* were worn during study or meals by the observant.

Newly arrived rabbis to America were bewildered by the voluntary nature of temple affiliation and the casual attitude of the congregation. One could drop in or out at will. In Germany, membership in the Jewish community had not been voluntary but was imposed by the power of taxation. The *Kirchensteuer* (church tax) was part of the general income tax levied upon the general population. In order to separate himself from his community, a Jew had to submit a written declaration to this effect before a civil court. This system tended to secure the authority of the rabbi to a greater degree than in America where the position of the rabbi often depended on the good will of the temple board and the members of the congregation.

In addition to their cultural displacement, the refugee rabbis who had either been brought to this country by affidavits of support provided by relatives or came as non-quota immigrants, having received contracts from small congregations, had to cope with grave emotional problems. To be sure, compared with refugee physicians, lawyers and other professionals, they had the great advantage of being able to remain in their profession, without undergoing new study and examination. American seminaries were generous enough to recognize the *semichah* (ordination) of the European schools, and the rabbinical organizations (Central Conference of American Rabbis and Rabbinical Assembly) graciously accepted the many arrived rabbis as members in good standing. Thus these rabbis were able almost immediately to provide, albeit modestly, for their families.

Immigrant rabbis had come from Nazi Germany to a country yet largely untouched by the gathering storm of Europe. In addition to their desperate struggle with the English language, they were besieged by letters pleading for help from relatives caught in the trap of Hitler's expanding empire. From the beginning of the deportations in 1940 letters came from the ghettos of Poland and elsewhere, and a rabbi without means or influence could do little to help members of his family to escape. These rabbis had to accept their powerlessness in addition to coping with congregation demands. This was a time without rabbinical networks, support groups or placement committees, and it was only through the generosity of their congregations and the warm understanding of their American colleagues that many of these rabbis survived the first difficult years.

Expectations of rabbis, particularly by the smaller American congregations, were quite different from those placed upon their European counterparts. In German-speaking countries the rabbis were more removed, more sheltered from the organizational requirements of their congregations. It was quite novel to them that they were expected to be administrators, fundraisers and organizers of religious schools. In Germany teachers' seminaries trained religious educators; other professionals were entrusted with administrative duties, leaving the rabbi free for study, preparation of sermons and lectures, and the teaching of religion classes in the public schools, adult education and pastoral work. Thus refugee rabbis faced a radical change in their role as preachers and teachers, faced with unfamiliar prayerbooks, forms of liturgy, and the social setting of the American synagogue. Considering the initial barrier of language and custom, as well as the emotional ballast that the "refugee" carried within his soul, it is quite remarkable that most of the younger rabbis handled this challenge successfully. As time passed, many who had grimly witnessed the destruction of their synagogue experienced the joy of presiding over the building of new houses of worship in this country.

Why did a considerable number of rabbis coming from the more traditional environment of the German synagogue choose to join the Reform movement? Many were sincerely attracted to the liberal spirit of their new congregations, while for others affiliation was a matter of economic survival. It may be argued that because of the German background of many Reform congregations the warm hand of hospitality was more easily extended to the newcomers. Many Conservative congregations were still conscious of their Eastern European origins and could not quite so easily welcome German-speaking rabbis who—strangely enough—had very little knowledge of Yiddish.

Rabbis educated in German schools—with few exceptions—did not understand or speak Yiddish. Jews who had immigrated from Eastern Europe after the First World War sought to acquire fluency in German, and the same was true of students who had come to the Rabbinic seminaries from Poland. Yiddish language and literature were not part of the curricula of the seminaries which concentrated on the study of Hebrew and Aramaic sources.

When German refugee rabbis were invited to American congregations with an Eastern European background, members wanted them to feel at home by addressing them in Yiddish, only to meet some embarrassed disclaimers. This, in turn, led some to the conclusion that the newcomers had an aversion to *"mamme loshen"* as ignorance was mistaken for arrogance. It was only in their new American milieu that some of the immigrant rabbis acquired a workable knowledge of Yiddish and an appreciation of the culture and literature which the language had produced.

This language barrier was a particular disadvantage in Conservative congregations. People who felt that German Jews had looked down upon them as cultural inferiors when they or their parents had come to this country earlier may now have felt that German rabbis showed a regrettable lack of understanding for their particular background and values.

Thus traditional rabbis may have felt somewhat alienated in the Conservative movement. In a touching recollection of his father's life, Dr. Ismar Schorsch, now the chancellor of the Jewish Theological Seminary in New York, recounts some of the difficulties which Rabbi Emil Schorsch encountered when he came from the large congregation of Hanover, Germany, to the small conservative congregation of Pottstown, Pennsylvania, to which he devoted the rest of his career. Dr. Schorsch writes, "Soon after his arrival he accepted an invitation to become the rabbi of a small Conservative congregation in southeastern Pennsylvania. Founded in the late 1800s by Hungarian and Russian immigrants who, in effect, kept their minute books in German, Congregation Mercy and Truth of Pottstown in 1940 had a membership of some 150 families but a generation or two removed from Eastern Europe. Thus its new rabbi was enveloped by a twofold sense of estrangement: in an alien tongue he would serve Jews who often bore deep antipathy toward the Jewish community from which he stemmed."[11]

The refugee rabbis' educational background and their understanding of Jewish values and traditions also influenced their careers in this country. Most of them had received their secondary education at a "humanistic *Gymnasium*," with its emphasis upon classical languages and literature. A thorough knowledge of Latin and Greek, as well as of French, English, mathematics, history and the natural sciences was the admission ticket to the universities, with their rigorous and disciplined methods of instruction. Study at the seminary had exposed the candidates for the rabbinate to great scholars and teachers, imbued with the spirit of *Wissenschaft des Judentums,* always seeking a synthesis between tradition and the demands of objective scholarly investigation. The "historic positive" emphasis of the Breslau Seminary may serve as an example.

Many of the younger rabbis who came to this country grew up during the years after the First World War when Jewish life in German-speaking countries experienced an important revival. Zionism became a consuming issue, and thinkers of the stature of Hermann Cohen, Franz Rosenzweig, Martin Buber, Eduard Strauss, and Ernst Simon inspired young Jews; a vigorous youth movement—Blauweiss, Kameraden, and other groups— led to a reexamination of traditional values; and the *Lehrhaus* concept opened the doors to a deepening of Jewish consciousness and knowledge.

The faculties of the seminaries emphasized Hebrew scholarship with only minor attention given to practical rabbinics. This set apart refugee rabbis, to some extent, from their American colleagues. Their homiletic training had stressed reliance on sources in the Torah and Talmud from which conclusions may be drawn about current events. Academic preoccupations sometimes led to admonitions by members of the congregation "not to talk over their heads." The "folksy" approach of the American pulpit had to be learned. In addition, German rabbis had no formal training in pastoral care and counseling techniques and had to acquire these skills by trial and error. While congregations in Germany were somewhat static and tradition-bound, the freedom and mobility of American religious life required radical readjustment. The immigrant rabbis had to discover the role of the rabbi as a practitioner of "public relations." In Nazi Germany relations between Synagogue and Church had been almost completely severed. The warm welcome extended by Christian churches to refugee rabbis, particularly in smaller communities, and their sincere interest in their experiences called for a new outlook. Invitations to speak to church groups and civic clubs were sometimes overwhelming. These new tasks required adaption and adjustment on the part of the refugee rabbis, at which they most often succeeded.

Considering these difficulties of adjustment to the American Jewish environment, a few of the older rabbis who had served prominent congregations in Germany formed their own refugee congregations in metropolitan areas such as New York, Chicago, and Cincinnati in response to the needs of the new immigrants. *Frankfurt on the Hudson* by Steven Lowenstein[12] describes one segment of immigrant society, the German-Jewish community of Washington Heights in New York City, with a detailed analysis of its structure and culture from 1933 to 1983. The heavily concentrated Central European refugees in this area belonged to a wide range of religious institutions, from the moderate Reform congregation Hebrew Tabernacle, through Conservative and Orthodox groups to the recreation of the *Trennungsorthodoxie,* a movement of religious secession from the general Jewish community, begun by the famous Rabbi Samson Raphael Hirsch in Frankfurt in the middle of the nineteenth century, and brought to new life in this country by Rabbi Isaac Breuer and his followers (*K'hal Adath Jeshurun*). Of over a dozen synagogues founded in Washington Heights, eight were still active in the early 1990s, most of them representing the Orthodox wing of Judaism.

Interestingly, the one Reform congregation (Hebrew Tabernacle) not originally founded by refugees acquired a German character. Rabbi Robert Lehman, a native of Germany has been with the congregation for many years. An important Conservative congregation, Beth Hillel, which merged with the Orthodox congregation Beth Israel in 1980, was founded in 1940 by Rabbi Leo Baerwald of Munich whose spiritual leadership had a pervasive influence on the immigrant community.[14] The total membership of the German-Jewish congregations in Washington Heights at its peak probably exceeded 6,000 families, representing a majority of the immigrant Jewish community.[15] In midtown Manhattan, the most influential and successful immigrant congregation was Habonim, founded by Rabbi Hugo Hahn of Essen in November 1939 following *Kristallnacht*.[16] Its Rabbi Emeritus, Bernard Cohn is himself the son of the German refugee rabbi, Emil Bernhard Cohn of Bonn and Berlin.

Most of the congregations founded by refugee rabbis for new immigrants served the needs of their constituents by maintaining the familiar liturgy and music, and slowly, with the growth of a new generation, earned entry into the organized American Jewish community. Some of these new congregations were originally sponsored by already established American congregations which provided space for worship and financial support.

Quite a few rabbis remained in the smaller congregations of the Midwest, South and West, either by necessity or by choice. Before the development of rabbinic placement committees promotion of rabbis was supervised by the seminaries and their organizational affiliates. As a matter of course, preference was given to graduates of American seminaries who were placed in larger congregations through personal recommendation. Therefore many refugee rabbis were not offered the opportunities to move on from the smaller congregations once they had settled there. Despite the economic constraints of the smaller congregations which led many rabbis to supplement their income by accepting teaching positions at local colleges, these congregations offered certain advantages. The relationship between rabbi and congregation was based upon trust and mutual affection, particularly when the rabbi served successive generations and participated in life-cycle events of families, all of whose members had been his students at one time or another. Thus he could remain faithful to the ideal of the *Seelsorger,* an untranslatable term embodying the pastoral work of the rabbi as well as his special involvement with every family of his congregation.

In the smaller cities, the rabbi also occupied a respectful place in the general community as a member of the clergy and friend of ministers, priests and their flocks, and as a lecturer and teacher in churches, youth camps, colleges and civic groups. He became a figure of authority representing Judaism to the establishment. Having come to America as a fugitive from oppression, the refugee rabbi aroused both the curiosity and sympathy of the people with whom he worked.

In 1935 the arrival on the campus of the Hebrew Union College in Cincinnati of five young men who had begun their studies at the *Hochschule* in Berlin was a notable event. Over the years, Leo Lichtenberg, Wolli Kaelter, Herman Schaalman, W. Gunther Plaut, and Alfred Wolf would have a remarkable impact, attaining prominence as rabbis, scholars, and community leaders.

Their experiences upon their arrival in Cincinnati foretold the cultural and religious shock sustained by most of the refugee rabbis who came to American congregations in later years. The five students, wearing their fedoras to the Rockdale Avenue Temple, were almost ejected by Rabbi David Philipson, a stalwart of the Reform movement. Gunther Plaut in his autobiography[17] describes quite humorously the clash between the traditions brought from Germany and the customs of classic Reform Judaism still prevalent at the College. For example, the recital of the *bircat hamazon* after meals by the arrivals from Germany caused consternation. Ironically, this prayer has today become standard practice, at least in its abbreviated form, in youth camps and at congregational gatherings.

Half a century later, Rabbi Plaut describes this German influence in his essay, *The Elusive German-Jewish Heritage in America:*

> Contrast this with the year 1983 in America. In Los Angeles, at the annual convention of the Central Conference of American Rabbis, a German-born president (Herman Schaalman) was yielding the gavel to another president of like origin (the writer); and at the same time the presidents of the other three Reform institutions were all German-born as well: the Union of American Hebrew Congregations (Alexander Schindler), the Hebrew Union College-Jewish Institute of Religion (Alfred Gottschalk), and the World Union for Progressive Judaism (Gerard Daniel). Since that time the president of the Jewish Theological Seminary (Ismar Schorsch) has also joined this surprising constellation of German-Jewish influence. One might be tempted to apply the well known words coined in a different context: *anachnu kahn,* "we are still here."[18]

215

In a similar vein, Joseph Glaser, addressing the Central Conference of American Rabbis,[17] said: "There is a grim justice to be noted here, an ironic triumph. Snatched from the very heart of the fire that consumed six million of our people, these five labor now in the upbuilding and perpetuation of that which was destined for oblivion, not as if nothing happened, but in spite of that which happened. We have said it so often that it sometimes appears almost trite, but at this moment, there is a compelling freshness to the defiant words, *Am Yisrael Chai*—"the People of Israel Lives."

Within the framework of this study it is not possible to mention all the rabbis who arrived in this country as refugees, rebuilt their lives, established their reputations in their communities and beyond, and made important contributions to America's Jewish organizations. In studying the biographies of these "refugee rabbis," it became evident that they took their vocation seriously and willingly accepted the burdens of adapting to their new culture. Regardless of which branch of American Judaism they served, they were committed to teach Torah according to their own understanding, relating it to the problems of life. Steering away from a fashionable pietism which mistakes symbolism for substance, they remained faithful to the goals of *Wissenschaft des Judentums,* seeking to explore the genesis and evolution of our faith, preferring the discovery of modest truths to the dissemination of scholarly propaganda. Most of them remained true to the theistic essence of classic Judaism, were rarely found in the ranks of the humanists,[20] and were not greatly attracted to the naturalism of the Reconstructionist movement.

The oppression, persecution and powerlessness which they all experienced strengthened their faith in the meaning of Jewish existence and in an unfathomable Deity who challenges our ability to maintain *Emunah*. This "trust" supports the religious person even in the extremities of life. The "refugee rabbis" sought to carry out the tasks assigned to them to the American Jewish community, whether great or humble, with dignity and dedication. They knew that "they would not be able to complete the work, but neither did they have the right to desist from it."[21]

NOTES

1. I wish to express my gratitude for their valuable counsel and assistance to Dr. Abraham Peck of the American Jewish Archives in Cincinnati, to Dr. Diane Spielmann of the Leo Baeck Foundation in New York, to Dr. Ida Selavan, Judaica Library of the Hebrew Union College/Jewish Institute of Religion, to Robert Singerman, Jewish Studies

Bibliographer at the University of Florida, to Fay Hirschberg, Hilda Lichtenberg Weltman and Ruth Nussbaum as well as to my cherished colleagues, rabbis Stanley Dreyfus, Joseph Glaser, Max Gruenewald, Harry Hyman, Walter Jacob, Alfred Jospe, Wolli Kaelter, Robert Lehman, Gunther Plaut, Frank Plotke, David Polish, Herman Schaalman, Ismar Schorsch, Michael Szenes, Isaac Trainin, Leo Trepp, Theodore Wiener, Alfred Wolf and Selig Auerbach.

2. *Das Jüdisch-Theologische Seminar, Fraenkelscher Stiftung,* founded in 1854 by Zacharias Frankel, and considered the fountainhead of modern Conservative Judaism, closed its doors forever after *Kristallnacht.*

3. *Die Hochschule für die Wissenschaft des Judentums* was founded in 1870 and opened its doors in 1872. At the insistence of the Prussian authorities the school had to be called *Lehranstalt* instead of *Hochschule* ("training school" instead of "academy") from 1883 to 1922 and again after 1934. The school continued to function on a limited scale until 1941.

4. The national rabbinical seminary of Hungary, founded in Budapest in 1877, functioning under the supervision of the Hungarian Ministry of Education, maintained close ties with the Breslau Seminary. Exchanges of faculty were not uncommon. Rabbi Michael Guttman, Professor of Talmud, served at different times as the rabbi of both institutions.

5. Alfred Jospe in "Das Seminar," 387.

6. After the war, Rabbi Paul Holzer returned to Germany (1951), where he served as principal rabbi of Nordrhein Westfalen in Dortmund.

7. After his immigration to the USA in 1948 Rabbi Schwarz served Temple Beth El in Benton Harbor, Michigan, until his retirement.

8. Rabbi Rothschild served as editor of the journal *Tradition und Erneuerung* (Tradition and Renewal), which was published by the Union for Religious Liberal Judaism in Switzerland.

9. The concept of the *"Einheitsgemeinde"* was based on the historic institution of the *"Kehilla,"* the centralized Jewish community of each city which organized and supervised all synagogues, schools, welfare agencies, and other associations. The principle of centrality was extended to regional organizations, such as the *Preussische Landesverband Jüdischer Gemeinden* (Prussian State Association of Jewish Congregations), or the *Oberrat* (Superior Council) in the states of Southern Germany. The Weimar Constitution of 1919 provided that religious associations should administer their affairs independently, without undue interference by state or civil authorities.

10. In my home community of Stuttgart the men who were called to the reading of the Torah were for many years required to wear a high silk hat or *Zylinder.* It was customary for men to keep their *zylinders* in the wardrobe of the synagogue where they exchanged them for their street hats on Saturday morning. During the High Holydays the rabbis had to look out on a veritable ocean of *zylinders.*

11. Rabbi Ismar Schorsch, *Rabbi Emil Schorsch,* Proceedings of the 1982 Convention of the Rabbinic Assembly, 164ff.

12. Steven M. Lowenstein, *Frankfurt on the Hudson* (Detroit, 1989).

13. Ibid., 114ff.

14. See the summary on p. 110.

15. Ibid., 114ff.

16. *Living Legacy,* Essays in Honor of Hugo Hahn (New York: Congregation Habonim, 1963), especially the essay "A Rabbi from Germany" by S.F. Brodnitz.

17. W. Gunther Plaut, *Unfinished Business, an Autobiography* (Toronto, 1981).

18. W. Gunther Plaut, *The German-Jewish Legacy in America* (American Jewish

Archives, November 1988), 274.

19. *Yearbook of the Central Conference of American Rabbis* (Jerusalem, 1981), 91:158.

20. See e.g., Sherwin T. Wine, *Judaism Beyond God* (Society for Humanistic Judaism, 1985).

21. Pirke Abot II, 21.

PART VI

The God-Seeking Intellectuals

A Walk on the Crest*

Michael Weinrich

MARTIN BUBER HAS DEFINED HIMSELF as an "atypical man."[1] While such a self-definition may imply a degree of vanity, this definition does hold true for many aspects of Buber's personality. This essay will deal with the atypical Buber as he is rarely characterized by his biographers and adherents: surprisingly, he is neither the "typical" Jew, nor the "typical" German, nor is he the "typical prophet of Judaism among the nations."

Yet it is not enough simply to classify Buber for he himself resisted being placed in one category or the other. Buber oscillated constantly between two worlds—German and Jewish—and therefore we must examine Buber's place in both of these worlds to understand the man.

Martin Buber's Jewish faith was by no means representative of "traditional" Judaism, but was, above all, a break with tradition. In opposition to traditional Judaism, Buber makes a distinction between religion and religiosity. Religion is rigid, Buber felt, confined by institution, rite and dogma, while religiosity refers to the inner element of the life of faith. This religiosity requires a kind of revival, as Buber envisioned it, "a Judaism, which is again alive in all its senses, active with all its strength, and joined into a holy community [so] that there is no other path away from the present Jewish existence than through renunciation and a new beginning."[2]

Buber noted, however, that religiosity is more than the singular act of the charismatic or the belief of the visionary or mystic and often seeks form in religion. But religion may be too narrow or too strict to contain such religiosity, Buber felt, and from this premise stems his criticism of religious tradition. He took aim at official Judaism for its "rabbinism," its untimely legality, its "rationalism," its ethical narrowness, and instead sought "the genesis of that under-ground Judaism,"[3] that is the elusive encounter with God.

Again and again Buber emphasized the immediacy or directness of the relationship with God: "The immediacy is the specifically religious substance of Judaism. Jewish religiosity is neither based on a statement of faith, nor on an ethical prescription."[4] As such, God is not the object of our reflection, but the transcendent point of reference of our human existence. God only can be addressed, not discussed.

The inner history of Judaism according to Buber is characterized by the struggle between prophet and priest. As archetypes of this struggle he cites Moses and Aaron: Moses as the prophet is committed to the truth and lets himself be guided exclusively by the voice of God, whereas Aaron as the priest is interested in power and thus his task is to reconcile the voice of God with the voices of the people.

Indeed, Buber saw the whole of world history, not Judaism alone, as a "dialogue between God and his creatures in which the human being is a genuine, legitimate partner."[5] For Buber, religious truth, which finds expression in faith, is a dynamic process which emerges through the encounter between the human being and God: "Religious truth, as distinct from philosophy, is not a maxim, but a way, not a thesis, but a process."[6]

In spite of this conceptual approach, Buber felt, there will always be an insurmountable distance between man and God which can only be overcome by action, action which is inextricably tied to ethics. Already before World War I, Buber had formulated a mystical faith: "Any construction of a 'pure ethics' of Judaism has to be fundamentally wrong. The essence of Judaism is where the Immediate is a veiled countenance of God that wants to be revealed in the human act."[7] Thus pure faith fulfills itself in the act.

The basis for all action is the possibility of a return from a mistaken action or misguided path. As human beings we are free to seek to encounter God: "Thus it is not a matter of proclaiming an 'ideal' and of demanding, defending and waiting for its realisation, but of starting out again every morning with the realisation of the right without knowing how far one gets today but knowing that the next day a new beginning can be made—and that in this Every-Day our perfecting and our perfection is concealed."[8]

Ultimately, Buber defined human action as the process of unification which includes the two dimensions which for Buber make up the essence of Judaism. The first dimension aims at the immediacy of the relationship with God, which is experienced, at least momentarily, in the encounter with Him. Second, unification is necessary in the community among humans: "Those humans, who promote community and therefore living union with each other, realize the image of the one God in the dimension of the world seesawing in conflict. All sanctification is unification...the highest level of sanctification of the world, however, is the unification of the community of humans in the face of God."[9] Thus unification can only be achieved through the synthesis of both dimensions.

If we examine this certainly most incomplete and daring outline of Buber's Judaism, we encounter a religion of action, of event, which continuously has to be recaptured spiritually. In one sense, Buber's Judaism remains representative and "typical"; and in the German-speaking regions there certainly exist a number of non-Jews who attained their idea of Judaism exclusively through Martin Buber. Walter Kaufmann mentions incidentally, though embarrassingly to the point, this peculiar perception in Germany: "If some Christians call him [i.e. Buber] the 'representative' of Judaism, all one can say is that he cannot be blamed for his contemporary lack of rivals."[10]

However, Buber was not the "typical Jew"—if there is such a thing—as many like to regard him. The Jewish discussion of Buber is internationally quite controversial, and even in Israel there are only a few who discuss him seriously. This, however, does not mean that Buber is a marginal phenomenon of Judaism. What makes Buber 'an atypical Jew' is his detachment from halakhic Law.

Buber did not accept historical Jewish tradition as described in the Torah and its interpretations. Buber summarized his attitude towards the Law in the following statement: "God's Torah...comprises laws,...but it is not itself essentially Law..."[11] 'Law' is the Greek mistranslation of Torah, which in the Hebrew Bible means: "Guideline, direction, instruction, advice, teaching."[12] Thus Buber rejected viewing the Torah as a concrete fixed Law. For Buber, only the instruction that reveals itself again and again is important; a Law that already exists is contradictory to his concept of revelation. By installing the Law as fixed, the living essence of the Law withers away[13] and becomes a rigid ethical principle. Thus for Buber, Judaism before the era of emancipation was enslaved not only from the outside by the "host nations," but also from the inside

223

by the "despotism of the Law": "There was no personal, emotionally rooted action: only action in accordance with the Law could persist. There was no independent, creative thought: Only the brooding on the books and the thousands of commentaries on those commentaries was allowed to be discussed. Of course, there always have been heretics, but what could the heretic do against the Law?"[14]

The preconditions for a rebirth of Judaism can only be created by a liberation from this coercion, Buber felt, which inevitably entailed assimilation. Buber regarded the conditions for a revival of Judaism as better among European Jewry, which had undergone emancipation, than among the Orthodox. With this belief, he took his place quite consciously among the heretics, and, in fact, he kept as much distance from the traditional synagogue as he did from the worship services of liberal Reform Judaism.[15] As for the revival of Judaism, Buber was always nearer to revolution than to evolution.

In his written response to Buber's "Lectures on Judaism" in 1923, Franz Rosenzweig asked whether the law that Buber envisions is really "the Jewish Law, the Law of millennia, that which has been studied and lived out, contemplated and praised, the Law for every day and death...Certainly the Torah, written as well as oral, was given to Moses at Sinai, but has it not been created before the world?" For Rosenzweig the Law has a specific cutting edge for the criticism of religion because it defies religious and moral paganism. In contrast to the nations, whose emergence remains obscure, to "Israel her way has been proclaimed already in the cradle;...the birth itself became the great moment of life, the mere existence itself became bound to its calling."[17] At the same time, the Law is in a constant condition of expansion, as it not only prohibits but in fact creates spaces for the permitted precisely through its prohibitions. For Rosenzweig this permission matters, as it is not an initiation of arbitrariness but remains the content of the Torah. "We neither know the limits nor how far back we can fasten the pegs of the tent of the Torah...."[18] Thus the Torah in its concentration on action is oriented towards the future. A legalistic interpretation, as Rosenzweig regards Buber's, is a crude narrowing, if not even a caricature. "Torah is more than Law, but Torah is the Law," responds Nahum Glatzer to Buber's statement on the Law.[19] As opposed to Buber's skepticism regarding all institutions, reflecting his anarchistic streak, Rosenzweig maintains that only the Jewish community can secure Jewish life and survival.

An incident reported by Ernst Simon, Buber's co-editor of *Der Jude*, is emblematic for Buber: "…I told him about my personal encounter with the Jewish way of life. Despite the objective danger of petrification and the…subjective danger of compulsion-neurosis, for me it had become a daily opportunity to serve God, an opportunity in which I could have confidence. 'This confidence is exactly what I do not have,' was Buber's response. With that we finally left it."[20] Buber himself writes: "I do not have anything but to live with fear and trembling; I do not have anything but the certainty that we have part in the revelation."[21] Buber again and again refers to the sought-for immediacy with God back to the prophetic experiences of the Bible. The ideal of immediacy surpasses the concreteness of the Law. Thus, despite Buber's emphasis on human action, the concept of the spirit becomes the most significant.

The concreteness of halakhic thought remained for the most part obscure to Buber. When he emigrated to Palestine from Germany in 1938, he was met with disappointment. As Eliezer Schweid put it, "The *Aggadah* of Judaism came to its fore in all its beauty through Buber's words. [In Israel] they could not recognize their reality of life, their halakhically rigid truth,"[22] in Buber's words. In Israel Buber lived often in painful isolation, because his life-work, which was based on dialogue, found less appreciation among his own people than among the nations of the world.

Therefore we see that Buber was no "typical" Jewish theologian, who interacts with the various traditions of his people to know them and himself better. Instead, Buber never dealt exclusively with the Jewish people; he rather aimed at the whole world and, knowing the whole, discovered individual parts of his own tradition. As he stated, "The history of Judaism and the history of great Jews is in its essence nothing else than a presentation of the primordial human, all-human process, here only especially concentrated and elucidated."[23] Jewish religiosity is in the first place a "generally human act." From the very beginning Buber pursued theology in the world forum, an approach that particularly reflects the problems of adapting theology to modern times. Perhaps in his concentration on the universal modern mentality, his understanding of the peculiarities of Judaism became obscured.

If we remember Buber's persistent alienation in Israel, we can conclude that he was in many ways a "typical German," closer to the German philosophers and scholars than to the Jewish theologians. There are in fact many examples of Buber's special rootedness in German intellectual life. Even at a young age he was attracted to German culture and stood aloof from traditional Judaism. Haim Gordon reports that the young Buber did not include in his Bar Mitzvah speech the biblical portion of the week but a verse from Schiller.[24]

Indeed his friend Gustav Landauer accused Buber of "aestheticism and formalism."[25] Buber's way of thought, especially concerning the renewal of Judaism, remained largely a factor of the pathos of language. In a certain sense Buber remained an aesthete who found satisfaction in the perfection of his creation of words. In any case Buber could not imagine an essential conflict between being a Jew and being part of German culture. Thus he underestimated the growth of anti-Semitism far into the Nazi era, apparently believing that Jews could survive in a secure ghetto in the hope of better times.

To be sure, Buber regarded National Socialism as a painful end to the German-Jewish symbiosis, but even after 1945 in writing to Nahum N. Glatzer he could still affirm the German language. "That you found attraction in the 'Gog' only in the German version I can understand very well. A love-affair like mine with the German language is simply an objective fact."[26] By contrast, modern Hebrew always remained a little unfamiliar to him. Exactly because Buber was not a philosopher or theologian, but a writer, his "rootedness in German culture and language was particularly deep."[27] And it comes most likely from the depth of his soul when he writes to Hans Trueb (December 20, 1945): "I may tell you that my separation from Germany has caused me much pain and still does."[28]

Language and culture have not been the only factors that influenced Buber. In the immediate context of the outbreak of World War I he made an extensive confession about Germany which today seems rather unbelievable. On September 30th, 1914, Buber wrote Hans Kohn:

> What you tell me about the atmosphere has somehow disappointed me. Here it is completely different: never has the term "people" become so much reality for me as in these weeks. Among the Jews as well a serious, noble sentiment prevails.... Among the millions who volunteered, there have been Karl Wolfskehl and Friedrich Gundolf....I myself unfortunately do not have any prospect of being useful; but I try to participate in my way....[29]

The immediate contact which Buber sought with German culture makes clear his interest in Christianity, which was claimed to be intrinsic to German culture. For example, in his theology Buber gives prominence to texts which also had an important role in the Christian tradition. This background helps explain the astonishing resonance which Buber has found among Christians. Despite his many philosophical writings, he has not been a *philosopher,* but a philosophical poet. His pencil was not sharpened by a critically balanced consciousness of method and concept. In his writings, impression and association, emphasis and linguistic onomatopoeia remain dominant. Buber also knew that there is no "typical" reality but that reality demands constant shaping, which has to fail from the very beginning, if one regards oneself as sufficiently supplied with concepts.

Buber's consistent criticism of the halakhah can best be understood as a product of the German-European tradition of an emancipated bourgeoisie. The unrestricted emphasis on individual freedom and the individual's sovereignty as opposed to all tradition is a cornerstone of modern European intellectual life. Yet despite his spiritual-emotional assimilation or rootedness in the German *Bildung*'s bourgeoisie, Buber was not the typical German Jew. Rather he addressed the assimilated Jews to remind them of their Judaism, to warn them of destructive self-abandonment and to show them the glories and attractions of a renewed Judaism.

Buber seems a sort of Jewish Schleiermacher, who also addressed the despisers of religion, to regain them for religion without attacking their educated contemporaries. Through Buber, Schleiermacher's work can become more graphic and alive, because Buber is historically closer to our time. Both Buber and Schleiermacher deal in apologetics; however, Christianity has been more susceptible to the apologetic tack, for while Schleiermacher has greatly influenced Christian theology, Buber barely has found a response within Jewish theology. Indeed, Buber's work is now predominantly followed by Christians, most likely because of his concessions to the interest of apologetics.

Finally, Buber did create for many Jews in Germany a connection with their forgotten Jewishness. Precisely because he was a German Jew, his voice was an energetic and charismatic warning against assimilation and self-abandonment. In this context, then, can we understand his Zionism: he joined the German emphasis of the spirit with the Jewish insistence on realization. The fact that he used an evidently European and particularly German intellectual background, from which he originated as an active participant, to urge a revival of Judaism, does not completely conceal his deepest intentions. In addressing assimilated Jews in Germany Buber in fact drew from Jewish sources and thus cannot be regarded as a representative of German culture.

Martin Buber can also be viewed as a prophet of Judaism among the nations; yet he cannot be labelled a "typical" prophet as the prophet is essentially an atypical personality. Jochanan Bloch (1919-1979), philosophy professor at Ben-Gurion University who studied Buber's life, calls him the unordained representative of Judaism to non-Jews whose wandering between the German and the Jewish worlds prevented him from becoming completely at home in either.[30] Yet precisely this ecumenicity served his "prophetic" activity.

One might object to designating Buber a prophet. But surely he was a herald and messenger of Judaism to the nations, dominated as was his work from the very beginning by the impulses of the mediator and diplomat. On the one hand, Buber's role was as a skeptical and even somewhat vehement voice of warning, calling for a return from the road to ruin. On the other hand, the designation of prophet makes it possible to do justice to his specific emphasis on theo-politics and the concept of realization, which shapes all his writings. In addition, the role of prophet does to a certain degree correspond to his self-consciousness, his very awareness that he was atypical.

Even after his emigration to Palestine in 1938, Buber remained a "wanderer between two worlds," between his people and the nations. Thus Shalom Ben-Chorin observes: "As much as Buber remained on the threshold between philosophy and theology, he also remained on the threshold between European culture in its German-Austrian variant and Israeli-Jewish humanistic culture."[31] And adds Robert Weltsch: "Buber is as are only a few others a genuine witness of the creative symbiosis between Judaism and Europe."[32]

Buber himself talked about the German-Jewish symbiosis after his emigration to Palestine, breaking his public silence about National Socialism to lament the loss of that symbiosis. "When it will be renewed," he wrote in 1939, "the symbiosis will by necessity link up with the values which had been its basis and to those works which emerged from it. But the symbiosis itself has come to an end and cannot return."[33] This lament shows us the anguish of a man who had been torn from his "organic context."[34] Buber had been convinced of the specific fruitfulness of the German-Jewish encounter. Though he knew about the "invisible clause of dismissal," inherent in every covenant of history,[35] he nevertheless emphasized that precisely the tense incompatibility between two cultures which are oriented towards one another allows for their specific productivity. In this sense only has the German-Jewish symbiosis been singled out by history. "The short productivity of the German-Jewish [symbiosis]," he says, "which in fact first made itself known when Goethe became inspired by Spinoza, or even before that, when Luther became inspired by the spirit of the Hebrew Bible, was a genuine and a natural one, even though it hardly lasted half a century."[36] Buber's works thrived fully on this cultural contrast. The loss of this dialogue therefore entailed for him a painful diminution of spiritual life.

The genocide of European Jewry committed by Nazi fascism has all but erased the character of this German-Jewish symbiosis. The German Jewry for whom Buber and Rosenzweig had translated the Bible no longer exists. When Christians today hold that translation in their hands, we must remember that it had not been written for us but for the now empty Jewish synagogues in our neighborhoods. To avoid robbing Buber of his Judaism, we have to remain conscious of his mission to us in his translation. As Christians, we must contribute to the dialogue or rather establish it in the first place. What matters is the liveliness of the German-Jewish dialogue despite prevailing differences, a liveliness that Buber perhaps envisioned when he admitted that he had undertaken a Jewish mission towards Christians with his Biblical-translation, despite his radical rejection of missionizing.[37]

There is probably no Jew who has influenced Christian theology as much as has Martin Buber, who initiated a lively encounter in which we are still engaged today. Helmut Gollwitzer regards it as a small sign of comfort that through Buber, "in the context of Christian theology which contributed significantly to the occidental contempt of the Jews, there emerged among a few the willingness to learn this Jewish teaching of a Jew."[38] While Gershom Scholem had been right to claim that there no longer exists a German-Jewish symbiosis, it is our task to refute him today and in the future.

Martin Buber incorporates for Christians "a perception of Judaism, which seems to be authentic and modern and fulfills their anticipations."[39] And herein lies our challenge: without diminishing Buber's merits as Israel's prophet among the nations and with gratefulness for Buber's prophetic allusions, we must go even further. We must pass through the gate that Buber has opened to learn that we still have a long way to go. It is up to us to realize and continue the Buber heritage. To continue, however, means not only to heed the voice of the "atypical" man Buber but to seek dialogue with all other voices which have either spoken to us in the past or speak to us today.

NOTES

*This essay is based on the author's book on Martin Buber's thought, *Grenzgänger: Martin Buber's Anstösse für Weitergehen* (Ch. Kaiser, München, 1987).

1. Cf. Martin Buber, "Antwort" (Answer), in: *Martin Buber,* ed. P. A. Schilpp and M. Friedman (Stuttgart, 1963), 589-638, 602; with a few editorial changes this text is also included in his *Collected Works,* 1109-22 (see note 11 below).

2. Martin Buber, *Der Jude und sein Judentum* (Köln, 1963), 65ff.

3. Ibid., 69.

4. Ibid., 72.

5. Ibid., 189.

6. Ibid., 133, cf. 188.

7. Ibid., 74.

8. Ibid., 245.

9. Ibid., 237.

10. W. Kaufmann, "Buber's religiöse Bedeutung" (Buber's Religious Importance), in: *Martin Buber,* ed. P. A. Schilpp and M. Friedman, 487, 571-88.

11. Martin Buber, *Werke* (Collected Works). *Erster Band: Schriften zur Philosophie,* München u. (Heidelberg, 1962), 691

12. Ibid., 690.

13. Martin Buber, *Werke. Zweiter Band: Schriften zur Bibel,* München u. (Heidelberg, 1964).

14. *Die jüdische Bewegung* (The Jewish Movement), 1916, quoted according to G. Scholem, "Martin Buber's Auffassung vom Judentum" (Buber's Perception of Judaism), in: *Judaica* 2 (Frankfurt, 1970), 143.

15. Cf. also Sch. Ben-Chorin, *Zwiegespräche mit Martin Buber* (Dialogues with Martin Buber) (Gerlingen, 1978), 72ff.

16. F. Rosenzweig, "Die Bauleute" (The Construction Workers), in: *Zur jüdischen Erziehung* (On Jewish Education) (Berlin, 1937), 59.

17. Ibid., 61f.

18. Ibid., 68f.

19. N.N. Glatzer, "Buber als Interpreter der Bibel" (Buber as Interpreter of the Bible), in: *Martin Buber,* ed. P. A. Schilp and M. Friedman, 346-63.

20. E. Simon, "'Angst und Vertrauen' bei Martin Buber" (Fear and Trust in Martin Buber's Works), in *Leben als Begegnung: Ein Jahrhundert Martin Buber (1878-1978)* (Life as Encounter: One Century with Martin Buber), Lectures and Essays, 2d ed., ed. P. von der Osten-Sacken (Berlin, 1982), 28-41.

21. Buber, "Antwort," 597.

22. E. Schweid, "Martin Buber und Aharon (David) Gordon: *Eine Gegenüberstellung*" (A Juxtaposition), in *Martin Buber, Bilanz seines Denkens* (An Account of His Thought), ed. J. Bloch and H. Gordon (Freiburg, 1983), 285.

23. Martin Buber, *Der Jude und sein Judentum,* 241.

24. H. Gordon, "Der geborene Ästhet: Eine neue Deutung von Buber's Leben" (The

Born Aestheticist: A New Interpretation of Buber's Life), in: *Martin Buber, Bilanz seines Denkens*, ed. J. Bloch and H. Gordon (Freiburg, 1983), 45-60.

25. "In spite of all your opposition I call this aestheticism and formalism. And I say that you—facing yourself—have no right to participate in the public debate on the current political events which are called World War, and to integrate this chaos into your beautiful and wise generalities. The result is something completely inadequate and upsetting." It is worth reading the whole of Landauer's letter, dated on the 12th of May, 1916; see *Letters*, hg. Band I, 433-38.

26. Martin Buber, *Briefwechsel aus sieben Jahrzehnten* (Letters), Band III, ed. G. Schaeder (Heidelberg, 1972-1975), 223.

27. M. Wyschogrod, "Buber's Beurteilung des Christentums aus jüdischer Perspektive" (Buber's Assessement of Christianity from a Jewish Perspective), in J. Bloch and H. Gordon, op. cit., 470-86. In a letter to H. Gordon on September 7, 1934, Buber himself emphasizes that he was a writer: "I am actually a *German* writer" (Buber's emphasis), in *Letters*, Band II, 553.

28. *Letters*, Band II, 96.

29. *Letters*, Band I, 370f.

30. Cf. J. Bloch, "Eröffnungsworte" (Opening Remarks), in *Martin Buber, Bilanz seines Denkens*, ed. J. Bloch and H. Gordon (Freiburg, 1983), p. 18.

31. Sch. Ben-Chorin, *Zwiegespräche mit Martin Buber* (Dialogues with Martin Buber), 52.

32. R. Weltsch, "Martin Bubers Bedeutung für das jüdische Bewusstsein im 20. Jahrhundert" (Martin Buber's Importance for Jewish Consciousness in the Twentieth Century), in: *Martin Buber 1878/1978*, ed. W. Zink (Bonn, 1978), 17-27.

33. *Der Jude und sein Judentum*, 546.

34. Ibid., 644.

35. Ibid., 216.

36. Ibid., 645.

37. *Werke*, Zweiter Band, 1182.

38. H. Gollwitzer, "Martin Bubers Bedeutung für die protestantische Theologie," in *Martin Buber, Bilanz seines Denkens*, ed. J. Bloch and H. Gordon (Freiburg, 1983), 402-23.

39. Schweid, op. cit., 270.

THE YOKE OF
THE KINGDOM IN JERUSALEM

Paul Mendes-Flohr

"Such is the generation of
them that seek after Him,
That seek Thy Face."
—Psalm 24:6

ON THURSDAY EVENING THE THIRTEENTH OF JULY 1939, a small group of
intellectuals gathered in the spacious Jerusalem residence of Judah L.
Magnes (1877-1948).[1] They were members of a newly formed religious
circle, *Ha'ol* (the Yoke). The circle apparently grew out of weekly
meetings that took place alternately at the homes of Martin Buber (1878-
1965) and Magnes.[2] At the time, Buber lived in an apartment near the
Ratisbonne monastery bordering the Rehavia neighborhood of Jerusalem, and Magnes resided in a simple but spacious home he had built on
Alfasi Street, situated in the heart of Rehavia, which was often referred
to as "kleiner Berlin" because of its great concentration of Central
European Jewish immigrants. *Ha'ol* would fit well into the emerging
cultural landscape of Rehavia, not only because the Hebrew of its
members bore the distinctive accent and cadence of their native German
but also because their discourse displayed the peculiar philosophical
inflections of educated Central European Jewish intellectuals struggling
to comprehend Judaism—to define their relationship to the tradition of
Israel and to God in light of the modern sensibility.

Each of the participants in *Ha'ol* was a member of the faculty of the
Hebrew University, except for Magnes who at the time was president of
the university. Each of these men at this inaugural meeting of *Ha'ol* was
an immigrant from Central Europe, aside from Magnes who hailed from

Oakland, California and had settled in Jerusalem in 1922 where he was instrumental in the establishment of the Hebrew University, serving as its first chancellor. Each of the individuals whom Magnes hosted in his home that evening had made a distinguished contribution to the renaissance of Jewish thought and scholarship in this century: Yitzhak Fritz Baer (1888-1979), Shmuel Hugo Bergmann (1883-1975), Martin Buber (1878-1965), Julius Guttmann (1880-1950), Gershom Scholem (1897-1982), and Ernst Akiva Simon (1899-1988).[3]

These individuals also represented an elite of Central European Jewry who, aside from Buber, had settled in Jerusalem in the 1920s and early 1930s. In Jerusalem they constituted a unique community. Recalling life in Jerusalem in this period, the Prague-born historian Hans Kohn (1891-1971) observed that:[4]

> the Jewish community [of Jerusalem] was still fairly small; people knew each other, and life was simple....There were no luxuries and few people were preoccupied with making money. Hardly anyone we knew had come to escape persecution or to improve his economic situation. Rather they came out of what might be called "idealism," for want of a better word. There were many brilliant and remarkable men and women among them. For a community its size, cultural life among the Jews in Jerusalem was of great intensity and creativity.

The alliance between the Central European intellectuals of *Ha'ol* and Magnes, the former American rabbi, proved uniquely propitious. The differences of background were mitigated by the fact that Magnes, a child of German immigrants to the United States,[5] spoke German and had, indeed, earned a doctorate from the University of Heidelberg. Nonetheless, his *yekke* friends never ceased to regard him as an American. With allusion to Magnes' pacifism and his imperious management of the affairs of the fledgling Hebrew University, Scholem somewhat derisively referred to him as a unique combination of "a Jewish Quaker and an American boss."[6] Nonetheless, Magnes' religious idealism and energetic organizational skills endeared him to Scholem and the other intellectuals who would join *Ha'ol*. The *yekkes,* for their part, helped Magnes to articulate his religious program within the conceptual refinements of European theological discourse.

Several weeks before *Ha'ol*'s first meeting in July 1939, Magnes had circulated a proposal for the group, which he initially called *mevaqshey panekha* ("Those who seek Thy Face").[7] Explaining the name, an allusion to Psalm 24:6,[8] Magnes notes that it refers to all those who seek the

God of Israel, indeed, all "those who have not yet found the path [to Him] and…[don't know]…if they ever will, although their search for the path is the deepest, most burning desire of their lives."[9]

Magnes tellingly adds that the search is guided by "faith and theology but *not* religion." For "when one says 'religion,' one implies that the path has already been found, and one is already committed to the official articles and beliefs [of a given religious tradition]."[10] Rather, the society Magnes proposed would address the question: "Is there any possibility of knowing God's 'Face' either by direct communication or [by means of] an authoritative tradition, or by virtue of His deeds?"

Written under the impact of the ominous events in Germany—the Munich Pact of September 1938, in which Chamberlain yielded to Hitler's nefarious designs on Czechoslovakia, and *Kristallnacht* of November 1938[11]—Magnes' proposal was animated by a sense of urgent, indeed, defiant affirmation of God's presence in history.

This was not Magnes' first attempt to establish such a religious association. In late 1928, he solicited the enthusiastic support of Hans Kohn and Shmuel Hugo Bergmann, both formerly of Prague.[12] Together they drafted a five-page proposal, the preamble to which reads:[13]

> [The members of the Association] are united in seeking the intellectual basis of faith and in their endeavor to live in accordance with the mandate of 'God within' each. This does not necessarily mean a confession of faith in a Supreme Being. It means an abiding interest in the problems of religion and a vital and honest quest of answers to these problems.

This effort proved fruitless, as was a later proposal to found a "Community of Hebrew Religious Morality."[14]

After more than ten years of consultations and draft proposals, Magnes realized his envisioned society, *Ha'ol.* This association, as were its ill-fated predecessors, was borne up by a sense of religious crisis. In a letter to Mahatma Gandhi on behalf of *Ha'ol,* Buber explained the spiritual crisis of his generation:[15]

> …Jewry of today is in the throes of a serious crisis in the matter of faith. It seems to me that the lack of faith of present day humanity, its inability truly to believe in God, finds its concentrated expression in this crisis of Jewry, darker, more fraught with danger, more fateful than anywhere else in the world.

Buber further explained to the revered Indian leader that "neither is this crisis resolved here in Palestine; indeed we recognize its severity here even more than elsewhere among Jews."[16] But, Buber continued, it was the conviction of the members of *Ha'ol* that Zionism and the return of the Jews to their ancestral land provided the basis for the renewal of Israel's faith.

It was this affirmation of the spiritual possibilities of Zionism that brought Buber and Magnes together and linked their lives in a common spiritual—and political—endeavor. On the occasion of Buber's fiftieth birthday, Magnes sent his friend greetings in which he rapsodically spoke of Zion's promise for the "deepening" and "renewal" of religious faith:[17]

> Here the soil is ready for this work [of renewal]. Here the sources of Judaism flow, partially deep underground, hidden below the rubble of centuries, and which one must first bring forth. The Bible, the language, the land, the landscape, a millennial culture and categories of thought [animating] the Mishna and Gemara, the history of the Orient aside the magnificent Jewish-European development, mysticism and rational philosophy—all are the inexhaustible sources of Judaism in Palestine.

Magnes concluded his greetings with an appeal to Buber to hasten his *aliyah* and discover the sources of Judaism that lay within the bosom of Palestine: "The living waters [of Judaism] bid you to drink of them."[18] Buber, then in Germany, would accept the invitation only in the spring of 1938, ten years later.

Neither Buber's nor Magnes' faith in the promise of Zionism was naïve, however. Magnes especially was burdened by a deep pessimism. "Below my placid surface," he noted in a journal entry from February 1937, "I am racked by religious doubt, by pessimism as to the world and Palestine."[19] Such troubled musings, which harken back to his youth, are recurrent in his journals, growing in frequency and intensity with the ascendency of what he regarded a morally myopic nationalism among the Jews of Palestine, and with the tragic events unfolding in Europe.[20]

It was these doubts that prompted Magnes' efforts to establish a new religious community—or theological "platform" as he put it. Significantly, he held that "this platform would and could not unfortunately be a Synagogue."[21] For though the society he envisioned would be comprised of people who passionately "seek God," most "have not found the path...and who knows if they ever will find it. Nonetheless, the most burning and deepest aspiration of their lives is the search for this path."[22] And in this quest they will perforce be guided by "faith, theology, but not," the former rabbi unabashedly emphasized, "religion."[23] Lamentably, Magnes observed, "when one says religion one means one has already found the path [to God] and is bound to officially prescribed articles of faith."[24]

What was urgently required, in Magnes' judgment, was a radical re-thinking of the fundamentals of faith and Judaism. In contemporary parlance, one might describe Magnes' program a "deconstruction" of Judaism, a concerted effort to get "behind" the texts and fundamental concepts of the tradition, radically to re-think them in order, of course, to reconstruct and reevaluate their meaning for us.[25]

The protocol of the meeting of July 1939 of *Ha'ol* offers a unique glimpse into their "deconstructive" deliberations.[26] The session was de-voted to perhaps the most vital topic facing modern Jews confronting their tradition: "What is the Torah to us?" Scholem opened with a brief statement which was then discussed by his colleagues. Despite the truncated rhythms of the stenographer's abridged transcription of the original proceedings, the notes—translated here from the Hebrew—marvelously reflect the tenor of *Ha'ol*'s theological reflections, the probing, irreverent yet manifestly affectionate scrutiny of the basic principles of Israel's faith. The protocol deserves to be cited in full:

SCHOLEM: The Torah is the sounding of a supernal voice that obliges one in an absolute manner. It does not acknowledge the autonomy of the individual. To be sure, Jeremiah was promised a "Torah of the heart"; but only at the end of days. The *hasidim,* in fact, did make an attempt to prepare the "Torah of the heart." A Hasidic work interprets a passage in Deuteronomy 17 [:18f.] on the king of Israel—"and he shall write for himself in a book a copy of the Torah..., and it shall be with him, and he shall read in it all the days of his life..."—such that the king will read the Torah within him, that is within himself.[27] This autono-mous conception of the Torah, however, is not [at all] compatible with the Traditional conception. Torah has two meanings: the designation of a path and transmission of something. Everything in the world, even a person, can be "Torah," but there *never* is Torah without supernal authority. The Torah is the Creator's dialogue with human beings, prayer is human beings' dialogue with the Creator. There is no Written Torah without the Oral Torah. Were we to desire to restrict the Torah to the Torah transmitted in writing, we would not be able to read even the Pentateuch but only the Ten Commandments. It follows that even the Torah [i.e., Scripture] is already Oral Torah. The Torah is understandable only as Oral Torah, only through its relativization. In itself it is the perfect Torah without a blemish, and only through its mediation, the Oral Torah, is it rendered intelligible.

From all this, however, it follows that [our understanding of] the Torah develops and changes, and according to its very nature it [the Torah as we understand it through the ever-evolving Oral Torah] cannot be rendered a unified system. The Torah is rather a continuum of questions and answers. Nonetheless, in spite of this development, there is nothing arbitrary about it whatsoever. [Although] every generation wishes "its" Torah to be the divine voice of revelation, there is no place here for the individual's freedom of decision. In principle, therefore, Orthodoxy is correct.

But as regards ourselves, we are unable to accept the Oral Torah of Orthodoxy. Yet with respect to the Written Torah it is incumbent upon us to recall that nothing therein is in itself fixed without the exegesis of the Oral Torah. We must therefore wait for *our* own Oral Torah which will have to be binding for us, leaving no room for free, non-authoritative decision. There is no Torah without revelation (*matan Torah*) and there is no Torah without heteronomy (*heternomiah*) and there is no Torah without an authoritative tradition.

BUBER: It is not necessary to assume that the source of Oral Torah must be in exegesis. The Oral Torah may have its source in a [single] word.

GUTTMANN: Scholem's position leads to utter subjectivism. According to him the Oral Torah is a function without a specific content. How can such a Torah be the possession of a collective? We must be beholden to the *content* of the [Written] Torah [i.e, the *mitzvot*].

SIMON: Scholem's view may be summarized thus: Had God brought us to Mount Sinai but not given us the Torah [i.e, the *mitzvot*], we should have been content (*dayyenu*).[28] [In my opinion, however], we must view the *mitzvot* as an echo of the Lord's words [*ke-hed devrey ha-gevurah*]. [On the other hand], we cannot give up our autonomy. Were someone to demonstrate to me that the Oral Law understands the commandment "not to kill" as a prohibition against the killing of Jews by Jews alone, I would not accept this explanation of the commandment and I would rely on my autonomy.

BAER: The theological question is of secondary importance. What is important is the responsibility of man before God and the organization of his life in accordance with this responsibility. This was the greatness of the Talmud. The Torah demands righteousness and justice. This is the task that lies before us: the creation of a social order that is in consonance with the Hebrew [concept of] justice. It is possible to *prepare* for the days of the Messiah. If we do not upbuild the Land [of Israel] with righteousness and justice, all is lost. This is the conclusion to be drawn from our history.

BUBER: [I wish to emphasize], there is no messianic politics. It is impossible to say that this prepares the coming of the Messiah and that this does not. Baer is right, however, when he implies that the deeds of human beings may elicit [a new] revelation—and revelation may also come from within a society. Revelation need not necessarily be transmitted through a voice; it can come by means of something, by an event.

MAGNES: According to the accepted understanding, the Oral Torah is a fence around the Torah [i.e., the Written Torah and its *mitzvot*];[29] according to Scholem it is liberation from the Written Torah. This is the position of the Gospels. This position constitutes a negation of the Torah. The strength of Orthodoxy was in its commonly accepted exegesis. This is also the principle of Catholicism. Scholem's view is precisely the opposite.

SCHOLEM: To a known degree we are anarchists. But our anarchism is *transitional*, for we are the living example that this [our anarchism] does not remove us from Judaism. We are not a generation without *mitzvot*, but our *mitzvot* are without authority. I do not have a feeling of inferiority with respect to those who observe [the Law]. We are not less legitimate than our forefathers; they merely had a clearer text. Perhaps we are anarchists but we oppose anarchy.

ADDENDUM TO THE PROTOCOL SUBMITTED BY MAGNES: At the end of his lecture Scholem remarked: "I believe in God, this is the basis of my life and faith. All the rest [of Judaism] is in doubt and open to debate."[30]

In the light of the religious anarchism which Scholem believed characterized his colleagues, it is seemingly paradoxical that they chose to call their group *Ha'ol* (the Yoke)—a name expressly taken from a Rabbinic Midrash: "Take upon yourselves the Yoke of the Kingdom of Heaven and judge one another in the fear of God and act toward one another in loving kindness" (*Sifre Deuteronomy* 32:29).[31] *Ha'ol*, accordingly, defined itself as "a group of friends whom a single question has brought together: 'Are we Jews merely a persecuted people asking for mercy or have we a message which we want both to proclaim and to carry out? Are we conscious of the Yoke which our Father has placed upon us?'"[32]

Prima facie, this conviction that Israel must assume "the Yoke of God" would seem to contradict *Ha'ol*'s religious anarchism, not to say theological agnosticism. In a speech to open the academic year 1944-45 at the Hebrew University, Magnes addressed this paradox. For he who seeks God, Magnes told the students, "can do no other than to persist in his quest to the last, to keep on inquiring, struggling, challenging. He will not be granted tranquility of soul. But if it be given him to renew the forces of his being day by day and constantly to be among the seekers, the rebellious—that is the crown of his life and the height of his desire."[33]

The search for God's Face, Magnes contends, is thus to be accompanied by an existential affirmation of God's rule in the world, the rule of "justice and mercy, equity and liberty."[34] Hence, as Magnes explained in yet another address to the students of the Hebrew University, morality—or rather what he would call prophetic morality, that is, bad politics and public policy based on the considerations of "absolute" or prophetic morality—is ultimately an act of faith. Indeed, morality is the only sure path by which we, as ordinary human beings not graced with special divine knowledge, can "draw near to the supreme reality, the God of Israel."[35]

Bergmann discerned in Magnes a "tragic faith," a breakthrough from the depths of despair" to an affirmation of God's rule.[36] This "tragic faith" is not to be understood merely as a defiant refusal to yield to despair, nor is it to be regarded as an endorsement of an "as-if" theology favored by neo-Kantians and pragmatic philosophers who hold that to uphold values formerly supported by religious belief it is necessary to act "as if" one still affirmed God's reality. Magnes, as did all the members of *Ha'ol,* emphatically rejected such pragmatic "theology" as intellectually unsatisfactory, indeed dishonest.[37] To affirm God as a "useful fiction" struck them as scandalous, an affront both to reason and the ultimate reality of God and His rule to which they remained true.[38]

In his letter to Gandhi, Buber had occasion to elaborate the theological presuppositions of *Ha'ol.* Reconstituted in Zion as an organic community, Buber explained to the Mahatma, the Jews—scarred by the humiliations of the Diaspora and bewildered by their hasty passage through the purgatory of secularization—have the unique opportunity of healing the crisis of faith, not only for themselves but also for humanity at large:[39]

240

There is no solution to be found in the life of isolated and abandoned individuals, although one may hope that the spark of faith will be kindled in their great need. The true solution can only issue from the life of a community which begins to carry out the will of God, *often without being aware of doing so, without believing that God exists and that is His will.*

And Buber further explained that at this delicate juncture in the spiritual history of Israel, "believing people" should not stand apart from those who have lost faith but should support their effort to restore to Israel its secular dignity. They should "neither dictate nor demand, neither urge nor preach," rather it is incumbent upon them to share in the life of the nation, to "help, wait and [be] ready for when it will be their turn to give the true answer to the enquirer." Hence, Buber concludes, "the Yoke of the Kingdom of God" must now be borne in the public secular sphere. "This is the innermost truth of Jewish life in the Land; perhaps it may be of significance for the solution of this crisis of faith not only for Jewry but all humanity. The contact of this people with this Land is not a matter of sacred ancient history: we sense here a secret still more hidden."[40]

As "servants of God,"[41] as Magnes somewhat sententiously put it, the members of the *Ha'ol* pursued a social and political activism, particularly on behalf of what they deemed to be the most exigent issue facing the Jewish community in Palestine: the need to promote Arab-Jewish rapprochement. It is thus not surprising that their energy was soon deflected from *Ha'ol* with its largely theological focus to more concretely political activities sponsored by other organizations, activities which in time led to the demise of Magnes' religious society.[42] Political engagement—affirming the divine principles of justice and compassion—was, of course, no digression. For those who had resolved to bear "the Yoke of the Kingdom of Heaven" it was a necessary corollary of the abiding quest for God's Face.

NOTES

1. The day of the week and time of the meeting are determined by the Hebrew date, 27 Tammuz 5699, given together with the secular date on the protocol of the meeting. (On the protocol, cf. note 26, below.) The venue of the meeting was described to me by Fania Scholem, the wife of Gershom Scholem, in a discussion I had with her in the winter of 1986, but it may have taken place at the home of Martin Buber; cf. following note. Magnes' secretary, Lili Jerusalem (currently a member of Kibbutz Givat Hayim), also recalls that "a meeting of *Ha'ol* took place in the home of Magnes on Alfasi Street and

that afterwards she "accompanied Buber home and along the way we discussed the question of faith and unbelief." Letter to me, dated April 1, 1990. Given the theme of Mrs. Jerusalem's discussion with Buber, it is likely that the meeting of *Ha'ol* that they attended that evening in the home of Magnes was, indeed, the meeting—devoted to the question of authority and faith in Judaism—considered in this article.

2. On these meetings, cf. S. H. Bergmann, *Tagebücher und Briefe,* ed. Miriam Sambursky (Königstein/Ts.: Jüdischer Verlag bei Athenäum Verlag, 1985), I: 4906-499.

3. It seems that in the weekly meetings of *Ha'ol* Robert Weltsch (1890-1982) also occasionally participated. Cf. Bergmann, op. cit., 496.

4. Hans Kohn, *Living in a World Revolution: My Encounters with History* (New York, 1932), 143f.

5. Magnes' mother, Sophie (Abrahamson), was born in Filehne, in eastern Prussia. Her family came to San Francisco in the 1860s. "From her mother Sophie imbibed a love for German culture; that and the presence of the Abrahamson grandparents exposed the Magnes children to the German language and culture." Arthur A. Goren, introduction, ed., *Dissenter in Zion: From the Writings of Judah L. Magnes* (Cambridge: Harvard University Press, 1982), 5. Although Magnes' father David was Polish born, German-Jewish culture seems to have been dominant in the younger Magnes' upbringing.

6. Oral communication from Shmuel Sambursky (1900-1990), professor emeritus of the history of science at the Hebrew University, September 1982.

7. Magnes' draft proposal is cited in full by S. H. Bergmann, "J. L. Magnes Seeks His God: On the First Anniversary of his Death." *Ha-aretz* (Tel Aviv daily) (October 17 1949), 2.

8. Cf. the epigram to this essay. "Thy Face" (*panekha*) may also be translated as "Your Presence." Cf. Mitchell Dahood, ed. and trans., *Psalms I* (Anchor Bible 12) (New York, 1965), 153.

9. Cited in Bergmann, "J. L. Magnes Seeks his God," 2.

10. Ibid.

11. Bergmann, "J. L. Magnes Seeks his God," 2.

12. Goren, *Dissenter in Zion,* 51.

13. In a letter, dated January 13, 1929, Hans Kohn sent Buber a copy of the proposal written in English. Cf. Martin Buber Archive, Jerusalem, varia 350, Mappe vav 371. Magnes' draft proposal and Buber's response is discussed in detail in my, "The Appeal of the Incorrigible Idealist," in *Like All the Nations? The Life and Legacy of Judah L. Magnes,* ed. William M. Brinner and Moses Rischin (Albany: State University of New York Press, 1987), 145f.

14. On "A Community of Hebrew Religious Morality," see *Judah Leib Magnes Papers,* Central Archives for the History of the Jewish People, Jerusalem, Mappe 2436, document no. 143 (B of F)—Magnes' five-page Hebrew outline of the community's program. The terminology and governing concepts of this document reflect the influence of the Zionist philosopher Aaron David Gordon (1856-1922) and Buber.

15. Buber to Gandhi, letter dated April 1939, included in *Two Letters to Gandhi from Martin Buber and J. L. Magnes.* Pamphlet no. 1 of the Group "The Bond" (Jerusalem, 1939), 10. Before being dispatched to Gandhi, the letters were read before the weekly meetings of *Ha'ol* (cf. note 1, above). Cf. Bergmann, op. cit., 495, 496, 499. According to Bergmann, the letters were actually sent on the 12th of March 1939. Ibid., 499. A reply from Gandhi was never received.

16. Buber to Gandhi, letter dated April 1939, p. 11.

17. Magnes, "Al Har Hazophim." *Der Jude: Sonderheft zu Martin Buber's fünfzig-sten Geburtstag* (Berlin, 1928), 50. The title of Magnes' article, written in German,

is a transliteration of the Hebrew, "On Mount Scopus," i.e., the site of the Hebrew University campus.

18. Ibid., 51.

19. Journal entry from February 22, 1937, in Goren, *Dissenter in Zion,* 324. Magnes discerned in Buber a similar pessimism, cf. Magnes, "He Who Sees Reality in its Totality." For Professor Buber on his seventieth birthday (1948), *Ner,* nos. 9-10 (1965), 20-21 (Hebrew). On pessimism—or rather the tragic sense—prompting Buber's affirmative faith, see his revealing discussion of Kafka in his *Two Types of Faith.* trans. N. P. Goldhawk (New York, 1989), 162-67. Cf. my discussion of Buber and Kafka, in "Martin Buber and the Metaphysicians of Contempt," in J. Reinharz, *Living with Anti-Semitism: Modern Jewish Responses* (Hanover/London: University Press of New England, 1987), 163f.

20. Cf. "I am racked by...skepticism as to efficacy of the pacifist point of view; by loathing of German heathenism; by pity for the suffering of Spain and other millions; by disillusionism; as to Russia as evidenced by the recent trials, by –, by –. And yet I am happy.—What a confusion! I do not envy those whose lives are less confusing. 'At sixty' the battle is still attractive. But the pain, deep down, is sometimes unbearable." Journal entry of from February 22, 1937, in Goren, *Dissenter in Zion,* 324.

21. From a fragment of a letter (first page is missing) from Magnes apparently to Felix Warburg; from the context the letter seems to be from 1929. *Judah Leib Magnes Papers,* miscellany. Cf. "...Alas, I have no confidence that the official communities of the *galut* [Diaspora] will seize this unparalleled opportunity to make Judaism a vital, spiritual force at this critical period of history....Nevertheless, there are happily, throughout the *galut* Jewish groups (*most of them, strangely enough, outside the synagogue*) which have been loyal and who will continue to prove their loyalty to this truly religious ideal." Magnes, "*Eretz Israel* and the *Galut.*" Address delivered in Jerusalem, May 22, 1923, in Goren, *Dissenter in Zion,* 213 (emphasis added).

22. Cited in Bergmann, "J. L. Magnes Seeks His God," 2.

23. Ibid.

24. The rejection, in the name of faith, of "religion"—that is the formal, institutional expression of religious faith—was rather fashionable in post-World War I theology. Cf. my "Law and Sacrament: Ritual Observance in Twentieth-Century Jewish Thought," in Arthur Green, *Jewish Spirituality: From the Sixteenth Century to the Present* (New York, 1987), 337 n. 20.

25. *Ha'ol* would, then, not endorse the premise of deconstructionism regarding the intrinsic elusiveness of truth and meaning. Rather they pursued a radical re-thinking of the basic concepts of Judaism for the sake of its renewal as a spiritual matrix of meaning and truth.

26. The protocol consists of two typewritten pages in Hebrew. The second page of the protocol was discovered several years ago by Professor Arthur Goren of the Hebrew University among the Judah Leib Magnes Papers (Mappe 2273; *Ha'ol*). The first page of the protocol was subsequently found among the papers of Gershom Scholem by Dr. Avraham Shapira. I wish to thank Professor Goren and Dr. Shapira for bringing my attention to these documents. The protocol in its entirety was first published in my "Law and Sacrament," 321-22. The original Hebrew version, with my commentary, now appears in G. Scholem, *Od Davar,* ed. Avraham Shapira (Tel Aviv: Am Oved, 1989), 95-98, and 516f.

27. The protocol does not provide the source of this exegesis; Scholem probably has in mind the commentary of Kalonymous Kalman Epstein of Cracow; cf. his *Ma'or wa-Shemesh* (Breslau, 1841-42; reprint Tel Aviv, 1965), 220a.

243

28. Simon, of course, is here citing the well-known thanksgiving hymn, *"Dayenu,"* of the Passover Haggadah.

29. Cf. *Pirque 'Avot* 3:13: "Tradition is a fence around the Torah." A standard rabbinic commentary explains this famous dictum from the Mishnah thus: "The Oral Torah—[the tradition] which is passed from one generation to another—is a hedge around the Written Torah, for without this tradition we would not understand the meaning of the [Written] Torah and its Laws. And we should be like a vineyard without a fence and everyone would do as he pleases, explaining and interpreting the Torah as he pleases." Pinhas Kahtai, *Commentary to the Mishnah* [Hebrew], 9th ed. (Jerusalem: Keter, 1971), II:359.

30. The varied theological issues of this protocol are discussed at length in my aforementioned essay, "Law and Sacrament."

31. Cited on the title page of the pamphlet mentioned in note 14 above.

32. Cited on inside cover of ibid.

33. Magnes, "For Thy Sake We Killed All the Day Long" (Psalm 44:23), Address at the opening of the academic year 1944-45 of the Hebrew University (November 1, 1944), in Magnes, *In the Perplexity of the Times* (Jerusalem, 1946), 67.

34. Magnes, "The Source of Prophetic Morality," Opening address for the academic year 1943-44 of the Hebrew University (November 14, 1943), in Magnes, *In the Perplexity of the Times*, 59.

35. Ibid., 61.

36. S. H. Bergmann, *Faith and Reason: An Introduction to Modern Jewish Thought,* trans. A. Jospe (New York, 1961), 142.

37. Cf. Magnes' critique of Mordecai Kaplan's theological pragmatism, in Goren, *Dissenter in Zion,* 193-94. Similarly, while a member of the American rabbinate, Magnes was decidedly uncomfortable with the sentimental-cum-cultural reasons marshalled by his colleagues in support of a more traditional attitude toward the *mitzvot.* Cf. ibid., 222-25, 267-68. His diaries and few public pronouncements on the subject reveal a Jew in anguished search for a theology sanctioning a life of prayer and ritual devotion. Cf. "I stand in reverence (or respect) and read and repeat the prayers and am sometimes moved, particularly by the prayers of believers, but I do not *pray,* or at least I do not pray to *Him.* Yet I believe that I should, and others like me, continue to read Psalms and other literature, to ponder, to hope, to complain to Him (just as though there were a Him) to deepen our lives, and perhaps..." The parenthetical statement would seem to be an endorsement of an "as-if" theology, but it is qualified by the "perhaps" which Magnes elaborates in an adjacent note in his journal. Cf. "I can only read and read and seek and ask—and wait. Perhaps the vision will be vouchsafed to me, too, some day....Who are the others for whom this bums as a fire or a light or a hell. I wish I might know them and learn from them and be kindled by them." Magnes, Journal entries from October 24 and 25, 1937. Cited in Goren, op. cit., 52.

38. See Nahum N. Glatzer's exposition of Franz Rosenzweig's critique of the "as if" philosophy propounded by the neo-Kantian scholar Hans Vaihinger, in Rosenzweig, *Understanding the Sick and Healthy: A View of World, Man, and God,* trans. not stated, ed. and introd. by N. N. Glatzer (New York, 1955), 14f. Cf. "Rosenzweig, in contrast to Vaihinger, considers man as a whole whose reason is not divided into a theoretical and practical aspect. He cannot believe therefore that the 'as if' approach can bring man 'inner and outer peace.' Far from being able to cure the invalid [i.e., the modern individual afflicted by theological doubt] the notion of 'as if' can only add to his confusion." Ibid., 15. Rosenzweig's critique, it would seem, exercised a strong influence on his generation of Jews seeking to reappropriate traditional faith.

39. Letter to Gandhi, April 1939, op. cit., 11 (italics added).

40. Ibid.

41. Cited in Bergmann, "J. L. Magnes Seeks His God," 2.

42. *Ha'ol* did in fact contemplate some political activity but largely confined these efforts to clarifying the ethical-religious issues involved in the political challenges then facing the Jewish people. Cf. Bergmann, "J. L. Magnes Seeks His God," 2. See also the one publication issued by *Ha'ol,* namely, *Two Letters to Gandhi* (cf. note 13 above). Most of the members of *Ha'ol* joined the League for Arab-Jewish Rapprochement, founded in April 1939, and the Ichud, a political association founded in August 1942 by Buber and Magnes and which promoted a humanistic conception of Arab-Jewish reconciliation. See *A Land of Two Peoples. Martin Buber on Jews and Arabs,* ed. with commentary by Paul Mendes-Flohr (New York, 1982), 134-35, 137-38, 148-49.

PART VII

The Arts

Problems of Identity
in the Art of German Jews

Ziva Amishai-Maisels

JEWISH ARTISTS IN GERMANY in the modern era were subject to two divergent desires. On the one hand, they wished to be fully integrated into German art and culture and often joined avant-garde movements in order to make a more decisive contribution. On the other hand, at some point in their careers, often under the influence of external pressures, they usually felt a need to express themselves in their art as Jews. For many of these artists, the interplay between these two factors was problematic, and each artist responded differently depending on his own background and the pressure of events in his time.

One of the sources of the problems encountered by German-Jewish artists was the thorny, uneven path of the Jewish Enlightenment and Emancipation in Germany. Although Moses Mendelssohn (1729-1786) spearheaded the Enlightenment in the mid-eighteenth century, equal rights for German Jews were obtained only piecemeal in the early nineteenth century as a result of Napoleon's ongoing conquest of Germany. After his defeat in 1814, these rights were withdrawn by many of the German states, and the reactionary wave which then swept over Germany found expression in displays of open anti-Semitism. Although attempts were made to restore these rights in 1848-1849, complete success was achieved only in 1869-1870.[1] Thus for one hundred years, enlightened German Jews were on an embattled seesaw, encouraged when rights were given to them and dashed down when they were withdrawn. Even after 1870, there remained a constant undercurrent of anti-Semitism in Germany which grew to immense proportions in the

1920s and 1930s and culminated in the Holocaust. Whereas this pressure caused some Jews to emphasize their Judaism, others tried to prove themselves more German than the Germans, affirming that they were "German and not Jewish" or "Germans of the Mosaic faith." These developments directly affected the lives of German-Jewish artists and their work shows their reaction to this ever-changing situation.

Since the Enlightenment dawned before the Emancipation, several Jewish artists converted to Christianity in order to practice their art and further their careers. This was already true in the case of Ismael Israel Mengs (1688-1764) who became a court painter in Dresden and dedicated his son Anton Raffael Mengs (1728-1779) to art not only by naming him after famous artists, training him and taking him to study in Italy, but by raising him as a Christian.[2] The younger Mengs thus followed quite a different path than did his contemporary, Moses Mendelssohn. Rather than retaining the best of both cultures, Jewish and German, he entirely abandoned the former to become a moving force in the latter, pioneering Neo-Classicism in close collaboration with J.J. Winckelmann.

Mengs' path was followed by several artists who grew up in Germany after the French Revolution and witnessed the adoption and repeal of Jewish rights in the early nineteenth century. Although their conversions were usually as complete as that of Mengs, some of them consciously or unconsciously expressed a rationalization of their conversion in their art. A few of them, such as Philipp Veit (1793-1877), Wilhelm Schadow (1788-1862) and Eduard Bendemann (1811-1889), belonged to the Nazarene school which tried to revive German Christian art and included in its ranks several Protestants who converted to Catholicism while working in Rome.

Veit, a grandson of Moses Mendelssohn, converted as a result of his upbringing. After his parents, Dorothea Mendelssohn and Simon Veit were divorced when Philipp was six years old, he was raised by his mother who converted to Protestantism when she married Wilhelm von Schlegel. Simon Veit reclaimed his son when he was 13 and tried to raise him as a Jew, but Philipp rebelled and entered the art academy in Dresden in 1809. While visiting his mother in Vienna in 1810, he converted to Catholicism, two years after his mother and stepfather had done so. His belief that Jews were doomed to damnation is seen from his comment to Moritz Oppenheim on his grandfather's adherence to Judaism: "Who knows what punishment he is now suffering for that!"[3]

After fighting in the German army against Napoleon (1811-14) and being made an officer, Veit arrived in Rome in 1815, fitting into the Nazarene group thanks to both his German patriotism and his Catholicism. Shortly after his arrival, he was apparently instrumental in obtaining for the Nazarenes the commission to decorate the reception room of his relative, the new Prussian consul Jacob Salomon Bartholdy (1779-1825), who had converted to Christianity in 1805.[4] Although the original project was for a simple design of arabesques, the Nazarenes soon substituted for it a cycle of the story of Joseph. It is not clear who suggested this substitution, which derived both from the Nazarenes' interest in the Bible and from Bartholdy's reluctance to have a New Testament theme in his house.[5] However, this choice of subject is a direct allegory on Bartholdy's position as consul: like Joseph, he was a Jew who gained high political office, assuming the dress, manners and, in this case, the religion, of a non-Jewish court. Although his Jewish "brothers" had difficulty "recognizing" him, he benefited at least two of them who had followed in his footsteps, Veit and Schadow, by commissioning them to paint the frescoes. By using this subject, Veit, Schadow and the other Nazarenes expressed their view that Bartholdy had a Jewish precedent for his actions and this may have been the light by which Veit saw his own conversion.

Bendemann, coming from a different background, took a different view of his conversion. The son of a Jewish banker in Berlin, Bendemann had converted under the influence of his teacher, Wilhelm Schadow, at about the time he married Schadow's sister, Lida.[6] His conversion may have been one of ambition rather than conviction, as shortly afterwards he was appointed Professor at the Dresden Academy, eventually succeeding Schadow as director of the Düsseldorf Academy.[7] Shortly before his conversion, he painted *The Mourning Jews in Exile* (1832), based on Psalm 137, in which an old man, women and children sit by the waters of Babylon, their harp broken and hung on a willow (fig. 1). Their withdrawn poses, the way they turn from each other in their isolation, and the entire expression of the painting convey a lack of hope in their redemption. At about the time he converted, Bendemann expressed this despair a second time, in his *Jeremiah on the Ruins of Jerusalem* (ca. 1834-36). Here the prophet sits mourning amidst the ruins and corpses, unable to avert the catastrophe. Bendemann repeated this theme towards the end of his life in *The Jews Being Led Away to the Babylonian Captivity* (1872), where masses of Jews are led away by Nebuchadnezzar to

251

Fig. 1. Eduard Bendemann, *The Mourning Jews in Exile,*
1832, Wallraf-Richartz-Museum, Cologne.

unending exile.[8] Since these subjects were not specifically commissioned, they apparently express Bendemann's own despair at the fate of Judaism, a despair that formed the background, or the rationalization, for his conversion to Christianity.

Moritz Oppenheim (1800-1882), who was also affiliated with the Nazarenes in Rome, was exceptional in that he did not convert and expressed his Judaism in his art in a more positive way. Oppenheim had witnessed the humiliation of the Jews in the Roman ghetto and was under strong pressure from Veit and the other Nazarenes to convert.[9] Despite this, he clung to his Judaism and made contact with the Rothschilds, who became his patrons, thus giving him the means to remain a Jewish artist. Oppenheim followed the normative development of nineteenth-century German academic art: at first adopting the Nazarene's style and religious and historical iconography, he then turned to the Biedermeier school's more naturalistic style and use of genre scenes with piquant anecdotal details.[10] In many of these works, his Judaism is evident only in small details. For example, when *Moses hands over the Leadership to Joshua* (1841), he gives him both the Ten Commandments and the Scrolls of the Law, expressing the idea that the whole Torah was given to Moses on Sinai.[11]

While his portraits also seem at first a part of normative German art, a closer examination suggests that his work is more complex. Whereas several of his sitters were staunch Jews who had succeeded in the modern world, such as members of the Rothschild family, many others were converted Jews, such as Heinrich Heine, Ludwig Börne, Dr. Salomon Steibel, Ferdinand Hiller and Fanny Hensel-Mendelssohn.[12] Oppenheim's portraits thus mirror the choices open to Jews in Germany during this period and show his involvement with those who made these choices.

These problematics are even more obvious in a group of works in which Oppenheim stressed the conflict between Christians and Jews, made a claim for Jewish rights, and protested against conversion. The earliest of these works, *The Return of the Jewish Volunteer from the Wars of Liberation to His Family Still Living According to the Old Tradition* (1833-34), stresses the loyalty of the Jews to Germany in a war whose success ironically stripped them of their rights. By showing the pronouncedly Jewish character of the soldier's family and home, he emphasized that Jews could make a contribution to Germany while retaining their faith. The painting is thus both an avowal of Oppenheim's position as a German-Jewish artist and a protest against the unfair repeal of Jewish rights after the Napoleonic wars. That the painting was understood in the latter sense at the time is evident in its donation by the Jews of Baden to Gabriel Riesser in gratitude for his constant fight in support of Jewish civil rights.[13]

The second scene, *Lavater and Lessing visit Moses Mendelssohn* (1856, fig. 2), depicting an episode that probably never took place, presents the Swiss clergyman Johann Caspar Lavater's written public challenge to Mendelssohn to either disprove Christianity or convert to it, and reveals Mendelssohn's affirmation of Judaism through his published answers to Lavater. Gotthold Ephraim Lessing is placed as a witness between the two, and his proximity to Mendelssohn reflects Lessing's position as Mendelssohn's friend and supporter in the Christian world.[14] Oppenheim suggests the intricacies of the dispute by placing a library full of books in the background and a chessboard between the protagonists; but the setup on the chessboard shows that Mendelssohn is winning, and the prominence of the Sabbath lamp above their heads conveys the idea that Mendelssohn remains within the framework of Judaism. The entrance of the woman with the tea tray, who is set right above Lavater's somewhat threatening walking stick, suggests that such disputes can end amicably.

Fig. 2. Moritz Oppenheim, *Lavater and Lessing Visit Moses Mendelssohn*, 1856, Judah L. Magnes Memorial Museum, Berkeley.

Fig. 3. Moritz Oppenheim, *The Jahrzeit*, 1871, Judah L.
Magnes Memorial Museum, Berkeley.

Shortly afterwards, Oppenheim took the opposite stand. His sketch
for the *Abduction of the Mortara Child* (1862) depicts the moment in
1858 when six-year-old Edgardo Mortara, who had been secretly bap-
tized by his nurse, is claimed by the Church and removed from his family
who try legally to have him restored in 1860, though to no avail.[15] Here,
responding indignantly to a contemporary event which reminds him of
his own experiences in the ghetto of Rome, Oppenheim stresses the
trauma of the family and the need for reform. This sketch remains,
however, an exception in his oeuvre, as his view of Judeo-Christian
relations in modern times was usually optimistic. For instance, in *The
Jahrzeit* (fig. 3) of 1871, he celebrates the recent extension of equal rights
to Jews in Germany. Here, during the Franco-Prussian war, Jewish
soldiers form a *minyan* in a French peasant's house so that one of them
can say *Kaddish*. They cover the cross on the wall but behind them stands
a small statue of Napoleon, the first granter of civil rights to German
Jewry. This work is almost a reprise of *The Return of the Jewish Volunteer*, emphasizing not only that he can return to his Jewish home once his

duty is done but that duty and religion are not in conflict and can be carried out simultaneously.[16]

To strengthen the roots of enlightened and emancipated Jewry, in the 1850s and 1860s Oppenheim began to paint genre scenes of Jewish life which parallel the Biedermeier scenes of Christian life that had been popular since the mid-1830s.[17] In these works, he created a roseate memory of Jewish ghetto life, stressing religious holidays, the general well-being, and the *heimische* atmosphere supposedly prevalent in Jewish families at the end of the eighteenth century. These works were reproduced with detailed explanations as *Scenes from Traditional Jewish Family Life* in the 1880s and were popular with both Jewish and Christian collectors, albeit for different reasons. Assimilated Jews were attracted to this nostalgic view of their forefathers' lifestyle which most of them had long given up, while Christians were curious about the mores and religion of those "exotic" Jews who were occupying an increasingly important place in German public life.[18]

Oppenheim is thus the first German-Jewish painter who clearly and continuously expressed the duality which was to become inherent to German-Jewish art. On the one hand, he assimilated stylistically and iconographically into the accepted norms of German art. On the other, he used his art to portray the dilemmas of Jewish life in Germany, to strengthen its roots among Jews and to prove its inherent beauty and worth to the Germans.

The major German-Jewish artist of the next generation was Max Liebermann (1847-1935), best known as the leader of German Impressionism and one of the founders of the Berlin Secession—a group of modern artists who broke with the academic German salon in the 1890s—and its longtime president. More than Oppenheim, Veit or the other artists mentioned here, Liebermann played a central role in the formation of modern German art. He began his career in the 1860s with detailed portrayals of the life of German and Dutch peasants. Gradually, he adopted an Impressionist brushstroke to render his constant interest in the effects of sunlight, turning in the 1890s to depictions of bourgeois life in Berlin. Liebermann considered himself so strongly integrated into German culture that in conversations with Chaim Nachman Bialik, whose portrait he was painting at the time, he stated that whereas Zionism was fine for oppressed Jews in other places, he was content to remain in his own land, where he felt completely free. This attitude was undermined only by the rise of Nazism and his subsequent expulsion from the Academy in 1933, events which led him to reassess both German-Jewish life and Zionism.[19]

Yet Liebermann had a side to his personality which is usually ignored in this picture of perfect assimilation. From the start of his artistic career, he sketched religious Jews, often in Eastern European garb. When abroad, he had a penchant for visiting and painting synagogues. In Amsterdam, he constantly painted the Jewish quarter, its markets and its gesticulating Jewish residents.[20] The synagogue interiors and sketches of Jewish characters were utilized in his *Twelve-year-old Christ in the Temple* (1879, fig. 4), in which he attempted to give the scene a Jewish, if not strictly historical perspective by placing it in a synagogue and using pronouncedly Jewish types, including both Eastern European and modern liberated Jews. This kind of setting was taken up five years later by Fritz von Uhde (1848-1911) who, strongly influenced by Liebermann, began to paint the life of Christ as set in nineteenth-century rural Germany.[21] But whereas von Uhde, a Protestant, achieved popularity because of this approach, Liebermann's painting was attacked by critics who considered it the height of impertinence for a Jew to depict Christ in such a way, even categorizing the fair-haired Italian boy he had used as a model for Jesus as particularly ugly and Jewish in type. Since Liebermann's painting had been inspired by a wish to combat anti-Semitism by stressing Jesus' Jewish background, these anti-Semitic outbursts made him so acutely uncomfortable that he stopped painting Biblical scenes for almost twenty years.[22] During that time, he expressed his Jewish identity through depictions of Amsterdam's Jewish quarter, revealing the meaning of these seemingly neutral townscapes only by their titles. When he returned to Biblical scenes after having completed a few illustrations for a Dutch Bible that was published in 1902, he carefully chose only "acceptable" themes. Thus *Samson and Delilah* (1902) depicts the popular *femme fatale* and was strongly influenced by Eduard Munch, and *The Good Samaritan* (1911) is based on von Uhde's now acceptable development of Liebermann's originally unacceptable modernization of Biblical scenes. *The Good Samaritan* was executed during the month von Uhde died, so that Liebermann may have been paying homage in it to his disciple, both by choosing one of von Uhde's themes, and perhaps by seeing that artist in the title role.[23]

It was only after this return to Biblical themes that Liebermann felt secure enough to support Jewish causes publicly. In 1914, appalled by the pogroms in Russia, he published a drawing of a screaming mother and

257

Fig. 4. Max Liebermann, *The Twelve-year-old
Christ in the Temple*, 1879, private collection.

her children fleeing from soldiers who strike down the father and labeled
it sarcastically: *'To my beloved Jews' (the Tsar)*. Shortly afterwards, he
depicted a ruined shtetl and gave it the caption, *In East Prussia*.[24] Almost
ten years later, responding to resurgent anti-Semitism and the growth of
the Nazi Party, he executed a lithograph memorializing the ten thousand
Jewish soldiers who died fighting for Germany during World War I. He
thus consciously reverted to Oppenheim's expression of Jewish patriotism as military service and sacrifice to Germany's cause.[25]

The attitude of Liebermann's associate, Lesser Ury (1861-1931), was somewhat more complex. He too started as a Naturalist and became an Impressionist in the late 1880s portraying bourgeois life in the streets and cafés of Berlin.[26] In the mid-nineties, however, Ury began to use a second, more academic style to depict allegorical and Biblical scenes. Whereas his early attempts at such scenes had concentrated, as had those of his teacher, Bendemann, on Jerusalem's destruction,[27] the First Zionist Congress gave his thoughts a more positive direction. In *Jerusalem* (1896, fig. 5), he did not portray the city but rather the yearning towards it as felt by the waters of Babylon.[28] Keeping in mind Bendemann's depressed rendering of this scene (fig. 1), Ury cautiously instilled it with hope. Old depressed men still sit in the foreground, withdrawn into themselves, and the most they can do is to pray. In the middle ground, their back to the viewer, sits the younger generation. While the woman weeps, the man beside her and the boy before him, look out past the river, over the horizon towards the Jerusalem of their dreams. Ury's painting is thus an immediate response to, and expression of, the shift from the despair of the older generation to the hope engendered in the young by the Zionist movement. The following year, he further answered Bendemann's view of Judaism in *Jeremiah*, who no longer sits bent over mourning the destruction of Jerusalem but lies relaxed in the desert,

Fig. 5. Lesser Ury, *Jerusalem*, 1896,
present whereabouts unknown.

gazing dreamily at the brilliant stars in the sky. This was an image of hope and prophecy more normative to depictions of Abraham than to those of Jeremiah.[29]

In these paintings, the style is so different from that of Ury's Impressionist works that one might think two different painters were involved. This change is not due to stylistic development: throughout his life Ury continued to use both styles, each with its own subject matter. The iconographic and stylistic dichotomy in his art expressed the dichotomy in his personality. The Impressionist Ury remained a Berliner, expressing German life and culture; the academic Ury expressed himself as a Jew through his Zionist and Biblical themes, and was upset that Jews did not respond by buying his Biblical paintings.[30]

Ury's dualism, this open adherence to Jewish and Zionist subject matter while staying in the mainstream of German art, was echoed in the works of two major German graphic artists: Ephraim Moise Lilien (1874-1925), an exponent of *Jugendstil*, who became the official artist of the Zionist Congress, and Hermann Struck (1876-1944), who was considered the master etcher in the Germany of his time and was also a delegate to the Zionist Congress.

Lilien espoused a two-pronged approach to German Jewry. First of all, he promoted the inculcation of Jewish values into German-Jewish culture. He designed the cover of *Ost und West,* the Berlin monthly magazine for Jewish culture and art, and worked for the *Jüdischer Verlag,* editing the Jewish art section of its first almanac. Yet at the same time, Lilien favored immigration to Palestine and it was he, rather than Ury, who established the classical depiction of longing to return to the Promised Land. In *Passover* and *The Jewish May* (fig. 6) as well as in his poster for the Zionist Congress of 1902, he depicted an old European Jew, trapped in a thornbush, whose thoughts turn longingly towards the Holy Land. This image reverses a popular German anti-Semitic type, the Jew in the thornbush, who appears in a story by the Brothers Grimm.[31] In utilizing this image in a Zionist context, Lilien suggests that the way to combat such anti-Semitism is to leave Germany and return to Palestine. He himself attempted to do this in 1906, when he went to Jerusalem to help Boris Schatz establish the Bezalel School of Art. Although he did not stay, he visited Palestine in 1910 and 1914 using the drawings and photographs he produced there as the basis of his illustrations for a German edition of the Bible. His Old Testament figures wear Bedouin costume, Herzl is depicted as Moses, and the New

Fig. 6. Ephraim Moise Lilien, *The Jewish May*, 1902, from
Morris Rosenfeld, *Die Lieder der Ghetto*, Berlin, 1902.

Testament is decorated with appropriate scenes from daily life in
Palestine to avoid portraying Christ.[32]

Hermann Struck's works seem, at first, less involved with Zionism.
He usually etched portraits and landscapes, while his Jewish themes
stress religious rituals and the physiognomy of the Jewish groups he met
in Eastern Europe during World War I. However, he signed all these
works in Hebrew to stress his Jewish identity, despite the danger of being
boycotted by anti-Semites.[33] Like Lilien, he too felt a stronger tie to
Palestine than to Germany. One room in his studio even served as a
meeting place for the *Mizrachi* faction of the Zionist Congress, so that
Struck would run back and forth between the meeting room and his art
students who were working in another room. In 1923, Struck moved to
Haifa, practicing and teaching his art there until his death.[34]

This "second generation" of German-Jewish artists made different
choices than those of the "first generation." After Oppenheim, artists no
longer feared to remain Jewish or to depict Jewish subjects. However, it
is not by chance that the most famous of these artists, and the one who
made the greatest contribution to German art *per se*, was Liebermann,
who openly acknowledged his Judaism but kept its expression in his art
to a minimum. Other Jewish artists of this generation either led a double
life (e.g. Ury) or eventually expressed their Jewish identity in their art and

261

lives. These artists rarely appear in books on German art, although Ury is occasionally mentioned for his Impressionist landscapes, Struck for his etchings, and Lilien for his adherence to *Jugendstil*. In stressing their Jewish side, they withdrew from the mainstream avant-garde movements to which they belonged, focusing their innovations on Jewish rather than on German art.

These tensions continued in the next generation of artists, active in the early twentieth century. Thus, for example, the director of the avant-garde Sturm gallery in Berlin so completely concealed his Judaism beneath a German veneer that he changed his name from Georg Lewin to Herwath Walden (1878-ca. 1941).[35] But two of the painters he exhibited in his gallery, Ludwig Meidner (1887-1968) and Jakob Steinhardt (1887-1968), reacted to their dual identity in quite a different way. Raised in traditional Jewish homes in small villages in Eastern Germany, they had taken up residence in Berlin during their youth. They had met by 1908, possibly through Struck with whom they had studied etching. Inspired by German Expressionist poetry and art, Meidner and Steinhardt joined forces to found the *Pathetiker* group which exhibited at the Sturm gallery in November 1912.[36] At this exhibition, both artists focused on apocalyptic destruction but the differences between them were already discernible. Meidner depicted the apocalyptic cataclysm as taking place in the modern world, giving his works a prophetic ring that echoed German Expressionist poetry (fig. 7). Steinhardt, also taking his cue from certain Expressionist writers, conveyed the same idea through Biblical imagery. He identified the seer-like artist with the prophets and portrayed *Jeremiah* (fig. 8) seated among the ruins of the world, not just of Jerusalem. In so doing, he opened himself to attack by Kurt Hiller (1885-1973), the Jewish critic and editor of *Die Aktion,* who deplored what he termed the Zionist tone of Steinhardt's works and suggested that the artist try to overcome it.[37]

This joint exhibition proved prophetic of the divergent paths the two friends would follow. Meidner maintained his generalized approach even when, during and after World War I, he adopted Steinhardt's now popular idea of the artist as a Biblical prophet, turning with equal fervor to the Old and the New Testaments, depicting St. Paul as often as Moses, and being especially attracted to the Biblical rebel, Korach.[38] Immediately after Hiller's review, Steinhardt attempted to develop a more general iconography but soon returned to an even more emphatically Jewish subject matter, depicting pogroms and praying Jews in a highly Expressionist style. After being quartered in the Lithuanian shtetls during World

Fig. 7. Ludwig Meidner, *Apocalyptic Landscape,*
1912, private collection.

War I, he became one of the major painters of that form of Jewish life.[39]
Thus, after the war, Meidner remained an integral part of the German
avant-garde, signing every available manifesto, while Steinhardt opted
instead to assume a major role in the flowering of Jewish culture in Berlin
in the early twenties.

In the mid-1920s, Steinhardt set his Jewish subjects aside to join the
avant-garde *Neue Sachlichkeit* movement, concentrating on landscapes
and portraits. However, affected by the rise of Nazism, he soon returned
to his shtetl scenes and tried through his 1930 *Sunday Preacher* to warn
the German people to repent of their present-day evil before it was too
late.[40] In 1933, one step ahead of the Gestapo, he escaped to Palestine,
where he immersed himself in painting the old streets of Jerusalem
inhabited by religious Jews who reminded him of those he had known in
Lithuania. While continuing to speak German, he abandoned that part of
his experience to stress the Jewish side more fully, finally returning to
Biblical themes. He became a major figure in Israeli art, and memories of
his German past appear only rarely in his art, usually in terms of Gothic

263

Fig. 8. Jakob Steinhardt, *Jeremiah*, 1912-13, private collection.

houses and as reworkings of the beggars and scenes of destruction he had depicted in his early works.[41]

During the same period, Meidner entered a new phase in his life and art. As Nazi power increased, Meidner became more religious, and, especially after he was labeled a degenerate artist by the Nazis and could find employment only in a Jewish school in Cologne, he concentrated on Biblical subjects and Jews in prayer, signing his works with a Hebrew initial and date. Turning his back gradually on his German past, he emphasized his Judaism. In 1939, just before the outbreak of war, he escaped to England, where he continued to work in this religious genre and drew apocalyptic scenes inspired by the Holocaust.[42] However, his lack of success led him in 1952 to return to Germany, where he became a leading spokesman for the earlier Expressionists. At this point, Meidner declared that he felt he had come home at last, and although it has been claimed that he remained religious, he utterly submerged himself once more in German art and culture.[43]

The works of Jankel Adler (1895-1949) show a reaction to German culture lying midway between that of Steinhardt and Meidner. Born in Lodz, Adler moved to Germany at the age of sixteen and soon joined the Young Rhineland group which tried to secure for artists of the Düsseldorf region their deserved place in German art. However, on returning in 1918-20 to his native Lodz, he helped found the Young Yiddish group of artists and writers. Resettling in Düsseldorf, he adopted the avant-garde *Neue Sachlichkeit* style, using it to express both German and Jewish subjects. Following German trends, he portrayed male-female relationships, workers and the poor, his style invoking a sense of mystery through strange perspectives and juxtapositions, strongly influenced by the Italian Giorgio de Chirico.[44] Occasionally, as in *Angelika* (1923) and *Judith* (1927-28), he added to the strangeness by inscribing Hebrew words in the background.[45] At the same time, he portrayed shtetl types from his native Poland, integrating this traditional subject once more into avant-garde art by means of the *Neue Sachlichkeit* style.[46] Like Steinhardt, but unlike Oppenheim, he specifically chose to portray traditional Eastern European Jews, the *Ostjuden* with their distinctive dress, rather than German Jews who were indistinguishable from their Christian neighbors. However, like Oppenheim, he depicted Jewish soldiers praying, their readily visible phylacteries stressing adherence to their religion (fig. 9).

In 1933, Adler fled Germany, leaving his Christian wife and daughter behind. After fighting with the Free Polish army against the Germans at the start of World War II, he was evacuated to Britain. Yet despite the more abstract style he had developed after 1933, he also expressed his anxiety about the war in a traditional Jewish way. In *Two Rabbis* (1942), for example, the wounded Jews who seem to be behind barbed wire extend a message to the Christian public asking for mercy, while the *Priest* (1942) gives his *kohen*'s blessing while hiding in a small closed room.[47] Many of his works of this period deal, however, not with Judaism *per se* but with the anxiety the Holocaust aroused in him. Before his death, Adler spoke of settling in Israel with his wife and child, rather than returning, like Meidner, to Germany.[48]

Other artists of this generation showed less interest in their Judaism, even when they suffered because of it. This was especially true of abstract artists, such as Anni Albers (b. 1899), who was affiliated with the *Bauhaus*. Such artists were for the most part uninterested in expressing their Judaism. With the rise of Hitler, they emigrated to America along with the other *Bauhaus* teachers, and continued working in their usual style as though nothing had happened.[49] The same can be said of Hans Richter (1888-1976), best known as a Dadaist. Richter, who had fought in the German army in World War I and then joined the Dada movement in Zurich, returned to Germany after the war, making his greatest contribution to art with his films. These were international in character, although in the mid-twenties several of them were marked protests against the German establishment. Richter was in Russia making an anti-Nazi film when Hitler came to power, but he soon moved back to Western Europe and in 1941 arrived in the United States, continuing to produce Dadaist and Surrealist films wherever he found himself.[50]

These artists reflect the international character of twentieth-century art in which artists move easily from one country to another, owing allegiance to Art itself rather than to their native land or to their religion. Their approach makes it difficult to categorize artists according to nationality. However, this specific identification was of primary concern to the Nazis, and those artists who happened to be Jewish suffered for it whether they identified with their religion or not.

Many German-Jewish artists succeeded in escaping from Germany in the 1930s. However, those who stayed in Europe, such as Felix Nussbaum (1904-1944), usually fell into Nazi hands and were killed. Having been expelled from the German Academy in Rome in 1933 for being *Jewish*, in 1935 Nussbaum settled in Belgium. Arrested in Belgium in 1940 for

Fig. 9. Jankel Adler, *Soldiers*, 1928,
present whereabouts unknown.

being *German*, he was deported to the St. Cyprien internment camp in the south of France, only to escape a few months later and return to Belgium, where he lived in hiding, without identity papers, running from one safe house to another. Although in an early self-portrait he had portrayed himself in the synagogue and he had painted Jews praying at St. Cyprien, his art does not usually utilize traditional Jewish iconography. Instead, he expressed the feelings of Jewish refugees living in constant fear of approaching death. He depicted himself and his friends in hiding, or wearing Jewish stars when they ventured outside, carrying the identity papers he lacked (fig. 10) or huddled together as Death comes to claim them.[51] In these works, Nussbaum expresses the ordeal inflicted by Germany on its Jewish citizens, who repeatedly escaped only to be caught again. His fears were fulfilled in 1944: trapped by the Nazis, he was deported to Auschwitz where he and his wife were gassed upon arrival.[52]

Genuine refuge was to be found in England (Meidner and Adler), America (Albers and Richter) and Palestine, to which Steinhardt made his way in 1933 and was soon joined by Mordechai Ardon (b. 1896, formerly Max Bronstein), Myron Sima (b.1902), Jacob Pins (b.1917), Eric Mendelssohn (1887-1953) and many other artists and architects. They brought with them the various styles then current in Germany—Expressionism, *Neue Sachlichkeit,* and the *Bauhaus*—and became the active force behind the new Bezalel School of Art and the Haifa Technion, changing the face of future Israeli art and architecture. Like Steinhardt, these artists all but rejected their German past. Although all of them reacted to the Holocaust at one point in their artistic development, they preferred to become assimilated into their new land and to express their new surroundings in their work. Yet they never really stopped being German: they preferred to speak German rather than Hebrew, and belonged to the German intellectual circles in Jerusalem and Haifa that strongly influenced culture in Palestine.[53]

Among these German artists, one, Lea Grundig (1906-1977), projected a more violent tension between her German and Jewish selves. Rebelling against her middle-class Jewish family, she married a Christian artist, Hans Grundig (1901-1958), and joined the Communist party. Their work focused at first on the condition of the poor, but they both soon turned to Communist-approved anti-Nazi polemics. While he used animal imagery to convey these ideas, she used human figures to warn of the threat of war and to protest anti-Semitism.[54] Yet her etchings for the series sarcastically entitled *The Jew is Guilty* (1935) are by no means philo-Semitic, for Lea showed absolute contempt for religious Jews. Her hostility to them in works such as *The Jewish Funeral* in this series surpasses her hostility to the Nazis, to the point that the rabbi leading the procession is almost worthy of *Der Stürmer.*[55] Her ambivalent feelings

Fig. 10. Felix Nussbaum, *Self-Portrait with Jewish Identity Card*, 1943, Kulturgeschichtliches Museum, Osnabrück.

towards Judaism are also perceptible in a self-portrait in which she wears a Stürmer mask around her neck, unhappily assuming the identity of the Jewish stereotype, much to the dismay of her family. In an early version of this work (fig. 11), other such masks appear above her on the wall, jeering at her for having to be identified as a Jew despite her antipathy to Judaism.[56]

In 1936 and again in 1938, the Grundigs were arrested for Communist

269

Fig. 11. Lea Grundig, *Stürmer Mask,* 1936, no. 4 of
The Jew is Guilty series of etchings, first state.

activities. Finally, while her husband was sent to Sachsenhausen without
her knowledge, Lea was allowed to join her family who had emigrated to
Palestine. She spent the war years there, rarely depicting local scenes,
although she produced one sympathetic portrayal of an old religious
couple walking in the streets of Jerusalem.[57] Instead, she concentrated on
illustrating events in Germany and Poland, trying to awaken people to

270

the atrocities there through albums such as *In the Valley of Slaughter* published in Tel Aviv in 1944. Although in Palestine she used her maiden name, Langer, the album was issued under her married name, for in it she identified with Hans, left behind in Germany. This album contains extremely strong depictions of the horrors of the concentration camps and the bravery of the ghetto revolt, and its imagery is by no means ambiguous. Yet her ambivalence to Judaism continued to seep through in her wartime *Ghetto* series where she pitied the starving ghetto inmates that she drew, but caricatured the greedy religious Jews, who almost seem responsible for their fate, and documented the in-fighting among the ghetto dwellers.[58]

Unlike other German artists who emigrated to Palestine, Grundig neither turned her back on Germany nor became acclimated to Palestine, despite the aid offered to her by influential patrons, such as Mordechai Narkiss, director of the Bezalel Museum. At the first opportunity, in 1949, she returned to Germany to rejoin Hans in Dresden, becoming one of the major art teachers of East Germany. She served as president of the Association of East German artists from 1964 to 1970 and sat on the Presidium of the Socialist Unity Party in 1967. During these years, she remained a political artist and, while her works contain a few echoes of her reactions to the Holocaust, they are primarily restricted to Communist protests against "Capitalist warmongering."[59]

With Lea Grundig, the art of German Jewry continues beyond the Holocaust. But her postwar work also takes us full circle back to a complete assimilation into her German surroundings and a conversion to a new religion—this time not Christianity, but Communism. Whereas German-Jewish artists enriched both German and Jewish art for over a century, with the Jews spreading the gospel of German art far and wide through their migrations, the unique play between German and Jewish art that had been a feature of this fruitful development came to an end with the Holocaust. Those artists who returned to Germany, such as Meidner and Grundig, became as highly assimilated into German culture as Veit and Bendemann had been at the beginning of the nineteenth century.

NOTES

1. Simon Dubnov, *History of the Jews* (New York, 1971-73), vol. 4, pp. 588-655; vol. 5, pp. 19-69, 255-74, 425-35.
2. Cecil Roth, *Jewish Art*, rev. ed. (Jerusalem, 1971), 190; and Thieme-Becker,

Allgemeines Lexikon der Bildenden Künstler (Leipzig, 1907-47), 24:390-93.

    3. Thieme-Becher, ibid., vol. 34, pp. 183-85; M. Spahn, *Philipp Veit* (Bielefeld, 1901), 3-25; Dubnov, ibid., 635-40; and Moritz Oppenheim, *Erinnerungen* (Frankfurt, 1924), 90.

    4. Bartholdy was the brother of Leah Salomon, who married Abraham Mendelssohn, Dorthea's brother and Philipp Veit's uncle (*Encyclopedia Judaica* [Jerusalem, 1971], vol. 11, cols. 1324-26, and vol. 14, col. 264; and Dubnov, ibid., 640-41). Since Bartholdy and his sister and brother-in-law had converted, they would have had no problem in staying in touch with the Schlegels and with Veit. See the summary of Bartholdy's career and his letter to Abraham Mendelssohn in Alfred Kuhn, *Peter Cornelius* (Berlin, 1921), 112-16.

    5. William Vaughan (*German Romantic Painting* [New Haven, 1980], 178-79), credits the idea to Veit, Schadow and Cornelius, while Kuhn (p. 117) credits Overbeck. For the suggestion that the "Jewish" Bartholdy felt a New Testament story would be too polemical, see David Koch, *Peter Cornelius* (Stuttgart, 1905), 74. For illustrations and the most recent research on these paintings, see Robert McVaugh, "A revised reconstruction of the Casa Bartholdy Fresco Cycle," *Art Bulletin* 66 (Sept. 1984), 442-52.

    6. Wilhelm Schadow (1788-1862) was the son of the sculptor Gottfried Schadow and a Jewish convert to Catholicism, Marianne Devidels. Although by Jewish law he would be considered Jewish, he was raised a Protestant, like his father, and converted to Catholicism in Italy, ca. 1813-14 (Thieme-Becker, ibid., vol. 29, pp. 541-47).

    7. Ibid., vol. 3, pp. 300-01; Roth, 193-94; and J. Schrattenholz, *Eduard Bendemann* (Berlin, 1891).

    8. *Ost und West* 1 (Jan. 1901), cols. 15-16; vol. 3 (Aug. 1903), cols. 557-58; vol. 14 (Sept.-Dec. 1914), cols. 653-54. See, however, his undated *Zion and Babylon,* ibid., vol. 3 (Mar. 1903), cols. 153-54.

    9. Oppenheim, *Erinnerungen*, 33-42, 45-49, 51-52, 54-59, 66-69; and Jerusalem, Israel Museum, *Moritz Oppenheim, The First Jewish Painter* (Autumn 1983), English side, p. 63.

    10. E.g. Jerusalem, *Oppenheim*, 1983, English side, pp. 6, 9-11, 24-26, 81, 83; Hebrew side, pp. 3, 12-13, 15, 53-54.

    11. Ibid., Hebrew side, p. 23. This was a commissioned work and the subject was probably chosen by those placing the commission (ibid., no. II.14).

    12. Ibid., English side, pp. 14, 16, 18, 20-22, 78-81; Hebrew side, pp. 6, 16, 18-19, 34, 38; Dubnov, vol. 4, pp. 635-45; *Encyclopedia Judaica*, vol. 4, cols. 1166-68; vol. 8, cols. 270-75, 490-91; and Oppenheim, *Erinnerungen*, 88-93. Fanny Hensel-Mendelssohn was the daughter of Abraham Mendelssohn, who was mentioned above in connection with Jacob Bartholdy, and was the sister of Felix Mendelssohn. She was married to a painter. The others seem to have converted mostly for professional advancement, although Hiller, like Bendemann, expressed his despair with the fate of Judaism in his oratorio, *The Destruction of Jerusalem* (1840).

    13. Jerusalem, *Oppenheim*, 1983, English side, pp. 23, 27; Hebrew side p. 24; and Dubnov, vol. 4, pp. 329-30.

    14. Jerusalem, *Oppenheim*, 1983, Hebrew side, p. 20; and *Encyclopedia Judaica*, vol. 11, cols. 1331-32, 1339-40.

    15. Oppenheim, *Erinnerungen*, p. 39; *Encyclopedia Judaica*, vol. 12, cols. 354-55.

    16. Jerusalem, *Oppenheim*, 1983. English side, pp. 48-49, 52.

    17. E.g. Arthur Roessler, *Ferdinand Georg Waldmüller,* Vienna, n.d., pls. 92-106.

    18. Moritz Oppenheim, *Bilder aus dem altjüdische Familienleben nach Original-Gemälden,* Frankfurt-am-Main, 1882; and Ismar Schorsch, "Art As Social History:

Oppenheim and the German-Jewish Vision of Emancipation," in Jerusalem, *Oppenheim,* 1983, 31-61.

19. Ferdinand Stuttmann, *Max Liebermann* (Hannover, 1961), 80-81. In the letter to Bialik cited here, Liebermann recalls his conversation and states that he was wrong.

20. Berlin, Nationalgalerie, *Max Liebermann in seiner Zeit* (Sept. 6-Nov. 4, 1979), 22, 192-93, 230, 478-79, 600, 606-7, 609-10, 612-13; and Max J. Friedländer, *Max Liebermann* (Berlin, n.d.), 55.

21. Berlin, *Liebermann* (1979), 30-31, 482-85; Ziva Amishai-Maisels, "The Jewish Jesus," *Journal of Jewish Art* 9 (1982), 98-99; and Gustav Keyssner, *Uhde,* Stuttgart (1921), ix-xiii, pls. 23-26, 30-33, 35-37, 49-51, 53-54, 56-60, 64-66, 68, 77-78, 94, 100.

22. Amishai-Maisels, "Jewish Jesus," 99; Erich Hancke, *Max Liebermann* (Berlin, 1923), 133-42; and Hans Ostwald, *Das Liebermann-Buch* (Berlin, 1930), 128-34.

23. For Liebermann's later Biblical paintings and his illustrations for a Dutch Bible, see Berlin, *Liebermann* (1979), 294-95, 568-69, 622. Von Uhde's *The Good Samaritan* of 1901 takes place in a narrow ghetto street (Keyssner, *Uhde,* pl. 94). Uhde had been sick for a long time and died in February at the time Liebermann was working on the final painting. Liebermann had also been ill and had been operated on in 1910 at the time he did his first sketch of the theme (Berlin, *Leibermann* [1979], p. 622).

24. *Ost und West* 14 (Sept.-Dec. 1914), cols. 641-42; and *Kriegszeit,* no. 21 (Jan. 6, 1915), 3.

25. Berlin, *Liebermann* (1979), 640-41.

26. Alfred Donath, *Lesser Ury* (Berlin, 1921), pls. 6-13, 20, 23-24, 38-39, 41-45.

27. Martin Buber, *Lesser Ury* (Berlin, 1903), 51; and *Ost und West* 5 (Jan. 1905), col. 11.

28. Donath, pl. 449.

29. Ibid., pls. 17-18

30. Lesser Ury, "Gedanken über jüdische Kunst," *Ost und West* 1 (Feb. 1901), cols. 145-6.

31. Milly Heyd, "Lilien and Beardsley," *Journal of Jewish Art* 7 (1980), 60-63, where a visual source for this motif is discussed; and Jakob and Wilhelm Grimm, "The Jew among Thorns," *The Complete Household Tales* (New York, 1962), pp. 564-69.

32. Beer Sheba, *E.M. Lilien in the Middle East* (Ben Gurion University, 1988), cover and passim; *Die Bibel,* illustrated by E.M. Lilien (Berlin, 1912); and *E.M. Lilien and Photography* (Tel Aviv: Tel Aviv Museum, 1990).

33. Arnold Fortlage and Karl Schwartz, *Das Graphische Werk von Hermann Struck* (Berlin, 1911); Arnold Zweig, *Das Ostjüdische Antlitz* (Berlin, 1919); and Hermann Struck, *Skizzen aus Litauen Weissrussland und Kurland* (Berlin, 1916).

34. Isaac Mann, ed., *Hermann Struck, Ha'Adam veha'Aman* (Tel Aviv, 1954), 32. The Mizrachi faction to which Struck belonged had a religious Zionist orientation whose motto was "The Land of Israel for the People of Israel according to the Torah of Israel."

35. *Encyclopedia Judaica* 16, cols. 248-49.

36. Ziva Amishai-Maisels, *Jakob Steinhardt: Etchings and Lithographs* (Jerusalem, 1981), 10 and nos. 42, 49; Thomas Grochowiak, *Ludwig Meidner* (Recklinghausen, 1966), 38-39; and Rudolf Pfefferkorn, *Jakob Steinhardt* (Berlin, 1967), ix. pl. 2. The name *Pathetiker* was chosen to stress that their works elicit pathos and is their own variation on the term "Expressionism."

37. Amishai-Maisels, *Steinhardt: Etchings and Lithographs,* nos. 50-58; Pfefferkorn,

pls. 4, 7; Grochowiak, pls. 33-34, 37, VI; and Kurt Hiller," Ausstellung der Pathetiker,"
Die Aktion no. 48 (Nov. 27, 1912), cols. 1514-16. Meidner's depiction of *Job* (no. 15)
was not criticized as it was overshadowed by his secular renderings of destruction.

38. Grochowiak, pls. 61-63. 65, 67-78, XV. During and after the war, Biblical
subjects were often treated in avant-garde German art without the artists being criticized
for Jewish, Zionist or Christian tendencies. Steinhardt's works had simply come before
his time, like Liebermann's *Christ in the Temple.*

39. Leon Kolb, *The Woodcuts of Jakob Steinhardt* (Los Angeles, 1959), nos. 1-64,
74, 79, 99-116, 120-24; Amishai-Maisels, *Steinhardt: Etchings and Lithographs,* nos. 59-
154, 184-208, 219-23; Pfefferkorn, pls. 5-6, 20; Hans Tietze, *Jakob Steinhardt* (Berlin,
1930), 2-3, 14, and unnumbered pls. from 1918-24.

40. Tietze, unnumbered pls. from 1925-30; Amishai-Maisels, *Steinhardt: Etchings
and Lithographs,* nos. 157-83, 209-17, 224-46; Pfefferkorn, pls. 13, 21-23, 26-27; and
Kolb, nos. 126-31, 134-36, 140-42.

41. Pfefferkorn, pls. 28-29, 33, 48-49, 55, 58-59; Kolb, nos. 143-47, 149-52, 178-
89, 202a-144, 221-32, 234-34a, 236-39, 241-250, 257-58, 263-68, 270-85, 304-6, 310,
314-17, 325, 334-43, 350-71, 399-409, 416-18, 430, 432, 434-36, 438-45; and Eli Bar-
On and Ziva Amishai-Maisels, *The Late Woodcuts of Jakob Steinhardt* (Nahariya, 1987),
nos. 446-58, 474-76, 483-87, 521-38, 541-50.

42. Grochowiak, pls. 145-49, 152-54, 158, 162-64, XXI, XXIV; Ziva Amishai-
Maisels, *Depiction and Interpretation: The Influence of the Holocaust on the Visual Arts,*
forthcoming, Part II, Chap. 6.

43. Grochowiak, p. 210; Joseph Paul Hodin, *Ludwig Meidner, seine Kunst, seine
Persönlichkeit, seine Zeit* (Darmstadt, 1973), 88-89; and Hans Tramer, "Das Judenproblem
im Leben und Werk Ludwig Meidners," *Bulletin des Leo Baeck Instituts,* n.s., vol. 16-17
(1977-78), 119, 125.

44. Düsseldorf, Städtische Kunsthalle, *Jankel Adler* (Nov. 1-Dec. 8, 1985), nos. 4,
6-8, 15-27, 30, 32-42, 47-49, 52-55, 64-67.

45. Ibid., nos. 9, 31.

46. Ibid., nos. 2-3, 5, 10-12, 35, 43-45, 57, 62-63, 68-69.

47. Ibid., nos. 92-93, 99, 114.

48. Ibid., nos. 85-89, 94-96, 98, 107, 110-13, 115; Ziva Amishai-Maisels, "The
Iconographic Uses of Abstraction in Jankel Adler's Late Works," *Artibus et Historiae,* no.
17 (1988), 55-70; and Anna Klapheck, *Jankel Adler* (Recklinghausen, 1966), 20.

49. Another German-Jewish abstract artist, Otto Freundlich (1878-1944),
was really associated more with the Paris Abstraction-Creation group than with
German artists. Arrested in Paris in 1939 and deported in 1943 to Poland and then to
Maidanek, he does not seem to have reacted in his art to his Judaism (*Otto Freundlich*
[Cologne, 1978]; and Jerusalem, Israel Museum, *Homage to Otto Freundlich* [Sept.-Oct.
1978]).

50. Hans Richter, *Hans Richter* (New York, 1971), passim.

51. Peter Junk and Wendelin Zimmer, *Felix Nussbaum, Leben und Werk* (Cologne,
1982), 31, 147, 154, 157, 159, 178-79, 182-92, nos. 231, 233, 257, 259, 281.

52. Ibid., 193-97.

53. For a discussion of this development, see Gideon Ofrat, *The New Bezalel*
(Jerusalem, 1987), passim; Tel Aviv Tel, Aviv Museum, *Mordechai Ardon—A Retro-
spective* (May-July 1978); Chicago, Maurice Spertus Museum of Judaica, *Miron Sima*
(1977); Jerusalem, Israel Museum, *Pins, Woodcuts 1942-1985* (Summer, 1985); and
Wolf von Eckardt, *Eric Mendelssohn* (New York, 1960), 23-26, figs. 44-45, pls. 47-
72, 102-3. See also the comments of Werner Haftmann as to why he did not include

those artists persecuted by the Nazis in his book (*Banned and Persecuted* [Cologne, 1986], 365).

54. For information on the Grundigs, see Wolfgang Hütt, *Lea Grundig* (Dresden, 1969), passim; and Günter Feist, *Hans Grundig* (Dresden, 1979), passim.

55. Berlin, Ladengalerie, *Lea Grundig* (1973), no. 42.

56. Ibid., pls. 102-102a.

57. Hütt, pl. 43.

58. Ibid., pls. 50-52.

59. Ibid., passim; Berlin Altes Museum, *Weggefahrten Zeitgenossen* (Oct. 3-Dec. 31, 1979), passim.

Ludwig Altman (1910-1990) seated at the
organ of the Oranienburger Strasse Synagogue
in Berlin, 1934 (private collection).

A Jewish Organist in Berlin, 1933-1936

Ludwig Altman

MUSIC PLAYED AN IMPORTANT ROLE in the lives of German Jews. Many of the contributions of German-Jewish artists, composers, conductors, vocal and instrumental performers in the secular world are well known. Less well-known is the role Jews played in the field of liturgical music. In the preservation of the old chants as well as the composition of new music, these musicians expressed the religious fervor of the Jewish people. This essay will attempt to recreate the milieu and work of those Jewish musicians involved specifically with liturgical music in Germany, most particularly Berlin.

In the early thirties, of Germany's 550,000 Jews, 175,000 lived in Berlin. The *Jüdische Gemeinde* (Community) arranged for all religious services, Liberal as well as Conservative. The Liberal rite utilized one or two rabbis, one or two cantors, a mixed choir, choir director and an organist. The Conservative services did not use an organist and its choir was all male rather than mixed.

There was also a special bureau in Berlin under the direction of Eliezer Ehrenreich which determined which rabbis would officiate at the various synagogues. Ehrenreich was a gifted administrator who also was quite musical. As an organist I had the good fortune to work with some of the best of the German-Jewish rabbinate. Although there was no "official" contact between rabbi and organist, each rabbi's style influenced the atmosphere of the service and liturgy. Rabbis Manfred

Swarsensky, Van Der Zyl, Joachim Prinz, and Max Nussbaum were especially helpful to me; Rabbi Hermann Sanger, in particular, was extremely musical and supportive of the organists.

Before 1933 all organists for religious services were Gentiles. Jews could not play the organ on Shabbat since the organ was considered a mechanism which the Jew was not permitted to operate on that day. Ironically, it was the Nazi period which ended this restriction because the Third Reich did not want its Aryan organists "contaminated" by contact with their Jewish colleagues. Young Jewish organists all over the country finally had a chance to perform the Sabbath services.

Among the cantors, or rather the *obercantors*, Magnus Davidsohn especially liked to arrange musical matters with his organist. He was pompous yet at the same time poetic in that he liked the organist to literally depict feelings and situations as literally as possible through the medium of the large and beautiful instrument in the Fasanen Strasse Synagogue. His organist would have to jump on several pedal notes to depict storms or use the lovely solo stops for pastoral scenes. Obercantor Davidsohn was fortunate to have left Germany in time to reestablish himself in London. His organist, Richard Altman was not as lucky and perished in the Holocaust.

I also had the thrill of working with the obercantor Leo Gollanin, a Russian-born baritone with a wonderfully mellifluous warm voice and impeccable musicianship. Gollanin served at the largest synagogue, the Neue Synagoge located on Oranienburger Strasse. Erected in the 1860s it seated about 3,000 people and housed the biggest of all the synagogue organs in Berlin and all of Germany for that matter. I remember especially the echo organ played from the top manual which alone featured twenty stops. It was one of the few instruments in existence with four, rather than the usual three, manuals. The entire organ had a total of 91 stops. Other cantors of distinction with whom I worked were Wilhelm Friedmann and Julius Peissachowitch who alternated at the Prinzregenten Strasse and Levetzow Strasse synagogues.

In general, the relationship between cantor, organist and rabbi was harmonious and ran smoothly; less successful was that of the choir director and organist. Young organists sometimes felt they could do without choir directors altogether and direct the liturgy by themselves. I happened to witness a particular conflict during one rehearsal at the Friedenstempel. The organist, Hermann Schwartz, stepped off his organ bench to tie his shoelaces. The choir director, who had his back to

Schwartz and thus could not have seen him, stopped the choir and said with great conviction: "Everything sounds well, only the organ is far too loud." This patent nonsense circulated quickly and gleefully to everyone's delight, except that of the untoward choirmaster.

Of course there were exceptions to these conflicting relationships, particularly between the choir director, Dr. Oskar Guttmann, and myself as the organist of the Oranienburger Strasse Synagogue. Dr. Guttmann was a forward-looking musician who tried his best to bring about a degree of reform in composing new settings of the ancient prayers. He reestablished himself in New York, where he became the choir director of the prestigious De Sola Pool Sephardic synagogue, Shearith Israel.

The most outstanding of the choir conductors serving the Jewish community was undoubtedly Alexander Weinbaum. He introduced new service music, daring for the time, such as works composed by Ernest Bloch and Heinrich Schalit. Weinbaum was a musical dictator. One wrong note sung or played and a storm ensued. He presided over all examinations given for the position of organist, choir singer, cantor and choir director. His decisions carried the most influence, and all deferred to his musical judgment. I was highly honored to have been chosen by Mr. Weinbaum to play the organ for the first performances of Bloch's and Schalit's works in 1934.

There were many other choir conductors whose contributions enriched Jewish liturgical works, such as Leo Kopf who specialized in performing Handel oratorios with his own choral and orchestral ensembles; Oskar Guttmann with his oratorio "Bereshit"; and Arno Nadel, whose regular job as choir conductor for the Conservative rite allowed him to pursue poetry, painting, and writing with great success. Sadly, Nadel became another victim of the Holocaust.

How were the Jewish organists trained to perform the traditional liturgy of Liberal Judaism? The Jewish communities instituted courses at the beginning of each spring with the express purpose of readying upcoming organists, singers, and cantors for the High Holyday services. These services required additional personnel to perform in many locations in addition to the regular synagogues. At the end of the course an examination was given whose results determined the caliber of position one could attain for the High Holydays. The best job was, of course, in the hall of the Berlin Philharmonic Orchestra. This examination was also extremely important as a step towards obtaining an organist position in one of the seven regular Liberal synagogues. Most of the organists were striving for one of these positions, which we considered a job for life.

After taking these courses in the spring of 1933, I was sent to a large movie house in the north of Berlin where the services were to take place. I remember first and foremost the organ itself: it was the era of the silent movie and the organs were built to produce all types of sound effects to go along with the films. My choirmaster, Mr. Vogel, was obviously most unmusical. His preference for extremely loud music was clear at the first rehearsal and he had me, as the organist, pull stop after stop after stop. When I had no more stops to pull and told him so, he suspiciously asked if there was really absolutely nothing else left, to which I replied, "nothing left except the 'Donner und Blitzen' stop, which I'm sure you don't want sounded on our holiest festivals." Eagerly, Herr Vogel disagreed, telling me that when he so gestured, I should play that stop. Accordingly, whenever I got that signal, I gave a kick in the direction of that "Donner und Blitzen" stop and was rewarded with a big smile on the face of Herr Vogel.

This experience has a humorous postscript. Many years later, I gave a concert at Temple Emanu-El in San Francisco and Cantor Goldberg, who had officiated with me at the movie house and who had escaped Germany in time by coming to the United States, attended the concert. Reminiscing, Cantor Goldberg asked me if I knew the reason for Herr Vogel's request that I play so loud. I answered that I had never given it that much thought and if I had, I had assumed that Herr Vogel was hard of hearing. "Oh no," Cantor Goldberg replied, "he hated all cantors for some reason or other, and he used you to drown me out."

The music of the liturgy was not difficult, although it required basic musicianship as well as the ability to improvise, modulate and transpose. The organist had to accommodate each cantor's voice since naturally his talents were most effective when a pitch was chosen which was correct for his voice. Hence the accompanist had to be able to transpose the entire score on sight, from and into all twelve keys.

One example of the abilities required of the organist were at the High Holyday services performed in 1934 at the Berlin Philharmonic Hall. Because of the length of the services, two cantors led the liturgy, one a tenor, the other a bass-baritone. This was a challenge for the organist since the first cantor wanted his music transposed upward while the second cantor needed it transposed downward. Even more difficult, the organist had to "catch" the key in which the cantor was singing in order to be able to play the proper key to coincide with the entrance of the choir. On the other hand, not much in the line of organ solos or pedal virtuosity was expected, making the organist's job somewhat easier.

There were many organists, and we all knew each other if only by phone or mail. I remember Paul Lichtenstern who succeeded me as organist of the Neue Synagoge; Werner Baer who became a leading musician in Sydney, Australia; Max Janowski who for a while had the same organ teacher as I did and who after coming to Chicago became one of the most popular Jewish composers; Erwin Jospe, who served the synagogue in Chicago, moved to Los Angeles and finally to Israel where he worked for the opera in Tel Aviv. Of particular note was Hans Freyhan, my successor as a music critic for the *Central Verein Zeitung,* Germany's largest Jewish weekly. He took a special interest in the role the organ could play in the synagogue service, though he did not wish to serve as an organist because of his religious conviction as a Conservative Jew.

Three organists in particular, who in fact did *not* live in Berlin, made great contributions to Jewish music. Herbert Fromm was fortunate enough to leave Germany to become musical director of a large Reform temple in Buffalo, New York. From there he went to the prestigious Temple Isaiah in Boston as Organist/Choir Director, a position he held until his retirement.

The second, Hermann Berlinski, hailed from Leipzig and after coming to the United States became the organist of Temple Emanu-El in New York. He traveled widely, and in his organ recitals in this country as well as in Europe he regularly featured his own works, thus introducing Jewish organ music to a predominantly Christian audience. The third musician came from Mannheim where his father, Hugo Adler, served as a cantor as well as a composer who left a legacy of fine liturgical settings. His son, Samuel, reached higher and went further as a truly modern composer. After serving as musical director at one of the large temples in Dallas, he became professor of composition at the highly regarded Eastman School of Music in Rochester, New York. Much of Adler's music was designed for non-Jewish audiences, but he has also given the synagogue a share of his fine compositions.

While an increasingly oppressive regime forced the Jewish population in Germany into ever-greater reliance for cultural experiences on their synagogues, two organizations were established to promote musical and theatrical performances. Of these, the *Kulturbund Deutscher Juden* was formed in the beginning of 1933 through the initiative of Dr. Kurt

Singer. A personality of fascinating versatility, Singer was a medical doctor and an equally gifted and experienced musician who possessed charm, worldliness and leadership abilities. At the first meeting of the organization he informed us that the Nazi government had not only given permission for the creation of a Kulturbund, but had actually been helpful in setting it up. We found this almost unbelievable as our very life-style as Jews was *"verboten"* by the Nazis. I remember that Dr. Singer was asked how long, in his opinion, he thought the *Kulturbund* would exist. Dr. Singer thought for a minute or two before he answered that he believed it would be in existence for three years. His thought was, of course, that the Nazi regime would collapse during this time.

The Nazis not only permitted the *Kulturbund* to develop Jewish theatre, but they also made the Berliner Theatre available for opera performances, drama, lectures, and symphony orchestra performances. One of the high-ranking Nazis, Hans Hinkel, would often confer with Dr. Singer; Hinkel even had a box in the theatre which he often occupied. Many non-Jews were invited to the very popular performances and enjoyed the various programs. While the *Kulturbund* lasted, it did allow us an artistic outlet, provided a feeling of togetherness and complemented the field of secular music.

Many thousands of Berliners supported the project of course. The question arises, "Why did the Nazis show such kindness?" It seems that it fit their plan to be able to show how well they treated their Jewish citizens and that all the reports of mistreatment were untrue. There we were, still in good clothes, still reasonably well-nourished, with even a theatre in which to perform beautiful, uplifting music and in which every person was Jewish. We were made to fool a naïve foreign press.

Another institution entitled *Künstlerhilfe,* under the leadership of Dr. Hermann Schildberger, broadened the musical experiences of the Jews in Prussia by providing outstanding performers for small communities where only a few Jews still lived. Groups of two to four artists such as singers, instrumentalists, and *Reciters* were very popular and would present programs which related to the spiritual needs of the day. Dr. Schildberger combined his ability as an administrator with his knowledge and expertise as a musician. He also provided music for the one and only Reform synagogue in Berlin, located in the Joachimsthaler Strasse. The service was entirely in German and featured music chosen from the German classics, for example, Beethoven, Schubert, Brahms. The cantor's part was sung by Fritz Lechner, an artist of distinction with a beautiful bass-baritone voice who later became a highly regarded member of the Metropolitan Opera in New York. Fortunately, Dr. Schildberger left Germany in time to reestablish himself in Australia where he not only provided the music for synagogues in Melbourne but also developed the field of grand opera.

When I announced that I was leaving Germany around December 25, 1936, several Jewish leaders warned me that I would not find work in the U.S. where I was unknown. Eliezer Ehrenreich, who was responsible for hiring rabbis, cantors, choir personnel, and organists and for placing me at the organ of the Neue Synagoge on Oranienburger Strasse during my last year in Berlin, told me that the board of directors of the *Jüdische Gemeinde* wanted to appoint me permanent organist of the Neue Synagoge for life. Under those conditions, did I still want to leave? I stood there, realizing that this was a *Sternstück* (turning point) in my life, a decision of greatest consequence. Silently I asked myself if I could visualize my playing the organ thirty years hence. As I could not see this likelihood, I thought that it was better to leave while I was young. I thanked Mr. Ehrenreich sincerely and will always remember him. He was murdered in Ravensbruck.

When it came to my final good-bye to the Oranienburger Strasse Synagogue at the end of December, 1936, I looked once more through the *Gemeindepartitur,* the collection of liturgical music for all of the Liberal synagogues of Berlin, and stealthily, I tore out the Organ Prelude of *Kol Nidre.* For the 50 years I served Congregation Emanu-El, including my years as a chaplain's assistant in the U.S. Army during World War II, I played this prelude faithfully on Kol Nidre Eve. This was my bridge from the past to the present.

In 1964, my wife and I were officially invited by the Bonn Government to come to Germany where I was engaged to play organ recitals in various churches, the most prestigious being the Kaiser Wilhelm Gedächtnis Kirche in Berlin. My recital, a full program of Bach, Mendelssohn, and American music, was advertised all over town. The reception for Emmy and myself was moving. Four of my old teachers came, including Professor Hans Joachim Moser, director of the State Academy for Church and School Music which I attended from 1930 until I was expelled on the eve of my graduation in 1933. The entire press sent their music critics, ten in all, who had favorable things to say. The church was completely full and they ran out of programs. What a day!

PART VIII

Finis and Beyond

THE NAZI REVOLUTION:
A WAR AGAINST HUMAN RIGHTS*

Gerhard L. Weinberg

THE 14TH OF JULY has long been celebrated as the day on which the storming of the Bastille in 1789 symbolized for the French people and the whole world a liberation from royal bondage and an affirmation of human rights. When Lafayette gave George Washington the key to the Bastille, he demonstrated the symbolic tie between the French and American revolutions, events that opened the way for human rights not only in the two countries but, by the inspiration of example, throughout the world. Those who indeed saw in the American and French upheavals salutary lessons for their own societies often considered the 14th of July their own special day. Thus from the very beginning, the concept of human rights and equality was seen by both its supporters and its opponents as in some ways including the Jewish inhabitants of their society.

In the Germany of 1933, July 14 was the occasion for a distinct set of actions by the government, actions meant to revoke human rights rather than to uphold them. The new National Socialist regime, which had come to power earlier that year, had been consolidating its hold on the country during the preceding months. In what one leading scholar has called a "mammoth session of the cabinet,"[1] a series of major laws was enacted under the new procedures which had been instituted by the Enabling Act of March 23, 1933.[2] The Nazi Party was declared to be the only legal political party in the country, and all efforts to organize any other party were now made subject to severe penalties. In the future absence of genuine choice, the public could be periodically consulted in the plebiscites according to a format established that day. A new structure was to be provided for Germany's rural population and a new name and constitution decreed for the German Protestant Church. Under the terms of another law, those persons whom the regime did not like could be stripped of their citizenship and their property, a procedure that would be applied to Willy Brandt and Albert Einstein to mention only two examples.[3]

This framework within which the new state would function until its defeat in war, was set on July 14, 1933, and this choice of date was deliberate. The regime perceived itself as the antithesis of the ideals of 1776 America and 1789 France; its leaders had preached against these ideals in the years before 1933; and they saw themselves as reversing the impact of those ideals upon Germany in particular. The fact that notions about human rights exerted limited influence in Germany only encouraged this new regime: allowed to continue unchecked, these ideals might become established as an integral aspect of German society.

There has been in recent years a veritable flood of scholarly publications dealing with the topic of continuity in German history. We have been told in great detail that neither the revolution of 1918 nor that of 1933 was a revolution at all; that there were no substantial upheavals in German society on either occasion, and that the persistence of old elites, structures, and policy assured a continuum from the German Empire of the late nineteenth century until the defeat of 1945 and perhaps beyond. While these assertions hold elements of truth, particularly regarding the consistent presence of elite groups in Germany, they overlook critical moments in Germany's history when individuals fought for human rights or when these rights were removed by government. The government's use of troops to reestablish the Prussian autocracy in 1849, the constitutional breaches with which Otto von Bismarck began his role as minister-president of Prussia in 1862 and which he threatened at its end in 1890, the often successful efforts of the opponents of the Weimar Republic to murder its leading statesmen, and the tragically unsuccessful attempts of Hitler's German opponents to kill him which in turn led to their deaths by the hundreds—these tumultuous events involved fundamental disagreements over the definition of human rights and the proper institutions of the country.

If one may define the cause of human rights in modern German history as the concepts of public control of government policy, institutionalized protection of individual rights, and equality of citizens in the eyes of the law, then the great struggles for this cause become clear. It was in opposition to these concepts of human rights that the Prussian autocracy triumphed over the revolutionary movement of 1848-1849, that Bismarck won the constitutional conflict in Prussia and erected the German Empire of 1871—and it was the supporters of human rights who won the upheaval of 1918-1919.[4] The formation of the Weimar Republic in 1918 meant that for the first time in the history of the country the direction of policy was to be determined by freely elected representatives of the public. For the first time in the history of Germany, individual rights, including the right to oppose the government of the moment, were to be protected against the arbitrary exercise of executive authority; and for the first time, there would be equal status of all citizens in all parts of the country.

Those who hated the Weimar Republic, vilified its policies, shouted down or even shot down its leaders, and publicly promised the German people an alternative structure with authority vested in one leader, the submission of all rights to central authority, and the imposition of legal distinctions in status between different segments of the population, understood perhaps more clearly than some of their contemporaries that there had indeed been a revolution in Germany in 1918. These factions also realized that their own assumption of power would mark a dramatic break with the immediate past.

In this new break made by the Nazi revolution, human rights was tied to the question of race, an issue rooted in demographic and historic factors. The demographic factor was simply that the group immediately defined as racially distinct, dangerous, and to be degraded—namely the Jews—constituted less than 1% of the population and had for a century actually been declining as a proportion of the country's inhabitants. It was therefore electorally safe to attack this tiny group. Through propaganda, it was also simple to manipulate statistical slogans about them: if there were two Jews out of a hundred persons in some activity, that meant not that it was 98% non-Jewish but that there was a 220% over-representation of Jews.

Historically the emancipation of Germany's Jews was closely intertwined with the spread of human rights ideas in Central Europe, from the impact of the French Revolution and Napoleon at the beginning of the nineteenth century to the Weimar Constitution of 1919. Already in the first decade of the nineteenth century, one of the Prussian reform's leading opponents, von der Marwitz, had attacked the reformers for trying to create what he called *ein neumodischer Judenstaat*, a new-fangled Jew-state. Resentment against France for the Napoleonic Wars and for the First World War could be safely and effectively focused on the Jews as beneficiaries of the legal equality for all citizens, which had spread through Europe since Napoleonic times and, reaching Germany, had taken form in the Weimar Republic. Legal discriminations against Jews were, therefore, part of the Nazi Party's program of 1920. These discriminations were applauded with fervor in the years from 1920 to 1933, implemented immediately after the Nazi seizure of power, and always publicly boasted about as one of the regime's greatest accomplishments, up to and including the mass murders of World War II.[5] It was in this way that the opposition to parliamentary government and human rights was joined with anti-French and anti-Semitic agitation in the Germany of the 1920s.

The question of race was also of enormous substantive importance because it signified what might be called the new alternative vision of the society to be constructed in stages beginning in 1933. The Nazi Party's perception of the past, present, and future in racial terms was opposed not only to the politically egalitarian society of Weimar but also to the allegedly racially blind society of pre-1918 Germany. The Second Empire was seen by the Nazis as hopelessly negligent in this regard, and the new party asserted that it had been this negligence above all else which had been responsible for Germany's defeat in the war in 1918 by its domestic rather than its foreign enemies. The new government would certainly follow a different path and hence assure itself of a different fate.

The discriminations against Jews would be matched by new racial policies within the so-called Aryan community. The centrality of racial doctrine in the system was affirmed by a law of July 14, 1933, calling for the compulsory sterilization of those whom the regime defined as afflicted with hereditary ailments—characteristically the first of the Nazi regime's laws in the area of family and marriage.[6] In addition there were laws providing forgivable loans for early marriage and medals for numerous children and a massive euthanasia system to remove those who were considered unworthy of continued life and an unproductive drain on the nation's resources. The racially unified society to be developed by these processes would conquer the lands it needed to feed itself, and, by expelling or exterminating those living there, provide the basis for an ever-expanding agriculturally settled population. The numerous children raised on the newly conquered lands would more than make up for the casualties incurred in the wars required for the conquests and would in turn provide both the need for additional conquests and the human resources to accomplish them. What would happen when the ever-expanding Germanic settlements eventually met on the other side of the globe was left hazy; but in the meantime, the regime took for granted that its populace would require dictatorship, and boasted about this observation as a sign of superior insight into the nature of the universe.

In the area of women's rights, the new regime would also alter the direction of the evolution of German society. It can certainly be argued that the advances of women in Germany had been minimal before 1933 but even these few were perceived as part and parcel of the movement for human equality that National Socialists wanted to reverse. The possibility—even if rarely realized—of women rising to positions of political, professional, academic, or economic power was too horrendous for the Nazis to contemplate. The new government would block all such avenues and redirect women into a totally patriarchal society where women with healthy bodies brought vast numbers of healthy children into the service of the fatherland. Other pursuits would be closed to women as far as practicable. The already existing discrepancy in the sex ratio as a result of World War I, which would be greatly accentuated by World War II, was to be resolved by the encouragement of illegitimacy.[7] For the years after World War II there were projects planned for a new form of polygamy which a British scholar has dubbed the National Socialist principle of crop rotation.[8] The fact that parental rights over raising children could be withdrawn if the parents were deemed politically unreliable is evidence that the Nazi policies had nothing to do with the maintenance of the family as an institution: the production of children for the all-powerful German state was what counted.

The symbols, the rites, and the procedures of the new state all exemplified the deliberate format of this new society. The supreme and constantly reiterated ritual of the new society was the parade—thousands marching in cadence and in uniform. This was not a novel means of mass transportation; in fact the parades went from one nowhere to another nowhere and often imposed stupendous and energy-consuming burdens on the public transportation system. Their purpose lay in the march itself: in its ritualistic submerging of all individuality, in its insistence on a publicly visible community of preferably indistinguishable human beings ordered by a will exterior to themselves and thus as effective a rite for those marching as for those summoned to cheer in anonymous masses as onlookers.

The mass march contrasts dramatically with the symbolic act of the alternative form of society in which each person goes individually into the secrecy of the voting booth and quietly chooses the direction in which he or she prefers to be led. And if the elections for all sorts of offices to which Americans and the French are called sometimes come with a frequency that seems as tiring as the endless marching of the Third Reich looks in the newsreels, it is because the founders of both types of systems understood the power of habit and the formation of social cohesion somewhat better than a cynical world may be willing to admit.

The other aspect of cohesive uniformity in the Nazi state is the treatment accorded to outcasts, whether from the supposedly superior or the supposedly inferior racial group. Many have heard of the case of Private Slovik, the one American soldier executed for desertion in World War II. The corresponding figure for the German army, however, is substantially higher than 20,000—an almost incredible statistic which cannot be precisely given because in the last months of the war soldiers were shot after summary proceedings of which no records were kept or if kept did not survive. If this was the treatment accorded to individual members of the superior Aryan group, it may be easier to comprehend why it has been so difficult to determine precise and accurate figures on the number of Jews murdered en masse by the National Socialists. The murderers thought it critical to record that twelve Paraguayan peso notes valued at 60 pfennigs each had been taken from the victims so that the Reichsbank could properly credit the account of the SS with RM 7.20;[9] but as for the number of dead, that was certainly not of equal significance.

If the individual and the rights of the individual were to play no role in the new society and if the state as an entity, directed by the will of a dictator, was to command everything, then the permanent visible symbolism of such a political and social structure was, most appropriately, to be found in its buildings. Designed by Adolf Hitler himself during the 1920s for future construction, developed and begun in a number of cities in the 1930s and 1940s, the buildings of the Third Reich were to be characterized by their colossal size on the one hand and the absence of human amenities on the other.

Hitler and his associates attached great significance to these mammoth construction projects which were to transform the appearance of

Berlin and more than twenty other cities. The largest single building, on which the architectural firms were still working in the spring of 1945, was to be the world assembly hall in Berlin, reaching almost one thousand feet into the sky and topped off by the eagle of the German Reich holding the globe in its claws. The drawings and some of the models of the hall survive as does one of the soil test forms from the beginning of construction. Designed to overwhelm both those inside and those outside, this structure would hold 150,000 to 200,000 persons—but they would all have to stand. When it came to the needs of the government, on the other hand, the frailties of mere mortals were given some consideration: the over 400,000 spectators who were expected to view the annual Nazi Party rally in the projected new monster stadium in Nuremberg would reach their lofty perches in elevators with a capacity of 32,000 and would be provided with special glasses so that they could actually see what was transpiring on the necessarily distant stadium floor.[10] It is also interesting to note that the construction plans for all cities, suburbs, and villages omit entirely one type of structure previously characteristic of German and other European communities: there would be no churches.[11]

Within the new museum structures and opera houses, concert halls and ministerial buildings, there would be only artistic works and performances which conformed to state rules, just as the libraries would hold only books and newspapers approved by the state and party censors. The German citizens, in order to be "nationalized" to a common standard, would be exposed exclusively to such art forms and cultural artifacts as the state authorized. No literary works out of harmony with the new standards would be published. Those musical forms which were perceived as alien to the Aryan race—jazz as one example—would disappear from the radio and the record shops, and most modern art could be seen only when included in an exhibition of "Degenerate Art" sent on tour to exemplify the alleged horrors of decadence.

The formation of human consciousness in a new mold, the Nazi regime felt, required the greatest caution lest people be contaminated. The creations of Walt Disney, for example, were banned simply because of his Jewish ancestry. While Disney's creations seem hardly a threat, the regime felt that the less obvious the censored object's distinctiveness, the greater the danger of unrecognized and hence most insidious infiltration. The guardians of the new system would accordingly exercise the greatest vigilance at precisely those points at which the ordinary and perhaps insufficiently alert German was most likely to become infected by undesirable cultural influences. This may sound rather like a description of earlier measures of the South African government or the utopia of the Moral Majority, but this description summarized the policies of a regime that feared spontaneity and creativity and which insisted that there could be no sphere outside state control for the unfettered flourishing of the human spirit.

Many of the plans and projects for the National Socialist version of urban, rural, and cultural renewal were cut short by war and defeat. They are important to consider, however, because a revolution halted in its tracks cannot be understood unless attention is paid to its planned destination. The National Socialist program did, however, bring to fruition as early as 1942 one of its underlying goals: the submission of the individual's right to that of the leader. The following episode will illustrate the realization of this policy.

In the crisis on the Eastern Front in the winter of 1941-1942, as the German army met its first serious defeat before Moscow, one of the German commanders, General Erich Hoepner, saved a corps of tens of thousands of men by ordering it to pull back, a step he took without Hitler's prior approval. The dictator was livid and on January 8, 1942, ordered Hoepner not only removed from command but deprived of his pension and the right to wear his uniform as well. Hitler was thereupon told by several officers at headquarters that he could not order these last two measures by fiat: Hoepner could be deprived of his rights as an inactive four-star general only by a formal court-martial proceeding. Naturally Hitler's mood was not improved by this piece of information, and the dictator decided to alter these rules, although no court-martial proceedings were initiated against Hoepner.

Once the Eastern front situation had been temporarily stabilized, Hitler summoned the Reichstag on April 26, 1942, for what would turn out to be its last session until October 1990 when Germany was reunited. The purpose of the meeting was to approve a proposal formulated by Hitler and presented by Hermann Göring, the President of the Reichstag. The proposal provided that the Führer could assign anyone of any rank to any position of his choice, could punish in any way he saw fit any person who did not carry out Hitler's orders, and that this could be done without regard to legal procedures or earned rights.[12] There would be no procedures and no rights protecting any individual in the Third Reich which could not be forfeited at the whim of the dictator, and with this proposal the Nazi system broke fully with the legal traditions of the old regime in Prussia as well as the Weimar Republic. The end of all human rights had been formally confirmed with great publicity and to loud applause. The fact that this highly acclaimed action, stripping all Germans of any procedural and substantive rights vis-à-vis their own government, occurred in the same month as the beginning of mass killing by the use of gas in Auschwitz is a coincidence in timing but not in essence. No rights for Germans and no life for others.

Persons deprived of their peculiar and special qualities as human beings are converted into the equivalent of inanimate objects. The regime's reference to its own citizens as *Menschenmaterial*, "human material," illuminates the point linguistically. The state then disposes of its own people as it does of any other resource—German trees and rocks have no rights, so why should German persons? Thus if Germans have no rights, anyone designated as non-German is barely worth counting. And where appropriate for the momentary benefit of the regime, even the allegedly scientific and unalterable racial distinctions could be amended: a prominent German airman, Erhard Milch, who rose to the rank of field marshal had only to have his mother certify in writing that she had committed adultery in order to clear up an otherwise embarrassing racial blemish in his ancestry.

In just twelve short years, from 1933 to 1945, the National Socialist revolution had gone extraordinarily far. The world had been turned upside down, tens of millions had died. In comparison with the Soviet Union by 1929 or Italy by 1934, the dozen years of National Socialist rule had much more dramatically altered not only the country in which the new regime had come to power but the rest of the world as well.

The National Socialists expected that their empire would last at least a thousand years and hoped that even its ruins would inspire subsequent millennia by its imposing and ubiquitous presence. With its rusting steel rods and crumbling cement, a reinforced concrete building is extremely unaesthetic once it is wrecked. Hitler therefore accepted the recommendation of his master builder Albert Speer that only stone would be used for the construction of the regime's monumental buildings. Like the picturesque Roman ruins which centuries later testify throughout Western and Central Europe and the Mediterranean to the glory of the Roman Empire, so the Third Reich's structures would evoke admiration and perhaps imitation even in their ruined state into a far distant future.[13] In reality, the great projects were never completed, and the Germany of 1945 was instead a land of endless rubble piles. A vast quantity of this rubble was made into a real hill in the middle of Berlin: the highest monument of the Third Reich is not a metal eagle holding the globe above the winter clouds but a new ski run in the old capital.

NOTES

*This is a revised version of a paper originally presented at Emory University in 1983.

1. Karl Dietrich Bracher (with Wolfgang Sauer and Gerhard Schulz), *Die Nationalsozialistische Machtergreifung*, 2d ed. (Cologne: Westdeutscher Verlag, 1962), 214.

2. On the Enabling Act, see ibid., 152ff. For a semi-official presentation of the laws of July 14, 1933, see the first volume, entitled "Die Nationalsozialistische Revolution 1933," in Paul Meier-Benneckenstein, ed., *Dokumente der Deutschen Politik* (Berlin: Juncker und Dünnhaupt, 1939), 70, 179-80, 204-6, 244, 376-77.

3. See Hans-Georg Lehmann, *In Acht und Bann; Politische Emigration, NS-Ausbürgerung und Wiedergutmachung am Beispiel Willy Brandts* (München: C.H. Beck, 1976), esp. pp. 49-53.

4. For a fine review of the whole issue see Dietrich Orlow, "1918/19: A German Revolution," *German Studies Review* 5, no. 2 (May 1982), 187-203.

5. Hans-Heinrich Wilhelm, "Wie geheim war die 'Endlösung'?" in *Miscellanea: Festschrift für Helmut Krausnick,* ed. Wolfgang Benz (Stuttgart: Deutsche Verlags-Anstalt, 1980), 131-48.

6. This point is made in the useful survey by Dorothee Klinksiek, *Die Frau im NS-Staat* (Stuttgart: Deutsche Verlags-Anstalt, 1982), 72-74.

7. Himmler's notorious order of October 28, 1939, the so-called Kinder-Erlass, or "directive for children," has been reprinted in Klinksiek, 153-54. The official newspaper of the SS, *Das Schwarze Korps,* wrote on January 4, 1940: "A young woman who by one means or another evades her highest responsibility, that of giving birth inside or outside of marriage, is as much a deserter as a man who refuses to serve in the army." The German text and related materials can be found in Willi A. Boelke, ed., *Kriegspropaganda 1939-1941: Geheime Ministerkonferenzen im Reichspropagandaministerium* (Stuttgart: Deutsche Verlags-Anstalt, 1982), 270.

8. Hugh R. Trevor-Roper, ed., *The Bormann Letters* (London: Weidenfeld and Nicolson, 1954), xx. The subject itself comes up elsewhere in the records as well; see Oron J. Hale, ed., "Adolf Hitler and the Postwar German Birthrate," *Journal of Central European Affairs* 17 (1957), 166-73.

9. The example is taken from a long list included in the report on the "Reinhard" murder operation in Poland by Odilo Globocznik to Heinrich Himmler and can be found in *Trial of the Major War Criminals before the International Military Tribunal* 34 (Nuremberg, 1949), 86.

10. Jost Dülffer, Jochen Tiess, and Josef Henke, eds., *Hitlers Städte: Eine Dokumentation* (Cologne: Böhlau, 1978), 24.

11. Ibid., 20.

12. Max Domarus, ed., *Hitler; Reden und Proklamationen, 1932-1945* 2 (Neustadt a.d. Aisch: Verlagsdruckerei Schmidt, 1963), 1877.

13. Albert Speer, *Erinnerungen* (Frankfurt-am-Main: Propyläen, 1969), 69.

THE HOLOCAUST AND AMERICAN INTELLIGENCE

Barry M. Katz

NAZI GERMANY'S CHIEF PROPAGANDIST, Joseph Goebbels, is said to have scoffed at the news that "a pack of Jewish scribblers" had been brought to Washington in 1941 to staff the newly created intelligence agency that would become the Office of Strategic Services (OSS). There is a hint of truth in this odd charge, however, for the American administration, called upon to create *ex nihilo* an agency that could operate at the same level of professionalism as the British, Soviet, and German intelligence services, did indeed make an unprecedented appeal to the academic community for assistance.

While OSS's reputation as a select coterie of socialites and adventurers is not wholly undeserved, its Research and Analysis branch (R&A) sheltered a community of American and European refugee scholars who helped to keep the fate of Europe's Jews from disappearing entirely from the American military and diplomatic agenda. The record of the OSS in regard to the Nazi program of genocide is not, in the final analysis, particularly impressive, but it is a far cry from the ignorance and indifference that prevailed elsewhere in the U.S. government.[1] In this essay I will describe the formation of the Research and Analysis branch and attempt to review its work with particular reference to the fate of Europe's Jews.[2]

FORMATION OF THE RESEARCH AND ANALYSIS BRANCH

The groundwork for America's first central intelligence agency was laid by a presidential order of June, 1941 to create an office charged with the collection, evaluation, and distribution of foreign intelligence. Although the Office of Strategic Services would later be most famous for the overseas exploits of its several "operational" branches, General William J. Donovan, who directed the organization throughout its brief lifetime, always acknowledged that the heart of the organization lay in its essentially academic functions of research and analysis and its reliance upon "good old-fashioned intellectual sweat."[3] These academic tasks were overseen by the Harvard University historian William L. Langer who, with the assistance of the American Council of Learned Societies, Librarian of Congress Archibald MacLeish, and a group of scholarly advisors, began in July 1941 to recruit a professional staff drawn from across the spectrum of the social sciences. Over the next twelve months, academic specialists in fields ranging from classical philology to neoclassical economics descended upon Washington, bringing with them their most promising graduate students, and set up shop at the Research and Analysis branch headquarters at Twenty-third Street and E.

By mid-1942 Langer's recruiting drive and the moral imperatives of the war had attracted a faculty that could rival any university: the OSS Economics Division produced five future presidents of the American Economic Association, including a Nobel laureate; virtually all of the founders of the postwar discipline of Sovietology won their stripes in R&A; and of its forty professional historians, no less than seven would rise to the presidency of the American Historical Association—a fact that scarcely accounts for the neglect of the OSS's Research and Analysis branch in the scholarship on World War II, on the roots of American intelligence, and, most significantly, perhaps, on the leading currents of modern American intellectual history.[4]

In spring, 1943, as the tide of World War II was turning in favor of the Allies, the directors of the Research and Analysis branch began a fresh recruiting drive whose results were, if anything, even more astonishing. Although there was express resistance in the government to employing "enemy aliens," William Langer recognized that within the community of Jewish refugee scholars in America resided yet another reserve of skilled experts. These scholars were fluent in the European languages, attuned to the intricacies of European party politics, and alert to points of strength, vulnerability, and resistance in Germany and German-occupied territories.

Walter Dorn and Eugene N. Anderson, two American-born but German-trained historians, spearheaded the recruitment of what became quite literally a staff of "foreign intelligence" experts who were hired with greater concern for their intellectual acumen than for political consistency: among them were social theorists Franz Neumann, Herbert Marcuse, and Otto Kirchheimer of the neo-Marxist *Institut für Sozial-forschung* of Frankfurt; jurist Henry Kellerman and political scientist John Herz; Hamburg art historian Richard Krautheimer; economists Wassily Leontief, Paul A. Baran, and Walter Levy; and Hajo Holborn and Felix Gilbert, the two outstanding representatives of a tradition of German historiography with its roots in Meinecke, Burckhardt, and Ranke. Altogether, only about two dozen European refugee scholars found employment in OSS, but their presence was felt in a manner quite disproportionate to their numbers.

One of the principal motivations in recruiting the scholarly community to the work of intelligence was for their presumed expertise in working with published materials. The primary source material used by R&A—the official reports, statistical data, personal memoirs, and so forth—were the stock-in-trade of the professional scholar. "Despite the glamorized notions which have gathered about some of the activities of OSS," remarked one eminent scholar, "the work of R&A was a real research slugging match,"[5] and the great majority of its operations were conducted not behind enemy lines but behind desks in the Library of Congress.

A second source of intelligence came from German radio broadcasts and from the official Nazi press which they obtained on a regular basis from Allen Dulles at the OSS Outpost in Bern. Analysts such as Herbert Marcuse and historians Leonard Krieger and Franklin Ford became quite adept at interpreting such fragments both for unintended insights into the functioning of the Nazi control apparatus and for their reverse value in the conduct of political and psychological warfare. Finally, a considerable volume of "raw" intelligence reached them through the overseas activities of the OSS Special Operations (SO) and Secret Intelligence (SI) branches, from the foreign contacts cultivated by OSS members in London, Bern, Stockholm, Lisbon, and Algiers, from sympathetic allies in the British intelligence services, and, when relations were good, from the various regional desks of the U.S. State Department.

By mid-1943, however, when the Central European Section of the Research and Analysis branch was already fully staffed and operational, somewhere between 2.5 and 3 million European Jews had already been massacred. We must turn, then, to the central questions of this essay: With regard to Nazi Germany's war against the Jews, what did American intelligence know, what interpretation was given to the information they possessed, and what did they attempt to do with it?

MONITORING THE WAR

Despite allegations regarding their inaction, the Central European scholars of R&A did attempt to monitor the fate of the European Jews. An early report produced on May 14, 1942 already observed that "the pattern of German violence includes the systematic extermination of the Jews," and from the time the unit was fully operational in the spring of 1943, R&A analysts reported on Europe's Jews on a fairly regular basis.[6] Throughout much of 1944 they applied this accumulated intelligence to the program of postwar denazification and military occupation and by the end of that year to the indictments being drafted against the principal Nazi war criminals. By this time, of course, the dimensions of the European catastrophe had become evident far beyond the government. But there are clear indications, however, that from the beginning of the war, the R&A scholars understood quite explicitly that the Nazis and their accomplices were engaged neither in "conventional" anti-Semitic persecutions nor merely random acts of terroristic violence but in a systematic campaign of mass murder.

The reports released by the Central European unit of R&A revealed, slowly but consistently, the magnitude of the atrocities in Europe. In May 1943, in an R&A weekly intelligence bulletin, Franz Neumann described the "complete liquidation of the Warsaw ghetto" as the "most recent stage in the long process of the extermination of the Jews,"[7] and sporadic reports of this sort continued to appear throughout the summer. In October Leonard Krieger reported on the arrival in Denmark of Adolf Eichmann, "SS Gruppenfuehrer and head of the *Zentralstelle für Jüdische Auswanderung*," which the young historian interpreted as marking "the final campaign to rid Europe of the Jews."[8] Two weeks later Felix Gilbert submitted a brief report on the "Mass Murder of Russian Jews by the Wehrmacht."[9] Shortly thereafter Samuel Sharp, one of the Section's experts on Polish affairs, confirmed that "some 3,000,000 Jews of Europe have been executed or have perished since the war began (in Poland alone an estimated 1,600,000)" and confessed that "there has been a tendency to consider the figures and details as more or less exaggerated simply because it had been difficult to believe that even the Nazis could apply such methods of mass extermination." He left no doubt, however, that "the orders to exterminate the Polish Jews can be traced all the way up to Himmler and Hitler."[10]

The Research and Analysis branch had by this time completed a major part of its projected documentation of *German Military Government over Europe, 1939-1943,* a multi-volume study of the Nazi agencies for the subjugation and exploitation of conquered territories. While these papers concentrated heavily upon legal, administrative, and organizational matters, their authors made a serious attempt to report on the measures taken against Jews in the fifteen European countries they studied. In their research on Poland, they broke through the veil of Nazi propaganda and surmised with reasonable accuracy that "insofar as the Jews have been left alive in the G[eneral] G[overnment], it has been largely for the purpose of exploiting them for manual labor." Initially, they reported, the Polish Jews were subjected to legal disenfranchisement, segregation, and ghettoization; their research revealed that, "In the latter part of 1942, however, and during 1943, the ghettos were largely liquidated and their inhabitants partly executed, partly allowed to die under harsh conditions, and partly sent away for forced labor. As a result of Nazi policy of the past four years, the Jewish population originally resident in the area of the General Government, totaling some one and three-quarters million people, has been cut down to less than 15 per cent of its former size."[11]

While reports such as these were numerous, it should nonetheless be noted that by late 1943 the extermination program was already an "open secret"; that the murder of the Jews, which appears in retrospect as a crime of world-historical proportions, was not at the time an all-consuming obsession of OSS; that the flamboyant General Donovan, briefed by Jan Karski at the Polish Embassy in Washington in summer, 1943, was more interested in the reception given the Polish courier by "his boys" in Spain than in Karski's reports about the death camps in the East; that as late as August 1944 an OSS economist attached to the 15th Air Force could urge the bombing of a small synthetic oil refinery at Polish Oswiecim without mentioning the other facility in the town the Germans had renamed Auschwitz.[12] Despite these tendencies, the evidence challenges the picture of naïveté or indifference regarding Europe's Jews that is typically ascribed to U.S. intelligence during the war.

As the war drew to a close, the Central European unit of the Research and Analysis branch focussed increasingly on the anticipated postwar constellation of power, on the military governance and denazification of Germany, and on the problem of war criminals. Shortly after Hitler's suicide in Berlin, a staff of some two dozen researchers began a nine-part research series on "Nazi Plans for Dominating Germany and Europe" for the use of the War Crimes staff, producing some of the most complete documentation then available on the magnitude of the catastrophe.

Of all the manifold levels of Nazi criminality, none was more horrifying or more resistant to rational analysis than the criminal conspiracy to exterminate the European Jews. The researchers at the R&A branch now faced the task of explicating such an incomprehensible event. Having reported regularly on incidents of official violence and terrorism, on mass deportations from the western countries that had fallen under German occupation, on the liquidation of the Polish ghettos, and on the network of concentration camps in Germany, the R&A scholars now attempted to establish for the Nuremberg prosecutors that these numerous acts had been elements of a single, indivisible crime: "It is the purpose of the Prosecution to demonstrate the existence of a common plan or enterprise of the German Government, the Nazi Party, and the German military, industrial, and financial leaders to achieve world domination by war. The destruction of the Jewish people as a whole, although an end in itself, was at the same time linked to and closely tied up with this aim of world conquest."[13] They estimated that some 5,700,000 noncombatant Jewish civilians had been systematically slaughtered in the course of the Nazi extermination program, the implications of which, for "the future of the Jewish people and of mankind," could at that time only be guessed.

The theoretically minded scholars of the Research and Analysis branch were not content, however, with a chilling post-mortem on European Jewry. The destruction of an entire people seems finally to have been intelligible to them only insofar as it could be reduced to some larger pragmatic design, however sick or evil. In this premature effort to theorize the Holocaust, Franz Neumann, whose Marxian analysis of the Nazi "Behemoth" served as "a kind of bible for people working on Nazi Germany,"[14] ranked as the acknowledged intellectual leader of the group. Neumann assumed that the Nazi leadership was too cynical or too sophisticated to believe its own crude anti-Semitic propaganda and that "measures against the Jews are always the 'spearhead' for general oppression," the "domestic testing-ground for universal terrorist methods directed against all groups and institutions that are not fully subservient to the Nazi system."[15] National Socialism, which had allegedly abolished the class struggle, needed an enemy whose very existence could serve to integrate the antagonistic groups within the society, and the Jews alone could fulfill this requirement for reasons which Neumann described:

1. The Jew was the weakest enemy of Nazism; the attack on him was therefore the most promising and the least risky one.

2. The Jew was the one enemy against whom the Nazis could hope to unite otherwise divergent masses of supporters.

3. The elimination of the Jew, as competitor, would be most profitable to the petite bourgeoisie which furnished the largest mass support for the Nazi movement.

4. The Jew was found in all countries. Nazi anti-Semitism was therefore a convenient means for mobilizing potential Nazi allies in foreign countries...

5. The ubiquity of the Jew as arch-enemy provided the Nazis with a justification for carrying the struggle for power beyond the frontiers of the Reich.[16]

This narrowly instrumental analysis, which insisted that the Nazi genocide must be serviceable to some larger political requirement, had already found its way into the second edition of Neumann's *Behemoth* (1944) where he added that "the extermination of the Jews is only the means to the attainment of the ultimate objective, namely the destruction of free institutions, beliefs, and groups."[17] Possibly their greatest error lay in this reluctance to see the murder of the Jews as a deliberate policy, *an sich und für sich*, irreducible to any larger necessity or design.

THE OSS AND AMERICAN POLICY

Much attention has focused on a seeming discrepancy between the "output" of the Research and Analysis branch with some of the incoming materials received by OSS on matters pertinent to the slaughter of the European Jews. Many times a particular transcription of an interview or communique turned up in the OSS archives which allegedly demonstrates that OSS was in possession of vital information but nonchalantly "filed it away." Some of these reports include the following:[18]

- OSS 24728: signal dated November 15, 1942 on the murder of Jews in the Baltic regions.

- OSS 26896: cable from Lisbon, dated April 10, 1942, from British officer who had escaped by hiding in ghetto in Warsaw: "Germany is no longer persecuting the Jews. It is physically exterminating them."

- OSS 27275: dated March 14, 1942 and possibly transmitted from the Polish underground through a Swedish businessman in Poland, on the "systematic liquidation of the Jews."

- OSS 58603: statement by Treblinka escapee David Milgrom, August 30, 1943, forwarded by Melbourne, American Vice Consul in Istanbul, January 13, 1944.

- OSS 88254: report of repatriated French officer on the mass execution of the Jewish population of Rawa Russka.

- OSS 95436: statement by an escaped Polish medical student on April 15, 1943, dated Geneva, November 1, 1943.

It has been alleged that OSS received materials of this sort, but because of its "minimal interest in the extermination of the Jews...the OSS did nothing with it."[19] While it is difficult to trace the route of an incoming cable, dispatch, or intercept through the sprawling and grievously uncoordinated agency, enough evidence has been gathered to dispel these hasty suppositions. More importantly, however, such allegations misconstrue the reality of the wartime Office of Strategic Services. Unlike its successor, America's first central intelligence agency did not have the power to affect American policy in any decisive way.

The OSS in general and its Research and Analysis branch in particular were fragile and vulnerable latecomers in the intelligence marketplace, both in Washington and worldwide, and drifted in an uncharted netherworld between the military and diplomatic establishments. From the very outset William Langer had been instructed by his superiors to regard the branch as a service organization whose "sole purpose" was to transform raw intelligence data into concise, factual, and rigorously objective analyses for the use of government agencies and "not to suggest, recommend, or in any way determine the strategy or the tactical decisions of the war."[20] OSS had entered a crowded field and barely survived its ongoing jurisdictional rivalries with the Departments of State and War.

Ironically, perhaps, the greatest accomplishments of the Research and Analysis branch and also its greatest failures lay in Langer's insistence that "there is no future in R&A as a pressure group," and that on the first suspicion of pleading a special cause "we will very soon lose our entree to all policy-makers other than those already committed to the same special cause."[21] In the face of the "derision, suspicion, and outright and avowed hostility" that R&A encountered elsewhere in the government and even among the more operational branches of OSS, it was crucial to the branch's existence that it gain a reputation for disinterested professionalism in the eyes of those entitled to participate in the policy-making process.

The work of R&A was, accordingly, pursued within the overarching structure of American military and diplomatic strategy—both of which were predicated upon the prior defeat of the German armies—a strategy that was not wholly inconsistent, it may be noted, with R&A's own analysis of the nature of Nazi totalitarianism. Even within the constraints of this grand strategy, however, iconoclastic scholars of the Research and Analysis branch reported on any number of matters that had been declared subsidiary, irrelevant, or even prejudicial to the prosecution of the war. Unfortunately, these reports did not amount to much, for it is likely that the great majority of them were not read much beyond the agency itself. It was always grounds for celebration when a kind word was received from some undersecretary or intelligence colonel who had happened across one of their papers and found it interesting. The mandate of Research and Analysis branch was limited and did not include the rescue of the European Jews.

This essay should not be misconstrued as an apologia for OSS's Research and Analysis branch, an agency that did some outstanding analytical work under the most challenging of circumstances but that was, in the last analysis, a marginal part of the overall war effort. It may well be the frustration and demoralization that prevailed among the many of the research analysts of the Office of Strategic Services that best illuminates the utter paralysis of the American government in the face of the greatest calamity in the history of the Jewish people.

The failures and successes of the R&A branch point inevitably to one question: What might OSS, the U.S. government, or the Allies have done to rescue the Jews? It is possible, to be sure, to imagine less restrictive immigration and refugee policies, or conjecture about military operations that might have been mounted on behalf of those trapped in Europe. As the late Lucy S. Dawidowicz has argued, however, such speculations have tended to obscure the real issue, "How could one country—National Socialist Germany—have gained dominion so rapidly over

Europe and enlisted so many different peoples into the commission of mass murder?"[22] The paralysis, indifference, and even complicity of American government agencies forms only a grim chapter of a text that was written in Nazi Germany.

NOTES

1. Some of the writers who have addressed this problem include Arthur D. Morse, *While Six Million Died* (New York, 1967); Henry L. Feingold, *The Politics of Rescue: The Roosevelt Administration and the Holocaust, 1938-1945* (New Brunswick, N.J., 1970); Walter Laqueur, *The Terrible Secret* (London, 1980); Martin Gilbert, *Auschwitz and the Allies* (New York, 1981); David S. Wyman, *The Abandonment of the Jews: America and the Holocaust, 1941-1945* (New York, 1984); Monty Noam Penkower, *The Jews Were Expendable: Free World Diplomacy and the Holocaust* (Champaign-Urbana, 1984); Richard Breitman and Alan M. Kraut, *American Refugee Policy and European Jewry, 1933-1945* (Bloomington, 1987).

2. This essay was originally conceived in response to an inquiry from Arthur Schlesinger, Jr., himself a veteran of the OSS Research and Analysis branch. Preoccupied at that time by the daily flux of events, Schlesinger and other former members of R&A were unable, after the fact, to reconstruct anything like the "position" of the OSS on the campaign against the Jews of Europe.

3. Quoted in Corey Ford, *Donovan of OSS* (Boston, 1970), 148.

4. The exceptions are Alfons Sollner, ed., *Zur Archäologie der Demokratie in Deutschland*, vol. 1 of *Analysen von politischen Emigranten im amerikanischen Geheimdienst, 1943-1945* (Frankfurt, 1986) and Barry M. Katz, *Foreign Intelligence. Research and Analysis in the Office of Strategic Services, 1942-1945* (Cambridge, Mass., 1989). There are informative chapters on the Research and Analysis branch in Bradley F. Smith, *The Shadow Warriors: OSS and the Origins of the CIA* (New York, 1983) and Robin Winks, *Cloak and Gown: Scholars in the Secret War, 1939-1961* (New York, 1987).

5. Philip E. Mosely, "The Growth of Russian Studies," in *American Research on Russia*, ed. Harold H. Fisher (Bloomington, 1959).

6. R&A 605 (March 14, 1942), cited in Laqueur, *The Terrible Secret*, 246 n. 36.

7. R&A 1113.9 (May 18-24, 1943), Franz Neumann [signed article], "Anti-Semitism." *Psychological Warfare: Weekly Roundup.*

8. R&A 1113.29 (October 5-11, 1943), Leonard Krieger [signed article], "Germany and Denmark – The Danish Jews." *Psychological Warfare: Weekly Roundup.*

9. R&A 1113.31. (October 19-25, 1943), Felix Gilbert [signed article], *Psychological Warfare: Weekly Roundup.*

10. R&A 1113.34 (November 13, 1943), Samuel Sharp [signed article], "Mass Slaughter of Jews Confirmed." *Political Intelligence Report* no. 34, Central Europe.

11. R&A 878.3 (November 11, 1943), *German Military Government over Europe, 1939-1943. Methods and Organization of Nazi Controls: General Government (Poland)*, 22-24.

12. Jan Karski, personal communication, September 6, 1987. William Salant to Group Captain Luard (August 3, 1944), "Status of the Oil Attack" and "Minutes of the Mediterranean Oil Targets Committee, August 8, 1944": papers of William Salant generously made available to the author by Dr. Walter Salant.

13. R&A 3114.3, "Nazi Plans for Dominating Germany and Europe: The Criminal

Conspiracy Against the Jews," Draft for War Crimes Staff (August 13, 1945).

14. Felix Gilbert, personal communication in response to questions put to him by the author (January 10, 1986), referring to Franz Neumann's classic *Behemoth: The Structure and Practice of National Socialism* (New York, 1942; 2d ed., 1944).

15. R&A 1113.9 (May 18-24), Franz Neumann [signed article], "Anti-Semitism." *Psychological Warfare: Weekly Roundup.*

16. "Outline of R&A 3114: Nazi Plans to Dominate Europe" (June 12, 1945), 17.

17. Neumann, *Behemoth*, 551.

18. Since my own work has focused on materials produced, rather than received, by OSS, I have relied here upon the compilations of Raul Hilberg, *The Destruction of the European Jews*, 2d ed. (New York, 1985), 1126f, 1127f, and Walter Laqueur, *The Terrible Secret*, 236 nn. 31-38.

19. This is the conclusion drawn by, among others, David S. Wyman in his otherwise very important book, *The Abandonment of the Jews*, 314.

20. "Functions of the Research and Analysis Branch" (October 30, 1942), RG 226, Entry 145, Box 2, Folder 45.

21. Richard Hartshorne to Division and subdivision Chiefs, "Draft of Proposed Guide to Preparation of Political Reports," 1a: RG 226, Entry 37, Box 5, Folder: Projects Committee Correspondence; compare William L. Langer, "Scholarship and the Intelligence Problem," *Proceedings of the American Philosophical Society* 92, no. 1 (March 1948), 43-46.

22. Lucy S. Dawidowicz, "Could the United States Have Rescued the European Jews from Hitler?" in *This World* 12 (Fall 1985), 15-30.

The New Germany and the Old Burdens

Fred Rosenbaum and Winston Pickett

IN DECEMBER 1986, the West German city of Kassel honored its most prominent native son, Franz Rosenzweig, on the 100th anniversary of his birth. Seventy-five participants—most of them Jews—came from Europe, Israel, and the United States to celebrate one of German Jewry's last and brightest stars in a long line of philosophers beginning with Moses Mendelssohn. Lectures by the leading Jewish scholars were prepared, symposia on Rosenzweig's legacy were coordinated, and even an exhibit on his life was arranged in the town's most prestigious museum. It seemed that Rosenzweig, known most widely for his theological treatise *Stern der Erlösung* (Star of Redemption), for his elegant translation of the Bible with Martin Buber, and for his educational innovations through the establishment of the Frankfurt-based Freies Jüdisches Lehrhaus in 1920, was about to get his due.

The problem, however, lay in the conference's location. Kassel is in the heart of Germany. For many of the participants who were refugees from Central Europe, this was their first return to the seedbed of the Final Solution. One eminent German-born Israeli scholar had refused to attend unless the annihilation of six million Jews was put on the agenda.

There are important reasons for his concern. Culturally and demographically, Jewish life in Germany is a faint shadow of its former self. Before Hitler, German Jews numbered around 550,000, or approximately 1% of the population. Today, out of seventy-nine million inhabitants in the newly reunified Germany, Jews total approximately 29,000

309

individuals (about three in every 8,000)—a figure that does not include some 7,000 Israelis and 5,000 unregistered Jews. The absorption of East Germany in 1990, a nation of eighteen million people, accounts for less than a thousand in the Jewish population of the new country. Moreover, approximately 90% of all German Jews emigrated there from Eastern Europe—particularly Poland and Hungary—after the war. Facts such as these, repeatedly cited at the Kassel conference, became a frequent leitmotif: "There are still Jews in Germany, but German Jewry is no more."

Today, most of world Jewry regards Germany with bitterness, suspicion, and anxiety. Yet it has not been simply the process of fusing two divided states last joined under Hitler, nor the reports of anti-Semitism since the fall of the Berlin Wall on November 9, 1989 that have evoked memories of the nightmare years. It is the postwar period in its entirety. In the minds of many Jews, therefore, Germany is perpetually in the dock, locked in a kind of half-century-long Nuremberg Trial.

The evidence for the prosecution consists first in West Germany's half-hearted efforts at rooting out the perpetrators of the greatest crime in human history. In the years following the war, German courts prosecuted only 12,900 ex-Nazis; of these, 5,200 were imprisoned and only 76 sentenced to life—the maximum penalty allowed by a country that has outlawed capital punishment. Indeed, a number of former Nazi officials even became part of the government. Perhaps the most celebrated case was that of Hans Globke, a senior official in Hitler's Interior Ministry, who was alleged to have drafted significant sections of the Third Reich's anti-Jewish laws and who, from 1953 to 1963, became the Federal Republic's State Secretary to its first chancellor, Konrad Adenauer. Nor has West Germany's highest office been free of taint. Kurt Georg Kiesinger, who became chancellor in 1966, had himself been a member of the Nazi Party for twelve years.

In 1978, West Germany was rocked by the famous "Filbinger Affair." Hans Filbinger, then minister-president of Baden-Württemberg, was accused of sentencing teenage soldiers to death for desertion and for anti-Nazi utterances just before Germany's surrender in 1945. While the ensuing public scandal ultimately forced him to resign—which he did reluctantly and without contrition—Filbinger continued to live in his official residence and to command the respect of a broad sector of Germany society.

The view that Germans have been unwilling to reckon with their Nazi past gained further credence during events surrounding the Bitburg controversy in 1985. Many American Jews—Holocaust survivor and Nobel laureate Elie Wiesel most prominent among them—focused their outrage on the Reagan administration for its failure to understand the symbolic weight of laying a wreath for "innocent" German soldiers at a cemetery where SS men lay buried. But they did not forget that it was Chancellor Helmut Kohl who had not only invited the American president to participate in this act of "reconciliation" but who also had refused to change its emotionally charged venue. American Jews watched with consternation as Kohl claimed that he represented a new generation of German leaders no longer tainted by the guilt of a past for which it bore no personal responsibility. While much was made of the fact that Kohl was only 15 at the end of the war, American Jews shuddered at what they felt was his monumental arrogance for assuming that he could bring about the "normalization" of Germany in so facile a way.

In the wake of reunification, Jews have responded anxiously to the prospect of a German preponderance—both economic and political—in a newly configured Europe. Will a united Germany, free of the physical division that recalled its defeat by the Allies and the war it began, now consider the Holocaust as something simply to put behind it? For some critics the basis of that concern lies in the work of no less an honored stratum of German society than its professoriate.

In the mid-1980s, one of West Germany's most prominent and highly respected historians began to write in a vein that frankly shocked scholars on both sides of the Atlantic. To be sure, Ernst Nolte and his followers never denied that the Holocaust had occurred. What he and other well-known historians such as Andreas Hillgruber and Klaus Hildebrand did that was so disturbing, however, was to place the murder of the six million into a "context" which effectively minimized its meaning, thereby giving Holocaust revisionism a new and quite respectable face. The Holocaust, they said, was not a unique event, but one which could be compared to—and, moreover, equated with—other twentieth-century catastrophes such as the Armenian massacre, the Vietnam War and even the Soviet invasion of Afghanistan. Moreover, most of Hitler's murderous excesses, in Nolte's view, are to be understood as a response to the equally barbarous acts of the Bolsheviks—"Asiatic deeds," as he calls them—which began in the 1920s, two decades before Auschwitz. For the West Berlin professor, Nazism was a copy of the Soviet gulag system and also a reply to it—a defensive reaction to the Communist threat, and to

311

the alleged danger to Germany posed by the Jews. As "evidence" Nolte cited Chaim Weizmann's well-known declaration in 1939 that if war came to Europe, world Jewry would fight on Britain's side. So armed, Nolte proceeded to explain and even partially to justify Nazism's genocidal obsession with the Jews as "enemies of the Reich."

Nolte and his followers came under heavy fire by other prominent academics such as the renowned social philosopher, Jürgen Habermas. But the *Historikerstreit*[1] as it came to be known, left many with the uneasy feeling that the politician Kohl's attempts to bury the Nazi past had now been cloaked with the mantle of scholarly credibility.

For all of those disturbing developments, however, another truth begins to emerge: Bonn is *not* Weimar. By any standard, one must grant that the Federal Republic's own brand of representative democracy has outlived its predecessor more than three times over. Its economy, the third largest in the world after the United States and Japan, continues to have a stabilizing effect on its society. The deutsch mark is the most stable currency in Europe, and the country's inflation rate is the lowest of all the Common Market countries.

The self-perception of its democratic makeup appears to be equally strong. According to the Allensbach opinion poll, one of the country's most respected indices of its kind, no less than 71% of those interviewed in West Germany in 1978 considered democracy to be the "best form of government," while only 11% suggested "there is another that is better."[2] Another Allensbach survey revealed that the percentage of West Germans preferring a multiparty over a single-party system rose from 53 to 68% in the years between 1950 and 1978, while devotees of a one-party system dropped from 24 to 5% during that same period.[3] Further signs of health in Germany's democracy can be seen in its unusually decentralized federalism—a system of regionalized power-sharing by which most of the country's authority is vested in the hands of eleven *Länder*, or states (now swelled to seventeen with the addition of East Germany), which have ultimate jurisdiction over every aspect of government except foreign affairs, defense, currency, mail, telecommunications and railway transportation.

The most striking contrast between the histories of the Weimar Germany and the Federal Republic, however, may lie in the latter's integration with the West. Whereas Germany between the wars was in many ways isolated, the Federal Republic, and now a united Germany, has taken a leading role in NATO and the EEC; in 1992, of course, all trade barriers are scheduled to fall and a single European currency is expected in the year 2000.

Culturally, the West Germans appear thoroughly intertwined with their neighbors. They travel abroad more than any other people in the world, and no less than two-thirds of the young adults in the country speak English fairly well. To be sure, as the perceptive sociologist Ralf Dahrendorf wrote in 1965, the German personality has been characterized both by an inability to tolerate nonconformity and by an unwillingness to accept social and ethnic groups that include homosexuals, the disabled, foreigners, and Jews.[4] Nevertheless, there appear to be signs of loosening in the last twenty years, caused in part by the social changes that were put into motion by the student, youth, environmental and women's movements beginning in the late 1960s. Indeed, one observer noted in 1987 a tentative groping of West Germany's youth towards a more tolerant, pluralistic and informal society than would have been imaginable twenty or even ten years earlier.[5]

Part of this new mentality may have caught some of the participants at the Rosenzweig conference off-guard. In a country where collective amnesia about the Jews and the Holocaust was believed to be the prevailing disposition, they sensed a new social climate. That sense came when the pastor of Kassel's Huguenot church, where 1,500 townspeople, academics, government officials, and Israeli guests had assembled to hear the centenary's opening session, welcomed the throng with the Hebrew greeting, *b'ruchim haba'im*. Later, several meetings were devoted to German-Jewish relations. And midway through the week-long conference, at a Rosenzweig "memorial hour" held at city hall, Kassel Mayor Hans Eichel declared: "If we Germans are proud of Beethoven, we have to be ashamed of Auschwitz."

Are there, then, some West Germans indeed engaging in a *Bewältigung der Vergangenheit*—an honest, thoroughgoing process of coming to grips with their past?

Certainly from the founding of the FRG to the 1960s there was little or no interest in confronting the Holocaust. In the early years after the war, though, Adenauer was credited with courage and vision for having created and implemented a far-reaching agreement on reparations with Israel. Over the next decades, billions of deutsch marks in goods and cash would be sent to the new Jewish state. Yet in a way, this transfer of wealth, opposed by a large segment of the German population, may have helped inhibit introspection. *Wiedergutmachung*, literally "making good

313

again," as Adenauer's program was known, gave the impression in many quarters that material compensation was all that was needed to draw the proverbial *Schlußstrich,* the accountant's "bottom line" on twelve years of Nazi horrors.

Internally, with Germans fixing their attention on rebuilding their bombed-out cities and restoring an economy ravaged by war, scant attention in the press or the public schools was paid to the moral question raised by Germany's role in the annihilation of six million Jews. Other than being viewed as the product of one evil man, one mad genius who held the German nation under his spell, the Holocaust occupied little place in public dialogue.

In East Germany, of course, the past lay buried deep beneath the Communist government's creation myth which, in a recasting of history, sought to sever any connection between the German Democratic Republic and the Third Reich. In a remarkable sleight of hand, the GDR aligned itself so closely with the Soviet Union that a reading of the propaganda from that period almost leaves one with the impression that East Germany itself fought side by side with Stalin against Hitler, an idea which was reinforced by that country's celebration each year of May 8— the date the Red Army liberated Berlin—as a national holiday.

The first significant breakthrough of West Germany's resistance to remembrance came with the Israeli capture and trial of one of Hitler's top-ranking bureaucrats in the extermination of Europe's Jews, Adolf Eichmann. Put on trial in Jerusalem in 1960, an event widely broadcast in Israel and Germany alike, Eichmann revealed not only the "banality of evil," in the words of Hannah Arendt, but for the first time exposed the details and indeed the reality of the Holocaust to a critical segment of Germany's population: its youth. Here, in tedious but damning detail were the minutiae of the Third Reich's monstrous inhumanity laid out for a generation whose parents had remained all but silent on the issue. To his credit, it was Adenauer himself who, out of concern for the widening gulf of ignorance between the generations, had urged the state-run German television to carry the trial.

Not long afterwards, in 1963, Germany and indeed much of Europe was shaken by Rolf Hochhuth's *Der Stellvertreter* (The Deputy), a play which presented a scathing indictment of the silence of Pope Pius XXI and the complicity of the Catholic Church during the deportation of Jews from Rome in October 1943. Never before in Germany had the ethical issue of silence as a form of complicity been raised so forcefully. Even the

314

Lutheran Church found itself caught up in the ensuing controversy as it and other factions of the German public vainly sought to keep the play from being shown. Into this emerging climate of probing and introspection came another event that had far-reaching repercussions on the way Germans were to view the events of the past generation: the Six-Day War. The popular image of a tiny, beleaguered nation that had risen from the ashes of the Holocaust to defeat a vastly larger Arab army bent on its annihilation enabled West Germans to feel sympathy for Israel and prompted young Germans in particular to examine their own country's attempt at genocide a generation earlier. By the end of the 1960s, a serious consideration of the Third Reich began to emerge as part of a larger generational conflict in Germany—one that erupted in the form of militant demonstrations on the country's university campuses and which reflected the younger generation's desire to make a break with the bourgeois society that had nurtured them and their parents' criminal past. Slowly and painfully the subject of Jews, Germany and the Holocaust began to emerge from the historical closet.

This trend continued into the 1970s with the accession to power of the Social Democratic party, which, more than the Christian Democratic Union, seemed prepared to come to terms with the events of World War II. Nowhere was this more apparent than during Chancellor Willy Brandt's official visit to Poland in 1970, the year following his election. There, at the memorial to the Warsaw Ghetto uprising, Germany's head of government spontaneously dropped to his knees in silent reverence. And while many Germans recoiled at the gesture for having gone too far, it seemed to demonstrate to the world that a new mood of self-examination had come to Bonn.

Curiously enough, the single most important event contributing to the shift in German thinking on the Holocaust was an American import. In early 1979, following its debut on American television, West German television broadcast the NBC docudrama, *Holocaust*, the engaging, though somewhat frothy saga of the fictional Weiss family. By the completion of its airing, the program had attracted more viewers than any single program in German history (about 40% of the population), and public opinion polls revealed that it generated considerable sympathy for the suffering of the Jews during the Third Reich. In addition to debates in the media, there were other concrete results as well, as thousands of schools and colleges were prompted to organize discussions on the subject. Not long after the broadcast, the Bundestag,

315

reacting to popular pressure, canceled the statute of limitations on war crimes that was scheduled to expire shortly.

Additional signs showing a German willingness to effect some kind of reconciliation have emerged in the last decade in the growing number of cities and towns in West Germany sponsoring return visits by their former Jewish inhabitants. Frequently these visits accompany the government's reconstruction of former synagogues or memorials bearing tribute to the rich history of Jewish settlement throughout Germany, much of which dates from late antiquity. In some of the smaller towns, non-Jewish citizens groups have even taken to restoring on a volunteer basis Jewish graveyards and synagogues, a number of which had been converted after the war into barns and storage houses. Moreover, these phenomena are not kept from the public view. Television stations such as the Westdeutsche Rundfunk, which reaches thirty million, schedule programs on Israel, Jewish culture and German-Jewish history—including the Holocaust at least several times per week. These efforts, combined with federally mandated Holocaust education programs in the school system, have gone a long way toward keeping Germans aware of both the recent past and the role of Jews in German history.

Other positive changes, set in motion during the 1960s and 1970s, have left their mark as well. In response to the younger generation's thirst for Jewish culture and education, the state of Baden-Württemberg in 1979 created the *Jüdische Hochschule* in Heidelberg, which, despite its mostly non-Jewish student body, became the country's first rabbinical seminary to open since the end of the war. In 1963, the *Institut für die Geschichte der deutschen Juden* was founded in Hamburg and has developed a program of instruction and research in the area of German-Jewish history. A similar institute exists at the University of Duisburg. Even the international Rosenzweig conference held in Kassel and the opening of a large and well-equipped Jewish museum in Frankfurt in 1988 appear to be testimony to the government's officially stated desire to preserve Jewish culture in its midst.

The return to power of the CDU in 1982, however, has resulted in a number of countervailing trends. Chancellor Kohl, as his 1985 performance at Bitburg has shown, has proven himself far from sensitive to Jewish concerns. For many, however, his behavior that same year was more than offset by that of Federal President and former Wehrmacht officer Richard von Weizsäcker, who, on the fortieth anniversary of the German surrender of May 8, 1945, in a courageous speech to the

Bundestag, told the German public that the only way to come to terms with the shame and horror of their past is by continuing to remember it. He declared that "anyone who closes his eyes to the past is blind to the present" and that "anyone who refuses to remember the inhumanity done is prone to new risks of infection." Along with Habermas and the country's two most respected novelists, Günter Grass and Heinrich Böll, who have also spoken out in this vein, von Weizsäcker seemed to represent a German view that contrasted sharply with that of Kohl and Nolte. Indeed, half a century after Hitler, the newly reunited country appears deeply divided intellectually between those who would remember and those who would rather forget.

The complex relationship between the resistance to memory and anti-Semitism in the Federal Republic may be seen in two incidents which, like Bitburg, occurred during the pivotal anniversary year of 1985. Less than two weeks before President Reagan's visit, on April 25, an article published in the popular weekly magazine *Quick* brought to the surface a dramatic assortment of anti-Jewish canards. Appearing without a byline and titled "The Power of the Jews," the article made use of the public outrage over the Bitburg visit as proof that organized American Jewry—especially the "Jewish dominated" networks of ABC, CBS and NBC—were doing everything they could to sabotage an honorable attempt at German-American reconciliation. Even the prestigious conservative newspaper, the *Frankfurter Allgemeine Zeitung (FAZ)*, in a thinly veiled threat, editorialized that Jews should be careful not to overstrain relations because the consequences could only be negative for them and for Israel.[6] Meanwhile the *Quick* article, selectively ignoring all non-Jewish and interdenominational outrage over the visit as well as the pain that Jews themselves felt witnessing a ceremony that so clearly lumped together both Nazi victims and perpetrators, accused the Jews of "re-opening old German wounds."

This projection of German guilt onto the Jews themselves—what historian Hajo Funke calls an example of "modern post-Nazi anti-Semitism"[7]—was evident not only in the *Quick* article, but in public opinion as well. Roughly a third of the West German population, albeit the upper age groups, voiced similar attitudes both before and for several months after Reagan's visit to Bitburg.[8] Moreover, during the same period, the two largest Jewish communities in Germany, Berlin and Frankfurt, reported a sudden increase in anti-Jewish statements, while right-wing nationalists and neo-Nazis, capitalizing on the already poisoned public atmosphere, desecrated Frankfurt's Jewish cemetery and painted anti-Jewish slogans on gravestones in Berlin-Zehlendorf.[9] That such anti-Jewish feeling found a comparatively loud echo in the wake of the Bitburg visit seems to illustrate how a dormant prejudice can be activated by a controversy surrounding a symbolic act; it also shows how anti-Semitism can be employed by those refusing to take any responsibility for a murderous past.

The second event that provoked a resurfacing of anti-Jewish sentiments occurred less than five months after Bitburg, with the aborted staging of the late Rainer Werner Fassbinder's *Der Mühl, die Stadt, und der Tod* (Garbage, the City, and Death). On one level, this play is a scathing indictment of the unbridled real estate speculation and urban redevelopment that took place in Frankfurt after the war. Unfortunately, however, in personifying that trend, Fassbinder chose a business tycoon, modeled on a real-life person, who was ruthless, sex-crazed, power-hungry and—not incidentally—Jewish. In fact, his very status as a Jew in post-Holocaust Germany earned him a protected position and for decades kept him immune from public criticism. The other characters' reaction to "the Jew," as he is simply called, is predictable. One ex-Nazi declares: "I could sleep better if this bloodsucker had been sent to the gas chambers." Fassbinder, who had written the drama in 1975 and failed to have it staged at that time, maintained that his depiction of the Jew was not anti-Semitic. Through his characterization, the leftist playwright claimed, he had sought to criticize the insidious economic forces that propelled a Jew into that position in the first place and to peel back the layers of Jew-hatred that masquerade as philo-Semitism. The public's reaction to *Garbage* was less predictable, however. When, in 1985, after Fassbinder's death, Frankfurt's Kammerspieltheater tried again to produce the play, local Jews stormed the stage on the first night. The director claimed that the production, albeit in an extreme way, revealed that Nazi views were alive and well in Frankfurt, and declared its showing a matter of free speech. The play's opponents—among them the majority of Frankfurt politicians and even the conservative *FAZ*—argued that anti-Semites would exploit the play's most hateful sentiments, which in any case were intolerable for Jews to hear on a German stage. In the end, *Garbage* was canceled.

In its aftermath, however, the play left many Jewish critics troubled. The *FAZ*, which only months before had criticized the Jews for the furor surrounding Bitburg, now allowed conservatives "safely" to denounce

Fassbinder's purported anti-Semitism—regarded simply as anti-Jewish prejudice and virtually the only unacceptable legacy of the Nazi era—while distancing themselves from any denunciation of National Socialism itself.[10] This reaction from the respectable Right revealed a disturbing tendency evident in some government circles as well: criticizing contemporary manifestations of anti-Semitism while consciously refusing to deal with the infinitely greater crimes of a generation ago.

Some voices on the Left, meanwhile, claimed that the play was not about anti-Semitism at all but rather about real estate speculation. Their arguments for its performance on the grounds of free speech persisted in demonstrating that they still had not understood the kind of anti-Semitism that the Nazis embodied or that the Holocaust was qualitatively different from other Nazi crimes.[11] That most of the Left, which had turned viciously anti-Zionist in the past decade, remained virtually silent during the Fassbinder debate, moreover shows how they too were barely interested in reflecting on the extent that anti-Semitism remains alive in Germany or examining the nature of anti-Semitism at all.

As Hajo Funke has written, the public's response to Bitburg and the Fassbinder play points to "the psycho-historical core of the problem that characterizes the situation in Germany today: the fact that there has never been a true and wide public discussion and evaluation of the Nazi past in the postwar period."[12]

Ironically, though, the greatest challenge to Jewish life in Germany may not come from the political or social arena but from within. Many internal contradictions plague the community of 41,000, not least of all the fact that its three largest centers—Frankfurt, Munich and Berlin, each with roughly 5,000 Jews—continue to be magnets for Israeli and Soviet Jews, drawn to Germany for economic opportunity and possessing only a marginal interest in contributing to the development and continuity of Jewish life there. Indeed, even if that interest could be nurtured by some arm of outreach—a concept that has yet to take root in Germany except by Chabad Lubavitch *shlichim* (emissaries)—the biggest obstacle to fostering innovative Jewish life may be the *Gemeinde*-structure in which it operates. Unlike the United States, where new Jewish communities frequently emerge organically from a core of worshipers, a rabbi, and, more often than not, a place to pray, in Germany Jewish affairs are coordinated from the top down. Both the creation and direction of a *Gemeinde* is managed through a centralized leadership, which, in turn, has jurisdiction over all Jewish communal organizations and synagogues,

319

and even the rabbis themselves. This structure creates a built-in resistance to change and innovation. Its ultimate power, moreover, is strengthened by virtue of its quasi-governmental status, a sizable allocation of federal and state funds, and its close relationship to the top politicians in Bonn.

Indeed, one of the most frequent criticisms leveled at the West German–Jewish leadership since World War II has been its pro-government stance even in the face of policies obviously neither in its self-interest nor in that of world Jewry. In 1978, for example, when West Germany's *Zentralrat für die Juden in Deutschland* (Central Council of Jews in Germany) chose not to join, and even opposed, the chorus of those calling for the resignation of ex-Nazi Hans Filbinger, many younger German Jews accused the organized leadership of being too easily bought off by the political establishment. Perhaps the most vociferous and irreverent among them was Henryk Broder, who, in 1979 co-edited a book with the provocative title, *Foreign in Their Own Land: Jews of the Federal Republic*,[13] a collection of essays and first-person accounts which revealed the groundswell of dissatisfaction among postwar second-generation Jews.

Among the harshest criticisms were those leveled by Broder himself, both at Germany's mainstream Jewish community and the New Left, with whom he had earlier considered himself politically allied. Broder's Polish origins reflected the dominant East European pattern of Germany's Jews. On the one hand he exposed the anti-Semitic leanings of the pro-Palestinian New Left, whose ability to drain all meaning from the Holocaust became evident when it labeled Israel's war in Lebanon an act of Zionist genocide, equating Begin's bombing of Beirut with Hitler's liquidation of the Warsaw ghetto. On the other hand, he charged members of the Jewish establishment, and especially *Gemeinde* heads such as Berlin's rigid septuagenarian Heinz Galinski, with becoming latter-day *Hofjuden* (court Jews), seeking to bask in the warm glow of approval from West Germany's politicians.

Broder's criticisms and those leveled by other contributors to *Fremd im eigenem Land* were more than isolated accounts. They represented the frustration and anger of a younger generation of Central European Jews who had come to the realization by the early 1980s that rather than maintaining a "normal" Jewish life, their parents had been living a lie. Often invoking Theodor Adorno's trenchant aphorism describing the mentality of their elders—"In the house of the hangman, you don't mention the rope; it stirs up resentment"—they had begun to express their views on issues such as the failure of the Federal Republic to fulfill its claims to eradicate anti-Semitism and its poor record of denazification. To be sure, some, like Broder and Lea Fleischmann, author of a scathing autobiographical commentary, *Dies ist nicht mein Land: Eine Jüdin verlässt die Bundesrepublik* (This Is Not My Country: A Jew Leaves the Federal Republic), emigrated to Israel after voicing their complaints.[14] But other young Jewish intellectuals stayed to fight, staged demonstrations during the Bitburg visit in 1985, protested against the reunions of SS veterans' organizations in Bavaria, and, above all, successfully prevented the performance of the Fassbinder play. This was no longer a Jewish community satisfied with maintaining a low profile; instead, a new and more assertive German-Jewish political consciousness began to emerge for the first time since 1945.[15]

Unfortunately, the harshest critics of the insularity and unaccountability of the German-Jewish establishment felt vindicated in 1988 by what has come to be known as the sordid "Nachmann scandal." More than anyone else, it was Werner Nachmann, for twenty years the official Jewish voice in the Federal Republic, who had betrayed his own trust. A textile manufacturer who returned with his family to his native Germany from France after the war, Nachmann was one of a number of Jewish businessmen who capitalized on the *Wirtschaftswunder*, or postwar economic boom. But after he died suddenly of a heart attack on May 12, 1988, an investigation of his estate revealed that Nachmann, the respected chairman of the *Zentralrat* and the official Jewish liaison to ranking German politicians in the Bundestag and the Chancery itself, had embezzled more than thirty million deutsch marks (over $15 million) in reparation funds intended for Holocaust victims. He used the money to prop up an array of his own failing business ventures, to pay for his son's wedding and to set up a secret Swiss bank account for the funding of ransom demands should he ever be kidnapped by terrorists.

That Nachmann was able to amass such power not only reveals the undemocratic process of German-Jewish leadership but also points to a vicious circle of deferred responsibility. Moreover, except for a spate of reports that surrounded the first revelations of the Nachmann affair, an official examination of his business dealings as well as his financial and political ties to high officials in the Federal Republic has yet to be conducted.

Jewish life in Germany is problematic for other reasons as well. To be sure, the Jews of the Federal Republic have not lived "with their suitcases

321

packed," fearing pogroms or deportation, as have the majority of Polish, Rumanian, Czech and Hungarian Jews who returned to their native lands from displaced person and concentration camps. Nevertheless, the face of Germany's 64 scattered Jewish communities is rapidly changing. With the median age somewhere between 45 and 50, and a death rate seven times higher than the birth rate, most of the smaller Jewish communities will doubtless vanish forever. There is a dearth of rabbis, cantors and teachers, despite the fact that the *Hochschule für jüdische Studien* in Heidelberg was opened in 1979 to train them. At the *Hochschule,* the majority of instructors are either American Jews or Israelis on sabbatical leave, while most of the students are non-Jewish. More than 65% of Jews living in Germany intermarry, leaving keen observers such as West Berlin's Rabbi Ernst Stein to ponder the question of survival itself. According to Stein, half of whose community of 6,500 Jews consists of Soviet emigrés, the most active and knowledgeable in his flock are the several dozen converts who "after all are required to study for a year or more."[16]

Stein, like most religiously liberal rabbis on the continent a graduate of the Leo Baeck College for Jewish Studies in London, also bewails the refusal of the German-Jewish establishment to tolerate any form of Judaism other than Orthodoxy. Even in his own Pestalozzi Street Synagogue, the most "liberal" of Berlin's four Jewish houses of worship, women are still required to pray in a separate section despite the rabbi's strenuous efforts, during his decade of service, to introduce mixed seating.

A German refugee who as a teenager spent the war years in Shanghai, Stein lived in Israel, the United States and Britain before returning as a rabbi to his native land in 1980. A dissenter on many issues, he feels strongly that Germany's small Jewish community is anything but secure in the newly unified country. He points not only to anti-Semitic feelings, which in his view are deeply ingrained even in the younger generation, but also to anti-foreign sentiments in general among the German public. For decades the million Turkish guest-workers in the country have been the group most victimized by West German racism; only under the rarest circumstances can they or their German-born children become citizens. But Stein foresees even more serious social conflict now that the Berlin Wall is down: a surge of popular resentment against the tens of thousands of impoverished Polish refugees entering the large German cities and even against the former East Germans once the colossal costs of reunification become known to the taxpayer.

Stein's fears notwithstanding, most indications point to a Germany passing the new tests of its democracy. Neo-fascist parties, like the Republicans led by a former SS sergeant, represent but a tiny minority and have been in disarray since the fall of the Berlin Wall. Under West Germany's constitution, hate crimes, which include the dissemination of neo-Nazi propaganda, incitement to racial hatred or defamation of National Socialist victims, as well as the denial of the Holocaust, are punishable with fines or prison sentences. In sum, Germany has been practicing democracy for forty years. Politically and socially as well as economically the country bears little or no resemblance to the abject and isolated nation that allowed Hitler to come to power in 1933. As for the threat of remilitarization, perhaps Henryk Broder's sardonic comment fits best: "The majority of Germans have found out that it is more pleasant to live in a democracy, to travel, to shop and to consume, than to march, fight and die for the fatherland."[17]

A more important concern, perhaps, relates to Germany's desire for normalization. As long as the country remained partitioned, the argument goes, German life, given the enormity of the horror it unleashed, remained what the rest of the world preferred it to be: abnormal. The wall was universally perceived both as a punishment for and a reminder of Germany's responsibility for starting World War II and for the obliteration of an entire Jewish civilization. With the dismantling of the wall, the Germans will simply draw another kind of line—the *Schlußstrich*, that in effect declares: "Enough. Let's move on and leave the past."

Yet, co-existing with Germany's tendency to bury its history, is its record of repentance. The Third Reich and the mass murder of the Jews have been the subject of public discussion for years, not only in school curricula, university seminars, symposia, and public ceremonies but through the repeated presence of those themes in the mass media. It is impossible to open a newspaper, listen to the radio or watch television without encountering the treatment of German-Jewish history or the current relationship of Germany and the Jews. In the last decade, no other European country appears to have had as strong an interest in Jewish culture and history as the Federal Republic. In towns without even enough Jews for a minyan, old synagogues and graveyards have been renovated or restored and German-Jewish refugees are invited back for a visit—prompted in part by a commitment by politicians to preserve the memory of their former Jewish communities. While such actions may stem in part from a guilty conscience, they nevertheless represent a

323

confrontation with German history—one that hopefully will be carried out by a united Germany as well. Even before reunification, a newly reconstituted GDR showned signs of a willingness to engage in a *Bewältigung der Vergangenheit*—a coming to grips with its own past. On April 12, 1990, upon the installation of the country's first democratic government, East Germany ended forty years of official denial by accepting joint responsibility for Nazi crimes committed during the Third Reich, specifically singling out genocide and the "murder of Jewish women, men and children."[18] In addition, the official statement asked "Jews of the world to forgive us" and expressed the GDR's willingness to pay reparations to Holocaust victims and to seek diplomatic ties with Israel.

Without stifling Communist ideology, harsh curbs on the press and virtually complete isolation from Israel and world Jewry, will not the eighteen million former inhabitants of the GDR have a much better chance to face their history now, than they did under Ulbricht and Honecker?

In the end, however, the battle for memory and for a new German-Jewish identity will likely be waged on matters of historic symbolism like Bitburg and the Fassbinder play. It is uncanny that the Berlin Wall was breached on the evening of November 9, 1989, precisely the date of *Kristallnacht,* or the Night of Broken Glass, when, fifty-one years earlier, Nazi thugs burned to the ground nearly every synagogue in the Reich. As German youths from both sides of the wall took to the streets—this time to dismantle totalitarianism—Chancellor Kohl spoke of November 9 as a national holiday for the united Germany of the future. But will his country also look to the past and simultaneously mark this day as one of mourning as well as joy? And will Germany's Jews demand such an act of recognition from their government? The answers will tell us much about Germans and Jews in the period which follows the postwar era.

NOTES

1. See Richard Evans, *In Hitler's Shadow: West German Historians and the Attempt to Escape from the Nazi Past* (New York, 1989), 24ff.

2. See John Ardagh, *Germany and the Germans: An Anatomy of Society Today* (New York, 1987), 405.

3. Ibid.

4. Ralf Dahrendorf, *Society and Democracy in Germany* (Garden City, N.Y., 1969).

5. Ardagh, op. cit., 447.

6. In a forum with Andrei S. Markovits, Seyla Benhabib, Moshe Postone, see

"Rainer Werner Fassbinder's *Garbage, the City, and Death:* Renewed Antagonisms in the Complex Relationship Between Jews and Germans in the Federal Republic of Germany," *New German Critique* 38 (Spring/Summer 1986), 3-28.

7. Hajo Funke, "Bitburg, Jews, and Germans: A Case Study of Anti-Jewish Sentiment in Germany during May 1985," ibid., 62ff.

8. Ibid., 66.

9. Ibid., 67.

10. See article in note 6, a forum in *New German Critique* 38 (1986), 26.

11. Ibid., 23.

12. Funke, "Bitburg, Jews and Germans," 64.

13. Henryk M. Broder and Michel R. Lang, *Fremd in Eigenem Land: Juden in der Bundsrepublik* (Frankfurt-am-Main: Fischer Taschenbuch, 1979).

14. Fleischmann's second book bears the title, *Ich bin eine Israelin* (I am an Israeli). (Hamburg: Hoffmann and Campe, 1980).

15. Anson Rabinbach, "Reflections on Germans and Jews since Auschwitz," in *Germans and Jews Since the Holocaust: The Changing Situation in West Germany,* ed. Anson Rabinbach and Jack Zipes (New York, 1986), 10, and in *New German Critique* 38 (1986), 10.

16. Interview with Fred Rosenbaum, November 1982 and April 1990.

17. Interview with Winston Pickett, March 1990.

18. *The New York Times,* April 13, 1990, p. 1.

AFTERWORD

ON MEMORY AND RECONCILIATION*
Elie Wiesel

FORTY YEARS AFTER THE HOLOCAUST, I can speak about memory. But not about *Versöhnung,* or reconciliation. That subject comes less easily. A story by Rabbi Nachman of Bratslav will help explain:

Once upon a time, in a faraway land, the king had a vision of the future. A malediction would fall on his kingdom. The next harvest would be cursed and whoever would eat from it would lose his mind. "What shall we do?" the king asked his advisers and counselors. None could come up with an answer. Finally, the king found one. To his closest adviser, who was also his trusted friend, he said "I intend to take all the grain that remains from recent harvests and store it in huge granaries. No one but you will have access to it. And when the time of malediction arrives, and my people and I go mad, you and you alone will eat from the uncontaminated grain. You and only you will remain sane. But, you will have to pay a price for your salvation: you will go from town to town and you will scream louder and louder: 'Men and women, do not forget, do not forget that you are mad...'"

Hasn't this been the task given the Jewish people, to be the gatekeepers of memory, since our appearance on the stage of history? Surrounded by nations that believed in idolatry or practiced violence, our ancestors would urge these nations not to forget whatever has befallen the Jews throughout history. The message aroused resentment; it still does. When Holocaust survivors plead for remembrance today, they frequently encounter hostility and denial. People in general refuse to remember painful events; our natural instinct suppresses what hurts us. With survivors, this instinct is different. The more painful the memory, the harder we work to keep it alive and share it with our contemporaries and their descendants. Why? Not because we want to cling to morbidity. Our desire to remember is rooted in a different motivation: we wish to remain linked to our dead who, due to the murderer's inhuman cruelty, have vanished into nothingness. With the Holocaust our dead have even been denied burial rights: they do not lie in cemeteries. Our prayers, our hearts, our memories are their cemeteries.

But our commitment to remembrance is motivated by our compassion for the living as well. At various occasions I have said to two American presidents, Jimmy Carter and Ronald Reagan: We wish to remember not only for the sake of the dead; it is too late for the dead. It may even be too late for those who survived the dead. But it is not too late for our children. It is for their sake that we cultivate and celebrate memory.

We survivors are profoundly sensitive to children. We remember those who were not allowed to grow, to laugh, to play, to learn, to dream: there was no room for them in the Nazi vision of the world. Isolated, rejected, oppressed, beaten, hunted down like frightened animals: between one and one and a half million Jewish children perished during the Holocaust, killed in the dark kingdom of Night. Often we wonder how humanity could survive their death. We would like to believe that the innocence and beauty of a child is stronger than the vile instincts of the murderer. Novels and films have illustrated that belief: when facing a helpless child, the killer somehow forgets that he is a killer. Unfortunately, in the strange confrontation in the Third Reich between German killers and the Jewish children, the children lost. Good husbands and fathers would kill Jewish children and feel nothing.

It is for their sake that we remember. We remember the past for the sake of the future. If the planet is to survive, it will be because of our faith in memory. Yet it does not seem that the world will survive: there is too much hatred, too strong an attraction to violence. The future brings thoughts of fear: the world has not been punished for what it has done to the Jewish people, and to itself, for there is no punishment. The only conceivable punishment, I believe, would be the destruction of the planet, which naturally we would hope to prevent. However, the Jewish people's commitment to remembrance is not, nor has it ever been, formulated in terms of crime and punishment. We preserve memory, instead, for the salvation of humankind.

Yet how does one remember? We are often helpless, lacking the tools of the historian who knows what to look for and where. Historians are interested in facts and documents; we are interested in human beings. The agony of one person, the despair of one family in a ghetto cellar waiting for the "action" to end, the silent weeping of one mother putting her dead child to sleep—is this the "material" historians seek? I have found that tears and prayers contain as much truth as historical documents, if not more. Poets and chroniclers, the words of both must be remembered.

Another problem faces us in the sharing of memory. There will be events that we cannot recall, yet our memory of the Holocaust can be limited and still remain truthful. Human beings are of course incapable of encompassing their entire past but we must at least try. To forget is to affect not only the past but the present and the future, too.

As I review my own past, I see an adolescent, faceless and nameless, who could have been in my position now. In the week before the liberation of Buchenwald, thousands and thousands of inmates—mostly Jewish, at first—were removed and murdered before the arrival of the American liberators. Somehow—by miracle? no: by chance—I always remained behind. The last day I had gotten to the gate when we were sent back to the barracks: the daily quota had been attained. I remember those who were not sent back, those who passed the gate. I think of the one adolescent who was taken away, perhaps because I had been sent back. I do not know who he was and never will. But I do know that when I speak, I feel that he is measuring and judging my words. That is why we had better speak the truth.

Words are dangerous. How many words separated the publication of *Mein Kampf* and the opening of the first concentration camps? Hitler's criminal delusions quickly became reality. Why weren't his words taken seriously by the outside world? Now we have learned that words may be vehicles of life or death. They may be instruments of destruction and murder. However, it is our responsibility to change them into acts of compassion, prayers for joy, gestures of friendship and humaneness.

I have written many books in the last thirty years, putting words to my memory, yet the questions I had when I wrote the first paragraph have remained unanswered. I still do not know what made the victims of the Holocaust into the loneliest victims in history, nor do I know what provoked the metamorphosis of educated persons into consummate killers. Often, when I study the literature of the Third Reich I stumble upon the same conclusion: certain events cannot be explained simply because they cannot be understood. Only those who were there know what it meant. That is why writers are so poorly equipped: they do not know the language. We cannot tell the tale, that is why it must be told. This is paradoxical but we must not fear a paradox.

While memory may be at times painful, it is somehow a less difficult task than *Versöhnung*. The proper translation in English for *Versöhnung* lies between reconciliation and forgiveness. An example of our struggle with forgiveness lies in a painful episode in the young history of Israel. In 1952-53, West Germany and Israel negotiated a "reparations agreement." As a journalist, I covered the conference in the Dutch city of Vassenaar. In many of my reports I opposed Premier David Ben-Gurion's position. I understood his argument that the murderer should not inherit his victim's fortune, and I also knew that Israel needed money. While Ben-Gurion was probably right, even he did not advocate *Versöhnung*. To build bridges between governments and nations is one thing; to forget the abyss of blood that separated them is another.

During that period, many Jewish communities were discussing the subject of forgiveness. No one asked the French, the Dutch, the Poles, the Belgians, the Norwegians to forgive. Only the Jews have been asked, and by the world community, not by Germany. Had the Bundestag adopted a resolution asking the Jewish people to forgive Hitler's actions in the name of Germany, the Jewish spiritual and political leadership would have something to discuss. But a true and sincere plea from Germany for forgiveness has never been spoken. When journalists or colleagues question me, as an individual, about forgiveness, I can only respond: who am I to extend forgiveness? I do not believe in collective guilt, thus I cannot offer collective innocence. The Jewish tradition emphasizes the importance of bearing witness over rendering judgment, and in my work I have always served as witness, providing as accurate a testimony as memory allows.

The task of survivors, then, is to bear witness, and not to set people apart, but to bring them closer together. We can help them eliminate hate rather than deepen it, reduce violence rather than increase its pace. While I cannot free myself from nightmares filled with fear and trembling, I feel no hate. Reject hate, I plead. Hate and memory are incompatible, for hate distorts memory. Memory does not erect walls; it demolishes them. For example, several months ago some of my colleagues on the Holocaust Commission and I had an idea to establish a group of American and German scholars to study ways to teach the Holocaust. Had such a group existed before Ronald Reagan's 1985 visit to Bitburg, that scandal might have been avoided. When we met, it was already too late.

The meetings—held in New York and Berlin—were honest and

painful. In Berlin, we visited the Wannsee Palace, the place where, on January 20, 1942, Germany's highest officials, representing all the ministries, gathered and adopted the Final Solution. I felt like questioning the walls, the trees, the clouds—for living people somehow kept on avoiding the subject. What have we learned in that place? That objects and stones are qualified for immortality, whereas human beings are not?

It seems now that because humankind is forgetting its past, it is continually subject to new upheavals. Racism, bigotry, anti-Semitism, religious conflicts, wars, more and more wars: twenty-one million men and women and children have died in 40 wars since 1945. Terrorism has become a vicious and fanatic philosophy for cold-blooded murderers to justify their insane activities. There has been no worldwide outcry against such terrors, no summit of world leaders devoted to ending violence. Thus the fight for the survival of humanity is still to be won. Apparently the witness' testimony has fallen on deaf ears, on deaf hearts. Yet for the sake of the young generation in all countries, Jews must continue to remember and to testify. It will be the next generation's choice, even within the prison walls of dictatorships, to become either a Niemoller, a Bonhoffer, or a Mengele, an Eichmann. There were some decent people even in Hitler's Germany, but these future generations will have to answer why their numbers were so few.

Will memory bequeath reconciliation? An old Jewish story: Once upon a time a Just man decided to come to the most sinful of cities, Sodom, hoping to save its inhabitants from destruction. He was young, energetic, imaginative. Day after day, he would go from street to street, from marketplace to marketplace, carrying posters, urging people not to yield to hypocrisy and cruelty, not to betray one another, not to steal from one another. In the beginning, passers-by stopped and listened to him: after all, a Just man preaching in Sodom was an entertaining sight. Eventually they stopped listening. Still, he continued shouting. One day, a child stopped him in the street, and asked him: "Poor teacher, why do you yell so loudly? Don't you see it is hopeless?" "Yes, I do," answered the Just man to the child." In the beginning I was convinced that if I shout loud enough, I will manage to change them. Now I know I will never succeed in doing that. If I go on shouting and protesting and warning, it is because I do not want them to change me."

Maybe this is why we are so obstinate in trying to bear witness. We do not want "the others" to change us.

331

CONTRIBUTORS

LUDWIG ALTMAN, organist and choral director of Congregation Emanu-El from 1937 to 1987 and throughout the tenure of Rabbi Joseph Asher, was born in Breslau in 1910 and served as organist at the Neue Synagoge in Berlin from 1933 to 1936. Throughout his career as both organist and composer his recitals and compositions received world-wide acclaim.

ZIVA AMISHAI-MAISELS, Professor of Art History at the Hebrew University in Jerusalem, is the author of *Jakob Steinhardt: Etchings and Lithographs* and *Gauguin's Religious Themes* as well as many articles on Israeli and European Jewish artists.

JOSEPH ASHER was born in Heilbronn in 1921, raised in Wiesbaden, and received his rabbinical education at Etz Hayyim Yeshiva and Jews' College in London and at Hebrew Union College in Cincinnati. Before coming to Congregation Emanu-El, San Francisco in 1968, he served congregations in Melbourne, Australia; Olean, New York; Sarasota, Florida; Tuscaloosa, Alabama; and Greensboro, North Carolina.

RAPHAEL ASHER, a graduate of Hebrew Union College, Cincinnati, is rabbi of Congregation B'nai Tivah in Walnut Creek, California.

DAVID DALIN, Associate Professor of Jewish History at the University of Hartford, is the editor of *From Marxism to Judaism: The Collected Essays of Will Herberg* and the author of many articles. David is the son of Rabbi William Dalin of San Francisco who officiated in 1946 at the rededication of Rabbi Ansbacher's synagogue in Wiesbaden, initiating a long and close friendship between the Dalins and the Ashers.

DAVID ELLENSON is Professor of Jewish Religious Thought at Hebrew Union College in Los Angeles and Director of its School of Judaic Studies. His most recent works include *Tradition in Transition: Orthodoxy, Halakhah and the Boundaries of Modern Jewish Identity* and *Continuity and Innovation: Rabbi Esriel Hildesheimer and the Creation of a Modern Jewish Orthodoxy.*

IMMANUEL JAKOBOVITS, Chief Rabbi of the British Commonwealth, is the author of *Jewish Medical Ethics* and *Jewish Law Faces Modern Problems* as well as numerous articles on historical, political, and halakhic themes.

BARRY M. KATZ, Senior Lecturer in the Program in Values, Technology, Science and

Society at Stanford University, has written extensively on German culture and the O.S.S., and his books include *Foreign Intelligence: Research and Analysis in the Office of Strategic Services, 1942-1945* and *Technology and Culture: A Historical Romance.*

ROBERT KIRSCHNER, Rabbi of Congregation Emanu-El in San Francisco and Joseph Asher's associate from 1981 to 1985, received his doctorate in Near Eastern Studies from the University of California at Berkeley and is the author of *Rabbinic Responsa of the Holocaust Era.*

SIMCHA KLING, the late Rabbi Emeritus of Congregation Adath Jeshurun, Louisville, Kentucky, served concurrently for ten years with Joseph Asher at the Conservative and Reform congregations respectively in Greensboro, North Carolina, where they studied Torah together and became life-long friends. His books include *The People and Its Land, Embracing Judaism,* and biographies of numerous early Zionist leaders.

TRUDE MAURER, Assistant Professor of History at the University of Göttingen, received her doctorate at Tübingen and has visited Israel and the Soviet Union on research grants. She is the author of *Ostjuden in Deutschland* and numerous essays on German-Jewish and East European history.

PAUL MENDES-FLOHR is a member of the Department of Religious Thought at the Hebrew University of Jerusalem. His works include *A Land of Two Peoples: Martin Buber on Jews and Arabs* and *Contemporary Jewish Religious Thought,* edited with Arthur A. Cohen. He is the co-editor of *Jewish Thought: An International Journal of History and Philosophy.*

PETER VON DER OSTEN-SACKEN, Professor of Theology at the *Kirchliche Hochschule* and the Director of the *Institut für Kirche und Judentum* in Berlin, has been instrumental in bringing Jewish Studies professors and rabbis, including Joseph Asher, to the German campus. In addition to numerous articles on Jewish subjects, he is the author of *Christian-Jewish Dialogue* and the co-author of *Rabbi Akiva.*

JAKOB J. PETUCHOWSKI, the Sol and Arlene Bronstein Professor of Judaeo-Christian Studies and Research Professor of Jewish Theology and Liturgy at the Hebrew Union College – Jewish Institute of Religion in Cincinnati, is the author of many works including *Heirs of the Pharisees, Understanding Jewish Prayer,* and *Prayerbook Reform in Europe.*

WINSTON PICKETT, U.S. Bureau Chief for the *Jerusalem Report* in New York, studied in Göttingen, 1976-1977, on a research grant and received his doctorate from Hebrew Union College, Cincinnati.

W. GUNTHER PLAUT, Rabbi and Senior Scholar at Holy Blossom Temple in Toronto, is the author of *The Torah: A Modern Commentary, The Rise and Growth of Reform Judaism,* and *The Magen David – How It Became the Jewish Symbol.* Born in Muenster, Germany in 1912, he received his Doctor of Law degree in Berlin in 1934 and was ordained at Hebrew Union College, Cincinnati in 1939. He is a past president of the Central Conference of American Rabbis.

KARL RICHTER, Rabbi Emeritus of Sinai Temple, Michigan City, Indiana, now residing in Sarasota, Florida, was born in Stuttgart in 1910 and was ordained by the Jewish Theological Seminary of Breslau in 1935. A translator of scholarly texts for the Leo Baeck Institute in New York, he is the author of numerous articles.

MOSES RISCHIN is Professor of History at San Francisco State University, Director of the Western Jewish History Center of the Judah L. Magnes Museum in Berkeley, and a past president of the Immigration History Society. His books include *The Promised City: New York's Jews 1870-1914; Like All the Nations? The Life and Legacy of Judah L. Magnes; Grandma Never Lived in America: The New Journalism of Abraham Cahan*; and *Jews of the American West*.

FRED ROSENBAUM, Director of Lehrhaus Judaica in Berkeley, San Francisco, and Stanford, is the author of *Free To Choose: The Making of a Jewish Community* and *Architects of Reform: Congregational and Community Leadership, Emanu-El of San Francisco, 1849-1980*.

HERBERT STRAUSS, founder and Coordinator of Research for the Research Foundation for Jewish Immigration, New York, 1972-present, also founded and directed the Zentrum für Antisemitismusforschung at the Technical University in Berlin, 1982-1990. Born in Würzburg in 1918, he received his doctorate in 1946 at the University of Bern and was Professor of History at The City College, New York, from 1948 to 1982. He has published widely on Modern and German-Jewish history, migration history, and anti-Semitism, and is co-editor of the *International Biographical Dictionary of Central European Emigrés*.

GERHARD WEINBERG is the William Rand Kenan Jr. Professor of History at the University of North Carolina, Chapel Hill. His books include *World in the Balance: Behind the Scenes of World War II* and *The Foreign Policy of Hitler's Germany: Diplomatic Revolution in Europe, 1933-1936*.

WERNER WEINBERG is Professor Emeritus of Hebrew Language and Literature, Hebrew Union College, Cincinnati. Born in Rheda, Westphalia in 1915, he returned to Germany in 1965 on a grant to research vestigial Judeo-German for his book *Die Reste des Jüdisch-Deutschen*. He is currently working on a critical edition of Moses Mendelssohn's complete writings.

MICHAEL WEINRICH is Professor of Systematic Theology at the Universität Gesamthochschule in Paderborn, Germany. He has written extensively on German-Jewish and Christian theology in the twentieth century including *Grenzgänger: Martin Buber's Anstösse zum Weitergehen*.

ELIE WIESEL, Andrew W. Mellon Professor in the Humanities at Boston University, first chairperson of the United States Holocaust Commission, and Nobel Laureate for Peace, is the foremost literary witness to the Holocaust.

INDEX

Abrahams, Israel: editor of *Jewish Quarterly Review*, 99-102, 111-13; Jewish liturgy and, 110; responses to Christian scholars, 105-09

Academy for the Science of Judaism. *See* Graduate School for the Science of Judaism

Adass Yisroel (relig. assoc.), 57, 89, 161-62

Adenauer, Konrad, 310, 313, 314

Adler, Cyrus, 111-12

Adler, H. G., 66-67

Adler, Hugo, 281

Adler, Jankel, 265-66, 268; *illus.* 267

Adler, Samuel, 281

Adorno, Theodor, 320

Agnon, S. Y., 196

Agriculture, settlements in Palestine, 194, 197-200

Agudat Yisrael, 80, 165

Aktion, Die (period.), 262

Albers, Anni, 266, 268

Altman, Ludwig, 276-83; *illus.* 276

Altman, Richard, 278

Altmann, Alexander, 55, 77, 93, 208

American Economic Association, 298

American Hebrew Congregation, Union of, 215

American Historical Association, 298

Amidah (prayer), 91, 110-11, 171-72, 173, 181

Anderson, Eugene N., 298-99

Anglo-Jewish Exhibition (London, 1887), 100, 104

Anglo-Jewish scholarship, 8, 101-05. See also *Jewish Quarterly Review*

Annenberg Research Institute, 99. *See also* Dropsie College for Hebrew and Cognate Learning

Ansbacher, Jonah, 43, 45; *illus.* 24; Buchenwald experiences, 35-36, 40; ethical sense, 32, 34-35; patriotism of, 27, 37-38; religious standards,

26-30, 36, 42, 44, 48

Ansbacher, Joseph. *See* Asher, Joseph

Ansbacher, Rosa·Menke, 28, 29-30, 32, 35, 36, 37; *illus.* 38

Ansbacher, Solomon, 26, 27, 29

Ansbacher, Sulamith, 28, 33, 37

Anti-Semitism: Berlin, 57-59, 87, 145, 283; Christian scholarship and, 57-59, 105-09; East European Jewry in Germany and, 139-43, 146-47, 150, 153; Fassbinder play and, 318-19, 324; German-Jewish artists and, 249-50, 257, 260, 261, 263-65, 266-71; German-Jewish response to, 25, 206, 226, 250; in GFR, 317-21, 322; Jewish-Gentile League against, 142; Judeo-German and, 25, 128, 137; nineteenth-century Germany, 57-59, 69 *n.*36, 249; post-Nazi, 317-18; postwar German curriculum and, 19, 20, 330-31; after reunification, 310, 318-19, 322-23, 331; Science of Judaism and, 90, 93; Scottish Allied Forces and, 36, 40; settlements in Palestine and, 199; in Weimar Germany and, 53, 139-40, 142-51, 249-50; in Wiesbaden, 14-15, 16, 32, 35. *See also* Holocaust

Anti-Zionism, 43, 92, 93, 319

Arab-Israeli Six-Day War, German reaction to, 315

Arab-Jewish relations, 241, 315

Ardon, Mordechai (Max Bronstein), 268

Arlozorov, Chaim, 201

Artists, German-Jewish, 249-71; appeal for Christians, 256; anti-Semitism, reactions to, 249-50, 257, 260, 261, 263-65, 266-71; *Bauhaus* style, 266, 268; Biblical themes, 251-52, 257, 259-61, 262-65; Biedermeier school, 252, 256; conversions to Christianity, 250-52;

Berlin-Zehlendorf, desecration of Jewish gravestones, 318
Berliner Stadtmission (Urban Mission in Berlin), 57-58
Berlinski, Hermann, 281
Beth ha-Midrash (Vienna), 102-03
Beth Hakerem (teacher's college, Jerusalem), 90
Bezalel Museum, 271
Bezalel School of Art (Jerusalem), 260, 268
Bialik, Chaim Nachman, 256
Bible, 22, 136, 229, 251; German-Jewish artists and, 251-52, 257, 259-61, 262-65; Jewish scholarship and, 55, 81, 101-102; translation by Buber and Rosenzweig, 229, 309. *See also* Torah
Biedermeier school of art, 252, 256
Bismarck, Otto von, 288, 289
Bitburg cemetery, controversy over President Reagan's visit, 6, 310-11, 316-19, 321, 324, 330
Bloch, Ernest, 279
Bloch, Jochanan, 228
Blood libel, 20, 60
Blumenfeld, Kurt, 191-92, 201
Bodenheimer, Max, 189-92, 193
Bodleian Library, Oxford University (Eng.), 102, 109, 111
Bolshevism, 142; in German revisionist history, 311-12
Bonhoeffer, Dietrich, 71-72*n. 90*
Börne, Ludwig, 253
Bousset, Wilhelm, 106-07
Brandt, Willy, 5-6, 288, 315
Brazil, Liberal prayerbook in, 186
Breslau, Reform prayerbook, 177, 179
Breslau Jewish Theological Seminary (Ger.), 75, 178; East European students, 89-90, 206; founding, 56, 89, 206; Nazi victims, 207; positive historical emphasis, 162, 212
Breuer, Isaac, 74, 80-82, 163, 213
Breuer, Joseph, *Torah im Derekh Eretz* and, 161-63, 165
Breuer, Mordechai, 164-66
Breuer, Solomon *("Alte Rav")*, 26
British Jewry, 99-112; Anglo-Jewish scholarship, 101-05; German

refugees and, 33, 36, 208, 266, 268
British Mandate, 206, 208
British Museum, 109
Broder, Henryk, 320-21, 323
Bronstein, Max (Mordechai Ardon), 268
Buber, Martin, 221-30, 233-34; Gandhi letter, 235-36, 240-41; non-Jews and, 223, 225-30; prophetic tradition and, 221, 222, 225, 227-29; religious observance, 94, 221-25, 227; as teacher in Germany, 31, 67, 89; theology of, 221-25, 227; Zionist activities of, 200-01, 227-28, 236
Buchenwald concentration camp, 35-36, 40, 207, 329
Budapest, *Landesrabbinerschule*, 206
Buechler, Adolph, 110, 111

Cairo Genizah, 105, 109-12
California, Jewish pioneers, 47, 49
Callenberg, Johann Heinrich, 59, 117-18
Cambridge, Eng., 92
Cambridge University (Eng.), 104, 108
Cantors: Cantor Goldberg, 280; in pre-World War II Germany, 28, 34, 120, 185, 209, 277-83, 322
Carlebach, Joseph, 31-32
Carlebach, Shlomo, 42
Carter, Jimmy, 328
Cassel, David, 56
Catholic Church, 95, 239; conversion to, 250-51; deportation of Italian Jews and, 314; in Judeo-German, 133, 137
Cemeteries: Bitburg, 6, 310-11, 316-19, 321, 324, 330; desecration in German-Jewish, 318; restoration projects in German-Jewish, 316
Central Conference of American Rabbis, 174, 210, 215, 216
Central Council of Jews in Germany, 320
Central Union of German Citizens of the Jewish Faith, 178
Central Verein Zeitung (period.), 281
Centralverein deutscher Staatsbürger jüdischen Glaubens, 147-48, 149; definition of *Judentum*, 151

Chabad Lubavitch, in postwar Germany, 319
Chicago, 281; refugee rabbis' congregations in, 213
Chmelniecki pogroms, 129
Choirs, in German synagogues, 34, 175, 185, 209, 277, 278-81, 283
Christ. *See* Jesus
Christian Democratic Union (Ger.), 315, 316-17
Christian-Jewish relations: in Berlin, 7, 53-68; Buber and, 223, 226-27, 228-30; in Catholic South Germany, 95; depicted in Oppenheim's paintings, 253-55; *illus.* 254; dialogue concerning the Gospels, 7, 60-66, 108-09; dialogue, post-Holocaust, 229-30, 313; eighteenth century, 117-20, 121, 122, 123; historical scholarship and, 62-67, 105-09; housing and, 121-23; Jewish music and, 281, 282, 283; Judeo-German and, 129-30; missionary movement, 58-65, 69n.36, 117-20, 122, 123; preachers and rabbis, 55; refugee rabbis in America, 213. *See also* Conversion; German-Jewish relations; Missionary movement
Christian-Social Worker's Party (Ger.), 57
Christianity, 96; blood libel, 20, 60; Buber and, 226-27; Catholic Church, 95, 133, 137, 239, 250-51, 314; Christian scholarship, 105-09; Church tax, 209-10; German missionaries, 58-65, 69n.36,117-20, 122, 123; German Protestant Church, 288; Lutheran Church and Jewish question, 314-15; preachers and German Jewish sermons, 55; relation to Judaism, 20, 22, 60-62, 65, 67-68, 105-09
Cincinnati, refugee rabbis' congregations in, 213. *See also* Hebrew Union College
Citizenship: British, for refugee Jews, 37-38; German, for East European Jews, 144-45, 153
Civil rights movement, 4, 33, 40, 42
Cohen, Hermann, 73, 77, 75, 78, 79, 82, 83, 212

Cohn, Bernard, 214
Cohn, Elkan, 47
Cohn, Emil Bernhard, 214
Cologne, Ger., 3, 190, 265; Jewish Literary Society, 193; Jewish rights in Roman times, 92; Zionism in, 192, 193
Commission on Interfaith Activities of Reform Judaism, 6
Communism: German revisionist history and, 311-12, 324; the Grundigs and, 268-71
Concentration camps: depicted in Grundig's paintings, 270-71; *Mein Kampf* and, 329; network of, in Germany, 302. *See also* under specific names
Conservative Judaism, 5, 181, 281; *kashrut* and, 30; in nineteenth-century Berlin, 56-57; refugee German rabbis and, 211-12, 213-14; use of choirs, 277, 279
Conversion: of German Jews to Christianity, 189, 250-51, 253, 255; of German-Jewish artists to Christianity, 250-52; to Judaism, of Soviet emigrés to GFR, 322. *See also* Christian-Jewish relations; Missionary movement
Cox, Harvey, on German-Jewish relationship, 2
Critique of Judgment, The (Kant), 79
"Critique of Pure Reason" (Kant), 80
Culture and Science of the Jews, Association for, 54, 55, 88
Curriculum: on Holocaust, in Germany, 4-6, 18-23, 38-39, 314-16, 330-31; Jewish, in prewar Germany, 31-33

Dachau concentration camp, 207
Dada movement, 266
Dahrendorf, Ralf, on the German personality, 313
Daniel, Gerard, 215
Darkhe HaMishnah (Frankel), 75
Davidsohn, Magnus, 278
Dawidowicz, Lucy S., 305-06
De Sola Pool Sephardic synagogue (New York), 279
de le Roi, J. F., 59-70

Dead Sea Scrolls, 109
Degania (agrarian settlement, Pal.), 200
Deism, Science of Judaism and, 88
Democracy, 43; in GFR, 9, 312-13, 323
Deputy, The (Hochhuth), 314-15
Dessau, Ger., Jewish poorhouse in, 121
Deutsch Kreuz, 26
Deutsche Demokratische Partei (German Democratic Party), 142, 146-47
Deutschnationale Volkspartei, anti-Semitism of, 143
Diaspora, 97, 190, 240
Diels, Hermann, 94
Dietary laws, 27, 29-30, 36
Dietz, Judith, 5
Dilthey, Wilhelm, 94
"Doctrines of Judaism, The" (Elbogen), 93
Domin, Hilde, 72 *n.* 92
Donovan, William J., 298, 301
Dorn, Walter, 298-99
Dresden, Ger., 99, 250, 251, 271
Dropsie College for Hebrew and Cognate Learning (Philadelphia), 99, 100, 111, 179
Duisburg, University of (Ger.), 316
Dulles, Allen, 299
Dunera (ship), 36, 40
Düsseldorf Academy (Ger.), 251, 265

East European Jewry, 27, 89, 92, 121, 129, 139-53: attitude toward Hirsch, 160; in Conservative congregations, 211-12; German anti-Semitism and, 27, 139-43, 145, 146-47, 150, 153; German-Jewish response to immigration, 28-29, 89, 147-51, 206; Hebrew culture and, 189, 206; models for German-Jewish painters, 257, 261, 262-63, 265; organizations in Weimar Germany, 151-53; Orthodox movements and, 157, 164; population in Germany, 140-41, 195, 310; women's status, 120-21; Zionism and, 139, 149-50, 151-53, 189, 195-96, 206
Eastern Jews, League of, 151-53
Eckman, Julius, 47
Education: classical, 30, 44; expulsion

of Jewish students, 13, 18, 30-31; graduate institutions for Jewish studies in Germany, 55-57, 89-90; Holocaust curriculum in Germany, 4-6, 18-23, 38-39, 314-16, 330-31; humanistic *Gymnasia* in Europe, 212; Jewish, in Germany, 30-33, 44, 54-56, 120, 152, 172, 206-07, 210; Jewish, in England, 26, 33, 104, 208, 322; Lehrhaus concept, 212, 309; program for interfaith couples, 48; rabbinical, 26, 49, 55, 212-13; teachers' seminaries, 90, 210; *Torah im Derekh Eretz* and, 162, 164, 166, 169. *See also* Institutum Judaicum; Seminaries; *Wissenschaft des Judentums*
Eger, Akiba, 93
Ehrenreich, Eliezer, 277, 283
Eichel, Hans, 313
Eichmann, Adolf, 4, 314, 331
Eighteen Benedictions (*amidah*), 91, 111; changes in prayerbooks, 171-72, 173, 181
Einheitsgebetbuch (Union Prayer Book, Ger.), 177-78, 180-86
Einheitsgemeinde, 209, 217 *n.* 9. See also *Gemeinde*
Einhorn, David, 174, 178
Einstein, Albert, 288
Elbogen, Ismar, 56; Liberal prayerbook and, 178, 179, 181, 185; religiosity of, 91-93; scholarship of, 56, 90-110
Eliav, Mordecai, 194
Elizabeth II (q. Eng.), 37
Emancipation, 97, 117; German Jewry and, 1, 54, 74, 87, 249-50; revival of Judaism and, 224, 227; Science of Judaism and, 87, 88. *See also* Haskalah
Emanu-El Congregation (Greensboro, N.C.), 4
Emanu-El Congregation (New York), 281
Emanu-El Congregation (San Francisco), 7, 40, 42, 280, 283; German *Minhag*, 47-48; rabbis, 47
Emden, Jacob, 117
Enabling Act (Ger.,1933), 287-88
England: comparison between English

Germany—German Federal Republic

German Jewry: archives for, 94, 96; awareness, pre-World War II, 25-35; Baeck and, 178-79; characteristics of, 39, 43, 101, 175-76; dual loyalty of, 253, 255-56, 258; East European Jew, attitudes toward, 89, 140, 147-51, 196; education and, 30-33, 44, 54-57, 89-90, 120, 172, 206-07, 210, 212, 309; emancipation and, 1, 54, 74, 87, 249-50; *Gemeinde* structure, 28, 149-50, 152, 209, 217*n.9*, 277, 283, 319-20; German culture, attitude toward, 1, 26-27, 30, 38, 44, 74, 75, 101, 225-27; humor of, 44-45; identity issues, 149, 249-71; liturgical conservatism, 176-77, 180, 184-85; liturgical music, 277-83; living conditions, eighteenth century, 117-23, post-World War II, 8, 40, 66-67, 309-10, 319-24; *minhagim,* 44, 47, 176-77, 209; OSS monitoring of, 300-03; patriotism of, 26-27, 29, 34, 40, 253, 255-56, 258, 265, 266; philanthropy, 148-49, 152; refugee rabbis in America, 47-48, 205-16; revival after World War I, 212. *See also* Artists, German-Jewish; Judeo-German

German Military Government over Europe, 1939-1943 (OSS), 301

German National People's Party, 139

German Nationalist Jews, Union of (*Verband nationaldeutscher Juden*), 147

German Protestant Church, Nazi regime and, 288

German Rabbis, Federation of, 201

German Students, Association of, 58

German Zionist Organization, 191, 192

German-Jewish relations, 2-8, 30, 34, 96; Asher and, 3, 5, 13-23, 39-40; meetings of American and German scholars, 330-31; in post-Holocaust Germany, 313; reconciliation, 2, 6-7, 23, 315-16, 327-31; as symbiosis, 1, 26-27, 35, 54, 67, 226-27, 228-29; Taeubler on, 96;

Germania Judaica (Elbogen), 92

Germany, 87, 94, 287-90, 322

—German Empire (to 1918), 14, 27, 91, 103, 146; East European Jewish population, 140; East German Jewish population, 142-43; eighteenth-century Jewish life in, 117-23; factions within Zionism, 191-92, 193-94, 200-02; Jewish citizenship and, 26-27

—Weimar Republic (1918-1933), 27, 53, 91; East European Jews and, 139-53; *Gemeinde* structure, 28, 149-50, 152, 209, 217*n.9*, 277, 283; human rights, 140, 288-89, 290, 295

—Third Reich (1933-1945): army caricatured in "Hogan's Heroes," 44; censorship under, 293-94; construction projects, 292-93, 295-96; discussion of, in contemporary Germany, 323-24; explanations of, 302-03, 329-30; GDR propaganda and, 314; human rights, 287-96; Jewish community in, 13, 14-15, 25, 28, 30-35, 56, 94, 206-07, 278, 282; Jewish musicians, 278-83; OSS monitoring, 300-03; racism, 190-91, 195. *See also* Final Solution; Holocaust; National Socialism

—German Federal Republic (1945-1989), 2, 5; attitude toward Nazi annihilation of Jews, 22-23, 39, 309, 310-12, 313-21, 323-24; demoncracy and, 9, 312-13, 323; Jewish life in, 19, 20, 89, 309-10, 319-24; Holocaust curriculum, 4-6, 18-23, 38-39, 314-16, 330-31; political and economic situation of, 312-13, 325

—German Democratic Republic (1945-1989), 314, 324

—Reunified Germany (1989-), 312; Jews and, 310, 311, 322-24

Gesetz (faithfulness to the Law), 73, 76, 77-78

Gestapo, 6, 35, 263, 292, 300

Ghettos, 149; Jewish painters' depictions of, 256, 271; Roman, 252, 255; Warsaw, 300, 304, 315

Giessen, University of (Ger.), 120

Gilbert, Felix, 299, 300

Ginzberg, Louis, 105, 110

Ha'ol members, use of, 233; hymns, 34, 75; revival, pre-World War I, 189, 196, 201; scholarship in, at German seminaries, 212-13; use in postwar Germany, 313; use in synagogue service, 171-74, 209

Hegel, Georg Wilhelm Friedrich, 74, 82, 174

Heidelberg, Ger., 94, 123; *Jüdische Hochschule*, 316, 322; University of, 190, 234

Heidenheim, Wolf, 180-81

Heilbronn-am-Neckar, 28

Heine, Heinrich, 19, 54, 103, 253

Hempel, Johannes, 66

Hensel-Mendelssohn, Fanny, 253, 272n.12

Herford, H. Travers, 109

Herz, John, 299

Herzl, Theodor, 197, 199, 200, 260; Bodenheimer and, 189-90; Warburg and, 194; Wolffsohn and, 192, 193; Zionist Congress (1897), call for, 190, 191, 195, 201-02

Herzl forest (Pal.), 198

Heschel, Abraham Yehoshua, 56

Hess, Moses, 190

Hesse, state, Ger., 4, 19

Hibbat Zion, 190-91

High German, 119, 127

High Holydays, 4, 122, 134, 182; in early California, 47; German-Jewish organists and, 279; Liberal prayer-books and, 173, 180-81, 182-83; liturgy, 49-50, 176, 181, 283; silk hats for, 209, 217n.10

Hildebrand, Klaus, 311-12

Hildesheimer, Esriel, 57, 74-75, 89, 160-61, 206

Hildesheimer Seminary (Berlin), 26, 57, 89, 94, 160, 206, 207

Hillel, Elbogen and, 91

Hiller, Ferdinand, 254, 272n.12

Hiller, Kurt, 262

Hillgruber, Andreas, 311-12

Hinkel, Hans, 282

Hintze, Otto, 95

Hirsch, Samson Raphael, 47, 80, 81, 157-69; Asher and, 38, 49; debate over his teachings, 159-66; exponents

of his teachings, 163-66, 213; founder of Neo-Orthodoxy, 26, 28, 74-75, 157, 169; Maimonides and, 167; Munk's critique of, 168-69; Positive-Historical Judaism, response to, 74-76, 162; Torah, attitude toward, 49, 75-76, 160-61, 163-64, 165, 169

Hirschfeld, Otto, 94

Historians, 62-67, 93-98, 103, 105-09; German revisionism, 2, 311-12, 314, 323; historical scholarship of Judaism, 62-67, 97-98, 99-112, 160, 212-13; historicism, 74-76, 82-83, 87-88; organizations of, 101, 104, 298; in OSS, 298-99. *See also* Positive-Historical Judaism

"Historic Parallels in Jewish History" (Graetz), 100

Historikerstreit (Habermas), 312

Hitler, Adolf: annexation of Austria, 33; construction projects of, 292-93, 295-96; Hoepner and, 294-95; *kashrut* standards and rise of, 29-30; mass extermination and, 1, 87, 301, 309; *Mein Kampf*, 329; modern German youth and, 14-23; refugee rabbis and, 13, 210; suicide, 302; youth movement, 4, 15, 17, 18, 32. *See also,* Final Solution; Holocaust; National Socialism

Hochhuth, Rolf, 314-15

Hochschule fur jüdische Studien (Heidelberg), 316, 322

Hochschule für die Wissenschaft des Judentums (Berlin). *See* Graduate School for the Science of Judaism (Berlin)

Hoepner, Erich, 284, 294-95

Hoffmann, David, 160-61

"Hogan's Heroes," 44

Holborn, Hajo, 299

Holland, 47, 121; Amsterdam Jewish quarter, 257; Jewish National Fund in, 192; Liberal prayerbook, 186

Holocaust, 1, 2, 32, 249-50: destruction of German-Jewish roots and, 97; confrontation of, by Germans, 2, 22-23, 309-21, 324, 330-31; curriculum in Germany, 4, 6, 18-23, 38-39, 314-16, 330-31; effect on Orthodox movements, 158; Elbogen's works and, 92; German rabbis and, 35, 206-07, 216; German-Jewish artists and, 263-65, 266-69, 270-71; German-Jewish liturgists and, 278, 279, 280, 283; as historical paradox, 53-68; Marxist analysis of, 302-03; message of survivors, 327-31; OSS monitoring of, 297-06; reparations to victims, 313-14, 321, 324, 330; *unetaneh tokef* and, 50. *See also* Final Solution; Genocide; National Socialism

Holocaust (docudrama), 315-16

Holocaust Commission, 330

Holocaust Memorial Museum (Washington, D.C.), 6

Hora'at Sha'ah (emergency measure), 159, 161-63, 164, 166

Horeb (Hirsch), 164, 165

Hotel Kron-prinz (Wiesbaden), 29

House of Love and Prayer (San Francisco), 42

Human rights: in Germany, 288-89; history of, 142, 287-96

Humanism, 80-81, 88, 93-95, 195, 212, 228; classic German humanists, 168; Hirsch and, 158, 163-64, 167-68; religious humanists, 8, 233-41, 245*n.42*

Humboldt University (Berlin), 60

Hungary, 26, 102, 310

Huyton internment camp (Eng.), 36

Idelsohn, Abraham Z., 186

Identity, Jewish. *See* Jewish identity

"Image of Judaism in Kant, The" (Rotenstreich), 73

"*Imitatio Dei*" (Imitation of God), Rabbinic theology and, 105-06

Immigration: East European Jews to Germany,139-53; German Jews to America, 47, 205-16, 305; Yemenite Jews to Palestine, 199

Impressionism, German, 256, 259, 260, 262

Institut für die Geschichte der deutschen Juden (Hamburg), 316

Institutum Judaicum, 59-60, 64-66; missionaries' observations of Jewish life, 117-32

Intelligence services, U.S. *See* Office of Strategic Services

Intermarriage, 20, 48, 265-66, 268-71, 322

Isaiah Congregation (Boston), 281

Isaiah, 101, 184

Islam, 20, 96, 139

Isle of Man, internment camp, 36, 37

Israel, 6, 43, 129, 164, 165, 209, 309, 321; diplomatic ties with GDR, 324; efforts to establish state, 191, 195, 202; German television programming on, 316; GFR's reparations to, 313-14, 330; Israeli art, 263-65, 268; Israelis, in Germany, 309, 310, 313, 319, 322; Neo-Orthodoxy and statehood, 158-59; Six-Day War, 315; *Torah im Derekh Eretz* in, 169. See also *Eretz Yisrael;* Palestine; Zionism

Israelite Synagogue Community Adass Yisroel of Berlin, 55, 57

Israelitisches Gebetbuch (Seligmann), 175, 181, 186

Italy, 295, 314

Jacobs, Joseph, 104

Janowski, Max, 281

Jellinek, Adolph, 102

Jeremiah, 251, 259-60; *illus.* 264

Jerusalem, 90, 166, 192, 195, 197, 314; Central European Jewish immigrants in, 233-34; German-Jewish artists and, 259, 260, 268, 270; *Ha'ol* (the Yoke), 233-41; Temple references in prayerbook, 171, 172

Jeschurun (period.), 75, 161

Jesus, 120, 261; Baeck on, 62-64; Harnack's portrayal of, 61-64; Liebermann's painting of, 257; *illus.* 258; Rabbinic Judaism and, 106-08

Jewish Historical Society of England, 101, 104

Jewish Humanist Society, 195

Jewish identity, 20, 38, 95, 149, 152; as ethnic community compared to religious community, 149-53; national identification, 20; problems of, for German Jewish artists, 249-71; Science of Judaism and, 152

Nadel, Arno, 279
Napoleon, 87, 249, 251, 253, 255, 289-90; *illus.* 255
Narkiss, Mordechai, 271
Nathan der Weise (*Nathan the Wise*) (Lessing), 53,139
Nathanael (period.), 60
Nathanson, Joseph Saul, 102
National Socialism, 143, 291-92; American intelligence and, 297-06; blood libel and, 20; Buber's estimate of, 226, 228-29; Enabling Act (1933), 287-88, 290; modern Germany and, 319, 323; neo-Nazis in GFR, 317-18, 323; Nolte's defense of, 311-12; Old Testament scholarship, 65; policy to exterminate Jews, 302-03, 305-06; in postwar Germany, 6; theoretical analysis of leadership, 302-03; war against human rights, 287-96; war criminals, 300, 302, 310; youth movement, 4, 15, 17, 18, 32. *See also* Germany—Third Reich; Hitler, Adolf; Holocaust; *Kristallnacht*
Nationalism, Jewish: dual loyalty issue and, 201-02; spiritual dimension of, 201; support within Germany, 190, 191, 193, 195, 196, 202
Nationaljüdische Vereinigung, Die (Zionist society), 190
Naturalization, 144-45, 153
Nazarene school of art, 250, 251, 252
Nazism. *See* National Socialism
Neo-Classicism, in German art, 250
Neo-Orthodoxy, 8, 26, 27-28, 48. *See also* Hirsch, Samson Raphael
Netherlands. *See* Holland
Neubauer, Adolph, 102, 111
Neue Kusari: Ein Weg zum Judentum, Der (Breuer), 81
Neue Sachlichkeit school of art, 263, 265, 268
Neue Synagoge (Berlin). *See* Oranienburger Strasse Synagogue
Neue Zeit (period.), 142
Neumann, Franz, 299, 300, 302-03
New Israelite Synagogue (Berlin), 55
New Liberal Jewish Congregation (London), 208

New Testament, 60, 63-65, 67, 105, 108, 251, 257, 260-61, 262. *See also* Gospel(s)
New York City: Holocaust curriculum meetings, 331; refugee rabbis' congregations in, 213-14; Sephardic synagogue, 279
Newman, Louis, 47
Nineteen Letters on Judaism (Hirsch), 74, 157, 163, 165
Nobel, Nehemia Anton, 74, 76-79, 82
Nolte, Ernst, 311-12
Norden, Eduard, 94
North Africa, Jewish learning in, 109, 110, 112
Nuremberg, Ger., 26, 293
Nuremberg Trials, 302, 310
Nussbaum, Felix, 266-68; *illus.* 269
Nussbaum, Max, 278

Office of Strategic Services (OSS), Research and Analysis branch, 297-306; American policy and, 303-06; formation of, 297-300; monitoring of Holocaust, 300-04
'Olath Tamid prayerbook (Einhorn), 174, 178
Oldenburg, Ger., Hirsch in, 165, 166
Oppenheim, Moritz, 250, 252-56, 261, 265; *illus.* 254, 256
Oppenheimer, Franz, 199-200
Oppenheimer, Joseph Suess, 122
Oral tradition, 87, 162, 163, 165, 224, 237-38; Oral Law compared to Written Law, 74-76, 80-81, 237-40
Oranienburg-Sachsenhausen concentration camp, 207
Oranienburger Strasse Synagogue (Berlin), 186, 278, 279, 281, 283; *illus.* 276
Organists: Gentile, in German synagogue services, 278; German synagogue services and, 172, 277-83; training in Germany, 279-81, 283
Orthodox Judaism, 5, 13, 28, 34, 35, 40, 45, 48, 73-83, 322; Beth Din (Rabbinical court), 26, 31; Buber and, 223-24; concept of Torah, 237, 238; customs in religious services, 149, 150, 172, 176-77; doctrinal

rights and, 288, 289, 295; missionary work in, 58; relationship between Germans and Jews in, 54, 96; Yiddish in, 129

Prussian State and the Jews, The (Stern), 54, 96-97

Prussian Union of Jewish Communities, 177-78,180

Psalms, 44, 56, 233, 234

Pseudepigrapha, 108

Publications of the Institutum Judaicum in Berlin, 59, 60

Purim, 136

Quick (period.), 317

Rabbinate: Ansbacher-Asher tradition of, 13, 26, 33, 39, 40; conferences of German-born rabbis, 43; education in Germany, 212-13; English, and the Science of Judaism, 101; German refugees, 47-48, 205-16; German-Jewish, and organists, 277-78; in Hamburg, 31-32; ordination, 26, 102-03; organizations in America, 210, 214; refugee rabbis' impact 205-09; roles in Germany and America, 209-14; training in England, 104; victims of Holocaust, 207. *See also* Seminaries

Rabbinic court (Beth Din): Frankfurt, 31; London, 26

Rabbinic Judaism: Christian scholarship and, 105-09; Gospels and, 64, 103, 108-09; literature of, 64, 108-09; modern scholarship and, 105-10

Rabbinical Assembly (America), 210

Rabbinical Seminary for Orthodox Jews in Berlin, 57

Racism, in Germany, 289, 290-91, 292, 293, 295, 322

Rambam. *See* Maimonides

Rapoport, Solomon Judah, 102

"Reading of the Law and Prophets in a Triennial Cycle" (Buechler), 111

Reagan, Ronald: visit to Bitburg cemetery, 6, 310-11, 316, 317-18, 319, 321, 324, 330; Wiesel and, 6, 328

Reconciliation, in German Jewish relations, 13-23, 327-31

Reconstructionist Judaism, refugee German rabbis and, 216

Reform Judaism, 5, 6, 8, 13, 28, 45, 48, 49, 56, 75; Berlin synagogues, 282; Buber and, 224; Buffalo congregation, 281; challenge to Orthodoxy, 159; clash between German Reform and classic Reform in America, 215; in Europe, 157; immigrant rabbis and, 209, 211, 215-16; Jewish national purpose, view of, 158; prayerbook, 171-75, 181; refugee German rabbis and, 209, 211, 215-16

Reform Temple (Berlin), 209

Reformation, 88

Refugees: in Australia, 44; East European, in Germany, 139-40; *Einheitsgebetbuch* and, 185-86; in England, 36-53; German-Jewish artists as, 263, 265-69; impact of refugee rabbis, 205-16; Jewish scholars employed in OSS, 297, 298-99; moral obligation to, 146; Nussbaum's paintings of, 268; in post-World War II Germany, 40; return to Germany, 209, 266, 309, 316; from Russian pogroms, 194, 257; in Weimar Germany, 152; during World War I, 141

Reich and State Citizenship Law of 1913, 144

Reichert, Irving, 47

Religion Within the Limits of Reason Alone (Kant), 73-74, 76

Renaissance, 88

Revelation, in Judaism, 75, 80-81, 165, 177, 184, 223, 225, 238, 238. *See also* Torah

Revisionism, in post-Holocaust Germany, 2, 311-12, 314, 323

Richter, Hans, 266, 268

Riesser, Gabriel, 253

Ritschl, C., 55, 58

Rituals, 20, 34. *See also* Prayerbook

Rituel des Prières Journalières (prayerbook), 174

Rockdale Avenue Temple (Cincinnati), 215

"Roman State" (Taeubler), 95

Romania, 102, 103

Romanticism, 88
Rosenbluth, Pinhas, 201
Rosenthal, Erwin, 92-93
Rosenzweig, Franz, 212; Buber and, 224; on *Gesetz*, 77-78; commemoration of, 309, 313, 316; on Torah and the Law, 224, 244*n.38*
Rosh Hashanah, 4
Rotenstreich, Nathan, 73
Rothschild Family, 252-53
Rödelheim, Ger., 50
Ruppin, Arthur, 196-99, 201
Russia (to 1917): Jewish artists, 257-58, 262-63; revolution in, 141. *See also* East European Jews; Soviet Union
Russian Jews, League of (Ger.), 151
Russisch-Jüdisch Wissenschaftlicher Verein, Der (Jewish Russian Scientific Society), 196

Sabbath. *See* Shabbat
"Sabbath" (Nobel), 78-80
Sacrifices, modified prayerbook references to, 171, 182
Salanter, R. Israel, 157, 166
Salzberger, Georg, 208
Samson Raphael Hirsch School (Frankfurt-am-Main), 31
San Francisco, Ca., 2, 42-43; Emanu-El Congregation, 40, 42, 47-48, 280, 283
Sandmel, Samuel, 6
Sanger, Hermann, 44, 278
Sarasota, Fla., 13, 40
Saxony, state, Ger., 128, 144, 150
"Sayings of the Fathers" *(Pirke Avot)*, 28, 82, 244*n.29*
Schaalman, Herman, 215
Schadow, Wilhelm, 250, 251
Schalit, Heinrich, 279
Schapira, Hermann, 190-91, 192
Schatz, Boris, 260
Schechter, Solomon: Anglo-Jewish scholarship, influence on, 100, 102-12; in Berlin, 102-03, 106; Cambridge University and, 104, 108-09; co-editor of *JQR* in America, 111-12; Jewish Theological Seminary and, 104, 112; Jews' College and, 101,

103-04; responses to Christian scholars, 105-09; on Zunz, 55-56
Scheunenviertel (Berlin), 145, 147
Schildberger, Hermann, 282-83
Schiller, Johann Christoph Friedrich von, 130
Schindler, Alexander, 215
Schleiermacher, Friedrich, 55, 74, 93, 227
Schlesinger, Arthur, Jr., 306*n.2*
Schnorrer, 121
Schochet (ritual slaughterer), 28, 30
Scholarship: Anglo-Jewish, 99-112; Christian, 106-08; historical, 62-67, 97-98, 99-112, 160, 212-13; liturgical, 111. See also *Wissenschaft des Judentums*
Scholem, Gershom, 1, 81, 229, 234; concept of Torah, 237-38, 239
Schoolbook Institute (Braunschweig), 4
Schorsch, Emil, 212
Schorsch, Ismar, 100, 212, 215
Schurer, Emil, 105-06, 107-08
Schwartz, Hermann, 278-79
Science of Judaism. See *Wissenschaft des Judentums*
Scottish Allied Forces, German Jewish refugees and, 40
Secret State Archive *(Geheimes Staatsarchiv)*, 96
Secularist Judaism, 157
Seligmann, Caesar, 175-78, 180, 181, 186, 208
Semicha (rabbinical ordination), 26, 102-03
Seminaries, 55, 56-70, 77, 87; Berlin, 56-57; Central Europe, 206; England, 101, 208; post-Holocaust, in Baden-Württemberg, 316; refugee rabbis in, 212-13; for teachers, 90, 210; Third Reich Germany, 206-07. *See also* Breslau Jewish Theological Seminary; other specific names
Semitic languages, 87
Sephardic tradition: London synagogue, 104; New York synagogue, 279
Sermons, 55, 93, 182; Ansbacher, 27, 30; Asher, 4, 43, 44, 49; Sanger, 44; Zunz, 55
Service Manual, The (Krauskopf), 174

Service Ritual, The (Krauskopf), 174

Severing, Carl, 139

Shabbat: American Friday night services, 209; in Asher's home, 44; Belzer Rebbe and, 45; German sermons, 37, 55; Liberal Judaism and, 77-78, 173; as metaphysical bridge, 78-80; observance in prewar Germany, 31-32, 34; prayerbook and, 171, 173, 180-81; silk hats for Torah reading, 34, 209, 217*n. 10*

Shabhu'oth (Shavuot), 184

Shanghai, refugee German rabbis in, 208

Sharp, Samuel, 300

Shazar, Zalman, 195

Shearith Israel Congregation (New York), 279

Shechita (ritual slaughter), 28, 30

Shoah. See Final Solution; Holocaust

Siddur. See Prayerbooks

Siddur Sephath Emeth, 181

Silbergleit, Heinrich, 141

Silesian Dictionary of Writers, 55

Simon, Ernst Akiva, 212, 225, 234, 238

Sinai, giving of Torah at, 75, 77, 238, 252. *See also* Revelation; Torah

Singer, Kurt, 281-82

Six-Day War, German reaction to, 315

Sloss, Frank H., 49

Social Democratic Party (Ger.), 142, 146, 315, 316

Socialism, Jewish nationalism and, 196, 198

Society for the Promotion of Christianity Among the Jews, 58-59, 60.

"Some Rabbinic Parallels to the New Testament" (Schechter), 108

Soviet Union, 295; Jews from, in Germany, 319, 322; Jews murdered by Nazis, 300

Spain, Talmudic academies of, 110, 112

Spanier, Arthur, 96

Spector, Yitzchak Elchanan, 160

Speer, Albert, 295

Spinoza, Baruch, 78-79, 229

Spitzer, Joseph, 32

St. Cyprien internment camp, 267-68

Staatliches *Gymnasium* (Wiesbaden), 4, 13, 14; *illus.*16

Star of Redemption (Rosenzweig), 309

State Academy for Church and School Music (Ger.), 283

Stein, Ernst, 322-23

Steinhardt, Jakob, 262-65, 26; *illus.* 264

Steinheim, Solomon Ludwig, 83

Steinschneider, Moritz, 56, 87, 101, 103, 128

Stellvertreter, Der (The Deputy) (Hochhuth), 314-15

Stern, Guy, 72

Stern, Selma, 54, 95, 96, 97

Stoecker, Adolf, 57-58

Strack, Hermann Leberecht, 60

Strategic Services, Office of. *See* Office of Strategic Services

Strauss, Eduard, 212

Strauss, Herbert, 90-91

Struck, Hermann, 260, 261, 262

Sturm gallery (Berlin), 262

Sukkot, in San Francisco, 48

Switzerland: First Zionist Congress (Basle, 1877), 190, 191, 201, 259, 260, 261; refugee German rabbis in, 208

Sydney, Austr., 37

Symbiosis, German-Jewish, 1, 26-27, 35, 54, 67, 226-27, 228-29

Synagogues: Amsterdam, 257; Australia, 44; differences between German and East European, 150; destruction in Germany, 185, 206-07, 214, 324; in England, 37, 208; *Gemeinde* structure in Germany, 28, 149-50, 152, 209, 217*n.9*, 277, 283, 319-20; German and American rabbis' different roles, 209-14; German pulpits, 43, 55; immigrant German congregations in New York City, 213-14; modified traditional *siddurs* used in Germany, 172; prewar Germany, 26, 28, 34, 75; use of inns as, 121. *See also* under specific names

Syrkin, Nahman, 196

Taeubler, Eugen, 56, 90-91, 93-98

Talmud, 93, 97, 102, 105; Christian scholars and, 60, 107-08; study of,

94-95. *See also* World Zionist
Organization
Zionist Organization of Germany,
195. *See also* German Zionist
Organization
Zunz, Leopold: eulogy for, 60; philol-
ogy in works of, 87; Reform
prayerbook and, 174; Science of
Judaism and, 47, 56, 101, 103, 108,
128; sermons of, 55; studies of
Jewish liturgy, 54-55, 110
Zurich, Switz., 94, 266
Zylinder, 34, 209, 217 *n. 10*